A Stage or Two
BEYOND
CHRISTENDOM

A Stage or Two

BEYOND CHRISTENDOM

*A Social History
of the
Church of England in Derbyshire*

Michael Austin

Scarthin Books
Cromford

Published by Scarthin Books, Cromford, Derbyshire DE4 3QF

Printed by Bell and Bain, 303 Burnfield Road, Glasgow G46 7UQ

Typesetting by Techniset Typesetters, Newton-le-Willows, WA12 9BW

© Michael Austin 2001

ISBN 1 900446 03 0 paperback; ISBN 1 900446 04 9 hardback

First published 2001

To the congregations and clergy
of the diocese of Derby
on the seventy-fifth anniversary
of the founding of the diocese

and

to their sisters and brothers
in
Churches Together in Derbyshire

Foreword

The Bishop of Derby

The origin of this history of the diocese began as a bright idea about a way to celebrate the young diocese of Derby reaching its 75th anniversary. An approach quickly followed to Michael Austin as a natural author. He has deep roots in the diocese and with them strong affections, together with an established reputation as a local historian. His edition of Archdeacon Samuel Butler's visitation of Derbyshire churches in 1823 and 1824 is required reading for anyone preaching at a parish landmark event.

The original idea would have led not so much to a history as a chronicle – a schedule of people and events over just the last three quarters of the twentieth century. That might have been of interest to those whose names appeared, and just possibly to the few others who knew them. From the outset Michael was convincing about his plan to set the story of the diocese in the broader sweep of the history of Christianity in these islands.

As I read the unfolding story, the wise words of the Pharisee Gamaliel, reported in chapter 5 of the *Acts of the Apostles*, kept surfacing. His fellow members of the Sanhedrin wanted to put down the new Christian movement. He advocated an alternative: '...if this plan or undertaking is of human origin, it will fail; but if it is of God, you will not be able to overthrow it...' In Gamaliel's terms this book is the story of a miracle. The tale threads its way through political, economic and social trends and episodes which play their part in the flourishing or the withering, but never the quenching, of the Church. For those familiar with them, the words from St John's *Gospel* will come to mind: 'The light shines in the darkness, and the darkness did not overcome it.'

Every era has needed prophetic voices to challenge the Church's inherent human tendency to be inward looking and self-serving. Sometimes circumstances have converged to make fertile ground for the prophetic message. At other times its messengers have been persecuted or simply ignored. Yet at no time has the message been silenced.

While rejecting the cliche that history repeats itself, I encourage the use of this book for the perspective it gives to the Church as it moves from the second to the third millennium. We are each a part of the one saga, and the greatest mistake would be for the reader to go straight to the twentieth century, the part that may connect with their own personal experience.

The twentieth century concluded with the Church anxious about the crumbling of old securities such as changing patterns of social behaviour and the nature and shape of communities. The current spaghetti junction of possibilities suggests so many directions forward for the Church in England. In the late nineteen nineties the diocese of Derby responded to the plea, 'I wish the Church was going somewhere!' The responses, published as *A Better Way*, continue to inform and direct our shared endeavour as we approach our 75th anniversary, the trigger for this history.

Those who read it will be reminded that while the gospel of Jesus Christ is unchanging the Church is indeed called 'to proclaim it afresh in each generation.' The story of our past, together with much evidence from the present, indicate that St Paul was right when he spoke of the endemic human tendency 'to search for God and perhaps to grope for him ... though indeed he is not far from each of us' (*Acts* 17:27). This story prompts both our gratitude for those who have led past generations in that discovery, and our prayers for those yet to do so in the chapters still to be written.

✠ Jonathan Derby

Of all history, that of our own country is of the most importance, for want of a thorough knowledge of what has been, we are, in many cases, at a loss to account for what is, and still more at a loss to be able to show what ought to be.

William Cobbett
Advice to Young Men (1830)

Resurrection alters the past and changes it from a past which is death-dealing to a past which is life-giving.

H.R. Williams
True Resurrection (1972)

Contents

Contents

Illustrations

Abbreviations

ASB	The *Alternative Service Book 1980*
Austin 1966	M.R. Austin, *The Church of England in the town of Derby 1824 – 1885,* (unpublished University of Birmingham MA thesis, 1966).
Austin 1969	M.R. Austin, *The Church of England in the county of Derbyshire 1772 – 1832* (unpublished University of London PhD thesis, 1969).
BCP	*The Book of Common Prayer* (1662)
COD	*Concise Oxford Dictionary*
Cox, *Annals*	J.C. Cox, *Three Centuries of Derbyshire Annals*, i – ii, (1890)
Cox, *Churches*	J.C. Cox, *Notes on the Churches of Derbyshire*, i – iv, (1875 – 1879) (*Note: though Cox continues to be useful, information given by him should be treated with care*)
DAJ	*Derbyshire Archaeological Journal* (formerly *Journal of the Derbyshire Archaeological and Natural History Society*)
DASRS	*Derbyshire Archaeological Society Record Series*
DDN	*Derby Diocesan News*
DDRO	Derbyshire Record Office / Derby Diocesan Record Office
DNB	*Dictionary of National Biography*
DRS	Derbyshire Record Society

Abbreviations

LJRO   Lichfield Joint Record Office

Macmorran   K.M. Macmorran, E. Garth Moore, Timothy Briden, *A Handbook for Churchwardens and Parochial Church Councillors* (Mowbray 1989 edition).

NSM/SSM   Non-stipendiary, or self-supporting, minister.

ODCC   F.L. Cross (ed.) *The Oxford Dictionary of the Christian Church* (1958).

OED   *The Oxford English Dictionary*

PP   Parliamentary Papers

Turbutt   Gladwyn Turbutt, *A history of Derbyshire*, i - iv, (Merton Priory Press 1999)

VCHD   *Victoria County History of Derbyshire* (1907)

Introduction

ABOUT THE BOOK

This is a history for the general reader. It is *a social* history of the Church of England in Derbyshire. This means that it tells of the Church in its relationships with the wider community, and with the extent to which it influenced, or was influenced by, trends and movements in society generally. It is less concerned with the Church as an institution: its politics, its theological disputes, its parties, finances and structures or the careers of its clergy. For the historian, for whom social history 'touches upon human relationships in every part of life' as Edward Royle puts it, this distinction is far more theoretical than real. Therefore while the primary interest of this book is with the Church in its social relationships, the emphasis inevitably switches between the internal life of the Church on the one hand, and, on the other, the people and communities it served and serves.

As this is a book written for the general reader, I have tried to set the Derbyshire material in the wider national and historical context wherever possible. For this reason also I have added a glossary which provides a guide to the more esoteric terms and practices referred to in the text.

For reason of space, given the very long period that the book covers, much important material has been excluded. A subjective judgement had to be made about what was likely to be of general interest. So, for example, there is comparatively little on the very significant social issues of tithe, or the effect of the enclosures of commons on the incomes and social standing of the clergy, or the exercise of patronage. Where possible, footnotes indicate where further information on these and other matters can be obtained.

For this reason also the detailed story ends in 1990. There will be some church people who will be disappointed by this. But this is primarily a history and not a journal of record. If it were the latter I would be bound to include everything of note up to 2002. As it is the former, and as we are far too close to recent events for me to make impartial comment on them, it is well to leave these last years to later historians. That said, church people with personal knowledge of the 1990s were asked to express a view on these years, and a summary of their reflections is included at the end of chapter 16.

Because it is necessarily so selective, this is just one of several social histories of the Church in the county that could have been written.

It is a social history of *the Church of England* in the county. This is a more contentious matter. The history of the Church in Derbyshire can be traced back at least to the 7th century. Does this mean that I claim that St Chad was an Anglican and would have acknowledged the monarch as supreme governor of the Church and subscribed to the Thirty-Nine Articles of Religion had he lived in the reign of Elizabeth I, or welcomed (or not) the ordination of women to the priesthood had he lived in the late 20th century? Of course not. The claim is rather that as a branch of the western Church the history of the Church of England is continuous from the early days of Christianity in England, and that the Reformation did not break that continuity. That assertion has been much contested and there is no space to defend it here.

Yet this is no partisan, one-sided *apologia* for the Church of England, still less does it assume any superior place for it in the history of Christianity in England. Far from it. This story must be set alongside those of the other Churches in Derbyshire and be measured against them, for the witness of the saints, martyrs and confessors of the Roman Catholic Church and of Protestant non-conformity in the county have judged and humbled the Church of England, taught it much, and enriched it greatly.

But this story is not theirs. There is room in this book for nothing other than brief notice to be taken of their extraordinary contribution to Derbyshire's religious history, and to express here an eager hope that one day we may all truly be one. It is in this hope that the dedication is shared with the Church of England's sisters and brothers in its partner Churches in Derbyshire.

ABOUT THE TITLE

This is taken from the second part to Izaac Walton's *The Compleat Angler*, written by Charles Cotton, Walton's adopted son, and published with the fifth edition in 1676. Cotton has Piscator take 'a well-bred country gentleman', Viator, to the top of Hanson Toot on the Derbyshire-Staffordshire border. They have the following conversation:

Pisc.   Come, sir, now we are up the hill, and how do you?
Viat.   Why very well, I humbly thank you, sir, and warm enough, I assure

	you. What have we here, a church. As I am an honest man, a very pretty church! Have you churches in this country, sir?
Pisc.	You see we have: but, had you seen none, why should you make that doubt, sir?
Viat.	Why, if you will not be angry I'll tell you. I thought myself a stage or two beyond Christendom.

The church that Viator saw was Alstonefield in Staffordshire, 5 miles NNW of Ashbourne. The rarity of churches here was typical of the Peak district with its few parishes and few churches covering huge areas. For Daniel Defoe, when he reached the county during his tour through Great Britain in the 1720s, Derbyshire was 'a waste without tree or hedge.' The parish of Hartington, for example, stretched for twelve miles. It seemed to Viator that he was indeed 'beyond Christendom'. His exaggeration serves as a metaphor. As we begin the third millennium it seems to many that we have moved into a period in the history of the Church in western Europe which is indeed 'beyond Christendom'.

ABOUT THE DIOCESE

For much of its history, the Church of England in Derbyshire belonged to the diocese of Lichfield. St Chad made Lichfield his episcopal see in 669. The diocese was then coterminous with the huge kingdom of Mercia which covered virtually all of the Midlands and stretched from the Humber to the Wye and, to the south, almost as far as London. The see was moved from Lichfield to Chester in 1075 and to Coventry in 1095. Thus its bishops, at various times, held the title of bishops of Chester, of Coventry, and of Coventry and Lichfield. At the Restoration Bishop John Hacket took the title of bishop of Lichfield and Coventry. Since 1836, when the archdeaconry of Coventry was transferred to the diocese of Worcester, the bishops of the diocese have been bishops of Lichfield. The story of the separation of Derbyshire first to become part of the new diocese of Southwell in 1884 and then to become a diocese in its own right in 1927, is told in this book.

While it was within the diocese of Lichfield, the archdeaconry of Derby covered virtually the whole of the county, apart from the 25 or so parishes which, as 'peculiars', were outside the archdeacon's jurisdiction. However, until they were finally removed in 1897 there were boundary anomalies in the south of the county deriving from the Danish occupation. Stapenhill, Winshill and Croxall remain in what is now the archdeaconry of Derby but are no longer within the administrative county. Donisthorpe, Measham, Ravenstone, Stretton-en-le-Field and Willesley, parishes once within the county and comprising 'islands' surrounded by Leicestershire, and subsequently absorbed by it, remained in the rural deanery of Repton until 1928 when they were taken into the diocese of Leicester. Netherseal with Overseal and Woodville were transferred to the new diocese of Derby at the same time. In 1974 Abbeydale, Beighton, Dore, Frecheville and Hackenthorpe, Greenhill, Mosborough, Norton and Totley, together with the extraparochial Beauchief were transferred to the diocese of Sheffield (to which Norton Woodseats had been joined in 1914). There were consequential boundary changes to parishes remaining in the diocese: Dronfield, Hathersage, Holmesfield, and Ridgeway to which Basegreen St Peter's was transferred. Part of the parish of Kirkby-in-Ashfield in the diocese of Southwell was transferred to Pinxton at the same time. Where possible these, and subsequent, changes have been noted in the statistical summaries.

ABOUT PEOPLE

I am most grateful to the bishop of Derby who asked me to attempt to write this book as a contribution to the commemoration, in 2002, of the seventy-fifth anniversary of the founding of his diocese. He has supported and encouraged me throughout and has offered much informed and incisive criticism. I am deeply indebted to Dr Richard Clark, Gladwyn Turbutt and E.G. Power who read the original draft of the book in whole or in part and who made extensive detailed comments, offered further information and suggested forms of words. They saved me both from mistakes of fact and errors of judgement. Anything in either category that remains is entirely my responsibility of course. Dr Michael Watts offered helpful advice and information. I am grateful, too, to David Mitchell of Scarthin Books for his encouragement, his enthusiasm and his editorial skills. I have relied greatly on the advice and assistance of librarians and archivists, and my gratitude goes to the staffs of Lambeth Palace Library, Nottingham Central Library, the local studies libraries in Derby and Chesterfield, and particularly to Dr Margaret O'Sullivan and her colleagues at the Derbyshire Record Office/Derby Diocesan Record Office in Matlock. I am also grateful to Bob Carey, the Derby diocesan secretary, to James Battie, the diocesan registrar, and to Mrs Margaret Siddons. A special debt is owed to Cedric Blakey, Jennie Goodman and Tony Chesterman. Despite all this assistance there may be inadvertent and unacknowledged quotations in the text (sometimes expressions are absorbed into my own thinking and I believe them to be mine!) and for this I apologise. I acknowledge Oxford University Press for permission to use the quotation on page 128.

Above all, once again, Ann has remained patient and supportive through the course of yet another enthusiasm which distracted her husband!

ABOUT USAGE

It is difficult to be consistent in the use of capitals for the designations of the clergy, but why should the Bishop of Derby enjoy an upper case 'B', but the rector of Mugginton suffer a lower case 'r'? As the designations 'bishop', 'archdeacon' and 'provost' occur frequently in this book, and to avoid peppering the text with capital letters, I have followed the advice (there is no rule) of *The Economist Style Guide* (against Fowler's *Modern English Usage*) and, other than when a dignitary's name is mentioned, I have tended (though not always consistently) to be an egalitarian anti-capitalist in this regard!: so, for example, generally 'the bishop of Derby' but 'Bishop Rawlinson'. I have followed this practice with other designations, except for Reader and, generally, for Church/es to avoid confusion. Modern spellings have usually been adopted throughout.

A PERSONAL NOTE

I owe so much to Jack Richardson, archdeacon of Derby when I became vicar of Derby St Andrew in 1960, and to Ron Beddoes, then the provost: to Jack for the constancy of his prayers and the steadfastness of his friendship and support, and to Ron for his warm generosity of spirit, for the breadth both of his mind and of his imagination, and for the acuity of his intuition. Our friends from St Andrew's in the 1960s will know how much they too have meant to Ann and to me and to our family. In gratitude to them all, my royalties have been assigned to the diocese.

Michael Austin
Fiskerton, Nottinghamshire
The Feast of St Andrew, 30 November 2001

1

'His hand in the Trembling Air': the Celtic inheritance

Fifty years ago the historian S.C. Carpenter[1] wrote that the story of Christianity in England is

> the record of the response of one of the most interesting peoples of the world to a religion which has always been too spiritual for them perfectly to comprehend, too exacting for them completely to obey, yet so humane that the English, who are intensely human, have never been able either wholly to deny or wholly to resist its claim to sovereign rule.[2]

The history of the English Church, Carpenter continued, is the story of 'the English compromise with Christianity'.

As we commemorate the seventy-fifth anniversary of the founding of the diocese of Derby, the Church of England is a very different Church to the one in which so many contemporary Derbyshire Anglicans were nurtured. Styles of worship marginalised seventy-five years ago are dominant now; the Book of Common Prayer predominant then is marginalised now; the ordination of women, hardly contemplated then, is gladly welcomed by a majority now; the threat of formal institutional division within the Church of England arising, for some, from the ordination of women, and, for others, caused by supposedly liberal theological opinions and lax moral standards in the Church, is as real

---

[1] Master of the Temple, 1930–35, dean of Exeter 1935–50. From 1916–22 he was an examining chaplain for the bishop of Southwell when Derbyshire was part of that diocese. He preached in Derby Cathedral at a service of thanksgiving following its hallowing in 1927.

[2] S.C. Carpenter, *The Church in England 597–1688* (London, John Murray, 1954), 3. From a very different perspective, and much less elegantly, A.N. Wilson has recently said much the same thing, describing the English as both commonsensical and quasi-mystical (*God's Funeral*, Abacus 2000, 212).

now as it would have been hardly believable then; the relationship between the Christian churches and other faith communities which was hardly a matter for theological debate then is an urgent practical, social and theological issue now. Yet radical, prophetic, theological insights rejected then have survived to be rejected now; and organic Christian unity, desired then, while perhaps nearer, still remains unfulfilled now. That list of contrasts and comparisons could be continued almost endlessly.

As the twenty-first century begins the Church of England, more so than any of the other English Christian communions, continues to be witness not only to the English compromise with Christianity but also to its profound but ambivalent relationship to the political, social and economic world in which it is set and of which it is a part. The role of the Church of England, a Church established by law, is founded upon an essential and inevitable compromise. To that our history bears witness. But, except perhaps for the 16th and 17th centuries, the speed of change within the Church demanded by that compromise is faster, the theological acuity required to maintain it with integrity more profound, and the debate within the Church about its future direction and development more open than during any other period in the history of English Christianity.

And that history had a very early beginning. We do not know when the Gospel was first preached in England. We do not know who first preached it. That obscurity is itself hugely significant theologically. The all-powerful word was breathed quietly in the ear and the air scarcely trembled. Perhaps, among the Roman military, or the merchants and traders and slaves and other camp-followers, there were some who had heard the word about Jesus and had taken his message and ministry to heart.

So we do not know how the Gospel came to these islands, and we know virtually nothing about the Christian mission here for several hundred years. What little we know is spread over centuries of complex history and the telling of the story here must now become a little breathless.[1]

By whatever means that word came and by whom it was preached, Tertullian (c. 160–c. 220 AD), writing around 208, tells that parts of Roman Britain, unconquered by the legions, had fallen to Christ. A generation later the north African theologian Origen (c. 185–c. 254) recorded that there were Christians in Britain. What we can be reasonably certain of is that following the emperor

---

[1] For those who want a much more detailed study Gladwyn Turbutt has comprehensively surveyed Christianity in Derbyshire in this early period in the first volume of his *A History of Derbyshire* (1999).

Constantine's edict of toleration in 313 Christianity became the imperial religion in Roman Britain. After Constantine took undisputed control of the whole empire in 324, Christianity, or rather the official version of it, became the imperial religion. In Roman Britain Christianity never fully succeeded in winning the hearts of the people. The struggle with paganism was to continue, and, when the Roman legions left two hundred years later, Christianity was virtually obliterated, surviving in the Celtic monastic communities in the far west of these islands from which a new Christian mission was to arise and in which a monk called Chad was eventually to play his part.

In 313 the Christian Church in Britain was just beginning to be established, perhaps by imperial command. Before then it is probable that it had survived only in a few of the great Roman villas. To that earlier period belongs the story of Alban, the first British martyr, who is traditionally believed to have lost his life during the persecutions under Diocletian in 305. But, in 314, three British bishops attended the Council of Arles, accompanied by a priest and a deacon who may have represented a fourth. Perhaps Constantine sent them. These men were not diocesan bishops in the modern sense. As in the early Church these bishops would have had oversight of a bishopric which corresponded to a city, the principal area of civil administration, which in turn would have represented an identifiable social group.

British bishops attended the Council of Rimini, meeting under Constantius II, in 359. So poor were they that, alone of all the bishops attending the Council (who wished to maintain their independence from the state) their travel expenses were met by the Imperial Post. We have the impression that the Romano-British Church was far from strong and widespread. It was certainly not wealthy, and little tangible indication remains of its existence, important though that is. Certainly there is none in Derbyshire and we must rely on circumstantial evidence. At the fort at Little Chester a bas-relief of the god Mercury has been discovered, but whether there were Christians in its garrison and in those of the other Roman forts in Derbyshire we cannot tell. John Bestall speculated that the presence of a chapel in Chesterfield dedicated to St Helen, mother of Constantine, the first Roman emperor to become a Christian, might suggest continuity from a Christian presence in the Roman fort there.[1] Joseph Campbell has suggested recently that Christianity was more firmly established by the time that the legions left these islands than has

---

[1] John Bestall, *History of Chesterfield* (1974), i, 99.

been supposed, and that when Augustine came to Canterbury in 597 a centre of pilgrimage dedicated to St Alban would have been in existence for perhaps two centuries less than a hundred miles away.[1]

But though Christianity may eventually have become the imperial religion, as with all religions established and imposed by law, that fact alone could not win hearts and minds. Gladwyn Turbutt suggests that Wirksworth was the only place in Derbyshire where Christianity survived from Romano-British times. Mercury was a far more potent religious symbol for the legions than the cross of Christ.

In the fifth century AD the Roman armies surrendered their hold on Britain, leaving these islands open to invasion by Angles, Saxons and Jutes. These Germanic tribes virtually extinguished Christianity in those areas in which they settled. In Wales and Ireland, however, the Christian faith survived – just about, it seems, if we follow an admittedly unsympathetic contemporary source. The monk Gildas (c 500–c 570), the first British historian, writing from Brittany in 547 about the Celts, tells us that the Welsh clergy were 'unworthy wretches, wallowing, after the fashion of swine, in their old and unhappy puddle of intolerable wickedness.'[2] Yet the Celtic Church gave us David (d. c.601), abbot, bishop and evangelist, and founder of monasteries where men prayed and studied and kept a rule of life and from which the Gospel was preached. An early *Life* of David made him the founder of the double-monastery in Repton which was certainly in existence before the end of the 7th century. In Ireland, Columba (c 521-597), of royal lineage and fiery temperament, cursed the rich and blessed the poor until a petty dispute about ownership of a manuscript led to pressure on him to leave Ireland. Accompanied by a few companions he went to Iona where he established a monastic community which became a centre for prayer, evangelism and ministry in Scotland. There Columba died on 9 June 597, just a week after the baptism of Ethelbert, King of Kent, at the hands of the man who came from Rome to lead the attempt to convert the South, Augustine of Canterbury.

Augustine lacked the stature, wisdom and imagination of Gregory, the monk that would have led the Roman mission to England had the people of Rome not refused to let him come and who became, in 590, Pope Gregory I. Having encountered several forms of Christian worship and custom Augustine wrote to Gregory for advice. What should the English be given? Gregory advised

---

[1] Joseph Campbell, 'Britain AD 500', *History Today*, February 2000, 29–35.
[2] quoted in J.R.H. Moorman, *A History of the Church in England* (A. and C. Black, London 1954), 9.

Augustine to choose whatever is 'pious, religious and correct, and when you have, as it were, made them up into one body, let the minds of the English, as yet new to the faith, be accustomed thereto.'[1] Augustine lacked the theological skills and, above all, the imagination to follow this advice and to give to the English a form of Christian worship which sprang from their culture. So he gave us the alien Roman forms with which he was familiar. He lacked too not only the statesmanship but also the courtesy of Gregory. In 602, Bede tells us, he met the Celtic bishops on the south bank of the Severn (though the Trent makes better geographical sense[2]). These gaunt men, walking for days to meet the new archbishop, had decided that if he rose to meet them, and greeted them as brothers in friendship, they would know that here was a man sent by God. It is said that Augustine remained seated as the bishops approached. He required of them that they accept his authority, and that they change their centuries-old Christian customs, notably that they adjust the date on which they celebrated Easter to bring it into line with Roman custom. They refused to accept either Augustine's primacy or his demand for uniformity. This rupture took very many years to repair.

The story of the Church in a land covered by many rival kingdoms now becomes complex. The Roman mission extended to Northumbria under Paulinus while Augustine attempted, with little success, to move his mission beyond Kent into East Anglia and Wessex. War between rival kings, Christian and heathen, was, within a generation, to threaten the work done by Paulinus in the north, but, under the protection of the Christian king Oswald the Church in Northumbria took heart. It was strengthened by a fresh mission, this time from Scotland. Aidan, a monk from Lindisfarne, became bishop in Northumbria travelling the north-east on foot, preaching, baptising, building simple timber and wattle churches, and beginning in the north what was to become the heart of Christian ministry and witness for hundreds of years – the monastic life.

And now the story brings us closer to home. Bede (673–735), in his *A History of the English Church and People*, tells us that 'by the ministration of the holy priests Cedd and Chad ... the faith of Christ came to the province of the Mercians, which had never known it and returned to that of the East Saxons, which had let it die out'[3]. What happened was this. In 653 Paeda, prince of the

---

[1] for citation details, see Carpenter 6, n. 2
[2] I owe this suggestion to David Mitchell.
[3] Bede, *A History of the English Church and People*, (Penguin 1968), 34.

Middle Angles, had been baptised by Bishop Finan of Lindisfarne. Paeda asked the Christian king Oswy of Northumbria to send four priests to preach the Gospel among his people. These four were Cedd, Adda, Betti and Diuma. In 656 Finan consecrated Diuma to be the first bishop of the Middle Angles and Mercians with the *cathedra*, the 'seat', of his see at Repton. It is from this moment that the Christianisation of Derbyshire effectively began, and the later foundation of 'minster' churches (of which we will say more shortly) provided the mechanism by which early missionaries reached out to all parts of the county.

Diuma died shortly after becoming bishop. Three bishops followed him, the last, Jaruman, dying in 667. His place was taken, temporally, by Wilfred, one of the great missionary bishops, who had been made bishop of York three years earlier. Wilfred recommended that the *cathedra* of the see be moved to Lichfield (which had recently been given to him by King Wulfhere). Two years later, in 669, Chad was appointed bishop of Mercia and Lindsey.

Chad was the brother of Cedd, one of the four priests who had originally been sent to Repton. Repton soon became a double-monastery for monks and nuns similar to that at Whitby (ruled by the abbess Hilda, a woman of great ability and authority). Chad was a saintly man and his name is revered not only in Derbyshire but throughout the Midlands. Three Derbyshire churches of ancient foundation were dedicated to him: Barton Blount[1], Longford and Wilne. Chad was bishop for less than three years, dying in 672. After his death the vast diocese of Mercia was divided, leaving the see of Lichfield responsible for the present-day counties of Staffordshire, Derbyshire and Cheshire together with parts of Shropshire and Warwickshire.

Bede lists Chad's many virtues: 'continence, humility, right preaching, prayer, voluntary poverty, and many others.'[2] He was also 'filled with the fear of God', a God whose hand he believed was everywhere to be seen. He would 'call upon God for mercy', Bede tells us, whenever a gale arose. If that gale became a violent storm Chad would go into the church 'and devote all his thoughts to prayers and psalms continuously until the tempest had passed.' When his monks asked him why he did this Chad replied:

> Have you not read, *"The Lord thundered in the heavens, and the Highest gave his voice. He sent out His arrows and scattered them; He shot out*

---

[1] This parish was united with Church Broughton, and the church declared redundant, in 1976.
[2] Bede, op.cit. 210

lightnings and discomfited them"? For God stirs the air and raises the winds; He makes the lightning flash and thunders out of heaven, to move the inhabitants of the earth to fear Him, and to remind them of the judgement to come. He shatters their conceit and subdues their presumption by recalling to their minds that awful Day when heaven and earth will flame as He comes in the clouds with great power and majesty to judge the living and the dead. Therefore we should respond to His heavenly warnings with the fear and love we owe him, And whenever He raises His hand in the trembling air as if to strike, yet spares us still, we should hasten to implore His mercy, examining in our inmost hearts and purging the vileness of our sins, watchful over our lives lest we incur His just displeasure.[1]

That is the voice of authentic Celtic spirituality. There is no trace of superstition here, nor any hint of what we might today regard as literalism. This is theology as poetry and for this reason it is 'right preaching'. Father Chad, as Bede calls him, may not have been the first to bring word of the Gospel to Derbyshire's hills and valleys but he did bring to its service here a holy and prayerful and disciplined life, a care for the churches, and that theological imagination and sensitivity which is so profound a quality of true Celtic spirituality. Here was a man who diligently sought to do the things he learned from Scripture. He bids us now, thirteen centuries after his death, to see and hear the God who raises his hand in the trembling air! Today's Church in Derbyshire owes its establishment to all those early missionary priests of whom Chad was an extraordinary example.

---

[1] ibid., 211.

2

'Heaven as a rooftree': the Anglo-Saxon Church in Derbyshire

Caedmon, who died about 680, was the first English Christian poet – or at least the first that we know about. Bede says that Caedmon was a herdsman at the abbey at Whitby when Hilda was abbess. At parties he was not given to singing rowdy songs, and when he saw a harp coming his way, he would go home. One night, asleep beside his cows, Caedmon had a dream. Bede tells us: "'Sing me a song", a man said. "I don't know how to sing", Caedmon replied, "It is because I cannot sing that I left the feast and came here." The man who addressed him then said: "But you shall sing to me." "What shall I sing about?" he replied. "Sing about the Creation of all things," the other answered.' And, Bede says, Caedmon immediately began to sing verses in praise of God the Creator that he had never heard before, and that their theme ran thus:

> Praise we the Fashioner now of Heaven's fabric,
> The majesty of his might and his mind's wisdom,
> Work of the world-warden, worker of all wonders,
> How he is the Lord of Glory everlasting,
> Wrought first for the race of men Heaven as a rooftree,
> Then made he Middle Earth to be their mansion.

That is art, and it is the art of the same Saxon Church that provides our first physical evidence of Christianity in Derbyshire.

Archbishop Theodore died in 680. He was one of the great archbishops of Canterbury. He had succeeded in uniting the Church across the boundaries of the four English kingdoms of Mercia, Northumbria, East Anglia and Kent. He had given the Church in England the beginnings of a basic organisation, and had divided the huge diocese of Mercia. He has been credited with creating the parish system but this developed in a somewhat haphazard way during the next three hundred years as the monasteries withdrew into themselves, local lords built churches for the lands they controlled, and bishops and their secular clergy (that is those who had not taken monastic vows) took the initiative, such as it was, in promoting the Gospel and administering and regulating the Church. Theodore had convened great synods, first at Hertford in 673 and then at Hatfield in 680 which not only served the unity of the English Church and determined its structure (Hertford) and its doctrinal orthodoxy (Hatfield) but also acted as a curb on the power of the four kings. He also made the Church less monastic in orientation, bringing it closer to local communities. The parish priest, where there was one, was a tenant and servant of the local lord. As we will see, the parish priest was effectively a peasant, and Theodore tried to ensure that he was supported from the local lord's estates. Lay patronage thus has a very early origin.

Great names belong also to the next phase of our story. In this part of England, Mercia, under king Ethelbald, became increasingly powerful. To the north, Egfrid, king of Northumbria, made Cuthbert bishop of Lindisfarne, where Chad had been a monk. Cuthbert stands before us as the last great Celtic saint, a man who dreamed dreams and saw visions and preached the Gospel such, as Bede tells us, men 'flocked together to hear the word'. But, in Bede's rather idealistic account in his *History*, that was true of the clergy generally, for 'in those days, whenever a clerk or priest visited a town, English folk always used to gather at his call to hear the Word, eager to hear his message and even more eager to carry out what they had heard and understood'! Bede was privately to tell Egbert, first archbishop of York, a somewhat different story: that an ill-educated clergy visited some places very infrequently.

Cuthbert was special for 'he used mainly to visit and preach in the villages that lay far distant among high and inaccessible mountains, which others feared to visit and whose vulgarity and squalor daunted other teachers'[1]. S.C. Carpenter wrote that Cuthbert had 'a mysterious intimacy with brute creation.' This sense of oneness with nature, together with his rigorous asceticism, had led Cuthbert to embrace the life of a hermit on the island of

---

[1] ibid., 260

Farne, from where, in 685, he had been brought back as bishop of Lindisfarne. Increasing infirmity drew him back to Farne where he died in March 687.

Cuthbert is commemorated in the dedication of Doveridge parish church. Early Derbyshire dedications honour other Celtic saints: Oswald and Chad and Wilfrid and, as we will see, the Mercian royal saints Werburgh, Alkmund and Wystan. These Anglo-Saxon dedications witness to the vigour of the Church in these centuries.

In Mercia, Guthlac, scion of the royal house and a monk of the Celtic-style double-monastery at Repton, followed Cuthbert's example and withdrew to Crowland in the remote Lincolnshire fenlands where for perhaps twenty years he lived the life of a solitary anchorite. So it was that Repton had been a spiritual home to two saints, Chad, monk and bishop, and Guthlac, monk and hermit. These were years when English monasticism was the heart of the Church. Although Derbyshire was to have relatively few religious houses, its country-side was to hold monastic lands and rights of grazing, and the influence of the monasteries, not least in the ownership of parishes, was to be considerable. The dominant economic power of the monastic houses was often far from benign in later centuries and must be weighed against their importance as places of prayer and centres of administration and preaching. Holiness and wealth live uneasily together.

And so the Church grew such that by now – the middle of the seventh century – there were few parts of England where the Gospel had not been preached. The Church seems to have had little more than a missionary presence in Mercia much before this time, but then, from the time of Archbishop Theodore, a new policy for evangelising the countryside was embarked upon. This consisted of the establishment of a network of 'minster' (vernacular for *monasteria*) churches staffed by communities of clergy whose ministry it was to carry the Gospel to people in the surrounding *parochiae* (literally, the places where they sojourned). Together with Repton, minster churches were built at Wirksworth, Ashbourne, Bakewell, Chesterfield, Derby and Hope.[1] But how well estab-lished was the Church, by what means and for how long?

We have noted that the Romans left our islands in the fifth century. By the middle of the seventh the invading pagan Germanic peoples had been

---

[1] What is known of the establishment and early history of these great churches is set out in Turbutt, 288ff.

converted to Christianity. If we are to believe Bede in his letter to Egbert, little credit for this belongs to the Celtic church. Bede, who admittedly had little time for Celtic Christianity, criticised its priests for failing to convert the Anglo-Saxons. However, it seems that Augustine's Roman mission did not extend much beyond Kent. Even had there been numerous clergy who knew and taught the Faith well and faithfully this would not explain the rapidity and extent of the conversion of the English. But the clergy were not numerous. Bede complained to Archbishop Egbert that some places were only visited by a priest once a year. Generally all they were able to do was to keep the ordinances of the Church as best they could and try to insist, but with little success, that those they baptised did the same. Bede's, and especially Gildas's, criticisms of the clergy, while recognising that both observers had their theological and ecclesiastical agendas, must be taken seriously.

So how can the conversion be explained? The answer is very prosaic. The presence and example of great saints in the Celtic and English churches would not itself guarantee that the conversion went very deep. The fact is that Christianity was (and is) attractive to rulers. By employing such Biblical texts as Romans 13:1 it taught that the powers that be (whoever they may be) are ordained of God and that every soul must be subject to them. Further than this it offered kings a guarantee that paganism could not offer, the certainty of resurrection from death. Above all, this side of the grave, Christianity afforded access to a God who could win battles. Had not two bishops, as Bede records, baptised a British army *en masse* and, with three shouts of 'Alleluia!', led them to a bloodless victory over Saxon and Pict columns that fled naked in panic before them? That event, fact or legend, would have convinced subsequent Saxon kings, themselves the high priests of religion, that there was much to be said for Christianity. The Church has been both a school for saints whose eyes are fixed on heaven, and a political (and often military) reality firmly set on earth. The working relationship between the Church's eyes and feet is based upon a fundamental truth of the Incarnation but it is invariably expressed in uneasy theological, practical and political compromises.

Perhaps the conversion of the English was too rapid and too shallow, for with numerical consolidation came spiritual decline. To read Bede's *History* one would think that all was well with the English Church. In fact we know, from that letter that Bede wrote to Egbert, that he knew of many religious houses that did not live up to the monastic ideal, that many clergy were ill-educated and that the English were by no means as serious about Christianity as were their contemporaries in southern Europe.[1] During the following century a series of at least seven synods of Church and State for the lands south of the Humber were held at Clovesho (we do not know now where this was) to attempt reform. The most important of these were held in 747 and 803. The 747 synod was concerned with discipline. The clergy were to attend to their spiritual duties and learn what the words of divine service[2] meant 'lest they be found dumb and ignorant in those intercessions which they make to God for the sins of the people'; monks were to attend to their daily offices and dress in their habits; Sundays and saints' days were to be observed; lay people must learn to communicate (that is, to take the sacrament) at mass more often 'lest they grow weak for want of the salutary meat and drink'; and bishops were to travel about their dioceses and 'plainly teach those who rarely hear the word of God.' There can be no doubt that the state of the Church that is revealed here as in need of reform was the state of the Church in Derbyshire a mere seventy-five years after Chad's death.

To this period of slack obedience belongs a Mercian saint. Werburgh, who died about 699, was the daughter of the Mercian king Wulfhere and another saint, Ermenilda. Werburgh became a reforming abbess of the Benedictine monastic house in Ely and established new monasteries in Staffordshire and Northamptonshire. She is commemorated in the early dedications of the Derbyshire parish churches of Blackwell, Spondon, and in Derby.

The Clovesho reforms were short lived. A series of Danish raids starting with the destruction of the Lindisfarne monastery in 793 and extending down the east and along the south coasts led to full-scale invasion and conquest, with the Danes plundering churches, monasteries and convents across the whole country, except for Wessex (or such, it was said, as there was of Wessex). A spiritually weak Church was virtually obliterated within a few years of the reforms designed to renew it. By 866 York was a Danish city. Peterborough, it was said, 'which before was full rich, they reduced to nothing.' Mercia was overrun. In the winter of 873–4 the Danish army plundered and sacked the monastery at Repton, the mausoleum of the Mercian kings. The remains of 250 individuals have been found near the church.

Yet to this period belong two more Mercian royal saints: Alkmund and Wystan. Alkmund was a son of Alhred, king of Northumbria. We know little

---

[1] Though we should note that Christian cross symbols have been found in Anglo-Saxon graves in Derbyshire, for example at Benty Grange, showing that men and women died in the faith in which they had been baptised. For them, at least, conversion was no light thing.

[2] in Latin.

about him, except that he was killed about 800 AD at the behest of Eardwulf of Northumbria. His remains were to be interred in the minster church at Northworthy (the earlier name for Derby) later dedicated to Alkmund.[1] Wystan was the grandson of Wiglaf, king of Mercia. He was murdered in 849 and initially buried at Repton before his remains were taken to Evesham by the Dane Cnut for political reasons early in the 11th century. Repton parish church, together with its former chapelry of Bretby, are dedicated to Wystan. Miracles supposedly associated with the tombs of Werburgh, Alkmund and Wystan led to their canonisation. There may have been other early Derbyshire churches commemorating these local saints whose original dedications were not remembered, as so very many were not, after the Reformation.

Came the time, came Alfred, king of Wessex. The English victory of Ethandune over the Danes in 878 led to the Treaty of Wedmore (Chippenham) which divided England between the Saxons to the west and the Danes to the east. Inevitably the line passed through Mercia with what is now Derbyshire in Danish Mercia. One of the terms of the Treaty of Wedmore was that the Danish king, Guthrum, should be baptised taking the name Athelstan. Alfred was his sponsor. It was left to Alfred's children, Edward ('The Elder') and his sister Aethelflaed ('Lady of the Mercians') to reconquer the Danelaw, and in 917 Aethelflaed captured Derby and the surrounding area. This led effectively to the establishment of the present-day county of Derbyshire.

Now we can leave the wider story and turn to our own county. Apart from a tantalising glimpse of Christian symbolism found in Anglo-Saxon graves of the late seventh century, it is from the eighth century onwards that tangible evidence of Christianity begins to appear in the form of religious sculpture. Much of this material evidence is therefore what might be called Christian art, but specifically Christian art has never been an end in itself. It is, at this period, evidence of the existence of a Christian Church sufficiently well established (however fragile) and confident (however corrupt) to celebrate and promote the Gospel in the stone crosses and, later, in the fonts and door lintels and tympana and other sculptures that survive in some abundance in Derbyshire. Ancient and beautiful pre-Norman sculpture was recorded in detail in the *Victoria County History* of Derbyshire in 1905. It has been described, and

---

[1] See Derek and Marion Taulbut, *St Alkmund: a summary of his Life, Murder and Cults,* published for Duffield parish church, January 2000.

recent scholarship on the subject helpfully surveyed, by Gladwyn Turbutt.[1] It is to be found in the complete or virtually complete crosses in Bakewell and Eyam; cross-heads and fragments at Bradbourne; cross-shafts in Ashbourne, Aston, Bakewell, Blackwell, Bradbourne, Darley Dale, Derby, Eccles Pike, Hope, Norbury and Spondon; fragments of round-shaft sculptured crosses in Bakewell, Ludworth, Wilne and Fernilee Hall and recumbent coped monuments in Bakewell, Repton and Wirksworth. These sculptured stones are beautifully decorated with plaitwork and knotwork and loopwork and ringwork, with key-patterns and spirals and foliage, and with animal designs. These decorative features enrich depictions of the Annunciation, the Adoration of the Magi, the Flight into Egypt, Christ washing his disciples' feet, the Entry into Jerusalem, the Crucifixion and the Ascension and much else, and witness to the vigour of the pre-Conquest Church in Derbyshire.

A glance at a map of Derbyshire shows over how wide an area this pre-Norman sculptured stonework is to be found. The earliest evidence is the seventh century coped stone built in to the wall of the north aisle of Wirksworth parish church. The crosses in Bakewell, Bradbourne and Eyam seem to come from the eighth century, cross shafts in Norbury and Hope from the ninth and fragments of round-shaft sculptured crosses and coped stones in Bakewell and Wilne and Repton and in what was formerly Derby St Alkmund from the tenth century. As we shall see there is much in Derbyshire which tells of the Church in the Anglo-Norman period also. The men who carved this stonework for these churches would have been taught their faith within their walls. It is likely that their priests were too ill-educated to teach them much and would have scarce understood the meaning of the words of the liturgy they used, but they told the Bible stories and the craftsmen rendered them in stone. As these craftsmen and their families stood in church they would in turn have been taught by the stone Annunciation and the carved Crucifixion. These men are long dead and long forgotten. Their work remains to remind us of our unity with them of the communion of all the Derbyshire saints.

---

[1] ibid., i, 323–328.

3

'A Priest and a Church': the Anglo-Norman Church in Derbyshire

We must rush quickly through the next period of our history. In Danish England three kings of little account had succeeded Athelstan, though one, Edmund (940–946), had made a man with Danish parents, Oda, the twenty-second archbishop of Canterbury. The twenty-fifth archbishop, translated from London, was appointed in 960. His name was Dunstan. He died in 988, a holy and much loved man and one of the great archbishops. Ethelred had become king in 978. When the Danes came again this 'redeless' or poorly advised monarch seems never to have been where he was needed. In 1012 the Vikings captured Aelfheah, or Alphage, Ethelred's fourth archbishop of Canterbury. Refusing to be ransomed by taxing the poor, Alphage was imprisoned on a Danish ship, and, in 1012 was murdered by drunken sailors.

Ethelred fled to Normandy in 1013 and was eventually succeeded by Cnut, the first in a period when foreign kings ruled us. He died in 1035. Two inadequate kings followed him, but then, in 1043, Ethelred's only surviving son was crowned. His name was Edward and was to be known as 'the pacific king, the glory of England' and to be canonised a saint. In fact Edward was far from being a very successful king and too much has been claimed for him, but he stands in our history not least as the man who gave us the Abbey of St.Peter in Westminster. Edward the Confessor died on 3 January 1066, a week after the consecration of his abbey and at the beginning of a fateful year. Harold was crowned in Westminster Abbey as Edward's successor. He reigned for ten months before being killed near Hastings at the hands of that 'stark' man (as he was called) and the next invader, the 'brutal adventurer' William of Normandy.

The effect of this new conquest on the English Church was to be both complex and profound. By it the Church was bound finally and completely to European Catholicism. Our bishops were now often to be French and occasionally Italian by birth. This linkage did not mean that our clergy would necessarily be more faithful or be better educated. A Burgundian monk in 1001 had declared that there was scarcely a priest in Normandy who could read – a situation paralleled in the English Church as we have seen.

One modest consequence of our closer ties with continental catholicism was that compulsory celibacy was imposed on the clergy. There were many lawfully married clergy when Edward the Confessor died. Compulsory celibacy, imposed not without opposition during the reigns of William and his sons, affected not only the parish clergy but also the considerable army of professional men, and of what we would now call the civil service, almost all of whom were priests.

The most obvious and immediate effect of the Norman conquest on the English Church was in church building. Anglo-Saxon churches had been mainly built of wood, with little in stone (which makes the Saxon church stonework that survives so important). The Normans brought with them the Romanesque architectural style of solid round arches and massive columns. The building programme began almost immediately. A great church in Bury St.Edmunds was begun in 1070; Chester in 1075; Rochester and St.Albans in 1077; Winchester, Ely, Worcester and Lincoln in 1079; Gloucester in 1089; Carlisle in 1092 and Durham in 1093, all within thirty years of William's landing in Sussex. In Derbyshire, St Michael's Melbourne was added, early in the 12th century, to an already rich inheritance of major churches.

William's reforms of the English Church went much further than a church building programme. He divided the ecclesiastical from the civil courts in a separation of jurisdiction without which our system of common law could not have developed. He controlled the nomination of bishops and abbots in such a way as to benefit the reform of the Church. Most significantly William brought the wealth of the Church under his control thereby making it, as G.M. Trevelyan wrote, 'tolerable and useful' by requiring it to serve (at least up to a point) not merely the interests of the Church but also of learning and knowledge, and therefore the wider social good.

Little of this had immediate effect on the life and ministry of ordinary priests, poor Saxon peasants almost to a man and belonging to a subservient and powerless social group. From the Conquest to the 19th century the social status of the clergy was to rise slowly but steadily. We will see that the mediaeval Church attempted (not always successfully) to prevent villeins from being ordained, for they were not freemen. They were thus subject to their lords, and their service could be transferred to another. By the reigns of the Stuarts the parish clergy were drawn largely from the ranks of yeomen and occasionally from the gentry. By at least the 19th century the successors of Derbyshire's poor peasant-priests stood some chance of being aristocrats. The younger sons of aristocratic families were often presented to family livings. For example, Curzons were regularly presented to the family benefice of Mickleover, and by the eve of the first World War the Revd Lord Scarsdale had been rector of Kedleston for nearly sixty years. But in the 10th century this social climb from peasant to peer had yet to begin.

The Domesday Survey

How many of these peasant priests were there in Derbyshire and where were they? In 1085, the Saxon Chronicle records,

> at Gloucester at midwinter ... the King had deep speech with his counsellors ... and sent men all over England to each shire ... to find out... what or how much each landholder held ... in land and livestock, and what it was worth ....The returns were brought to him.

This became known as the Domesday survey. It was an inquest or investigation by commissioners, and conducted, under oath, in about seven months in 1085–6. What we call the Domesday Book is a revision of the commissioners' evidence complied in Winchester no later than 1089. There is evidence that the survey was not conducted uniformly and that there are many errors and omissions, but the Domesday Book is still an indispensable guide to the nature of English society at the beginning of the second millennium. It gives us our first statistical evidence for the Church in Derbyshire, and the names of two or three of its clergy.

Domesday was primarily a tax inspection. It was designed to make the collection of the Danegeld more effective. The Danegeld was an annual tax, probably imposed originally by Ethelred the Unready to buy off the Danish raiders, though the word *Danegeld* appears only after William's conquest. William's survey gave him valuable fiscal information but, more importantly, it gave him also some idea of who the local lords, or 'feudatories', were, what human and financial resources they commanded and therefore what power they had.

A typical Derbyshire entry is that of what would later be called a manor (an area under feudal lordship) in the Hammenstan (probably the Wirksworth) Wapentake. A wapentake was a hundred or division of a shire deriving from the days when land was under Danish control. The word comes from the Old Norse for 'weapon' and 'take' probably referring to voting in an assembly by show of weapons. Here is the entry:

> In DERELEIE [Darley] King Edward had 2 carucates of land (assessed) to the geld. in FARLEIE [Farley] and COTES [Cotes in Darley] and BERLEIE [Burley] (there is) 1 carucate of land and two bovates (assessed) to the geld. (There is) land for 3 ploughs. There the king has 1 plough; and 7 villeins who have 3 ploughs. There (is) a priest and a church and 12 acres of meadow. Wood(land) for pannage 2 leagues in length and 2 in breadth. In King Edward's time it was worth 40 shillings and 2 sestiers (*sextarii*) of honey; now (it is worth) 4 pounds.

A *carucate* was a 'ploughland' of eight *bovates*. Each bovate represented land assignable to one ox. A *plough* was an eight oxen 'great plough' and was the basis of the Domesday survey. The productivity of a manor was assessed by the number of ploughs that could be employed. A 'half-plough' thus represented land employing four oxen. Of the people on the manor by far the largest social class was that of the *villanus* or villein – a husbandman owing customary labour services to his lord and tied to his manor. Elsewhere there are references to *sokemen* (free peasant farmers), *serfs* (a diminishing group who had no personal rights or property and were the chattels of their owners), *bordars* (cottagers holding a small amount of land and owing labour services), and *censarii* (who paid rent in money, not labour).

To these five classes of peasant must be added a sixth, the priests, for they were peasants too, though in some places they were peasants of a somewhat superior sort. These men were the priests of the former 'minster' churches. Thus at Bakewell there were two priests who between them had the service of two villeins and five bordars and where no less than three carucates belonged to the church. At Ashbourne the priest had one carucate assessed for the geld or tax, and had under him two villeins and two bordars with half a plough. He also had a man who paid him 18 pence, the priest himself having a plough of his own. But peasant clergy of such relative status and affluence were few in number.

Bakewell and Ashbourne were 'minster' churches within the royal demesne or domain. Elsewhere, even on Derbyshire land whose tenants-in-chief were the bishop of Chester and Burton Abbey, the priests were not so fortunate. Bakewell and Repton (also within the royal demesne) were the only two manors (or parishes in today's terms) with two priests.

Before we consider the number and distribution of the clergy we should look briefly at the land-holdings of the two ecclesiastical tenants-in-chief, the bishop of Chester and Burton Abbey. In fact there was no diocesan bishop of Chester in the 11th century. The diocese was created by Henry VIII in 1541. The bishop of Lichfield at the time of the Domesday survey was Peter, consecrated by Lanfranc in 1072. In 1075 he removed the seat of his see to Chester because, the *VCHD* suggests, as a Norman ecclesiastic he followed continental practice and placed his seat in the most important city in his diocese, and Lichfield hardly counted as that. This may be so, but more prosaic reasons had to do with his own safety and the economic condition of Staffordshire. We might usefully note here that Peter's successor, Robert de Limesey, was to move the seat of the diocese to Coventry, though Lichfield seems always to have been effectively the centre of the bishop's ministry. It seems to have returned to Lichfield during the episcopate of Robert Peche, bishop from 1121 to 1127, who began work of restoration there.

In Derbyshire the Domesday survey shows that the bishop held the manor of Sawley, Draycott and Hopwell, where there was a priest and two churches, Long Eaton, which had no church or priest, and Bupton, part of the village of Longford, which had a priest and a church.

The Benedictine Burton Abbey was the only religious house to hold lands in Derbyshire at this time. Founded by a Mercian nobleman, Wulfric Spot, in about 1002 and endowed with a considerable landed estate, it had lost most of this by the time of the Conquest. It was subsequently endowed with the manors of Mickleover (which had once belonged to Edward the Confessor) and Caldwell (of which it was said that 'King William gave this manor to the monks *pro beneficio suo*') together with eight areas of sokeland. In none of these places did the Domesday commissioners record a priest or a church.

Six churches are recorded in the Domesday survey of Derby. These were to be the parishes of All Saints, St Alkmund, St Peter, St Michael and St Werburgh, together with another, long lost, but probably St Mary, owned by Burton Abbey and of which, around 1000 AD, one Godric was the priest, and which was also the mother church of the extensive manor of Mickleover (not recorded in the

Domesday survey). The survey records that before 1066 there were two churches, both 'in the King's lordship', one served by seven priests, the other by six. In 1086 four more churches were recorded. In addition, the Commissioners note, one Stori 'could make himself a church on his land' if he so chose. We also have recorded the names of two more Derbyshire Saxon clergy, Osmer and Godwin, each of whom had a land holding of one bovate. The burgesses of Derby were said to render to the king 12 thraves (or measures) of corn at Martinmas, of which the abbot of Burton received 40 sheaves.

The Domesday survey for Derbyshire records 46 priests and 43 churches in the rest of the county, though as a few churches are recorded with no priests, and *vice versa,* we may assume omissions from the survey and plump for a bare minimum of 49 manorial priests and 47 churches. As 346 places are mentioned in the Derbyshire Domesday we can assume widespread omissions. The existence of archaeological evidence of Saxon churches, or at least a Christian presence, in places not mentioned in the survey as possessing churches, suggests that the Church in Derbyshire was already more widespread at the time of the commissioners' inspection than Domesday records.[1]

The survey tells us that there was a priest and a church in 35 Derbyshire manors. Bakewell and Repton each had two priests – evidence, perhaps, of the continuation of colleges of priests at these two minster churches. In Weston-on-Trent and in Sawley/Draycott/Hopwell there was one priest and two churches. In Stainsby/Tunstall, South Wingfield, Eckington, Newton and in Lullington a priest but no church is recorded, though this may be merely a mistake. In Ednaston/Hulland there was 'half a church' and no priest, while in Brailsford there was a priest and half a church. Reference to a 'half church' indicates a church the ownership (and therefore the income) of which was shared between two neighbouring lords, usually following the partition of an estate. In some places in other counties ownership of churches was divided into smaller fractions.

These references to half-churches give us a clue to why local lords provided churches and priests for their manors. It was clearly no act of piety alone. Churches were sources of income for their owners, and this is why, though they seem not to have been asked specifically to do so, the commissioners included them in the survey. The priest carried out the Church's ordinances and said masses for his patron for a stipend. The owner, lay or ecclesiastical,

---

[1] For suggested explanations of apparent inconsistencies in the Domesday survey of churches and priests in Derbyshire see Turbutt, 435–6 and 455–6.

drew the income which the church attracted. This could be from land assigned to the church glebe, or from the customary payments of the people, such as marriage and burial fees. In the towns rental income could be considerable. As we have noted, the building of a church might be shared by neighbouring lords and the income it produced divided. Because churches were property they could be bought, sold, divided or sub-let. This was a not uncommon practice in the eleventh century.

There are two points to note here. The first is that until the fifteenth or sixteenth century, at least in the theory of English law, the fabric of the church belonged to the lord of the manor. He could grant a *beneficium* or 'favour' to any priest he chose to serve his church. The Church eventually succeeded (though with only partial success in some places) in ensuring that benefices were not given to serfs, for they were subject to their lords. The Synodical Statutes of, for example, William of Blois (1229) required that the clergy should not perform *opera servilia.* But, secondly, why was the bishop so little involved, for he ordained the priest and the priest owed him allegiance? For two possible reasons. The first is that the principle that the local lord owned the local place of worship pre-dated Christianity. Grant and tenure passed from pagan lord and pagan priest to Christian lord and Christian priest. The second reason is that a bishop with a huge diocese and few staff could hardly enforce his will upon local lords of the manor who, for whatever mercenary reason, maintained the fabric and services of the churches.

The evidence of the Church in Derbyshire from the Domesday survey must be treated with caution. We have seen that there were almost certainly more priests and churches than are recorded there. Nationally the Domesday evidence is very uneven. Churches and priests are hardly mentioned in the survey for Oxfordshire and Cambridgeshire, while less than a dozen are recorded in the whole of Cornwall and Devonshire. Compared to Derbyshire, the Nottinghamshire Domesday records more places with churches (72) in a county with fewer places (297). The commissioners in Staffordshire recorded only two places with churches, but 29 priests with no churches, in a county with a total of 342 places. In only a handful of counties, mostly in East Anglia and the south-east, were churches and priests mentioned in more than 255 of recorded places. Yet the Derbyshire Domesday at least gives us some basic statistical evidence of the Church's presence and a broad idea of its distribution.

Tangible evidence comes from the stonework left to us by the Anglo-Norman Church in the county. The *VCHD* historians described this in detail and there is no need to do so again here. They described examples of Norman sculpture from fonts in Ashover, Church Broughton, Mellor, Tissington and Youlgreave; from tympana and door lintels in Ashover, Ault Hucknall, Bolsover, Findern, Hognaston, Kedleston, Normanton, Swarkestone, Tissington, Whitwell, Willington, Parwich and Scarcliffe; and in chancel arches, arcades, windows and doorways, sepulchral slabs, and fragments built in to walls, in Ault Hucknall, Bakewell, Bradbourne, Darley, Duffield, Heath, Long Eaton, Shirley, Stanton-by-Bridge, Steetley and Wirksworth. The dedications of churches to Chad and Cuthbert and Wilfred, and, at Norbury, to Barlok, and to other Celtic saints is further evidence of the vitality of the pre-Norman Church in Derbyshire. And then we have the richness of Norman church architecture in the county from a later period, of which Melbourne is such a wonderful example and said by Bishop Hoskyns in 1914 to be one of the most beautiful (and, then, grossly under-insured!) churches in the world.

The caution with which we should treat the Domesday material is illustrated by the fact that no priest or church is recorded in twenty of the parishes in which there is evidence of the existence of the Anglo-Norman Church, and in seven other places for which there is evidence of pre-Conquest Anglo-Saxon church sculpture.

We must now leave the churches and the people and the priests recorded in Domesday. In the reign of William the Conqueror (and for centuries to come) the parish priests, almost all of them Saxons in his time, were as poor and insignificant and ill-educated as their Celtic predecessors. They were ill-equipped to do much more than carry out the Church's ordinances so far as they understood them. Yet, like Chad and Guthlac before them, many said their prayers, and were faithful, and, as did Chaucer's 'poore parson', followed 'Christes lore' with little thought of personal gain. We owe them so much.

Their lords and those that followed them built churches to the glory of God and to the furthering of their own spiritual security, social status and economic position. Eight Derbyshire churches lay claim to an origin between 700 and 1000 AD, no less than 34 were established in the 11th century, 44 in the 12th, 29 in the 13th, 20 in the 14th and 7 in the 15th centuries. These figures are only approximate, but they show the extent to which earlier churches were replaced and new churches were built in Derbyshire in the early Middle Ages – and what a legacy, and responsibility, we inherit.

4

'The blysse wyth-owten ende': mediaeval faith

With so much left unsaid, and great men and women and unknown saints left unrecorded, we must now move forward two hundred years to the 13th century, regarded as the greatest age in mediaeval history. It was the century of St Thomas Aquinas and St Francis of Assisi and of Dante, and, in our country, of Edward I and Roger Bacon. It was the century which began for us with King John and which ended with the first distant drumbeats of The Hundred Years War.

The ordinary people of the parishes of Derbyshire would not have been touched by these great men and events, or if they were, only very indirectly. For all but a few their lives were lived out in relative isolation within the parishes in which they lived and worked. The parish had originally been co-terminous with the manor or landholding of the local lord, who built a church for the people on his estate and which was regarded by him as his personal property. He appointed a priest who would obey the ordinances of the Church so far as he was able, pray for the soul of the lord of the manor, and care for the people.

Power and Patronage

As manors were broken up, added to, or changed hands, so the boundaries of what we now know as parishes had inevitably changed, though by the beginning of the century the overall pattern had remained virtually stable for 500 years. The patronage of parishes, originally generally in lay hands, was now more or less evenly divided between lay and ecclesiastical patrons. Among the latter were the monasteries endowed with lands and churches given by pious or self-interested wealthy families. Just over the border in Nottinghamshire, for example, the abbey of Welbeck, a Praemonstratensian house, owned eleven churches. In Derbyshire another Praemonstratensian abbey, Beauchief, owned Alfreton, providing a priest for the parish from among its own canons. It had also appropriated Dronfield, but had to supply a vicar together with his stipend, provide for the services in the parish church, and maintain its chancel. Darley Abbey, an Augustinian house, appropriated Crich in the 13th century, and, as we will see, was rebuked by the archbishop of Canterbury in 1280 for not taking its responsibilities there sufficiently seriously. The priory at Launde in Leicestershire, also an Augustinian house, appropriated Hathersage; and Tutbury priory the rectory of Church Broughton. Canons of the Augustinian priory of Dunstable, which owned considerable numbers of sheep in the Peak, regularly served Bradbourne. There are many other examples. Incidentally, monastic interests in the sheep-runs in the Peak were widespread. As an example, four monastic houses had granges in the parish of Hartington. Three were Cistercian houses: Combermere Abbey (Cheshire) with farming interests in Biggin, Garendon Abbey (Leicestershire) in Heathcote, and Merevale Abbey (Warwickshire) in Pilsbury, while the Augustinian priory of Dunstable (Bedfordshire) had holdings in Friden and Stanedge.[1]

The power of the Church stretched beyond the economic influence of the monastic houses. King John's submission to the Pope in 1213, following the lifting of his excommunication and deposition, enabled papal influence over presentation to benefices to be greatly extended. There is much evidence of widespread abuse of the system. In 1301, John, son of Octavian Brunforte, a member of the papal household, was given a canonry at Lichfield and the archdeaconry of Stafford even though he was only twelve years old and a foreign national. There is no evidence that he even visited this country. Successive archdeacons of Derby in these years were non-resident pluralists: Hugh Marreys was given the archdeaconry of Coventry, a canonry and prebendary in St Chad's, Shrewsbury, and the prebend of Pipa Parva in Lichfield in 1349, and, in 1353, the archdeaconry of Derby. His predecessor, John of Askeby, was also a notable collector of ecclesiastical offices, but notwithstanding this he 'experienced difficulty in adjusting income with expenditure' and was often before the justices for debt.[2] Nationally there were many far worse

---

[1] Peter Featherstone, *Biggin and Hartington Nether Quarter* (1998), 14.
[2] A.L. Browne, 'The Early Archdeacons of Derby', *DAJ*, Vol.60 1939, 75–79

examples. This systematic abuse caused widespread resentment which often led to violence. It was resented not because the parishes to which these men and boys were presented were left without clergy (they were not) but rather that English money – and large quantities of it – was flowing into foreign pockets.

However, if the rector was an absentee anyway, it mattered little that he was not ordained, and still less that he was an Italian and could not speak English. Many rectors were not ordained, or, if they were, they were in the minor orders of sub-deacon or acolyte. One might assume that vicars, appointed and paid to act vicariously for rectors, were necessarily priests, though this was often not the case. It has been estimated that the proportion of rectors in priest's orders in the diocese of Canterbury in the 13th century was no more than 20–25%. Among vicars the percentage of priests was about 80%[1]. In far larger dioceses like Lichfield, and with less conscientious bishops, these percentages may well have been lower. Parishes served by the monastic houses that owned them could fare better for priestly ministry.

Parishes and parsons

The widespread abuse of patronage did not mean that the parishes were without clergy. There were a very large number of men in a variety of holy orders. It has been reliably calculated that at the beginning of the 13th century there were about 9500 parishes and no less than 40000 clergy in England. This gives a ratio of four or five men for each parish! It has been said that in the 13th century England was 'swarming with clerics' of one sort or another, each of whom had to be supported, however modestly, by the parishes. In addition there were 17000 monks and friars, also dependent on the generosity of lay people.[2]

In England, the average parish covered about 4000 acres and would include, in addition to a village, outlying hamlets and farms which would often be at a considerable distance from the parish church. In north-western Derbyshire parishes were very much larger than this average. Chapels-of-ease were eventually provided to serve their outlying communities. In Derbyshire, for example, Ashbourne had nine chapels, and Bakewell perhaps as many as eleven. Inevitably some chapels developed a degree of independence from the parish church, though this diminution of the rights (and therefore the income) of the rector or vicar was strenuously resisted. A few chapels-of-ease were well

---

[1] J.R.H. Moorman, *Church Life in England in the Thirteenth Century*, (Cambridge,1945), 48.
[2] ibid., 53–55.

endowed, but the clergy serving the majority of them had to exist as best they could. The chapel of Chelmorton in the parish of Bakewell was worth sixty marks[1] a year. Of this, forty marks went to the prior of the Cluniac house in Lenton in Nottinghamshire, and the other twenty to the Dean and Chapter of Lichfield. The chaplain's income of a mere five marks was raised by the parishioners giving two and a half marks, the Dean and Chapter of Lichfield giving one mark from their twenty, and the neighbouring parish of Beeley contributing the remaining twenty shillings. Chelmorton had its own chaplain as did many other chapels-of-ease. Of Ashbourne's nine chapels, six had their own resident priest, with the other three being dependent on visits from the clergy of the parish church in Ashbourne.

The income of these parish churches and their chapels accrued to their lay or clerical rectors. It varied very widely. A papal financial assessment of the English church taken in 1291 shows that the richest living in England was Lindisfarne (explainable, but ironic) valued at £230. 15s. p.a., followed very closely by its mainland neighbour Bamburgh. Next in the list came Bakewell in Derbyshire at £194 p.a. That annual income contrasted sharply with the average of £20. 6s. 4d. for the parishes in the Derby deanery.

Chapels and Chantries

In addition to the parish churches and chapels-of-ease wealthy parishioners were often given episcopal permission to maintain private chapels. The earliest instance of this in the episcopal registers was at Tuxford in Nottinghamshire, where, in 1227, the rector was allowed to build a private chapel as he claimed that he lived too far from the parish church. In about 1224 the bishop of Lichfield, Alexander de Stavensby, gave authority for the establishing of a chapel in the manor house at Mapperley but in such a way as safeguarded the rights of the canons of Dale Abbey who were jointly patron and rector of Kirk Hallam. This is one of many examples of Derbyshire landed families and monastic houses having rights and responsibilities in what is now another administrative county. In Derbyshire there was, in the next century, a chapel in William of Wakebridge's house in his manor of Crich (where, in an inventory, it is listed after the pigsty and before the dovecote!).

---

[1] A mark was worth 160 pennies, i.e. 13s 4d, or 67p in today's currency. As a comparison, in 1410 it was considered that a knight could live on 100 marks a year, and an 'esquire' on 40 marks [Susan Wright, *The Derbyshire Gentry in the Fifteenth Century* (DRS, Vol. VIII, 1983), 3].

Then there were the endowed chantry chapels which, in many parishes, provided additional clergy to assist the parish priest. By the end of the 13th century private chapels in the homes of wealthy parishioners were quite common. At this time too the endowing of chantries in parish churches and cathedrals was growing. This was to become a scandal. Chantries were attractive to indolent clergy for the stipends were often at worst adequate, and there was little to do. In the 14th century Chaucer's poor parson refused to

> run to London to earn easy bread
> By singing masses for the wealthy dead.

Yet that primary function of a chantry, the singing of masses for the souls of the benefactor and members of his family and of his friends, was of immense value to the benefactors of a chantry, and many chantry priests evidently carried out the provisions of chantry endowments conscientiously. Chantry priests also often assisted the parish priest in his ministry and were effectively what we would now regard as assistant curates. Some chantries had secondary functions which benefited a wider number of people; many provided schools and hospitals and maintained bridges.[1] To endow a chantry chapel with land was a considerable expense, and only the wealthy could afford to do so. The less affluent gentry might pay a priest to pray for the benefactor's soul in the parish church.[2]

Most major parish churches had chantry chapels. As one example, Chesterfield had at least three in the parish church and at Walton. The gild chapel of St.Helen in the town was also probably a chantry chapel. In addition the master and brethren of Chesterfield's town and craft gilds made endowments so that masses could be said for them in the parish church.

The cartulary of the four Wakebridge chantries at Crich give a clear picture of the purposes for which chantries were endowed.[3] When the chantry of St Nicholas and St Catherine was dissolved it was said that it had been founded 'for the mayntaynynge of Godes service and for the socoure of pore folkes.' The chantry provided 10s for the poor each year, and its cantarist was obliged to

---

[1] St Mary's chapel on the Bridge in Derby was not a chantry chapel. The first bridge and chapel were built by the burgesses of Derby during the second half of the 13th century. Although the chapel was in the parish of St Alkmund's, it was a 'free chapel' and was served from All Saints until the College was dissolved under 2 Ed VI, 1548.

[2] Though in 1500 Anne Bradbourne (widow of John Bradbourne and by then the wife of John Kniveton), with kinsmen and neighbours, endowed a chantry for the Bradbourne family in Ashbourne [Susan M. Wright, op. cit., 25].

[3] Avrom Saltman, *The Cartulary of the Wakebridge Chantries at Crich*, (DAS Record Series, vol. 6, 1976), 1ff.

assist the incumbent of Crich on occasion. There is no evidence that the first cantarist, Richard Davy, performed his duties other than conscientiously and with conviction. The chantry of St Mary also provided assistance to the vicar of the parish on Sundays and on specified feast days. The cantarist of the chantry at Annesley (in Nottinghamshire but part of the Crich baronry) was obliged to assist the parish priest and to sing masses for villagers who lived too far away from the parish church to worship there regularly, while the Wakebridge chantry at Normanton in Nottinghamshire (actually a chapel-of-ease) served parishioners in an outlying part of the parish of Southwell.

The Wakebridge chantries at Crich and in Nottinghamshire are representative of many chantries whose priests assisted the parish priest and which also provided chapels in outlying areas of large parishes. Chantries had therefore important community functions as well as serving the eternal interests of their benefactors.

William of Wakebridge became something of an expert in the legal intricacies of founding chantries. He played a part in establishing a chantry in Bakewell parish church and also, apparently acting for the Newark town gilds, in Newark parish church where it became one of no less that fifteen endowed chantries served by a college of chantry priests.

In 1368 the income of the cantarist of the chantry benefice of St Nicholas and St Catherine in Crich parish church was twice that of the vicar of Crich. When the chantries were dissolved in 1547 the net revenues of this chantry were recorded as £12. 3s p.a. This was a considerable sum but it needs to be put in proportion. In November 1356, when William was beset by a riotous crowd in Hucknall, his horse, which had been driven away in the fracas, was valued at £10. The income of the vicar of Crich was low (at £6. 13s 4d in the *Valor Ecclesiastius* of 1535) because the surplus revenues of Crich parish church, after minimal sums necessary to provide for the clergy, had been given to the Augustinian priory (abbey) of Darley by the system of 'appropriations', the priory thereby becoming rector of the parish. The abbey took the bulk of the Crich revenues but did little in return. In 1280 the parishioners of Crich petitioned the archbishop of Canterbury, during his visitation of the diocese, to require the priory (where he was lodging at the time) to repair the nave of their parish church on the ground that the priory owned much land in the parish from which it drew a considerable income. Archbishop Pecham succeeded only in coercing the priory to meet part of a cost for which it was wholly responsible.

This more detailed account of the functions of the Crich chantries will have to serve as a general description of the functions of the many other chantries in Derbyshire. Not only in Crich but also in Tideswell the chantry priest was expected to assist the parish priest, as he was too in Bakewell. The priest of the Trinity Gild in Derby All Saints and the five gild priests at Chesterfield were expected to accept parish responsibilities also. In the large parish of Dronfield the gild priests were expected to administer the sacraments and 'to helpe otherwyse in tyme of necessite.'[1] At Eckington the two gild priests assisted in the parish when 'the Visitacyon of God cometh amongst them the parson and his parish prieste is not suffycent in time of necessite to mynystere there.' Some chantry and gild priests drew the short straw being required to 'synge morowe masse', or the very early mass, each day.[2] This was the duty of the Trinity gild priest in Derby All Saints.

When the chantries were dissolved the effect on the parishes they served was far greater than the dissolution of the monasteries. As many chantry chapels were in effect chapels-of-ease of their parish churches their dissolution robbed outlying hamlets of their church and their priest.

The great churches

To complete this very brief and highly selective account of the provision of churches and clergy in 13th century England, there were the great churches, the cathedrals and the collegiate foundations. Lichfield cathedral, as did all cathedrals, existed, effectively, solely for the maintenance of its dean and chapter. Its considerable revenues and rights of patronage were devoted to that end, even to the extent that priests were employed to relieve them of almost all of their spiritual duties. Some of the collegiate churches, of which Southwell Minster, together with Ripon, Beverley and St George's, Windsor was one, were of ancient foundation. They were communities or 'colleges' of secular clergy who lived together to serve the Minster and the parishes associated with it. Such were the colleges of the old Derbyshire minster churches like the 'great church' of Derby All Saints (where a building known as 'The College' still exists nearby, and which, nearly nine centuries later, was to house the diocesan offices of the new diocese of Derby). Again, that was the ideal. In practice the faithfulness of the canons was at best questionable. In the 13th century the

---

[1] *VCHD*, ii, 16.
[2] ibid.

canons of Southwell, in addition to the regular income deriving from their office, were paid to attend church! They received threepence for attending the night office of matins on ordinary days and sixpence on feast days. There were times when not one of the numerous canons of Southwell was in residence.

Worship and pastoral ministry

If we were able to attend worship in a Derbyshire village church in the 13th century what would we hear and see? The preface to the 1662 Book of Common Prayer, *Concerning the Service of the Church*, reminds us that 'heretofore there had been a great diversity in saying and singing in Churches within this Realm; some following *Salibury* Use, some *Hereford* Use, and some the Use of *Bangor*, some of *York*, some of *Lincoln* . . . ' Of these 'uses', or local modifications of the standard Roman liturgy, that of Salisbury or Sarum was the most widespread, but in the diocese of Lichfield there is evidence that we would probably hear the Latin rite of the mass according to the Lincoln Use.[1]

Numbers of those attending would, as a percentage of population, probably be much higher than it is today, though the impression that everyone went to church in the Middle Ages is false. In 1291 the archbishop of Canterbury, John Pecham, wrote to the archdeacon of Canterbury pressing him to appeal to the people to go to church. Papal legates and French abbots rode about the country making the same plea.

If more people attended church then than they do now, their unruly behaviour there would be much criticised by a worshipper today. Complaints of a lack of reverence by worshippers, and of dignity and care in the celebration of the mass by the clergy, were common in the 13th century. In these circumstances what was there to encourage people to go to church, or to take communion at mass when they did? Because most people communicated only on Easter Day, Alexander de Stavensby, bishop of Lichfield from 1224 to 1238 urged them to communicate three times a year.

In many parishes the church was the only covered public meeting place. Until at least the late 18th century churches were used for a wide range of secular purposes: in the Middle Ages for holding fairs and markets, as courts of law (as at Chapel-en-le-Frith), as temporary prisoner of war cages in the Civil War (Chapel-en-le-Frith in 1648 and Boylestone in 1644), and later for drawing

---

[1] Evidence comes from the Wakebridge chantries cartulary, see Saltmann, op.cit., 178.

lots for the militia, for the assessment of Poor Law cases, as coroner's courts, and for much else. For the mediaeval parishioner (and for centuries to come) there was little distinction between the religious and the secular use of the church (as in life generally), the sacring bell sounding when the priest elevated the Host marking the moment when, for a second or so, earth became heaven. There were no pews in early mediaeval churches to corral the people, and if the priest could not be heard, or understood if he could be, it is little wonder that the church was not given the respect which today even the casual visitor would give to it. So, it is no surprise that brawls in church were not rare. In 1322 Hugh de Meynell of Langley was involved in a violent disturbance in St Werburgh's in Derby, and blood was shed in a fight in St Peter's, Hope, in 1530.[1] The truth is that, as J.R.H. Moorman writing of the 13th century Church put it so well if somewhat idealistically:

> Apart from what the Church offered, there was little to make life gracious and benign. Village life was often rough, and coarse and brutal: but over it all lay the sweet influence of the Christian Church, which tried by ghostly counsel and by the recognised means of grace to set its members upon the 'strait and narrow way that leadeth unto life'.[2]

The 'gracious and benign' and the 'coarse and brutal' were sharply juxtaposed in the parish church.

Lack of knowledge of the Bible (few clergy possessed one), lack of understanding of the theology they would have to expound, and lack of instruction in the art of preaching ensured that sermons were very rare. It was the mendicant friars, who, following the example of St.Francis who followed his Lord, first preached to the people, eventually compelling the parish clergy to do so too. But that revival and challenge came later in the century. Taken together there is ample contemporary evidence to suggest that a modern worshipper would have found worship in a Derbyshire village church in the 13th century a far from uplifting experience. But we are not 13th century Derbyshire villagers. Whether or not the priest gabbled the Latin service in a whisper, whether or not the congregation joked or traded or fought or courted as he did so, and whether or not the church was cold, damp and decaying (as more often than not it was), when the sacring bell was rung and the Host was lifted high men and women would have known that something of huge significance was taking place before

---

[1] Turbutt, 704.
[2] J.R.H. Moorman, *Church Life* etc, 89.

their eyes: Christ had again come to them and to their community. In the 14th century they may have been taught the words of an elevation prayer which began 'Ihesu Lord, welcome thow be' and which ended 'Grawnte me the blysse wyth-owten ende.' This serves as a reminder that the Church over-intellectualises and sanitises its religion too readily. We destroy the sense of the holy when we make it a matter of manners or theology or intelligibility, or, worse, a means to the maintenance of social order. How else can we explain popular resistance in Derbyshire to the at best lack of sensitivity, and often gross crudity and violence, with which, as we will see, the agents of the Reformers were to carry out their task of stripping the altars of these same village churches three hundred years later?

However, the mediaeval church had its grievous abuses and we have listed but a few of them. Poor communications meant that even a resident and assiduous diocesan bishop had difficulty in maintaining oversight in his diocese. The size of several dioceses compounded the problem. In the 13th century the diocese of Coventry and Lichfield extended from Blackburn to Leamington Spa, an area now served by eight dioceses. And bishops were by no means always either resident or assiduous. Roger de Meyland was our bishop for 38 years from 1258. He knew little English and lived abroad. In 1282 the reforming archbishop of Canterbury, John Pecham, wrote to this negligent, absentee and pluralist bishop to tell him that he had recently carried out a visitation of his diocese. In admonishing the bishop he detailed the abuses that he had uncovered: churches had been appropriated by monastic houses without proper provision being made for the spiritual welfare of the parishioners, Confirmations had been neglected, and simony and incest were rife among the clergy. Worse, he said, the bishop had appeared to collude in this wickedness. Pecham wrote also to the Dean and Chapter of Lichfield complaining that their bishop had winked at many of these evils. The effect of this lack of oversight on the more remote and least accessible parishes in Derbyshire must have been very considerable. There were obviously many sinners. That the Church survived and was to flourish suggests that there were also many saints. That the grace of God is not dependent for its working on the holiness of the Church could not be better demonstrated.

One snapshot of the pastoral ministry of the clergy is provided by the mortality rates for beneficed clergy at the time of the Black Death. Bubonic plague is first recorded in England in 1348. By May 1350 the major epidemic had ended. The number of those who died was immense, estimates suggesting that 50% of the population died in some parts of the country. The parish clergy were among the hardest hit as their ministry brought them into daily contact with the disease both through visiting and caring for the sick and in burying the dead. In the county tables showing maximum mortality rates for beneficed clergy, Derbyshire heads the list with 58%. However, neighbouring Nottinghamshire and Leicestershire with 36% come well down the list with Staffordshire with 34% and Cheshire with 33% at the bottom. There is no satisfactory explanation for this discrepancy. Areas of Nottinghamshire with a low rate of clergy mortality were adjacent to parts of Derbyshire with a high rate. Within Derbyshire the mortality rates also varied considerably between deaneries:

Repton	75%	Chesterfield	51%
Derby	68%	High Peak	50%
Castillar[1]	56%	Ashbourne	42%

Seventy-seven parish priests died and 22 resigned. In Derby the incumbents of St Peter's and St Michael's died and the vicar of St Werburgh's resigned. Two priests of the chantry of Our Lady in St Peter's died. At least eight parishes twice lost their incumbents in a very short time. Three successive incumbents of Pentrich all died in the same year. The abbots of Beauchief, Dale and Darley abbeys, the prior of Gresley, the prior of the Dominican house in Derby and the prioress of King's Mead were all killed by the plague as must have been many monks and nuns.[2]

The monastic houses

With a note of this faithful ministry we must leave the parishes of mediaeval Derbyshire and turn to an even older embodiment of the Church's presence in the community, Derbyshire's monastic houses.

By 1200 the simplicity of life of the first monastic houses had long gone, and many monasteries had become businesses with very considerable land-holdings employing large numbers of men and enjoying incomes rivalled only by rich families. This wealth was the undoing of the monasteries. It encouraged kings to impose huge tax burdens on them and, during times of civil disturbance, soldiers and the general populace to raid, pillage and burn them. Potential

[1] in the south-west of the county, roughly corresponding to the Appletree Hundred.
[2] Cox, *Churches*, iv., viii.

benefactors of monasteries compared the wealth of the monks with the poverty and holiness of the wandering friars, the Dominicans and the Franciscans, who began to preach and teach in England early in the 13th century. By its close each had over fifty houses in England and Wales. These friaries joined the houses of the older monastic orders in the county.

There is space here only to list Derbyshire's monastic houses. The outline history of each is to be found in *VCHD* vol. ii and in Gladwyn Turbutt's *A History of Derbyshire,* vol. ii. The Priory of King's Mead (established c. 1150-60) was a house for Benedictine nuns a mile or so from Darley Abbey. The Priory of St James in Derby (c. 1140) was a house for Cluniac monks. The Augustinian order had houses for its canons at Darley Abbey (c 1146), Breadsall (c. 1266), Repton (c. 1172), Calke (c. 1115-20) and Gresley (c. 1100-35). Premonstratensian canons were to be found at Beauchief Abbey (c. 1173) and there was another house of the same order at Dale (c. 1200). The Knights Hospitallers had a preceptory, or subordinate house, at Yeaveley (c. 1189-99), and the Knights of St Lazarus had a preceptory at Locko (meaning the enclosure of a lazar- or leper-house) by c. 1190. The Dominican Friars had a house in the parish of St Werburgh in Derby by 1238. There were hospitals served by men and women under monastic vows in Alkmonton, dedicated to St Leonard, the patron saint of prisoners and captives (c. 1100), and in Chesterfield, also dedicated to St Leonard (c. 1170). There were three hospitals in Derby: dedicated to St James (attached to the Cluniac house), St Leonard (c. 1150) and St Helen (c. 1150). Between Hope and Castleton there was, by about 1150, a hospital dedicated to St Mary.

These were the religious houses, that is communities under monastic vows, in Derbyshire. We have already seen the dominant influence that monastic houses had on the economy of many parishes in the county. This influence was largely negative. Gladwyn Turbutt has shown how much revenue from appropriated benefices flowed from the county to cathedral deans and chapters and monastic houses outside it, with very little returning as stipends and for church maintenance. In the county, monastic houses held 23 benefices (Darley Abbey alone holding nine) with often scant regard for the maintenance of the Church's worship and ministry. As one other glaring example, when the archbishop of Canterbury, John Pecham, held his visitation of the diocese of Coventry and Lichfield in 1279-80 he discovered that the dean and chapter of Lichfield took the revenues of its very wealthy benefice of Bakewell, amounting to £194 p.a., paying the vicar a mere £13 6s. 8d. From this pittance he had to support himself, two priests, a deacon and a subdeacon. The latter two had to beg. John Pecham ordered the dean and chapter to increase the vicar of Bakewell's stipend to allow him to feed his curates and to give them a housing allowance.[1] We have already noted that during the same visitation the archbishop had to take the monks of Darley Abbey to task for their stinginess in maintaining their Crich benefice.

There was some marginal excuse for this meanness. The establishing of a monastic house on a viable basis could take a long time. Lay benefactors had to make money available by giving land or income from land. Not infrequently this initial endowment was not sufficient and attempts to found a house failed. This happened at Dale, to take just one example.[2] Sometime when Stephen was king (between 1135 and 1154) a baker from Derby gave up his trade to become a hermit in Depedale, in the manor of Ockbrook, building himself a chapel there. The baker-hermit was supported from a tithe on a mill in Alvaston owned by Ralph, son of Geremund. In following years successive attempts by the Grendon family, part owners of the manor, to establish a monastic house in Depedale failed. The first to try living there were canons from the Augustinian priory of Calke. They stayed for 30 years but were eventually sent back to Calke for infringing the forest laws. Then, in about 1185, six canons from the Premonstratensian house at Tupholme were sent to Depedale and a priory was established. After seven years they were recalled by the abbot of Tupholme. The prior of Depedale refused to leave his mistress and had to be brought back to Tupholme forcibly, where he committed suicide. The priory was by now derelict and the Grendon family then turned to the Premonstratensian house of Welbeck for help. The abbot sent canons to Depedale, but after five years, disappointed, it is said, with the poverty of the place, he recalled them. Eventually sufficient finance was made available and canons from Newhouse, the senior Premonstratensian house in England, established an abbey at Dale which was to last until the dissolution of the monasteries in 1538/9. Given that history it is little wonder that the canons of Dale developed a lucrative line in money-lending[3], a not unimportant service for the local community.

While that is a long and even sad tale it points to the importance of the monastic life for lay people and for the surrounding population as well as for the members of the communities themselves. We must not assume that the

---

[1] Turbutt, 724–5.
[2] For a full account see Avrom Saltman, *The Cartulary of Dale Abbey* (1967), DASRS, vol 2 for 1966.
[3] J.R.H. Moorman, *Church Life* etc, 363.

Grendon family's eternal self-interest was the only motive for its persistent attempts to establish a house of prayer in Depedale.

The Forests

In this very truncated account there is one last thing to say about parish, priest, people and monk in early mediaeval Derbyshire. If we plot the Anglo-Saxon and Domesday evidence for the Church on a map of the county, the distribution is reasonably even. The exception, of course, is the 40 square miles or so of the north-west of the county which comprised the king's forest of the High Peak. We must pay some attention to this wild and lawless area and the attractions it offered to a few of the clergy[1].

It was forest not because it was woodland (which much it was not) but because 'forest' means that which is 'outside', that is, it was regarded as waste and an area reserved for the king for sport, as was Duffield Frith (or forest) to the south. However, it was by no means completely beyond the reach of the Church. Forest law was administered in forest halls or *Camera in foresta regia Pecci* to which a chapel was attached.

The justice seat or principal administrative centre of the Peak forest was roughly in the middle in an extra-parochial area which was to become Chapel-en-le-Frith — the chapel in the forest. The accounts of Gervase de Bernake, bailiff of the Peak forest for 1255-6 record that he gave vestments, an altar-cloth made from an old chasuble, a silver chalice, an old missal and an old gradual[2] to the chapel together with some tables and a chessboard and two tuns of wine (but only one full) to the hall.

Offenders were arraigned at the justice seat (which was often held in other places for convenience). These frequently included those who had charge of the forest on behalf of the king. Up to 2000 head of deer were taken illegally by William de Ferrers, earl of Derby, during the years when he was bailiff (1216–1222). At the same court the earl's hunting companions were also charged. Five of these offenders were clergy. It was an offence repeated by Robert, earl Ferrers, in 1264. Eight of the 38 named with the earl were knights and one was a priest, Master Nicholas de Marnham, rector of Doddington in Lincolnshire.

---

[1] What follows is taken in the main from *VCHD*, i, 397–425, but note, in addition, the survey of the parishes and extra-parochial areas in the Peak Forest in Anthea Jones, *A Thousand Years of the English Parish* (The Windrush Press 2000), 80–87.

[2] A set of antiphons or sentences, usually from the Psalms, to be sung immediately after the Epistle in the mass.

In 1268 clergy were convicted of poaching or receiving. They included the rectors of Manchester, Denbigh and Tankersley, the vicar of Sheffield, and Augustine, the chaplain of Penniston. The court records show that William de Bradshawe, a parson, was charged with killing a doe at Kinder in 1280, though he subsequently appealed to the ecclesiastical court in York. One monk, Peter, the prior of Ecclesfield, was charged with the offence of harbouring a poacher. He was bailed by the abbot of Welbeck, the Praemonstratensian abbey in Nottinghamshire.

In Duffield Frith the account of the Belper ward for 1272–3 mentions a chapel attached to the Belper manor house and established for the use of foresters. The chaplain was John, who held land from which he derived his income. A woddmote or forest court was held in Belper in May 1466. Among those presented was William, son of Thomas Eyton (vicar of Wirksworth from 1432 to 1487) who, with two others, was charged with entering Duffield forest on several occasions accompanied by four greyhounds.

In 1503 Thomas Savage was appointed by Henry VII as bailiff, receiver, collector and barmaster of the High Peak. He was also archbishop of York, but his appointment to these posts was not incongruous as his chief delight was said by a contemporary to be 'in the sound of the huntsman's horn and the baying of his hounds'! Thomas Savage died in 1507. His successor as bailiff, Christopher Bainbridge, was made a cardinal in 1511 and poisoned in Rome in 1514. He was succeeded by Thomas Wolsey.

With this name we enter that time of fundamental revolt, seemingly against all that we have just described, that we call The Reformation.

5

'Cast away your beads': the Reformation in Derbyshire

We begin with the obvious question. Why did the mediaeval Catholic Church in England effectively, and certainly legally, cease to exist within a generation in the sixteenth century? Was it because it was too rich and too powerful? Perhaps, but it had been rich and powerful for centuries before but there had been no Reformation then. In any case, rich as its dignitaries were, in the parishes the clergy were close to the people and most were poor providing the context of the holy – what John Moorman romantically called the 'sweet influence' – within easy reach of which both poor and rich lived out their everyday lives. Was it because the call for theological reform became so insistent that it had to be answered? Yet radical theological reformers had been preaching and writing and suffering for their faith in the fifteenth century, but the Reformation did not take place then. Was it because there were abuses and corruptions in the Church? But these had existed for centuries. Geoffrey Chaucer wrote of them in the fourteenth century, but there was no Reformation then. Did the Reformation take place because European nation states had begun to assert their independence from papal domination? Yet Spain and France asserted their independence but experienced no radical reformation. Was it because the Renaissance encouraged scepticism and freedom of thought? Perhaps, but some of the greatest Renaissance figures, while they were critical of the Church and sought its reform in the light of the New Learning, were by means revolution-aries and certainly not Protestants. The archetypal English Renaissance Man, Sir Thomas More, was executed for refusing to renounce papal supremacy. Was the Reformation the result of a cry for religious liberty? Were men and women thenceforth free to worship God as they chose? By no means. Such an idea would have been vigorously repudiated by Luther and Calvin. Did the Reformation mark a time when lay people began to make their voice heard? Was Protestantism primarily an anti-clerical lay movement? Was there widespread popular disillusion with the Church? No, and in any case lay protest against the privileges and power of the clergy had been voiced well before the sixteenth century.

Perhaps the Reformation occurred when it did for a more mundane reason. During the preceding centuries written English gradually replaced Latin and French as the vehicle of intellectual debate. Increasingly, lay people entered an intellectual culture previously reserved to the educated (though not most parochial) clergy. As the Bible became available in English, beginning with the translations of Wyclif's Latin text at the end of the 14th century, so the educational partition between clergy and laity began to be dismantled. However, the Bible in English was available to very few, and Wyclif's Bible remained the only English text until Tyndale published his version of the New Testament in 1526.

Lacking confident answers to our question it has been argued that the term 'the Reformation' is little more than a kind of marker which historians attach to a series of by no means necessarily connected social, political and religious movements. Yet if we cannot be dogmatic about the causes of the Reformation we can be more sure of its results. In England it was eventually to give rise (amongst much else) both to a national Church which, it was claimed, was catholic but reformed, and to other Christian Churches which could not, for conscience sake, conform to this new uniformity in either theology or church order.

In the second decade of the sixteenth century these many factors which gave rise to the Reformation were becoming interdependent though its consequences were well in the future. The initial English challenge to Roman supremacy was due not to disagreements over belief, for Henry VIII always remained Catholic in faith and observance, but for dynastic reasons. He wanted a male heir. His first queen, Catherine of Aragon, bore him four sons and three daughters. Apart from Princess Mary, all were born dead or survived for no more than a few days. To secure what he hoped would be a legitimate male heir, Henry, after much legal debate, eventually petitioned Rome to have his marriage to Catherine set aside. When Pope Clement VII refused, Henry renounced the papal supremacy and made himself head of the English Church.

The English Reformation had four phases. In the first, while Henry was alive, reformation extended little further than the government and management of the Church, the curtailing of its privileges and the appropriation of its finances. By claiming to be the spiritual as well as the temporal head of the Church Henry became, effectively, an absolute monarch. He wielded his power nakedly and put down dissent without mercy. Monasteries were dissolved and their revenues taken by the state. This had little direct effect on parishioners. To a tenant there was little to choose between monastic and lay landowners, and to an impoverished vicar it made little difference whether he was kept poor by a lay rector or a monastic house. However, when, in 1548, the chantries and gild endowments in parish churches were suppressed, the lives of ordinary parishioners were touched directly. Not only did the rich benefactor of a chantry and the member of a parish or trade gild lose the comfort of masses said for their souls, but perhaps more importantly at a social level parishes also lost the schools (as at Hathersage and Melbourne), hospitals and almshouses (as at Alkmonton) and other amenities financed by many chantries, as well as the services of the chantry priests who assisted the parish clergy in their ministry.

In one matter Henry's appropriating of the Church's property and revenues might have been to the benefit of the Church in Derbyshire. In about 1540 Henry was encouraged by his Nottinghamshire-born archbishop of Canterbury, Thomas Cranmer, to establish new dioceses financed from appropriated Church revenues. One of these would have been a separate diocese for Derbyshire and Nottinghamshire. Henry nominated one Dr Cocks (possibly a leading reformer, Dr Richard Cox, who became bishop of Ely in 1559) as its first bishop and named Southwell as the cathedral town. The large sum of £1003 was assigned to the support of the new cathedral and its bishop with two-thirds assigned to the cathedral and one-third to the bishop. Nothing came of the proposal as Henry found more pressing need for the money. In the event only six new dioceses were created. The diocese of Southwell was not to be established for nearly three and a half centuries.

Thus far reform would have been barely noticed by a Derbyshire parishioner. The worship offered in his parish church continued as before except, eventually, in one matter where the influence of more radical reformers was seen: in 1536 Henry allowed a Bible in English to be placed in every parish church.

Some information about the incomes, and therefore of the social position, of the parochial clergy at this time is provided by the *Valor Ecclesiasticus*, a survey of ecclesiastical revenues ordered by Henry VIII in 1534 in order to estimate additional Church income he might acquire. The figures provided in the *kinges bookes* of 1535 are suspect and probably underestimate the then value of livings, especially of rectories, and the list does not contain the income for all the beneficed clergy and curates in the county. Despite the defects in the list, the information it contains suggests that Derbyshire clergy in Henry's reign were far from well provided for. Unappropriated rectories ranged in value from £3 2s 1d (Hartshorne) to £41 3s 4d (Eckington) and averaged slightly over £11. Vicarages ranged from £3 8s 8d (Longford) to £41 7s 9d (Wirksworth, due to tithes on lead) and averaged about £10. Endowed chantry and gild priests received incomes ranging from £2 (Derby St Peter) to £12 4s 4d (Crich), averaging about £4 13s.[1]

The suppression of Derbyshire's monastic houses and its chantries was swiftly accomplished. In 1535 commissioners were sent into every county to compel the acceptance of the king's authority by every monastery and priory. Their work was easily accomplished in Derbyshire as the religious houses were relatively few in number and modest in value. It seems that at least 48 monks and nuns in the county signed away their religious houses between 1536 and 1540. Fifty-nine monks were allowed to become beneficed clergy and 43 religious received pensions.[2] The suppression of the chantries was set in hand by Henry in 1545 and completed under a fresh Act of Parliament under Edward VI in 1548. Their loss was far more significant for the parishes. In Derbyshire some large parishes were effectively deprived of their outlying chapels and the chantry clergy that served them. A record of 1555 of the pensions paid to former chantry priests lists a minimum of 53 in Derbyshire who were dispossessed in 1547.[3] Ann Middlemas Johnson estimates that following the dissolutions of 1548, 159 clergy were effectively deprived of their ministry.[4]

The outlying chantry chapels were left uncared-for with everything of any worth taken away. An inventory of all churches and chapels taken in 1549 had revealed more of value that could be made available to the royal exchequer, while another taken in 1553 was designed more to impose Protestantism than to raise income, though this was the ostensible reason. In the parish churches and chapels-of-ease the commissioners left only a chalice, a bell and a surplice. The scale of destruction was huge. No item listed in the inventories of Derby All Saints survived. Charles Oman suggested in 1961[5] that only three medieval

---

[1] I am indebted to Dr Richard Clark for this information.
[2] This and much of the detail that follows is derived from Ann Middlemas Johnson, 'The Reformation clergy of Derbyshire', *DAJ*, 1980, 49-63, which gives much more information than there is space for here.
[3] *VCHD*, ii, 18.
[4] op.cit., 53.
[5] *DAJ*, 81.

patens survived, at Dronfield, Shirley and Hartshorne.[1]

During this second phase of the English Reformation, in the reign of the boy king Edward VI (1547–53), the movement towards doctrinal reform in this country was greatly strengthened by the presence in the two universities of major figures from the continental Protestant churches, invited here by Thomas Cranmer. These men, among the most distinguished of whom were the Italian Peter Martyr, the German Martin Bucer, and the Pole John a Lasco, in the main tended towards the theological position of the Swiss reformer Ulrich Zwingli whose theology of the eucharist was more radical than that of the more conservative Protestant position of Martin Luther. For this reason Lutheran Protestantism had little influence here in these critical years. However, so rapid had been the changes in theology and liturgy that the gap between the beliefs and practices of the university theologians and those of Derbyshire priests and parishioners was wide.

To these years belong the first editions of Cranmer's English Prayer Book, the conservative book of 1549 and the more fundamentally Protestant book of 1552, the compilation of which had been influenced by the radical European reformers. It would have been difficult to enforce their observance in the more remote Derbyshire parishes. England was a patchwork of local jurisdictions and loyalties. The topography of Derbyshire affected its social and religious history profoundly. An overall even conformity was never possible, and, especially in the north of the county, was resisted, though there was never any organised opposition to reform parallel to the uprisings in Lincolnshire and in Yorkshire in 1536.

Derbyshire was, and remained for many years, traditionalist in religion. When Henry VIII's vicar-general, Thomas Cromwell, sent an officer to Buxton to despoil the shrine of St Anne not only of its image of the saint but also of the 'cruchys, schertes, and schetes, with wax offeryd', he found that the devotion of the ordinary people was not as easily destroyed and was forced to 'lokk ... upp and seal ... the bathys and welles ... thatt non schall enter to washe them'[2]. A well chapel dedicated to St Anne may have stood on the site of the present church of St Anne erected in 1625. The 'cruchys' would have been hung on its walls in gratitude to the patron saint for the curative powers of the waters. In Chesterfield, William Ludeham, a hermit of the chapel of

---

[1] there may have been at least one other, at Radbourne.
[2] Eamon Duffy, *The Stripping of the Altars: traditional religion in England 1400-1580* (1992), 385.

St Thomas, was arrested for claiming that as it was treasonable to pluck down the King's arms, 'What shall he do then that doth pluck down churches and images, being but a mortal man as we be?'[1]

The third phase of the Reformation in England was one of reaction and resistance. Henry's daughter Mary succeeded Edward VI in 1553. She restored papal allegiance and Catholic worship though she retained the revenues of the dissolved monasteries and chantries which remained in the hands of the Crown, though much had already been dispersed. The European reformers hurriedly returned home. Together with very many Protestant believers in London, East Anglia and the south-east – the heartland of the English Reformation – Mary handed over to be burnt at the stake 20 clergy including five bishops, among them the archbishop of Canterbury, Thomas Cranmer. By far the majority of those executed were, however, tradesmen and labourers. Fifty were women. The executions for heresy carried out during the four years of Mary's reign far exceeded those under Henry VIII and Edward VI. Almost 300 men and women are known to have been burnt for heresy. In addition, very many died in prison awaiting trial. Inevitably the majority died in the Protestant heartlands. Fifty-eight died for their faith in Middlesex and London, more than 50 in Kent and in Essex, with 40 in Sussex. One of the women died in Derbyshire. Her name was Joan Waste, a 'Poore Blind Woman' of twenty-two, who used to attend her parish church of All Saints in Derby each day where the parish clerk read the New Testament to her. Her heresy was that she denied the doctrine of transubstantiation. The bishop of Coventry and Lichfield, Ralph Bayne, accused her. The Chancellor of the diocese and incumbent of two Derbyshire parishes, Anthony Draycott, preached to her and denounced her, threatening her with eternal damnation. She did not recant, and with that she was taken out and burnt to death in Windmill Pit. The date of her martrydom was 1 August 1556. In 1553 a priest at Derby All Saints, Richard Jordan or Jurdan, had been accused of the same heresy before Bishop Bayne. He admitted it, but recanted,[2] and possibly later became curate of Brampton. Three years after Joan Waste's martyrdom Bishop Bayne and Anthony Draycott refused to take the oath acknowledging Queen Elizabeth as supreme governor of the Church and were deprived. Ralph Bayne died the same year. The imprisonments, burnings and deprivations did nothing to endear Mary, married to Philip

---

[1] cited in Eamon Duffy, ibid., 406.
[2] Ann Middlemas Johnson, op.cit., 56.

of hated Spain, to the English people.

In one matter the Reformation had a public face in some Derbyshire parishes. In 1549 the clergy had been allowed to marry. Under Mary these married clergy were deprived of their livings but, if they renounced their wives, they could be presented to benefices elsewhere. About one third of the clergy in Essex had to leave their benefices for this reason. The fact that only one tenth of the clergy had to do so in the entire diocese of York is but one illustration of the varied pattern of the English Reformation: it engaged the south and east much more than the north and the west to which Derbyshire belonged. In the diocese of Coventry and Lichfield 42 priests were arraigned before the bishop, Ralph Bayne, in March 1553-4 and accused of marrying. Of these eight were Derbyshire priests, or less than 6% of the clergy in the county. All were deprived of their benefices, though it seems that one, Thomas Gosnell of Trusley was subsequently reinstated to a curacy at Stretton-en-le-Field. Robert Ashton, pluralist vicar of Longford and rector of Mucklestone in Staffordshire was deprived but had been reinstated to Mucklestone by 1564. George Davye or Davys was curate of Scropton in 1553-4 and was deprived, as were Nicholas Cotton, vicar of Mickleover, William Wayne of Marston-on-Dove, John Dawson, vicar of Melbourne, Peter Hart, rector of Matlock, and Bernard Brandon or Brande, vicar of Pentrich. In recording these names Ann Middlemas Johnson says that 'there is little doubt that the parish clergy of Derbyshire found themselves facing a most bewildering upheaval in their religious lives. Under Henry they could not marry, under Edward they could; they were forbidden to marry under Mary, but Elizabeth allowed it.'[1] As Ms Johnson points out, their marital status was by no means the only source of confusion for Derbyshire clergy in the period between the last years of Henry's reign and the beginning of Elizabeth's, so rapid and fundamental were the political and theological changes. What were they to believe? What were they to teach? We should have some sympathy for them when, under threat of deprivation and even of death, they changed their minds.

Elizabeth came to the throne in 1558. With her the fourth phase of the Reformation begins. Elizabeth faced a difficult task. Most Englishmen probably remained conservative in their religious views. They were Catholic by tradition and in sentiment but they disliked being subject to the Pope and

---

[1] ibid., 58.

they feared Spain, though, if Catholic Spain were to invade Protestant England could Elizabeth be sure that English Catholics would not collaborate with the invader? The toleration of any religious belief or none which so marks today's society was alien to Elizabeth's time. Religion united or it divided society, and thus it had deeply social and political aspects.

The result of the queen's attempt to unite the country came to be called the Elizabethan Settlement, under which a national Church was established by law – a Church which would later claim to be both Catholic and reformed. The English Prayer Book of 1552 was restored though with subtle modifications which steered it in a Catholic direction. Elizabeth styled herself not supreme head (as her father had done) but supreme governor 'in so far as the laws of Christ allow.' An Act of Uniformity in 1559 made this settlement binding on all Englishmen under penalties which, as threats of invasion by Spain became greater, were enforced with increasing severity.

Inevitably there were Derbyshire clergy who refused to conform. John Ramridge, archdeacon of Derby and rector of Longford was deprived in 1559. Henry Comberford, rector of Norbury and precentor of Lichfield, and Anthony Draycott rector of North Wingfield, vicar of Wirksworth, and Bishop Baynes' chancellor, were also deprived. In 1558 Nicholas Holmes resigned his Elvaston benefice, as did his successor William Robinson, before they could be deprived. Some clergy managed to avoid subscribing to the 1559 Act and remained in their parishes. It is a mark of how conservative and traditionalist the Church in Derbyshire was that less than a third of its beneficed clergy subscribed.

In 1565, their bishop, Thomas Bentham, bishop of Coventry and Lichfield from 1560 to 1579 and a convinced Protestant who had lived in exile in Zurich and Basel during Mary Tudor's reign, felt compelled by this lack of conformity to require his clergy to 'call upon the people daily that they cast away their beads with all their superstitions that they do use' and the clergy themselves to 'cast away your Mass-books, your portesses and all other books of Latin service' and not to use the traditional hearse candles. He required churchwardens to fine those using their rosary beads one shilling for every offence. He seems to have attempted to prevent the people from intoning Psalm 130 for their dead friends or from following the custom of laying corpses at roadside crosses on the way to burial. As further evidence of the persistence of traditional devotion a generation after Henry VIII's death Bishop Bentham also required his clergy to remove any ritual accoutrements 'which be laid up in secret places in your church.'[1] If the bishop thought it necessary to issue these injunctions to the diocese as a whole we can be reasonably confident that the Reformation had hardly penetrated to the more inaccessible Derbyshire parishes. In 1584 William Overton, bishop of Coventry and Lichfield 1579-1609 asked church-wardens, in articles of enquiry,

> Whether your minister or any other of your parish be known or suspected as favourers of the Romish church, superiority or religion; and whether any renegade Jesuits or counterfeit massing-priests, going not according to the order of their professions, are known or suspected to frequent or haunt to any person or persons within your parish, sometime for a shift to lie or lurk with them; and whether they or any schoolmaster, or any other pretending the name of a servant, are suspected to allure and persuade any within your parishes from the true sincerity of the Gospel now by public authority established to the using of mattins, beads, and such other vain popish trish-trash, or any unlawful popish books . . .[2]

The churchwardens of Derby St Michael reported that their incumbent, Michael Babington, had been away overseas for five or six years and was 'Suspected to be a papiste.'

Another of Overton's visitation articles, aimed at rooting out traditional religion, asked 'whether any within your parish be suspected to use sorcery, witchcraft, charms, unlawful prayers, or invocations in Latin or English; namely midwives in time of women's travail with child, and who resort to such for help or counsel?' There was no question aimed at detecting Puritan sympathies among the clergy such as a refusal to wear a surplice or sign with the cross at baptism.

In contrast to these indications of the survival of traditional religious practices there is some evidence that what Keith Thomas describes as a 'distaste for any religious rite smacking of magic' had spread among ordinary people, perhaps combined with a resentment of the economic status of the Church. He cites an early seventeenth century diarist who recorded how 'four

---

[1] Eamon Duffy, op.cit., 572.

[2] from W.P.M.Kennedy, *Elizabethan Episcopal Administration, (1924)*. I am grateful to Dr Richard Clark for this reference.

drunken fellows' in Derbyshire drove a recently calved cow into church 'and that which is appointed for churching a woman was read . . . for the cow, and led her about the font: a wicked and horrible fact.'[1] For Thomas this and much other evidence suggests that 'the decline of old Catholic beliefs was not the result of persecution; it reflected a change in the popular conception of religion'. Though this is a view which is much disputed, the fact that so many Derbyshire churches had to be renamed after the Reformation because their pre-Reformation dedications had simply been forgotten might lead to the same conclusion.[2]

Bishop Overton's articles of enquiry asked also for information about the performance of church services, the fabric and furnishings of the churches themselves, and much else, including whether 'your minister keep any suspected woman in his house' and whether he was 'given to drunkenness or idleness; or is a haunter of taverns' or whether the clergy be 'hunters, hawkers, dicers, carders, tablers, swearers, or any ways give any evil example of life . . .' To this question the wardens of Ilkeston answered that 'Our vicar ys a carder and dycer at Alehouses he ys suspected to keepe one Anne Webster . . . which went awaye about May Day last with child . . .' The vicar of Pentrich was suspected of having two wives. He lived in a vicarage 'in great decaye' and, little wonder, 'the vicars zeale ys smale.'

By no means all the churchwardens replied. The impression one receives from those that did suggests that not a few church buildings in Elizabethan Derbyshire were in poor repair and that the pastoral zeal and morality of some of the clergy were not such as parishioners had the right to expect. But that is an obvious conclusion, and much the same could be said of any period up to the mid-19th century.

Elizabeth's settlement could not be accepted by resolute Roman Catholics or the stricter Protestants. About 1570 the term *recusant*, 'refuser', which had earlier had a wider meaning came to be applied exclusively to Roman Catholics (a term which also dates from this time) who refused to conform. To begin with there was a degree of indulgence for recusants and fines for their refusal to conform were not always exacted, but by 1562 recusants were being noted, lists drawn up and arrests being made. Pope Pius V declared that it was

---

[1] Keith Thomas, *Religion and the Decline of Magic* (Penguin 1991), 87.
[2] Further to this see Richard Clark, 'The dedications of mediaeval churches in Derbyshire: their survival and change from the Reformation to the present day', *DAJ* 112 (1992), 49–61.

sinful to conform. The Northern Rebellion of 1569 taking up the cause of Mary, Queen of Scots, and the papal bull of 1570 which declared that Elizabeth was 'the pretended Queen of England, the servant of wickedness' confirmed government fears that every Roman Catholic was potentially a traitor. Recusancy was now a criminal offence. The conspiracy to free Mary, Queen of Scots, involving, perhaps unwillingly as its leader, Anthony Babington of Dethick, later added to the sense of threat.

Anthony Babington was a covert Roman Catholic. Considerable areas of the north of Derbyshire were strongly recusant, and remained so. In Elizabeth's reign the Eyres of Hassop and the Fitzherberts of Padley and Norbury, the Poles, and the Hunlokes of West Hallam and Wingerworth were notable recusant families exercising considerable influence. Together with the northern counties, Wales and the marches, Derbyshire, Staffordshire and Warwickshire had significant numbers of recusants. The penal legislation of 1559 left those in the High Peak, and in most of northern England, relatively untouched. A Roman Catholic bishop, Nicholas Pursglove, formerly bishop of Hull, who did not oppose the Elizabethan Settlement though he refused to subscribe to it, lived in the High Peak in peaceful retirement.[1] Tideswell had a Catholic school. For many years Mary of Scotland had lived in genteel captivity in Sheffield, South Wingfield and Chatsworth and had been welcomed locally. But in the south of the county Sir Thomas Fitzherbert of Norbury, and lord of the manor of Padley, refused to take the oath of Supremacy in 1559 and spent the rest of his life in prison, dying in the Tower of London in 1591. His story is one of extraordinary steadfastness, courage and devotion. His brother-in-law John Sacheverell of Morley was imprisoned elsewhere in London. In 1581 a list of recusants in Derbyshire was compiled by an agent of the Privy Council, said to have been a servant of Lady Petre's. It contains 10 names including Sir Thomas Fitzherbert and John Fitzherbert. In March 1596 twenty-five Roman Catholics were convicted for refusing to attend Hathersage parish church.[2]

The story of the Padley Fitzherberts and of the priest-martyrs is well known. Two Derbyshire-born priests, Nicholas Garlick and Robert Ludlam, were arrested at Padley on 12 July 1588, and, with another priest, Richard Simpson, were tried on 23 July and, having spent their last night in its chapel, were brutally executed at St.Mary's Bridge in Derby the next day. Those who had

---

[1] The commissioners of recusants said of him in 1561 that he was 'very wealthy, stiff with papistry, and of estimation in the country.'

[2] PRO, E377/8. I am grateful to Dr Richard Clark for this reference.

given Nicholas Garlick and Robert Ludlam shelter at Padley, John Fitzherbert, his son Anthony and three of his daughters were arrested, together with ten men working on the estate. The penalty for harbouring priests was death but this was not exacted in the case of the Padley Fitzherberts. John was imprisoned, first in Derby for two years, and then in London where he died on 9 November 1590. In December 1588 nearly 40 Roman Catholics were in prison in Derby including some of the tenants and servants of the Fitzherberts[1].

Another name on the 1581 list is that of Sir Thomas Gerard of Etwall. He had to answer the charge that he was a recusant but was allowed to remain at liberty by agreeing to attend services (though not holy Communion) in his parish church at Etwall. On one occasion his rather more resolute brother Nicholas, badly disabled with gout, was staying with him. Much against his will Nicholas was carried to Etwall parish church one Sunday. As soon as the minister (probably the incumbent, Edward More) began the Prayer Book service of Morning Prayer Nicholas began reciting the psalms in Latin in a loud voice. When he had reached the third psalm the vicar gave up the struggle and had Nicholas carried back to his brother's house! Thomas Gerard was later to adopt a more rigorous stance and was imprisoned in the Tower from 1567 to 1570 and again from September 1586 to August 1588 followed by further imprisonments.[2]

From this period, too, a relatively small number of Protestants, polemically styled 'Puritans', began to exert influence. These were those who, while conforming to Elizabeth's settlement, wished for a Church further purified of what they held to be unscriptural elements. Their preferred title was 'the godly'. They were already beginning to make an impact. In 1574 Thomas Daubery, rector of Stretton-en-le-Field 1567–97 was ordered to wear a surplice by Bishop Bentham, as was Peter Ekersall, curate of nearby Measham. Ekersall is said to have voiced his own and his parishioners' objections to such effect that Bentham withdrew.[3] 'The godly' were to have their day in the century that was to follow.

---

[1] Turbutt, 981-2.

[2] *VCHD*, ii, 24.

[3] For further information about the Reformation in Derbyshire, noting particularly the impact of reformist ideas on the clergy indicated in their Wills, see Richard Clark's lecture, 'Some reflections on the Reformation in Derbyshire' given to the Derbyshire Archaeological Society in October 1989.

6

'Religion the cloake to cover their intentions': the custody battle for the Church, 1603 – 1649

We have already noticed that an assumption that the Church was reformed evenly and indiscriminately across the entire country is clearly wrong. Indeed, in at least one important area, that of canon (that is, Church) law and the operation of the ecclesiastical courts, fundamental reform would not be achieved for centuries. The truth is that while England in general during Elizabeth's reign may have been anti-Roman it was far from being fully Protestant. Even at the beginning of the eighteenth century it was Protestant more in what it opposed than in what it upheld.

The century that intervened saw a continuation of that process of religious development that we know as the Reformation. Its first six decades saw profound theological disputes, civil war, and the overthrow both of the monarchy and the Church of England of which the monarch was supreme governor. Clergy were once again deprived of their livings and a new form of church government, Presbyterianism, temporarily and unsuccessfully imposed – only for the monarchy and the Church of England of the bishops to be restored in 1660.

Under James I, Elizabeth's cousin, the Church of England saw a continuation of the uneasy consensus between bishops and Puritans. Having said that, we have covered over a multitude of complexities. The Church of James I, and more so that of his son Charles, was a Church riven by a fundamental dispute between rival claimants to Christian orthodoxy within the Church of England. It was not that Elizabeth's orthodox Anglican Church was now beset by a vehement sort of non-Anglican Protestantism. In fact the term 'Anglican' is not found in use before 1635. The notion that there was in these years an Anglican Church threatened by those set to destroy it from outside is quite false. Rather we have in the years leading to the Civil War in 1642 what a recent historian has described as a battle between two rival claims for custody of the Church. To describe this as a struggle between loyal Anglicans and Puritans outside the Church's jurisdiction is therefore to beg every question worth asking about this complex period in our history.[1]

These questions date back to Elizabeth's settlement. The settlement sought to achieve, as the Book of Common Prayer said of the Church of England's liturgy, a 'mean between two extremes', a *rapprochement* between those, including some bishops, who wished for further and deeper reformation, and those who believed that reformation had been achieved and perhaps had gone too far. The settlement satisfied neither extreme, and became less of a religious compromise between them and more of a political constraint on both of them.

The roots of the struggles within the Church of England in the 17th century are to be found there, and if we are to understand the often bitter theological and ethical disputes, the compromises, coalitions and accommodations, and the refusal of one side to acknowledge the legitimacy and integrity of the other within today's Church of England, we will find them already institutionalised in Elizabeth's religious settlement, a settlement which gave legal form to a reformation which was both incomplete and ambiguous.

The objections of 'the godly'

Within a few years of the beginning of the century a new reign began. Elizabeth died in 1603. On his way from Scotland to London in 1603 James I had been presented with a Puritan petition, moderate and conciliatory in tone, which requested that the godly be relieved of their 'common burden of rites and ceremonies': the sign of the Cross at baptism, the wearing of the surplice, the rite of Confirmation, bowing at the name of Jesus, and the reading of the Apocrypha in divine service. James called a conference at Hampton Court in which the Puritans presented their case. Their petition had said nothing about episcopacy, but the question of its legitimacy was now raised. James would have

---

[1] Conrad Russell, *The Causes of the English Civil War* (OUP 1990), 85ff.

none of this. He had seen presbyterian church government in Scotland and feared that the abolition of the bishops would inevitably lead to the abolition of his own role as the Church's supreme governor. 'If once you are out' he said to the bishops, 'and they [the Presbyterians] in place, I know what would become of my supremacy.'[1] A modest revision of the Prayer Book and a new and comprehensive set of canons consolidated both the king's authority and the Church's discipline. The canons required all that the Puritans had sought to remove: the cross at baptism, the ring in marriage, the wearing of the surplice, and kneeling to receive communion, and concluded by asserting that members of the Church of England acknowledge that

> the King's supremacy over the Church on causes ecclesiastical is legitimate; that the Church of England is a true and apostolic Church; that the Articles of Religion are scriptural and true; that the rites and ceremonies are such as can be used with a good conscience; and that the government of the Church by archbishops, bishops, and other clergy is agreeable to the Word of God.

Their refusal to subscribe to these canons compelled about ninety Puritan incumbents to leave their benefices. The words 'Puritan' and 'Papist' became terms of abuse flung at the other from each side. Those regarded by the 'godly' as papists were the bishops and clergy of the Church of England who upheld the theology and practices enshrined in the canons and who, in the main, adopted an anti-Calvinist, Arminian, theological position.

The objections of the godly were by no means confined to rites and ceremonies. They were rightly concerned at the low standard of the education of the clergy, and therefore of preaching, which was fundamental to the theology and ministry of the godly. In 1551 more than half of the clergy of Gloucestershire could not repeat the Ten Commandments and one in ten did not know where to find them. One in twelve could not name the author of the Lord's Prayer.[2] In 1583 it was said that the vicar of Blidworth in Nottinghamshire was apt to confuse Jesus with Judas. It is little wonder that parishioners were equally ignorant. A test applied to 'prove' witchcraft was to require old women to repeat the creed or the Lord's Prayer at their trials. Alice Gooderidge, arraigned for witchcraft at Derby assizes in 1597, failed

---

[1] A.Tindal Hart, *Clergy and Society 1600–1800* (SPCK 1968),27.
[2] citations in Christopher Hill, *Economic Problems of the Church from Archbishop Whitgift to the Long Parliament* (Oxford 1963), 206.

the test.[1] But had she known them she was probably too terrified to be able to repeat them.

In 1602 or 1603 a list of benefices and chapelries within the jurisdiction of the bishop of Coventry and Lichfield was compiled. It contains the names of 461 benefices and chapelries and 433 clergy in Staffordshire, Derbyshire, Shropshire and Warwickshire. Of the clergy in the diocese as a whole 110, or 25%, were graduates, but only 82, or 19% of the total, were licensed to preach. In the Derbyshire list there are 151 benefices and chapelries and 137 clergy. The ratio of clergy to parishes is lower at 91% but of the clergy 44 were graduates (32%) while 33 (24%) were licensed to preach. So Derbyshire had a considerably higher proportion of graduates and licensed preachers than in the diocese of Coventry and Lichfield as a whole.

Nevertheless the concerns of the godly were well founded. It would seem that a sermon was heard in only a quarter of the churches in Derbyshire – and then rarely as Elizabethan injunctions of 1559 required the clergy 'to preach in their own persons, once every quarter of the year at least one sermon, being licensed especially thereunto.' The number of licensed preachers had declined as Puritan clergy departed following the imposition of Elizabeth's Act of Uniformity. Parish clergy who were not licensed to preach the quarterly sermon were required by canon to find a clergyman who was. This led to resentment and dispute. At Clowne, at Michaelmas in 1583 the incumbent Richard Chapman, who in the 1602 list is described as having no degree and as 'no preacher' (that is, not licensed), declined to attend church when the licensed preacher arrived. His sexton, acting on Chapman's orders, refused to take the cushion into the pulpit. Richard Chapman and his sexton had to appear before the archdeacon's court to answer for this discourtesy. Some years later the entire congregation at Wirksworth left the parish church in 'clamorous fashion' when the licensed preacher entered the pulpit. The vicar, Michael Chapman, listed as a doctor of divinity, unusually seems not to have had a licence to preach[2], though he appears as a public preacher in a 1593 list. In many parishes there was no sermon from one year's end to another. This disturbed the Puritans, who regarded a non-preaching ministry as 'the sinne of sinnes,

---

[1] John Denison, *The most wonderfull and true storie of a certaine Witch named Alse Gooderidge of Stapenhill, who was arraigned and convicted at Darbie at the Assises there* (1597), 9, cited in James Sharpe, *Instruments of Darkness: Witchcraft in England 1550–1750* (Penguin 1997), 222–3.
[2] J.C.Cox, *Annals,* i, 244, and *VCHD,* ii, 22–3.

of the sin of soul-murther', and demanded sermons each week. The canons of 1604 met this demand, requiring beneficed clergy who were licensed preachers to preach each week, and those who were not to procure a licensed preacher to preach a sermon once a month. On the other Sundays the non-licensed clergyman was expected to read an authorised homily.

Within less than a generation the general educational standard of the clergy had risen. This was due in large part to the growth of the Tudor grammar schools which provided the revived universities of Oxford and Cambridge with bright undergraduates, but it was also due, not least, to the enforcing of the 1604 canons. Every preacher was to show his licence to the churchwardens and enter his name in the register of preachers together with that of the bishop who had licensed him. The Derbyshire list indicates that preacher's licences had been granted not only by the diocesan bishop but also by both archbishops and the bishops of Lincoln and Ely. Elsewhere in the diocese, clergy claimed to have licences of long-standing granted by Bishop Jewel of Salisbury, who had died in 1571, and Bishop Bentham of Coventry and Lichfield who died in 1579. The 1604 canons also required the clergy to catechise every Sunday and on Holy Days, to hear private confessions under conditions of strict secrecy, to dress modestly, not to lodge in taverns and not to play at 'dice, cards or tables'. Much else was enjoined by the canons to raise the standard of pastoral care and the conduct of public worship. In this the clergy were greatly helped by another outcome of the Hampton Court Conference of 1604. This was a new translation of the Bible, suggested by James I. It was published in 1611 but although it was 'Appointed to be read in churches' it received no formal authorisation.[1]

However, attempts to improve the general level of clergy incomes came to nothing in face of opposition from lay impropriators protective of their own income. Increased stipends would have reduced pluralism and therefore, notionally, raised educational and pastoral standards over time.

What effect did this policy of imposed uniformity have on the parishes and clergy? The picture is mixed. Nationally the policy resulted in Puritan clergy being excluded from appointment to benefices, though, in Derbyshire, at least one Puritan clergyman, William Whiting, was appointed after 1604, becoming

---

[1] 'Authorised Version' is thus a misnomer.

rector of Egginton in 1612. To combat this, wealthy Puritan laymen founded lectureships in major parish churches. In Derbyshire, for example, a Barbary merchant in London left money in 1608 to provide for a preacher in Ashbourne parish church. In 1631 a further £400 was subscribed so that a divinity lecture could be added.[1] On Sunday afternoons, clad in their Geneva gowns, Puritan lecturers could preach and pray as they wished in parish churches and frequently drew large congregations. Encouraged by the influential high church and anti-Puritan Bishop Laud of St.Davids, later to become successively bishop of Bath and Wells, of London and then archbishop of Canterbury, James issued a set of *Directions* which sought to regulate the Puritan parish lecturers.[2]

When Laud became archbishop in 1633 he conducted a metropolitical visitation. He enforced the restoration and repair of parish churches, and insisted that public worship should follow the Prayer Book, and that the communion table should be set up at the east end of the church 'where formerly the Altar stood'[3] and that it should be railed off. The clergy were required to wear the surplice (hated by Puritans). They were to celebrate holy Communion at least once a month, should hold services on Wednesdays and Fridays, should keep the Church's festivals and fasts and should themselves say the daily offices of Morning and Evening Prayer. Once again it is impossible to say how far these requirements were carried out by the clergy of Derbyshire, though there is no reason to suppose that the majority did not do as they were told, willingly or not. At least one incumbent, Richard Barlow, rector of Morton, acquiesced unwillingly. Having set up a communion table in the nave of his parish church in 1636 he was required to move it to the chancel.[4]

A set of 17 canons passed by the Convocations in 1640 sought to consolidate the Laudian Church of England. But the enforcing of uniformity was short-lived. In 1625 Charles I had succeeded his father. He was a man who, though more charismatic than his father, lacked his political sagacity.

---

[1] Christopher Hill, op. cit., 270. Godfrey Foljambe had endowed a lecturership in Chesterfield parish church in 1595, and, from as early as the 1570s, the Corporation of Derby supported a lectureship in Derby All Saints.

[2] Many of these lecturers were not ordained. As the title of a senior curate or associate minister the title still pertains in some city parishes.

[3] A plan, dated 1638, of the pews in Hayfield parish church shows the communion table in the restored position (*DDRO*).

[4] citation in Turbutt, n19, 1389.

7

'A Nailer hath confuted them all': Civil War, Commonwealth and Protectorate

The causes of the Civil War which began when Charles I raised his standard in Nottingham in 1642 were profoundly complex. It was certainly a struggle between king and Parliament as to who should rule England, but in the long term the causes of the conflict were to be found in the problem of governing three disparate countries with different cultures; in the difficulty of inadequate royal revenues at a time of rising inflation; and, most intractable of all, in the struggle between those who had fought for custody of the Church of England for two generations and more, with Parliament and the godly Puritans standing over against King Charles and Archbishop Laud's Church of England. Puritan and Parliament prevailed. Laud was executed in 1645 and his king in 1649.

The Presbyterians had temporarily carried the day in the custody battle for the Church. They were 'the godly' of the reigns of James I and Charles I who, disposing of 'prelatical' bishops, sought to establish a national Church governed by representative elders or presbyters from the parishes meeting in local 'classis' or 'colloquys', with regional synods and a national synod above them. This presbyterian system was never fully implemented in England and was in any case short-lived, for a radical alternative form of church government, hand-in-hand with a more radical politics, became dominant.

This was Independency. It rejected any notion of a state Church whether ruled by bishops or by presbyters. It claimed that each congregation should be independent, with freedom to govern itself outside the control of either Church or state – within limits, for Independency never recognised the Quakers and other radical religious groups. Independency was to become dominant during the ten years from 1649 to 1659 when Cromwell directed the destinies of England.

At the outbreak of the Civil War worshippers in many parish churches in Derbyshire would initially have noticed little difference (though at Derby All Saints, Henry Fisher removed the surplices on 17 June 1641 and all efforts to recover them failed) but this was to change radically as the years passed. By 1643 it seems that diocesan and archidiaconal administration had more or less collapsed in the diocese of Coventry and Lichfield. Throughout the entire war, and the Commonwealth and Protectorate that followed it, only 2425 incumbents from a national total of 8600 were evicted from their parishes, to be replaced by Presbyterian, Independent and Baptist 'intruded' ministers.

We know little about those who were removed from their benefices. Attention is often focused on the Presbyterian ministers who replaced them when it became their turn to be ejected on the restoration of king and Church and the imposition of the Act of Uniformity of 1662. But conscience cuts both ways; by 1645, out of 108 Derbyshire benefices perhaps 13 clergymen had been formally ejected – though for reasons other than for refusing to accept Presbyterian theology and church order, then still a matter for debate and resolution. It seems that these men were removed more for being on the losing side than over questions of theological principle. They were Robert Topham of Wirksworth, William Thorpe of Carsington and of Matlock, William Bott of Fenny Bentley, Thomas Chapman of Pentrich, Shirland Adams of Eyam and of Treeton, Yorkshire, Richard Clarke of Aston on Trent, Henry Cooke of Derby St Alkmund, William Greaves of Brailsford, George Holmes of Breadsall and of Clowne, George Mason of Bradley, Godfrey Oldfield, curate of Mellor, Anthony Topham of North Wingfield and Ralph Wells of Horsley.[1] A few others had left earlier to accompany the king's army, and several more resigned within a year or two. They and their families left their parishes on grounds of conscience. Already poor they became poorer still, losing their homes, their friends and their livelihood.

The week by week life of the parishes continued initially much as before. Administration by bishops and archdeacons, and the enforcement of their orders by the ecclesiastical courts, ceased, to be replaced by that of county

[1] I am grateful to Richard Clark for this and for other information in this chapter, the result of his own research.

committees. Instructions were issued in 1644 requiring 'the utter demolishing, removing, and taking away of all Monuments of Superstition' including 'Holy Water Fonts', the levelling of chancel steps (as a measure to eliminate what were regarded as superstitious papist practices), and the removal of the communion table from its Laudian position lengthwise against the east wall to an east-west orientation in the body of the nave. In some parts of the country Parliamentary commissioners enforced these injunctions ruthlessly, churchwardens' accounts later recording considerable expenditure in repairing the damage done. At Derby All Saints the chancel was levelled as early as 1641, and in 1646 the exceptional sum of £16.16s was spent in what seems to be the repair of wanton damage.[1] By the end of the century All Saints was said to be 'out of repaire and very ruinous'.[2] We might note here that churches were occasionally put to unusual uses in the Civil War. The Royalist Col Rowland Eyre, returning to Derbyshire with his regiment after the defeat at Marston Moor, billeted his soldiers in Boyleston parish church. Parliamentary dragoons under their local commander Sir John Gell surprised and captured the Royalists, later adding to the number in the temporary prison more Royalist troops captured in an assault at Burton-on-Trent.[3]

The major difference with which parishioners would have had to come to terms was the replacement of the Prayer Book by the *Directory of Public Worship* in January 1646, though this was never enforced other than in a piecemeal way. Sequestration committees were established and, in October 1646, an ordinance was passed under which parishes were to be grouped together in classical assemblies or *classes.* The Wirksworth classis was the only significant element of Presbyterian organisation in Derbyshire of which we have detailed knowledge, though there is no evidence that parliament ever approved a system of classes in Derbyshire.

The Wirksworth classis met monthly between 1651 and 1658. Its minute book survives showing that it dealt with such matters as the examination of ordination candidates, the administration of holy Communion to non-parishioners and the appointing of a day of 'humiliation' or fasting because of 'feavers and other sicknesses in divers places within the Classis'. It was concerned also to regulate the marriage of cousins and to discipline church

---

[1] Margaret A. Mallender, *The Great Church: A short history of the Cathedral Church of All Saints, Derby* (1977), 14.

[2] ibid., 16. It should not be assumed that this was entirely due to Puritan vandalism left unrepaired.

[3] Brian Stone, *Derbyshire in the Civil War*, (Scarthin Books 1992), 63.

elders for scandalous behaviour.

One of those who attended the meetings of the classis was Francis Topham, who became rector of Thorpe in 1633. He had submitted to Presbyterian theology and discipline. At the few meetings of the classis he attended he would have joined his far more enthusiastic brother Martin who became vicar of Wirksworth sometime before 1650 (succeeding his father, the ejected Robert Topham, incumbent since 1633). Francis insisted on imposing in his parish the fasts ordered by the classis, though he would have found them difficult to enforce, Thorpe and the surrounding country being predominately Royalist, with John Milward's sons serving with the king's forces and one of the Blores with the duke of Newcastle's. Francis Topham was succeeded in 1656 by Alexander Hamilton. He bent his conscience and conformed at the Restoration remaining incumbent until 1712 rebuilding the old and ruinous rectory and patiently copying out the parish registers and terrier.[1]

The quality of the ministry of intruded godly Puritans was often recognised. Joseph Swetnam had become rector of Dalbury in 1624. He later became rector of Whitwell and was minister of Derby All Saints by the late 1640s. He served as a captain of horse in the parliamentary army. By the 1650s, together with many other Presbyterian ministers, he had become uneasy with Cromwell's Independency, which initially he seems to have welcomed. He resigned (or, as Calamy said, he entered into a 'mixtly voluntary Secession') before the Act of Uniformity of 1662 was passed. He was said to be 'a man very well fitted to fill so August a Place as Allhallows in Derby. A very able Preacher and a great Master of Language'. Notwithstanding his resignation on grounds of conscience Swetman left 16 shillings a year from property he owned in Full Street to be paid to sixteen poor widows each Good Friday.[2]

'A new and heavenly-minded man': the Quakers in Derbyshire.

By far the most notable of the independent wandering preachers of the seventeenth century was the shoemaker son of a Leicestershire weaver. His name was George Fox (1624–1691). He was, one of his biographers wrote, a man 'that God had endued with a clear and wonderful depth, a discerner of others' spirits and very much a master of his own.' He was, William Penn said,

---

[1] E. Higham, 'The Ancient parish of Thorpe', *Southwell Diocesan Magazine*, September 1910.
[2] Mallender, op.cit., 14. Further to Swetnam, see J.T. Brighton, 'Royalists and Roundheads', *Journal of the Bakewell and District Historical Society*, Vol VIII, 1981.

both 'a bulky person' and 'a new and heavenly-minded man', though John Wesley was to remark that Fox was 'foul-mouthed to all that contradicted him.'[1]

Fox rode and walked the length of the country, and visited Ireland, the West Indies, North America and Holland, proclaiming that the truth was to be found in the voice of God speaking directly to the soul. His first journeys were to Derbyshire and he returned to the county time and again between 1647 and 1680, preaching, confronting and confounding the (initially Presbyterian) 'priests', as he called them, of the parish church 'steeple-houses', and encouraging those attracted by his evident sincerity and holiness of life to be his 'Friends of the Truth', later the Society of Friends.

Fox was imprisoned several times, first in Nottingham in 1649 (for 'a pretty long time') and notably in Derby in 1650 for almost a year, to be followed by further incarcerations in prisons in Launceston, Lancaster, Scarborough and Worcester. In Derby gaol Fox confronted magistrate Gervase Bennet. Fox, with John Fretwell of Stainsby, a husbandman, had been committed to Derby's house of correction charged with 'the avowed uttering and broaching of divers blasphemous opinions, contrary to the late act of Parliament, which, upon their examination before us, they have confessed.' In 1650 it was Bennet, Fox records in his *Journal*, 'who was the first that called us Quakers, because I bid them tremble at the word of the Lord.'

Fox's *Journal* was compiled towards the end of his life and many years after the events that it records. It is deeply influenced by Fox's reading of scripture, and one cannot always readily separate the events it describes from the biblical interpretation he attaches to them and which shapes his record.[2] What we can be sure of is both the warmth and the bitterness with which his preaching was received – preaching that was perceived to have a social content and a political edge. Fox's hearers were either for him or against him. As just one example here is Fox's record of a visit to Derbyshire in 1655:

> From thence [Nottinghamshire] . . . I passed . . . into DERBYSHIRE, where the Lord's power came over all; and many were turned from the darkness to the light, and from the power of Satan unto God, and came to receive the Holy Ghost. Great miracles were wrought in many places by the power of the Lord through several. In Derbyshire James Naylor met

---

[1] John Wesley, *Sermons on Several Occasions* (1866 ed.), ii, 310.
[2] On this see M.R. Austin, 'Bible and Event in the *Journal* of George Fox', *The Journal of Theological Studies*, April 1981, 82-100.

me, and told me, seven or eight priests had challenged him to a dispute. I had a travail in my spirit for him, and the Lord answered me, and I was moved to bid him go, and give him the victory of his power. And the Lord did so; inasmuch that the people saw the priests were foiled, and they cried , 'A Nailer, a Nailer, hath confuted them all.' After the dispute, he came to me again, praising the Lord. Thus was the Lord's day proclaimed and set over all their heads, and people began to see the apostacy [sic] and slavery they had been under to their hireling teachers for means; and they came to know their teacher, the Lord Jesus, who had purchased them, and made their peace between God and them. While we were here, Friends came out of Yorkshire to see us, and were glad of the prosperity of truth.[1]

In Fox's account of the incident we find several intertwined social, religious and psychological threads. Rejecting, and radically challenging, the spiritual authority of the well-educated and socially superior, Fox and his Friends claimed to hear their call direct from God. James Nayler subsequently told how the word of God came to him: 'I was at plough, meditating on the things of God, and suddenly I heard a voice saying unto me, "Get thee out from thy kindred and from thy father's house."' As with Fox's *Journal* the account seems to be deeply influenced by incidents in the Bible expressed in the words and cadences of the King James' version. For men and women like James Nayler and George Fox, to live by the word of God meant to take the Bible utterly seriously. Only in its light and by its power, they believed, was the truth proclaimed to 'the priests and preachers'. And when it was proclaimed, as Fox records in Derby in 1650, 'the power of God thundered amongst them, and they did fly like chaff before it.'

Those who followed George Fox in Derbyshire suffered for their deep convictions. Derby seems to have been the first place where a Quaker woman preached. Elizabeth Hooton was imprisoned in 1651 for interrupting a church service in Derby, as was Thomas Towndrow for doing so at Ashover in 1654. Most scandalously of all Jane Stones was imprisoned and whipped in 1657 for interrupting a meeting of the Wirksworth classis. She was condemned by the

---

[1] John Billingsley was the incumbent of Chesterfield at the time. For the background to this incident, which involved Billingsley and a bull-baiting, see Richard Clark, 'Why was the re-establishment of the Church of England in 1662 possible? Derbyshire: a provincial perspective', *Midland History* (Vol VIII 1983), 94.

local justices 'to be striped naked to the waste and whiped at the cartes taile in Wirksworth Market.'[1] There were supposedly godly ministers in the Wirksworth classis, but, in all periods, a notion of one's godliness and a sense of one's social position have gone easily hand in hand. J.A. Sharpe notes that at this time women preaching was but one aspect of the general spectacle of 'the lower orders developing ideas of religion whose immediate consequences were a direct attack on the social order.'[2]

John Gratin was another courageous Derbyshire Quaker. He lived in Monyash and became a 'Friend' in 1664. King and Church had been restored four years earlier. From his home Gratin preached widely in Derbyshire. This was in direct contravention of the Conventicle Act passed that year[3], and he was fined in Chesterfield and imprisoned in Derby.

With the spirit of independency in the ascendant, freedom of belief and worship was widely asserted, not least by those who, outside any Church or orthodoxy, Anglican, Presbyterian, Independent or Baptist, claimed, as did George Fox, a direct revelation from God. There were Fifth-Monarchy Men who were millenarians awaiting the Second Coming, and Philadelphians, and Ranters, Socinians (or Unitarians), the Sweet Singers of Israel, the Adamites (a sect with an ancient lineage whose adherents had a predilection for worshipping in the nude in all weathers), and many other mystical sects. One such was the Puritan and anti-Trinitarian sect of the Muggletonians led by Lodowick Muggleton (1609–1698) and his cousin John Reeve. In 1651, claiming the authority of direct spiritual revelations, Muggleton and Reeve announced that they were the two prophetic witnesses of Rev. 11:3. They denied the doctrine of the Holy Trinity asserting that God had possessed a human body, and that he had left Elijah in heaven as his vice-regent while he himself descended to die on the Cross. For these two the unforgivable sin was not to believe in them as true prophets. One of Muggleton's missionary journeys brought him to Derbyshire. He was arrested in Chesterfield in 1663 on information lodged by the vicar, John Coope, and charged with preaching anti-Trinitarian blasphemy. In fact

---

[1] *VCHD*, ii, 30. Whipping was a common law public punishment for misdemeanour. It was abolished for women in 1820. Its use for men became increasingly uncommon after this date, but it was not finally abolished until 1948.

[2] J.A. Sharpe, *Early Modern England: A Social History 1550-1750* (Arnold 1997), 250.

[3] This forbade any person over 16 years of age to be 'present at any assembly, conventicle or meeting, under cover or pretence of any exercise of religion, in other manner than according to the liturgy and practice of the Church of England.'

Coope had mistaken Muggleton for a Quaker and, having investigated his claims, pronounced him 'the soberest, wisest man of a fanatic that he had ever talked with'. Muggleton was committed to Derby gaol and after nine days was released on bail. In Derby Gervase Bennet engaged Muggleton in debate, but, it is said to the delight of his fellow magistrate, was no match for him. Extraordinarily, according to *DNB*, the last Muggletonian died in 1979.

8

'The Sovereign Prerogative': the restoration of king and Church

The restoration of king and Church in 1660 was at the same time a revolution. A Parliament controlled by Presbyterians, but frightened by an army seemingly composed of Independents and the wilder sort of separatist extremists, welcomed Charles II knowing well that the restoration of the monarchy, while securing the future against political and social radicalism, meant the end of presbyterian church government and a return of episcopacy. Initially there was a desire for a measure of *rapprochement*. The king and some of his bishops were prepared to revise the 1604 Prayer Book to appease the consciences of 'the godly', but the returning Laudian clergy, deeply conscious of the injustice they had suffered and with public opinion with them, would have none of this. A conference of both sides called by Charles in 1661 failed and an Act of Uniformity was passed requiring the re-ordination of those clergy not already episcopally ordained. It further demanded that all clergy take an oath of obedience to the king and that they undertake to uphold the doctrines and usages of the Church of England and not to promote change in either. On St.Bartholomew's Day 1662 about 1800 parish ministers nation-wide who had refused to take the oath, be re-ordained or to make these undertakings, were ejected from their livings and were subsequently subjected to the harsh provisions of the so-called Clarendon Code – the Test, Corporation, Conventicle, and Five Mile Acts which together were designed to restrict the exercise of their ministry and generally to inhibit nonconformity.

A few of the Anglican clergy who had been expelled from Derbyshire parishes in the 1640s returned to them. One was William Bott, rector of Norbury from 1642 until he was ejected. Another was Richard Clarke, rector of Aston from 1636, a 'Prelatical Divine, who had been Eject'd there many Years before.'[1] He too was reinstated in 1662. One other, the elderly Ezekiel Coachman, at one time rector of Walton-in-Trent, did not succeed in his claim for restoration.[2]

The majority of the formerly Presbyterian parish clergy in the county conformed. Thomas Bocking, incumbent of St Peter's, Hope, since 1650 remained there until 1672. There were many others. However, dedicated Presbyterians could no more accept the Church as restored in 1662 as those Anglican clergy they had replaced could in conscience become Presbyterians between 1645 and 1652. They are the true fathers of English nonconformity and we owe them much in Derbyshire.

With the coming into force of the Act of Uniformity on 24 August 1662, St Bartholomew's Day, two episcopally ordained clergy who had accepted Presbyterian church order and discipline in the county resigned. Thirteen ministers ordained as Presbyterians had resigned or had died between 1660 and 1662. At least 12 episcopally ordained clergy who had been incumbents of parishes in 1644 and had then accepted Presbyterian church order and discipline now accepted episcopal authority once more. Their number included men who had been prominent in the administration of the Church in the intervening years. Emmanuel Bourne, for example, rector of Ashover since 1621, had presided at the ordination of William Bagshawe to the Presbyterian ministry in 1650. Bourne had long been a noted Puritan. At this distance in time it is easy to criticise these men as vicars of Bray, but if, like many Presbyterian clergy, you believed that the rightful custody of the Church of England belonged to men of your mind, but that Independency would create anarchy and so destroy it, then submission to king and bishop once again might seem the only course by which the national Church could be preserved. Some Presbyterian ministers in Derbyshire, ejected in 1662, had previously prayed publicly for the restoration of the king for this reason.

It may be that, for this reason, Everard Pole changed his mind. Pole was rector of Mugginton from 1629 to 1674. On 3 May 1641 Parliament issued a 'Protestation' to be signed by members of both Houses, and by all office-holders in Church and State, by which they renounced popery and declared their allegiance to the 'true reformed Protestant religion expressed in the

---

[1] Edmund Calamy, *A Particular Account of the Ministers... silenced and ejected by the Act of Uniformity...* (1713), ii, 205.
[2] Cox, *Annals*, i, 337.

doctrine of the Church of England.' That Church of England was a Church from which all archbishops, bishops and other dignitaries had been 'utterly abolished', as a bill which passed its second reading later that month declared. Pole, together with his congregation, signed the 'Protestation' on 15 August 1641, thereby declaring his commitment to root and branch reform of the Church of England. He was ejected from his benefice in 1662 but almost immediately conformed and was restored.

The number of Derbyshire Presbyterian ministers who were ejected or resigned from their livings in 1662 because they refused to conform is uncertain, but it may be as high as 38. There were impressive men among them. We have already noted Joseph Swetnam. Two other Derby incumbents went with him, Luke Cranwell of St Peter's and Samuel Beresford of St Werburgh's. Another to be ejected was John Hieron, rector of Breadsall, together with his brother Samuel, rector of Shirley.

John Billingsley was also ejected. He had become vicar of Chesterfield in 1653 replacing the royalist William Edwards, vicar of the parish since 1638, who had died in 1650. Billingsley had been ordained a Presbyterian minister in St Andrew Undershaft in London in September 1649. He was presented with others at Derby Quarter Sessions in July 1661 for refusing to use the Book of Common Prayer and was removed from his benefice. He too had opposed Independency after Cromwell's death and was said to have prayed publicly for the king. For this he had to answer before the Council in London. The bishop of Lichfield and Coventry subsequently brought John Billingsley before his consistory court in 1662, later writing to the bishop of London that

> I convicted him by sufficient witness that in a farewell sermon August 23,
> he said that the prelatical Ministers, at least some, were put out for
> murder, drunkenness, whoredom etc.- but such as himself for being too
> holy and too careful of Religion.[1]

Another Presbyterian minister ejected in 1662 was the highly regarded John Oldfield (or Otefield as he signed in his parish registers). He was born near Chesterfield about 1627 and became rector of Carsington in 1650 in place of the ejected William Thorpe, incumbent since 1638. His parishioners, according to Edmund Calamy, one of the first historians of nonconformity, were 'very ticklish and capricious, very hard to be pleased in ministers.'

---

[1] J.M. Bestall and D.V. Fowkes, *History of Chesterfield*, vol ii, part 2 (Chesterfield 1984), 61-2.

Oldfield attended the first meeting of the Wirksworth classis on 16 December 1651 and was to be its moderator on fifteen occasions.

Following his ejection in 1662 Oldfield moved from place to place settling eventually in Alfreton where he died, aged 55, in 1682. He wrote a soliloquy after the passing of the 1662 Act of Uniformity. In 1855 Elizabeth Gaskell was to quote it in *North and South* as the inspiration for Richard Hale as he too leaves the Church of England's ministry for reasons of conscience:

> When thou canst no longer continue in thy work without dishonour to God, discredit to religion, foregoing thy integrity, wounding conscience, spoiling thy peace, and hazarding the loss of thy salvation; in a word, when the conditions upon which thou must continue (if thou wilt continue) in thy employments are sinful, and unwarranted by the word of God, thou mayest, yea, thou must, believe that God will turn thy very silence, suspension, deprivation, and laying aside, to His glory and the advancement of the Gospel's interest. When God will not use thee in one hand, yet He will in another.[1]

Oldfield had married Ann, the sister of Robert Porter. Porter had become vicar of Pentrich sometime before 1650 replacing Thomas Chapman. Chapman had initially accepted the new reforms but was later sequestered by the parliamentary commissioners for refusing to accept Presbyterian order and had died in 1652. Robert Porter was the moderator of the Wirksworth classis at its first recorded meeting on 16 December 1651. Ejected from Pentrich in 1662 he remained in the parish, preaching in his own house, until the Five Mile Act compelled him to move to Mansfield. He still preached occasionally at a house in Longcroft Fields. During Charles II's short-lived indulgence in 1672 he established a congregation in Mansfield, but, like the early Methodists in the next century, he attended services in the parish church and held his own meetings at other times. Calamy said of him that

> His Parts were great and quick, his Fancy was very Rich and Pregnant, and his Wit rendered him the Desire and Pleasure of Gentlemen in Conversation . . . .The People he settled amongst were Poor, but his Labours were great, and very prosperous among them.[2]

The best known of the Derbyshire ministers deprived in 1662 was William

---

[1] Elizabeth Gaskell, *North and South* (Penguin edition 1995), 36.

[2] E. Calamy, op.cit., ii, 180-2.

Bagshawe, Presbyterian vicar of Glossop. He was ejected with his curate Jonathan Twigg. Bagshawe, later to become a Congregationalist, was to be widely respected as 'The Apostle of the Peak' preaching regularly to ten congregations until his death in 1702.

As a strange legacy of the Restoration, the Glossop chapelry of St Mary Magdalene, Charlesworth, became an Independent chapel during Queen Anne's reign.[1] Richard Clark suggests that local inhabitants might have hired dissenting clergy to preach there after the Restoration. Notwithstanding this toleration, a century and a half later, as we will see, the Independent minister in Charlesworth was to harry the incumbent of the recently created Anglican parish unmercifully.

Much that was positive belongs to the period of the Commonwealth and the Protectorate that followed it. Parsonage houses were rebuilt (the vicarage at Kirk Langley is dated 1655), and, more remarkably, a chapel dedicated to St Charles, King and Martyr, was built in the extra-parochial peculiar of Peak Forest in 1657. Under Parliament the clergy were generally better paid than before, though their increased economic status was to be very short-lived, 74 of the 150 poorest benefices in the county augmented by Parliament's Committee for Plundered Ministers losing their increased income after 1660.[2] Of greater significance socially, the people had experienced a degree of freedom of choice in matters of religion. This had momentous implications for Church of England and Dissent alike. After the Act of Toleration of 1689 freedom to worship as one pleased (other than for Roman Catholics and Unitarians) was eventually interpreted as freedom not to worship at all. But between the Restoration in 1660 and the Act of Toleration thirty years later religious persecution returned as old scores were settled.

The new diocesan bishops in 1660 found much that was wanting in their dioceses. Although the parochial system had been maintained throughout the Civil War, the Commonwealth and the Protectorate, and the incomes of the poorer clergy had been raised, albeit temporarily, very many parish churches had been allowed to fall into disrepair, and a considerable number were to continue in that state until well into the 19th century. Confirmations had not been conducted, of course, and huge numbers now demanded it. In 1661 John

---

[1] A new building was erected in 1797.

[2] Richard Clark, 'A good and sufficient maintenance: the augmentation of parish livings in Derbyshire, 1645–1660', *DAJ*, (1980), 69ff.

Hacket, son of a London tailor, had become bishop of Coventry and Lichfield. On one journey through Shropshire and Staffordshire he confirmed 5384 people.[1]

The Gospel sacraments had also been neglected: Public baptism had been largely disregarded owing to the Puritan rejection of using the sign of the cross, though parish registers show that some baptisms had taken place. The eucharist had virtually ceased to be celebrated at all. Following the Restoration it was still to be only rarely celebrated; in most country parish churches no more than four times a year and then only as an adjunct to Morning Prayer. This continued in some parishes until the end of the 19th century – and this despite injunctions from archbishops and the example both of Wesley's Methodists and the founders of the Oxford Movement. Under the Protectorate marriage in church had been abolished and much irregularity in this and other matters affecting parishioners had to be addressed.

There was, therefore, much for the bishops to discover and much to do. There exists a book of *comperta and acta,* faults found by the bishop of Coventry and Lichfield and cases referred to the church courts from the archdeaconry of Derby in 1665.[2] Two years later Thomas Brown, archdeacon of Derby and vicar of Ashbourne from 1660 to 1669, sent searching articles of enquiry – a legal questionnaire – to churchwardens. They were under sworn oath to answer the questions correctly 'with all affection, favour, hatred, hope of reward and gain, or fear of displeasure or malice set aside.' The questions were very searching: Is there in the church a font of stone 'set up in the ancient usual place'? Is there the Book of Common Prayer, 'lately set forth by Act of Parliament'? Is there 'a convenient and decent Communion Table, with a Carpet of Silk, or some other decent stuff, continually laid upon it at the time of Divine Service'? And is the communion table 'so used out of time of Divine Service, as is not agreeable to the holy use of it, as by sitting on it, throwing hats on it, writing on it, or is it abused to other profaner uses'? Was their parson 'distinctly and reverently' saying the services 'by the Book of Common Prayer appointed', and did he have a licence to preach? And did he catechise the young for half an hour before Evening Prayer, and did he baptise or administer holy Communion in private houses 'otherwise than by Law . . . allowed'; and did he 'look carefully to the relief of the poor'; and did he use 'such decency and

---

[1] On coming to the diocese Hacket had found his cathedral virtually in ruins. He set about to restore it, much frustrated by his dean whom he eventually excommunicated.
[2] LJRO, B/V/1/72.

comeliness in his apparel as by the 47 Canon is enjoyned'. And 'if any person hath been dangerously sick in your Parish hath he neglected to visit him, and when any have been parting out of this life, hath he omitted to do his last duty in that behalf'? And do the parishioners attend church regularly, and do they behave themselves or 'do [they] give themselves to babling [sic], talking, or walking, and are not attentive to hear the Word preached or read'? And much else. These articles of enquiry were on a *pro forma* printed in London in 1665 and were evidently in use at least throughout the province of Canterbury. The churchwardens' replies do not survive, but the existence of the articles shows how concerned bishops and archdeacons were with the state of the Church of England for which they were now once again responsible.

With this quantity and detail of information coming back to them the bishops succeeded eventually in restoring the place of an episcopal Church of England in national and local life.[1] But they failed to maintain the clergy in the degree of economic security, however modest, that they had enjoyed under Cromwell. As the Parliamentary augmentations to clergy stipends had largely been paid from tithes on the sequestered estates of Parliament's opponents these payments ceased at the Restoration.[2] In addition, leases on dean and chapter and bishops' lands and property had fallen in by 1660. These leases could be renewed by the payment of fines or penalties. Diocesan bishops now had the opportunity to augment the income of the parochial clergy from this source. This they failed to do, generally taking this money for themselves.[3]

With the sometimes drastic decline in the incomes of the clergy after the Restoration went an inevitable lowering of their social position with the result that many were held in some contempt by their wealthy parishioners. Poor parsons could not afford to maintain already dilapidated parsonage houses, and to buy books and to educate their children and also to pay pensions to their predecessors, as they were required to do. In face of this they often had to take on additional curacies or farm their glebe themselves or accept pupils into their parsonages in order to supplement their income. Occasionally parish clergy practised medicine 'for want of other means', and indeed had done so since the Reformation. Some resorted to what today would be regarded as

---

[1] Confidence returned quickly in some places. In 1662 Sir Francis Burdett built the church at Foremark, a donative 'squire's church', with wrought-iron gates leading from the churchyard into the grounds of Foremark Hall.

[2] Further to this see Richard Clark, 'Why was the re-establishment of the Church of England in 1662 possible? Derbyshire: A provincial perspective', *Midland History*, (Vol VIII 1983), 85ff.

[3] Christopher Hill, cited in A. Tindal Hart, *Clergy and Society 1600-1800* (SPCK 1968), 58.

sorcery. In the 17th century, Keith Thomas records:

> When a woman was conscience-striken after hearing the warning in the
> Communion service against profane livers, the minister of Hope,
> Derbyshire, a Mr Jones[1] 'gave her an amulet, viz. some verses of *John I*
> written in a paper to hang about her neck, as also certain herbs to drive
> the devil out of her'.[2]

This need to supplement his income inevitably affected the standard of pastoral
care the parish priest provided.

Then, in 1665 and during this time of great religious, social and political
change, came the plague and the parish clergy and people were exposed to the
dangers to which their predecessors had been subjected when the Black Death
struck in the 14th century. The story of the coming of the plague to Eyam (an
isolated incident in Derbyshire), the leadership of its rector, William
Mompesson, and the courage and self-discipline of his parishioners is well
known.[3]

The 'Obstinate refusers': the Compton Census of 1676

Under Charles II's brief indulgence in 1672–3, 28 Presbyterian ministers and
eight Congregationalists were licensed in Derbyshire and 54 Presbyterian, 10
Congregationalist and two Baptist places of worship were allowed to open.
This period of relative freedom came to an end in March 1673.

William Brown's articles of enquiry in 1667 had required churchwardens to
return to him the names of 'Recusant Papists . . . or other Sectaries . . . or
Schismatics' and whether they 'do labour to seduce and withdraw others from
the Religion now established' and whether they 'do instruct their families or
children in Popish Religion, or refuse to entertain any, especially in place of
greatest service, or trust, but such as concur with them in their opinions' and
'how long have the said Popish Recusants abstained from Divine Service, or
from the Communion.' The drift of this enquiry is clear. The concern is as
much to do with political and social unity and control as it is with the
maintenance of the newly re-established conforming orthodoxy from which it
could not be separated. The one sustained the other.

---

[1] Possibly a curate. There seems to have been no incumbent of Hope of this name in the 17th century.
[2] Keith Thomas, op.cit., 328–9.
[3] see especially John Clifford, *Eyam Plague 1665-1666* (1989, revised 1995).

In 1676 this political concern took the form of a national census. The archbishop of Canterbury, Gilbert Shelden, ordered the bishop of London, the strongly Protestant Henry Compton, to request the bishops of the province to enquire from the parish clergy the 'number of persons, or at least families' within their parishes together with the number of those 'who either obstinately refuse, or wholly absent themselves from the communion of the Church of England'. Although this ambiguous phrasing produced figures that are equally ambiguous, they give us some idea of the proportions and distribution of Catholic and Protestant nonconformity in Derbyshire a decade before the Act of Toleration.

Derbyshire clergy made returns from 136 parishes, including chapelries. It seems from these that they estimated the numbers of 'obstinate' individuals (perhaps those of communicable age, that is, over the age of 16[1]) rather than families. That these are estimated figures rather than an actual count (which would have been impossible in the more populous parishes) is indicated, in many returns, by the rounded numbers. According to the Compton Census there were in these 136 Derbyshire parishes and chapelries 49418 'Conformists', 596 'Papists' and 921 'Nonconformists'. This might suggest that less than one in thirty of the population was an 'obstinate refuser' in Derbyshire at this time, but it would be foolish to assume that every conformist was so by genuine persuasion. Expediency rather than deep conviction would have prevailed for many. Within less than two centuries Protestant nonconformists were considerably to outnumber Anglicans in Derbyshire.

The distribution of Bishop Compton's 'obstinate refusers' in Derbyshire was predictable. The heartland of Roman Catholicism was in the north west of the county. There were estimated to be 140 'Papists' in Hathersage (compared to 440 Anglicans), 23 in Barlborough, 32 in Eckington, 30 in Tideswell and 65 in Bakewell. Further south Roman Catholics were more isolated. The exceptions were the 65 in Norbury (compared to 74 Anglicans) witnessing to the example of the Fitzherberts, and the 40 in West Hallam indicating the influence of the Powtrell family.

It is useful to note here that further enquiries into the strength of Roman Catholicism in the country were undertaken in 1705 and 1706, and also in 1767. From the Derbyshire returns to the 1676 Compton Census and to these 18th century enquiries, Richard Clark has estimated that the number of Roman

---

[1] M.R.Watts, *The Dissenters*, i, *From the Reformation to the French Revolution* (Oxford 1978), 491.

Catholics in the county, including children, in 1676 was 894; in 1705-6, 811 (though this figure is on the low side in Richard Clark's view); and 860 in 1767.[1]

Returning to the Compton Census of 1676, although Protestant non-conformity appears to have been strongest in those areas served by ministers ejected from their benefices in 1662, proportionately the numbers were still modest, with 200 adults in Bakewell (4235 Anglicans), 100 in Chesterfield (3394 Anglicans), 52 in Glossop, 40 in Brampton, 49 in the parish of Derby All Saints, and 40 in Derby St Peter's. There is little to explain the high figure of 40 nonconformists in Brailsford, where the incumbent also noted six 'Papists' and 254 'Conformists'.

This sharp and simple differentiation between conformists, papists and nonconformists is recognised, yet graciously undermined, in Izaac Walton's will which he drew up in August 1683, the year of his death. Walton was a staunch Anglican, the acquaintance of John Donne and the biographer of Richard Hooker. In his will he professed his faith in

> the only one God, who hath made the whole world, and me and all mankinde; to whome I shall give acount of all my actions, which are not to be justified, but I hope pardoned, for the merits of my Saviour Jesus.

With sensitivity and warm compassion for his friends he then continues:

> And because [the profession of] Christianity does, at this time, seime to be subdevided into papist and protestante, I take it, at least to be convenient, to declare my beleife to be, in all poynts of faith, as the Church of England now professeth. And this I doe the rather, because of a very long and very trew friendship with some of the Roman Church.

So it is that dogma surrenders to love.

But a period of further and rapid change, indeed of revolution, was coming. Charles II died in 1685 and his brother James II succeeded to the throne, and he was a known papist.

---

[1] For an account of these enquiries as they related to Derbyshire, for a helpful note on the Roman Catholic community in 1705-6, and a summary of the individual Roman Catholic communities in the county, see Richard Clark, *The Derbyshire Papist Returns of 1705-6*, Derbyshire Record Society Occasional Paper No. 5, 1983.

9

'All the signs of a declining state': the beginning of a new age, 1702–1824

The 'Glorious Revolution'

Almost immediately James II alarmed moderate Anglican opinion. He attended mass publicly, announced that those imprisoned for their religious beliefs should be released, and ordered the bishops to instruct their clergy to cease preaching against popery. He informed the French ambassador that he intended to grant religious and civil freedom to Roman Catholics. But his enthusiasm to unite the country around a new and inclusive conformity was struck a fatal blow by his bastard nephew the duke of Monmouth who mounted a Protestant insurrection from Holland. This was put down at the battle of Sedgemoor in July 1685 and was followed by the notorious Judge Jeffrey's 'bloody assize' circuit. The promised concessions to Roman Catholics followed, with significant appointments of known papists to Oxbridge college headships, and the creation of new monastic houses in London.

In all this James attempted to profess his religious toleration. In 1687 he issued Declarations of Indulgence in which he proclaimed his support for the Church of England but simultaneously suspended penalties against those who refused to conform: Protestant and Roman Catholic alike. After this declaration a Roman Catholic chapel was erected in North Lees, in the parish of Hathersage (where, at the Gaol Delivery[1] held on 11 March 1682, 103

---

[1] Gaols were used mainly to hold suspects. A commission of gaol delivery appointed people such as sergeants-at-arms and judges to bring out and try suspects by jury. They could otherwise stay in gaol for years.

recusants had been convicted, with a further 112 on 30 July 1683), an old Roman Catholic chapel was restored in Newbold, and the family chapels of the Hunlokes in Wingerworth and the Eyres in Hassop were opened to their tenants. James II's flight in 1688 prompted mobs to ransack the Newbold and North Lees chapels.[1]

Widespread discontent among those of influence and power, not least in Derbyshire, at the direction in which the Stuart dynasty was leading the country led to a secret invitation to William of Orange and his wife Mary, daughter of James by his first wife, to accept the English throne. William landed at Torbay on, of all dates, 5 November 1688. James II, the rightful king, fled to the Continent – dropping the Great Seal of England into the Thames as he did so, so it was said.

William III's accession could not be accepted by many, James II being still alive. Their refusal brought the deprivation of six bishops, including the archbishop of Canterbury, William Sancroft, Thomas Ken of Bath and Wells and Thomas White of Peterborough. Two others died before the sentence of deprivation could be carried out. These courageous men refused to accept that William was king *de jure*. Though they had vigorously opposed James II on the ground of his Roman Catholicism, they had taken oaths of allegiance to him as king by divine right. They could not now take a similar oath to William. They had no recourse but to go, together with 400 parish clergy. We honour them as the *non-jurors*. The most distinguished Derbyshire non-juror was Thomas Brown, archdeacon of Derby, vicar of Ashbourne and of Wirksworth and a prebendary of Lichfield. Henry Bardyn of Beighton was another Derbyshire non-juror.[2] With the retirement of these men of great integrity we move into the 18th century.

William III's accession brought some relief for Protestant Dissent. The Act of Toleration of 1689 granted to Dissenters a measure of freedom of worship. While not removing their civil disabilities or the repressive legislation of the Clarendon Code it amended the Five Mile and Conventicle Acts and allowed nonconformists to have their own chapels, provided that the diocesan bishop was told of their existence, and that their doors were kept unlocked. However, the Occasional Conformity Act of 1711 and the Schism Act of 1714 (passed, due to Tory reaction, under Queen Anne) brought back some of the sharpness of the old repression. Though both Acts were repealed in 1718 much of the Clarendon

---

[1] *VCHD*, 34.
[2] though not given by Cox as an incumbent of Beighton.

legislation remained on the statute book until the early 19th century allowing unsympathetic magistrates, including Anglican clergy that served on the bench, to harry nonconformists well into the second half of the 18th century. However, well before 1828 when the Test and Corporation Acts were eventually repealed, annual Acts of Indemnity had protected nonconformists from penalty.

To this period belongs the story of Henry Sacheverell (?1674–1724), a self-opinionated London clergyman and Tory pamphleteer. He was a distant cousin of George Sacheverell of Callow near Wirksworth. When George was made sheriff in 1709 he injudiciously invited Henry to preach the Assize sermon in Derby All Saints on 15 August. Henry, who should have been a non-juror, made bitter reference to those who had, in his view, 'shamefully betrayed and run down' the Church. He implicitly attacked the Revolution of 1688, and advocated passive resistance to secular, by which he meant Whig, encroachments. Though these were unpopular sentiments in Derbyshire[1], this sermon would have caused little more than a nine-days' wonder locally had not Henry repeated his views even more vociferously in a sermon before the Lord Mayor of London and the London Court of Aldermen in St Paul's on 5 November. In December the Whig dominated House of Commons con-demned both sermons as seditious, and Sacheverell was impeached for his 'high crimes and misdemeanours'. By a small majority (with more bishops against him than for him) but with popular London sentiment clearly on his side, Sacheverell was sentenced to the ridiculous penalty of suspension from preaching for three years. Queen Anne subsequently rewarded him by presenting him to the benefice of St Andrew's, Holborn. Sacheverell would have been forgotten had not the Whig government's over-reaction in impeach-ing him not been, in large part, the cause of their own downfall in 1710.

Relief under the 1689 Act did not extend to Roman Catholics or to Unitarians, the former because of the continuing political threat they were held to represent, and the latter because of their refusal to acknowledge the divinity of Christ.

Calm, consolidation, and nonconformity

The previous two hundred years had been centuries of almost unremitting religious and political conflict. By the end of the 17th century it seems almost

---

[1] The 1st duke of Devonshire, William Cavendish, signed the invitation to William III in June 1688.

as if men and women had become exhausted by it. The century that followed, known to historians as the Age of Reason, or The Enlightenment, had a very different feel to it. Protestant and Roman Catholic nonconformity came to be largely tolerated though still suffering degrees of civil disability which ranged in severity. The clergy of the Church of England ministered to all the people in their parishes, rich and poor alike, but, as a profession, they came more and more to be identified with those upon whose patronage they depended.[1] Most church people in most places – clergy and laymen, those of substance and those with little – would have rejected any notion that the Church of England and the conservative, influential, upper and middle strata of rural society were in any real sense distinct. The Church of England had become, in effect, landed society in one of its social contexts – the context of religious observance. It was to be awakened to its spiritual responsibilities by an Anglican high church clergyman. His name was John Wesley.

We know much about the Church of England in Derbyshire in the 18th and 19th centuries. In this chapter and the next all that can be done is to provide the most modest and highly selective of surveys. We begin with the clergy.

The clergy of Derbyshire: their income and social position

Every index of the financial state of the clergy in the county, from the 1535 *Valor Ecclesiasticus* to the archdeacon of Derby's visitation of those parishes in the county which were under his jurisdiction in 1823–4, pointed to the low value of most benefice incomes in Derbyshire. As late as 1884, and despite the augmentation of poor benefices by the Governors of Queen Anne's Bounty, the first bishop of Southwell, George Ridding, discovered that one fifth of the 482 benefices in his diocese were worth less than £150 p.a. The disproportionate number of 60 of these parishes were in Derbyshire. As we have noted, insufficient income for a parish priest inevitably meant that he had to augment it by additionally serving another parish, by taking pupils, by personally farming his glebe, or by other means. His pastoral ministry suffered accordingly.

Queen Anne had succeeded William in 1702. She was a devout woman of high church sympathies who felt deeply for the welfare of the clergy and therefore for the proper maintenance of the parochial ministry. Like her predecessors since Henry VIII she received into the royal exchequer the old mediaeval dues of

---

[1] For an account of Crown, ecclesiastical and lay patronage in Derbyshire in this period see Austin 1969, 76-89. The duke of Devonshire alone presented to 18 Derbyshire benefices in 1772, and to 20 in 1832.

'First Fruits and Tenths', consolidated into a fixed sum of about £16000 p.a. In 1704, prompted by two of her bishops, Gilbert Burnet of Salisbury and John Sharp, archbishop of York, Anne transferred these revenues to a fund from which the income of the poorer clergy could be augmented. Eleven parliamentary grants of £100000 each were to be added to the fund between 1809 and 1820.

The fund was known as Queen Anne's Bounty. It was administered by Governors in accordance with rules which some clergy found very restrictive. Particularly was this so with the regulation which laid down that, on augmentation, a parochial chapelry should be separated from its parish church and become what was then known as a perpetual curacy. This was resented by those incumbents who received an income from their chapelries. For example Ralph Heathcote, rector of Morton, complained in 1755 to the then Secretary of the Bounty, Henry Montague, that

> every Curacy or Chappel augmented by the Governors must from thence
> forward at least become a perpetual Cure and Benefice of itself separate
> and distinct from its Mother Church to which it may have formerly
> belonged; and not only so, but the Rectors or Vicars of the Mother
> Church are by the same Act debarred and excluded from having or
> receiving directly or indirectly any benefit or Advantage from the
> Augmentation, and consequently such augmented Curacy or Chappel
> must forever afterwards be constantly supplied and served by a separate
> and distinct Minister or Curate of its own.[1]

But this was exactly the point of the Bounty's rules. The augmenting of chapelries ensured the permanent maintenance of parochial ministry in them, admittedly at a minimum stipend. Many parochial chapelries acquired their baptism and marriage registers from the date of their augmentation.

The Bounty's grants were made in sums of £200 to purchase land from which income could be drawn. The livings were selected by lot (starting with the poorest first) or to meet benefactions of a similar, or greater, amount. Rules restricted the number of augmentations that could be made in any one year. The first Derbyshire augmentations of £200 were to match benefactions. They went to Castleton in 1714, to Atlow in 1716 and to Breaston and to Risley in 1719. The first grants of £200 by lot took much longer to arrive in the county.

---

[1] Austin 1969, 200–1.

They went to Ashford in 1731, to Turnditch in 1737 and to Willington in 1738. Between 1714 and 1845, 353 Bounty and parliamentary grants went to 103 poor Derbyshire benefices and chapelries. All the Bounty grants were of £200 but the subsequent parliamentary grants could be in larger multiples with £2000 going by lot to Darley in 1821 and £2200 to Ripley in 1822. These were considerable sums and they improved the incomes, and hopefully the quality of pastoral ministry, of some of the poorer Derbyshire clergy. But these augmentations did little to raise the poorest livings to an acceptable level. Following investment in land, increases in individual incomes averaged little more than 5% of the grant. In fact, in the 1820s, even following the application of parliamentary grants, it might take a decade or so to double the value of a poor living and to produce a barely acceptable stipend. John Bacon wrote in his introduction to the 1786 edition of the *Liber Regis*[1] that

> it will be the Work of Ages before all the Small Livings entitled to an Augmentation can receive any Benefit or Share therefrom; and of many Ages more before the Income of every Living will be so advanced as to afford a Competency for the Minister, supposing that Competency to amount to no more than 60 Pounds per Annum to each Living.

And so it turned out in Derbyshire. If no wealthy parishioner made a benefaction, or if the lot did not fall, a poor parson remained poor. These were 'starvings' and not 'livings' as one Derbyshire incumbent was later to say ruefully to the Secretary of the Bounty.[2] But not every Derbyshire parson was poor.

'Us Stationary country Gentlemen'

There is no doubt that the social position of many of the clergy of Derbyshire improved in the 18th century, and that this stemmed from their improved education, their family background in the county, and of course (at least for some) from their increased income. In 1772, 49 of the clergy of the county were Oxbridge graduates. Of these, 84% had been born in or close to the county. This indicates the settled nature of the middle social stratum of county society at the

---

[1] a survey, originally published in 1711 by John Ecton, of livings then under £80 a year. This was compiled to assist the Board of Queen Anne's Bounty. John Bacon's was an improved and updated edition.
[2] See Austin 1969, 194-212 for an account of the Bounty's augmentations to poor livings in Derbyshire up to 1832.

time and of the very close connection of the clergy to it. Eighteen of the 49 had been educated in Derbyshire. Twelve of these had attended Chesterfield Grammar School, 11 of whom had been at the school when William Burrow was its master from 1722 to 1752 and when it was said to be the leading school in the north of England.[1] For nine years it was attended by Erasmus Darwin. These men therefore shared a common background of interests, acquaintances and education which had existed since childhood. They belonged to a long-established, small and self-perpetuating county community of what was to be called, by the end of the century, the middle class.

A typical example of the relationship of the clergy, the professions and county society at a particular social level is to be found on the memorial erected to Godfrey Heathcote in Chesterfield parish church in 1775. He is styled a 'Gent', the second son of the same Ralph Heathcote, rector of Morton, whom we have already met defending his income. He married Dorothy, the daughter of James Cooke, rector of Barlborough. Godfrey practiced as a lawyer in Chesterfield holding the appointments of Steward and auditor to successive dukes of Devonshire.

Between 1772 and 1832 about one third of the clergy of Derbyshire whose family backgrounds I have been able to trace came from parsonage families. There was a marked tendency for the clergy to improve their social lot by judicious marriage into a wealthier set. Of Charles Stead Hope, son of Charles Hope, both of whom were incumbents of Derby parishes in the late 18th and early 19th centuries, it was said that 'like his father, not only as a theologian and a holder of a plurality, he secured an heiress for a helpmate'! Notices of the marriages of Derbyshire clergy in the 18th century in the *Derby Mercury* not infrequently mention that the clergyman has married 'a Lady of genteel Accomplishments and a plentiful Fortune'. They married the sisters and daughters of lawyers, the daughters of peers, the sisters of bishops, and others of 'very genteel Fortune and amiable Person'. There is only one notable example of a Derbyshire clergyman marrying into the family of one of the great industrial entrepreneurs, and then only well into the 19th century. This was Edward Abney, vicar of Derby St Alkmund 1841-1885, himself the descendent of an old Derbyshire family, who married Katherine, granddaughter of Jedediah Strutt of Belper in 1833. Contrast the social position of these Derbyshire clergy in the 18th century with their peasant status in the Domesday survey, and with

---

[1] C.V.Kendall and M.P.Jackson, *A History of the Free Grammar School, Chesterfield* (ms 1965), cited in Desmond King-Hele, *Erasmus Darwin* (Giles de la Mare 1999), 7.

Chaucer's 'Poore Parson' in the 14th century. Much of that rapid though limited rise in social status was achieved in the 18th century itself. Take three very contrasting Derbyshire clergymen of the time: William Bagshaw Stevens, Thomas Brown and Samuel Pegge.

Stevens was the somewhat idle Master of Repton School, minister of the donative chapel of Foremark and domestic chaplain to Sir Robert Burdett of Foremark Hall. Through his connection with the Burdetts Stevens met such leading men of his day as Charles James Fox, Erasmus Darwin of Breadsall (the remarkable grandfather of Charles) and Lord Lansdowne. Yet he met them only as domestic chaplain of Sir Robert and never on terms of social equality. The intimate side of Stevens' social life was supplied by his neighbours in Willington, the Spilsburys, the Ardens, Squire Barker (whom he characterised as a 'jumped-up townee'), the Dethics and Mrs Glover, and other local comfortably placed families such as the Dalbys of Castle Donnington and R.C. Greaves, the land-agent of Ingleby. Another neighbour was George Greaves, rector of Stanton-by-Bridge 1770–1828 and of Swarkestone 1795–1828, who, Stevens said, was a 'Jolly Priest' and 'abundant in good humour, an everlasting Talker . . . a man to be loved but not trusted'[1]. With these friends he could share the local gossip and an interest in literature. With them, too, Stevens could bemoan his lot in never securing a wealthy benefice, no matter how urgently he canvassed patrons while he waited, as he often indelicately put it, for some sick and elderly incumbent to 'drop'. Sir Robert Burdett was Stevens' patron but never his friend. As such Stevens prudently but quietly adopted Burdett's radical political position. It did him little good. Stevens' romance with Fanny Coutts, the daughter of the owner of the bank, was abruptly curtailed by her father, Fanny later marrying the much more socially acceptable heiress-hunter the first marquess of Bute.

At Tideswell, Parson Brown's very different circle consisted of farmers and merchants. Agriculture was the common interest. The farming family of the Bakers are repeatedly mentioned in Thomas Brown's diary, as is William Shaw, a farmer in Baslow, Thornhill the whitesmith, James Longden the wainwright and Edward Jackson, George Sheldon, Robert Bramwell and Edward Longdon, all farmers or merchants in his parish. In 1785, when Thomas Brown was then the curate of Tideswell, not only did he serve two curacies, keep a school and farm the parish glebe himself, but also added to his

---

[1] Georgina Galbraith, *The Journal of the Rev William Bagshaw Stevens,* (Oxford 1965), 518.

income by measuring hay as an independent assessor, and even occasionally by lettering a name board for a cart or painting a signboard for a house. His diaries record him preaching many sermons at club feasts and funerals for half a guinea or a guinea a time. His income in 1785 from all sources was £106 8s 8d, just exceeding, in Pickwickian fashion, his expenditure of £99. 1s 5d.[1] Brown had little contact with the wealthy gentry. He was himself a farmer, and farmers were his friends.

In contrast the letters of Samuel Pegge, rector of Whittington 1751-96, are full of references to his landed friends and acquaintances, such as Sir Henry Hunloke of Wingerworth and the Gells of Hopton Hall. Pegge wants to know if there is 'any truth in Mr Pelham of Brocklesby's paying his addresses to the Widow Waltham?', and regrets that his friend Hayman Rooke is not going to London 'as I was in hopes of hearing a whole Budget of News from you on your return; for you know how it is with us Stationary country Gentlemen – that a little London intelligence of almost any kind is always extremely agreeable to us . . . '[2] Another of his friends, from school-days, was the physician and scientist Erasmus Darwin.

'Are they not become saucy': the politics of clergy and people

The 18th century closed with threats of revolution from within and of invasion from without. To meet the threat of invasion from France three volunteer infantry corps were raised in Derbyshire in 1798. Their officers, which were to include five parish clergy, received their first commissions in 1803. As to threats of rebellion from within, closely dependent on their patrons as they were, most beneficed clergy saw it as their duty to uphold law and order and to preach the virtues of subordination. Radical agitation caused them grave disquiet. To take just two of many examples. In a sermon preached on the one hundredth anniversary of the revolution of 1688, Samuel Pegge asked

> in regard to the lower ranks of the People, where is that Order and Decorum, that Subordination, by which classes were wont to be distinguished? They are all Freemen indeed, as well as we, and we wish them to continue so; but are they not become saucy, insolent and impatient of all Controul, expecting, under the Cloke of Liberty, and of

---

[1] for references see Austin 1969, 116.
[2] letters to Rooke dated 4 April 1791, 16 January 1788, 8 August 1778 etc., quoted in Austin 1969, 72.

I know not what natural Rights, that every man should do just as he pleases, in spite of all legal Authority and Power? 'tis scandalous Licentiousness, tending to Levelling, Anarchy and Confusion.[1]

Pegge was expressing an opinion widely held in his circle. Robert Wilmot, rector of Morley and Smalley, offered similar opinions to his successors in the privacy of the Smalley parish registers. Noting in 1798 that the number of baptisms had not been proportionate to the increase in the population of his parish he argued that, apart from the attractions of Dissent, there was another principal reason:

For this circumstance I believe we are indebted to the works of the infamous Paine which have eradicated the principles of religion from the minds of the lower orders of the people; who, not having leisure to study what they read are caught by the sound of the words, and not by their meaning.[2]

Wilmot noted that 'the town and neighbourhood of Derby' was particularly influenced by English Jacobin agitation but claimed that only one man in his parish, named Alsop, had been 'dissaffected'. Yet had this dissaffected parishioner read, say, only Thomas Paine's *Age of Reason* published in 1794–5, the sound of the words could have possessed no clearer meaning. The Bible, Paine wrote, is 'a history of wickedness that has served to corrupt and brutalise mankind', and 'priests and conjurors are of the same trade'. To encourage such opinions was dangerous. When William Strutt, the Belper cotton manufacturer and a Unitarian, attempted to distribute Paine's *Rights of Man* to his employees in November 1792 he had his mill flooded and his books burned by a mob.[3]

But Strutt was an exception. An increasingly frightened manufacturing class relied on the clergy to apply moral sanctions. William Cantrell, curate of Derby St Michael, warned the poor in 1815, that 'a Rebellious Spirit is a national curse, and makes your Rulers obliged to oppress you.'[4] Thomas Gisborne, addressing members of the Derby Union of Operatives in 1834, condemned their union as

---

[1] S.Pegge, *A Sermon preached at Whittington . . . on the Grand Jubilee . . . of the Glorious Revolution MDCLXXXVIII*, (Chesterfield 1788), 15.
[2] Smalley parish register, 1798. See also 1792 and 1801 (a MS transcript by C. Kerry in Derby Library, acc. no. 4707, 57, 66–7).
[3] M.R.Watts, *The Dissenters*, i, (Oxford 1978), 528.
[4] W.C. [William Cantrell] *Seasonable Advice; or an antidote to the Poison of Disaffection*, (Derby 1815), vii-viii.

against the law of God, for how could they claim to love their neighbours if they were seeking to bring their employers 'into complete subjection.' He reminded them, as only an Anglican of the period could, that 'the law of God confirms, by its own authority, the law of the land.'[1] These were opinions expressed by Anglican clergy throughout Derbyshire in these years of social unrest.

Robert Wilmot died in 1803 aged 53. He was buried on 2 October, the Morley register recording that 'This funeral shewed an assembly of the whole Parish with tears and sadness on every face.' His humanity, and the inhumanity of the operation of the Poor Law, is illustrated by a note he added to the Smalley parish register opposite the entry for the burial of Samuel Liggat on 23 December 1785:

> The Poors' Rates of this Township having been very considerably increased, it was thought advisable to have a standing overseer and a meeting of the Parishioners was held to appoint a man to the office distinguished for extreme parsimony & hardness of heart. The result of the appointment was cruelty and oppression of the poor, and Samuel Liggat was absolutely starved to death. I was from home when he was buried, and did not know of his death till many months afterwards when, although I obtained sufficient information to convince me of the fact I could not obtain sufficient evidence to convict the overseer upon it, and therefore he escaped the punishment he deserved.[2]

Wilmot's sole dissaffected parishioner, Mr Alsop, would have needed little prompting to dream of revolutionary means of redress.

'The parson super-induced'

The comfortably placed beneficed clergy in the county moved most easily in those social circles appropriate to their background, income and connections. In 1802 Edward Pole, rector of Radbourne and a member of the principal land-owning family in the area, was chairman of the Derbyshire Agriculture and Breeding Society. Other clergy were stewards of the Assemblies held in Derby and Chesterfield, while almost all the wealthier beneficed clergy took out 'Gentlemen's' certificates each year to kill game. By the end of the century many incumbents had their incomes considerably increased as a result of

---

[1] Thomas Gisborne, *A Letter to the Members of the Derby Union of Operatives*, (1834), 7–8.
[2] Cox, *Churches*, iv, 352.

enclosure of commons and as time passed their rising income was reflected in the substantial size of new parsonage houses and the number of servants they were able to employ. As to the new parsonages, in October 1795 a contributor to *The Gentleman's Magazine* wrote of Christopher Alderson, the rector of Eckington, that 'his successors will be much indebted for the elegant improvements he has made to the rectory, which vies with many of the best houses in the country for real taste in its decorations'. It seems that Alderson had a reputation as a professional landscape architect for 'he is very happy in disposing pleasure grounds, and has been ... employed at Frogmore. Some specimens that I have seen deserve much praise, particularly at Ford House, Derbyshire ... '. At Eckington Alderson had laid out his rectory garden with 'a pretty piece of water, across which he had thrown a handsome bridge, and at one end placed a rustic temple.' As to servants, John Ward, vicar of Mickleover and his wife had no children, but, in 1811, could afford to employ four servants. No other family of the 117 listed in the parish had as many servants except a farmer, Thomas Mills, who also employed four servants, but three of these were farm labourers.

The most notorious example of clerical self-seeking in Derbyshire in the 18th century was that of John Taylor of Ashbourne. He was a notorious pluralist being rector of Bosworth and a prebendary of Westminster. He lived the life of a very wealthy country gentleman on an income of £7000 a year and counted the duke of Devonshire and Samuel Johnson among his friends. He rarely, if ever, visited his benefices and was much more interested in breeding cattle and dogs. Hester Thrale visited John Taylor in 1774. She noted 'his fine pictures which he does not understand the beauties of, [and] a glorious harpsichord which he sends for a young man out of the town to play upon.'[1] Boswell said of Taylor that 'his size and figure, and countenance and manner, were that of a hearty English Squire, with the parson super-induced.'[2] The fact that Taylor was ordained was to him of financial rather than of religious or social consequence, yet to his credit he had a social conscience. In a sermon preached in Ashbourne before the officers of a local benefit society he said that

> it is always to be remembered that a demand for support from your
> common fund is not a petition for charity, but a claim to justice. The
> relief thus demanded is not a gift but a debt. He that received it has first

[1] Turbutt, 1315.
[2] refs. in Austin 1969, 74.

purchased it. The denial of it therefore is a fraud and a robbery; and fraud the more atrocious and detestable as, by its nature, it must always be practised on the poor.[1]

'Lean, lank parsons': the curates of Derbyshire

Of course we have been telling here of the well-to-do clergy, their income coming from tithe (in kind or, increasingly, by commutation) and from leasing glebe and, above all, from their rights to newly enclosed common land[2]. The poorer incumbents were nowhere near so well placed as we have seen. In a visitation in 1823–4 the archdeacon of Derby, Samuel Butler, frequently described the parsonage houses in poorer benefices as less than adequate, that at Elmton, for example, being 'a small thatched cottage in decent repair, the habitation of a labourer & perfectly unfit for a clergyman.' Several benefices had no parsonage house at all. The various classes of curates were even worse off, the average stipend in Derbyshire for curates serving only one parish rising from £36 a year[3] in 1772 to £84 in 1830, and the stipend per curacy for those serving more than one parish rising from £28 to £66. Bearing in mind the changes in the value of money during this period, compare that average stipend with, as one of many examples, the income of £207 from his tithes on lead ore alone in 1829 reported by the vicar of Wirksworth (though this decreased by one third over the next two years in face of cheap imports of lead from Spain.) By 1830 the average national annual income for incumbents was £275. As late as 1853 the average income for curates was only £79. (Incidentally, Baptist and Congregationalist ministers received much the same.[4])

At least one poor and nameless 18th century Derbyshire curate, impoverished as he was, was content with his lot, being assured that his reward awaited him

---

[1] *Sermons of Different Subjects left for Publication by John Taylor LL.D.* (1789), *93.*

[2] On the important social issue of tithe in Derbyshire in this period see M.R. Austin 'Tithe and benefice incomes in Derbyshire', *DAJ*, 102, (1982), 118-24 and on the economic effect of enclosure see M.R. Austin, 'Enclosure and Benefice Incomes in Derbyshire 1772–1832', *DAJ*, 100, (1980), 88-94. Disputes over tithes were frequent. For example, papers relating to disputes at Eyam, Brassington and Staveley are preserved in the Derby Diocesan Record Office (under D2602 A/Pl 28/1–4, D5198 and D661 A/Pl 41 respectively).

[3] It seems reasonable to multiply gross clergy incomes for the period 1750–80 by 100 to give approximate comparable values in 1999. This multiple is too large for 1780–1803 when there was erosion of money values of about 40% [Desmond King-Hele, *Erasmus Darwin*, (1999), 27, and authorities.] Thus the average curate serving a single parish in 1772 would have received about £3600 in 1999 values.

[4] Michael R.Watts, *The Dissenters* (Oxford 1995), ii, 249.

elsewhere. He was resigned, he said,

> to my humble position, since, I am well convinced that the present will
> shortly be superseded by a very different sense of things. I know that the
> dissipated rich and the contented poor shall experience a reversal of
> condition: a reverse miserable to the one, but happy to the other . . . . A
> Curate therefore, how great soever the hardships under which he
> struggles, by continuing in the uniform, conscientious discharge of his
> duty, is surely a juster object of envy than the luxurious Dignitary . . . .
> If a provision in the Church more adequate to his necessities be
> unattainable by the Curate, none is better instructed how to make a
> virtue out of necessity: none can better fortify his mind against those
> bellows of adversity which may sink others, less supported by the aids
> of religion, into the gulphs of despair.[1]

How could absentee, pluralist incumbents get away with paying their curates
such low stipends? Adam Smith had no doubt as to the answer. In 1776, in his
seminal *An Inquiry into the Nature and Causes of the Wealth of Nations*, he
argued that the large number of pensions, scholarships, exhibitions, and
bursaries drew far more men to ordained ministry than would have been the
case had they had to pay for their education themselves. This being so

> the Church is crowded with many people who, in order to get
> employment, are willing to accept of a much smaller recompense than
> what such an education would otherwise have entitled them to; and in
> this manner the competition of the poor takes away the reward of the rich.

Attempts to raise curates' stipends by legal enactment were bound to fail, Smith
argued. In 1713, under 12 Anne c 12, bishops could compel payment of a
maximum stipend for curates of £50 and a minimum of £20, yet curates would
always accept a 'wretched maintenance' which was 'less than the legal allowance
on account of the indigence of their situation and the multitude of their
competitors.' The result was that many curates made do on a labourer's wage.
Smith noted that journeyman shoemakers in London earned £40 a year, while
'there is scarce an industrious workman of any kind in that metropolis who does
not earn more than twenty. This last sum indeed does not exceed what is
frequently earned by common labourers in many country parishes.'[2] It had

---

[1] *Derby Mercury*, 4 August 1791, letter from A Curate.
[2] Adam Smith, *Wealth of Nations,* i, (fourth edition 1786, reprinted 1869), 137–9.

been so for many centuries. Under the 14th century Statute of Labourers, 25 Edw. III, the wages of master masons, and even journeyman masons, were set at levels higher than the stipends of curates. In Adam Smith economics the universal law of the market is aways more powerful than laws made by interventionist parliaments!

Little wonder that Anna Seward, born in Eyam in 1747 the daughter of Thomas Seward, then its rector, could write, in 1767, of 'those lean, lank parsons which are sowed so thick over this country; most of them the starveling curates of their fat and jolly rectors, who live in gayer scenes and leave their clay-sunk parishes to the cheapest journeyman they can procure.'[1] Very much more could here be said both of the lean curates and their fat and pluralist rectors.[2]

Notwithstanding market forces, absentee incumbents occasionally had to make do with what curates they could find, or perhaps some did not care who they employed. The Morley parish register for 1764 notes that as 'In the years 64 and 63 the Revd John Bakewell of Derby was Curate, and he was a very negligent man and became afterwards insane, it is much to be feared that there were several omissions of entries in this register.'[3] John Bakewell's incumbent was the absentee pluralist Richard Wilmot, also a canon of Windsor and the vicar of Mickleover.

Sense and eccentricity

Together with the wealthy and the poor, the faithful, the idle and the wayward clergy, Derbyshire had its share of eccentric clergy, at least seen from our perspective. One of these was John Kennedy, born in 1698 and rector of Bradley from 1732 until his death in 1782. In 1762 he published a book on the chronology of the Bible. He proposed a date for the Creation based on calculations of the astronomical positions of the sun and moon in antiquity, evidence for which he believed he could find in the Pentateuch, the first five books of the Old Testament. So impressed was Samuel Johnson that he wrote

---

[1] W. Scott, *The Poetical Works of Anna Seward, with extracts from her literary correspondence* (Edinburgh 1810), i, cxcvii.

[2] Anna revered her father, yet, in April 1755, Thomas was installed as a prebend of Lichfield, and in June in the same year became also a prebend of Salisbury while, at the same time, it seems, rector of Kingsley in Staffordshire! Samuel Johnson said of him that he was 'a genteel, well-bred, dignified clergyman, who had lived much in the greater world.'

[3] The Morley Village History Committee, *A History of the Parish of Morley, Derbyshire* (Ilkeston 1977).

not only the book's concluding paragraph but also its dedication to the king. In recording this, the author of *The History and Topography of Ashbourn and the Valley of the Dove*, published in 1839, remarked that although Kennedy's book

> was the occasion of much controversy . . . . If it is true that the author's conclusions have never been satisfactorily refuted, they are worthy of some attention in the present day, when the assertions of certain geologists in reference to the age of the earth would seem directly to impugn the accuracy of the scriptural account of the creation.

So it was that a somewhat eccentric Derbyshire clergyman of the 18th century came to be mentioned at a time when the most far-reaching of the 19th century's pre-Darwinian scientific controversies was raging. His gravestone said of Kennedy that he was 'a good and learned man', though *DNB* says of him that he 'seems to have been of a quarrelsome disposition' producing books which 'display ingenuity in misapplying learning'!

At least three of Kennedy's Derbyshire clerical contemporaries were attracted to the new ideas and inventiveness which so marked the 18th century. Two were friends of Erasmus Darwin,[1] Richard Gifford (1725–1807) vicar of Duffield from 1759, and Abraham Bennet (1749–1799) curate of Wirksworth. The other was Charles Hope (1733–1799), the pluralist incumbent of three parishes in Derby, All Saints, St Alkmund's and St Werburgh's.

Richard Gifford was vicar of Duffield from 1759 until his death in 1807. From 1772 he held the benefice in plurality with that of North Ockendon in Essex, residing in Duffield in the winter months and in North Ockendon in the summer until 'rendered incapable of doing so by the effect of the Essex climate on his health.'[2] Gifford had pretensions as a poet, and was delighted when Samuel Johnson quoted his 'Contemplation, a Poem' in amended form under the word 'Wheel' in his *Dictionary*. In 1781 Gifford published *Outlines of an answer to Dr Priestley's Disquisitions relating to Matter and Spirit.*[3] He

---

[1] Darwin (1731–1802) moved from Lichfield to Derbyshire in 1781 on his marriage to Elizabeth Pole; first to Radburn Hall and then, in 1784, to Derby. He moved to Breadsall Priory a month before his death. As to Darwin's religious views, he is described by his recent biographer as a sceptical deist, and as somewhat anti-clerical [Desmond King-Hele, op. cit., 87, 89, 131 *passim*].,

[2] *DNB.*

[3] Joseph Priestley (1733–1804), nonconformist minister and chemist, discovered 'dephlogisticated air', oxygen, in 1774. Originally a Presbyterian minister, he became a leading Unitarian, and was a radical political and social reformer.

translated part of the Domesday survey for John Nichol's *Leicestershire*, and contributed occasional pieces to the *Gentleman's Magazine*. These literary efforts qualified him to be described by *DNB* as 'a miscellaneous writer'. But he was of independent mind and a strong whig in politics. With Robert Clive, incumbent of Moreton in Shropshire, he encouraged Erasmus Darwin to dip into metaphysics, receiving a letter from him discussing the philosophy of the leading 17th century apostle of free enquiry, John Locke.[1]

Abraham Bennet was altogether more distinguished. He was born in Taxal, and became successively curate of Tideswell (on £30 a year) and then of Wirksworth (on £60) where he remained until his death, serving four incumbents. He was, at the same time, domestic chaplain to the duke of Devonshire, and perpetual curate of Woburn and the duke of Bedford's librarian. From 1796 he was also vicar of Fenny Bentley. Bennet was a pioneer of electricity. His main research was in electrostatics, the study of stationary electrical discharges and their effects. His claim to the modest fame accorded to him is the invention, in 1786, of the gold-leaf electrometer, an instrument for detecting and measuring electrical discharges. Although Thomas Young is credited with first propounding, in 1801, the wave theory of light, Abraham Bennet had proposed, seven years earlier, that light must be caused by vibrations 'in the universally diffused caloric of matter of heat or fluid in light.' Bennet published *New Experiments in Electricity* in 1789, the year he was elected a Fellow of the Royal Society.

Charles Hope was an acquaintance of Darwin's. He was the only clergyman to be a member of the Derby Philosophical Society when it was established by Darwin in 1783. A letter of sympathy was sent by the Society to Joseph Priestley when his books and his scientific instruments were destroyed by a 'Church and King' loyalist mob in Birmingham in 1791. Charles Hope complained publicly that insufficient members of the Society were present when the letter was agreed, and he was expelled ('desired to withdraw his name') as a consequence. We will meet Hope's son, Charles Stead Hope, shortly.

'My own Best Endeavours': the teaching ministry of the clergy

What did these well-to-do or poor, eccentric or learned clergy teach? Some historians of the 18th century have generally been disparaging. They have

---

[1] Desmond King-Hele, op. cit., 87.

painted a picture of a socially subservient, somewhat self-seeking clergy concerned more with their own status than with their pastoral responsibilities and preaching a message acceptable only to those upon whom they were dependent for patronage. There is much truth in this criticism. Nevertheless there were faithful clergy caring for their people, dispensing much charity from a variety of sources, preaching the Gospel, and teaching the faith.

Teaching the Catechism as a preparation for Confirmation is one example which can be easily summarised. In 1771 the notorious the Hon. Brownlow North, half-brother of the prime minister Lord North, became bishop of Lichfield and Coventry. He was to be translated to Worcester in 1774 and thence to Winchester where, it was said, he was 'a nepotist who much dilapidated the revenues of the see.' He sent out articles of visitation in 1772. Among other questions he asked his clergy if, when teaching the Catechism, 'you either expound it to them yourself, or make use of some printed exposition: and what is it.' There are 31 replies to this question in the extant returns. The majority of the clergy used, as one of them put it, their 'own Best endeavours'. The rector of Breadsall used 'no printed form, but do it extempore etc', and at Brailsford, though the rector 'read Catechistical Lectures extracted from Newcome [P.Newcome, *A Catechistical Course of Sermons* (1702)] . . . I catechise the Children at the same time & expound it to them in the most familiar Manner I can.' The vicar of Derby St Alkmund, Thomas Manlove, expounded the Catechism 'from my memory, tho' I have a written exposition collected from my reading and my judgement. I chose this method, as I think I deliver myself more familiarly than I do by any written exposition.' At Langwith the rector made use 'of an exposition part my own, and part an extract from some of the best authors upon that subject', while Samuel Pegge, rector of Whittington, 'printed and gave away an Exposition of the Church Catechism'. The most popular authors of 'printed Expositions' were William Wake's *Principles of the Christian Religion* (1700) and Thomas Secker's *Lectures on the Church Catechism* (1769). Secker was a 'sober and judicious' archbishop of Canterbury from 1758 to his death in 1768. Others expositions, in addition to Newcome, were John Lewis's *The Church Catechism explain'd by way of question and answer and confirm'd by Scripture Proofs* (1700), Thomas Marshall's *The Catechism set forth in the Book of Common Prayer* (1679 and later editions to 1700), John Pearson's *Exposition of the Creed* (1659), John Williams' *A Brief Exposition of the Church Catechism* (1689), Adam Littleton's *Solomon's Gate: or, an Entrance into the Church, being a familiar explanation of*

the Grounds of Religion contained in the four Heads of Catechism (1662) and T.
Bate's *An Explication of the Church-Catechism* printed in about 1720. Bate was
rector of Swarkeston, donative curate of the peculiar of Calke and perpetual
curate of Ticknall. It seems that his exposition was written for the school in
Ticknall founded by Lady Harpur of Calke. Bate's book was used also by the
incumbent of Osmaston-by-Derby. At Kirk Ireton the rector, T. Gough,
expounded the Catechism 'assisted in the Creed by Bp Pearson, and in the
Lord's Prayer by Dr Lyttleton', while at Edale the incumbent used 'an extract
of my own from Lewis, Wake and Secker'.

It has been worth taking up some space with this summary. It suggests that
some clergy were taking their duty to prepare children for Confirmation
seriously and that they were following the thoroughly orthodox Anglican
divines who wrote at a time when the clear exposition of the doctrines of the
Prayer Book of a newly restored Church of England was held to be essential.
Certainly the 31 who answered this question took their responsibility
seriously, or at least they wrote what they thought their bishop would expect
to read. Yet it was only the children of the poor who were so instructed. In
1885 Thomas Mozley recorded that in 1820 his mother's friends 'laughed at
the idea of children of respectable people being examined for Confirmation.
They applied for tickets, and received them as a matter of course.'[1] No doubt
this was, in part, a reaction to the idea that 'respectable people' should be
examined in the Prayer Book Catechism. A candidate was there required to
acknowledge the duty 'to order myself lowly and reverently to all my betters'
and 'to do my duty in that state of life, unto which it shall please God to call me.'
That came uneasily to the lips of people of 'quality'. On 18 June 1795 'Clericus',
a correspondent to the *Derby Mercury*, reported that preparation for Confirmation was generally very poor: 'These examinations were very frequently
perform'd either in a very concise & careless manner, or not perform'd at all,
and the intent & meaning of Confirmation is very seldom mention'd'.

This is but one sample of the quality of pastoral concern. Much more could
be said: about the frequency and quality of preaching in Derbyshire, of Sunday
and weekday services, and of celebrations of holy Communion.[2] Self-seeking
though many of the clergy may have been, there were others who were faithful
and who exercised their pastoral ministry as well as they could from parsonages
and churches that were frequently ill-cared for.

---

[1] T. Mozley, *Reminiscences chiefly of towns, villages and schools* (1885), ii, 86.
[2] see Austin 1969, 124–8, 148–64.

'Going fast to decay': the parish churches of Derbyshire

In the late 17th and early 18th centuries, churches in the fashionable classical style were built in Derbyshire. Among them were Trusley (1713), its tower slanting slightly certainly since Archdeacon Butler's visit in 1824, its box pews socially graduated by size and the decoration of their door hinges; the octagon at Stoney Middleton; and the nave of Derby All Saints, the earlier building being virtually destroyed during the night of 18 February 1723 by a team of workmen employed by the vicar, Michael Hutchinson, because the patrons, the corporation of Derby, refused to rebuild what was probably a somewhat dilapidated church!

By the close of the 18th century the population of Derbyshire was growing rapidly. The first phase of industrialisation, centred on the lead and iron ore mining and framework knitting of the north and east of the county, was giving way to a second phase in which the application of coal to industrial processes led to a rapid growth in the iron industry and to a much more diversified economy. Industries ancillary to iron-smelting, such as limestone burning shared in the expansion, and the development of cotton spinning was to have far-reaching social and economic consequences.

How did the Church of England react to these social and economic changes? As a Church, working at diocesan level to a considered and agreed policy, it did nothing, and nor could it. The revival of the idea of the diocese as a coherent community of parishes organised to further the Gospel, minister to the people and maintain the Church did not come until the 19th century. In the 18th century Church expansion was haphazard to say the least.

In 1772 there were 179 benefices in Derbyshire of which no less than 25 were peculiars and therefore outside the bishop's jurisdiction. Large tracts of the county were unprovided with churches. Their scarcity on the Derbyshire/Staffordshire border is brought out well by Viator's comment in Walton's *The Compleat Angler* which provides this book's title. At this time the parish of Hope, for example, had two churches for the hamlets of Bradwell, Brough, Shapton, Aston, Thornhill, Woodlands, Highlow, Offerton, Abney, Grange, Fernalegh, Wardlow, Stokehall, Grindlow, Great and Little Hucklow, Whaley, Doveholes and Fairfield. The situation had not improved by 1832 when the vicar wrote to the Commissioners of Ecclesiastical Revenues to tell them that to make a tour of his eighteen hamlets he had to travel 'six and thirty miles at the least' and 'were it not for the vicinity of other Churches, or for

Methodist Chapels, several of them would be without opportunities of attending Divine Worship in my parish'. There were other examples like this. The vicar of Ashbourne, writing to the Commissioners, pointed out that his parish was more than twenty miles in circumference 'and that some of its Hamlets are so distant from the only Parish Church as not to be able to derive any benefit from it' citing Hulland as a particular case.

It was in just these large scattered parishes that villages were becoming manufacturing centres in the mid-18th century. In the parish of Hope, Pilkington noted in 1789, 'the mining business is the chief support of the inhabitants', while in Glossop it was spinning and weaving of cotton and woollen cloth. In the parish of Hartington, which extended for twelve miles along the western boundary of the county and was served only by its parish church and the dilapidated chapel at Earl Sterndale (where, as late as June 1823, the archdeacon reported that the building was ruinous with the wind and rain penetrating through the broken roof) the new industries were limestone burning and cotton, thread and linen manufacture. In the parish of Heanor, whose village and seven hamlets were served by the parish church alone, mining and stocking manufacture were the principal industries. Many more examples could be given.

In some areas, it was pointed out in 1811, particularly those in the new manufacturing districts, 'the Chapels of the Methodists seem the most rapidly increasing' and indeed it is easy to chart the progress of Methodism along the Erewash valley and across the north of the county where it established a presence in many places in which the Church of England was weak and where, in turn, it stimulated older Dissent in renewed activity.[1]

When he visited the churches under his jurisdiction in 1823-4, the archdeacon of Derby (and later bishop of Lichfield) Samuel Butler found one in seven neglected to a serious extent. There is compelling evidence that in 14% to 15% of the churches the minimum of care, if that, had been taken to preserve the fabric, that this was an improvement on an earlier age, and that standards were to improve still further by the 1840s.

In the churches that were in tolerable repair the fittings were often, in Butler's frequently used descriptions, 'mean', 'shabby' or 'tasteless'. Three examples of neglect within the space of a few miles were Osmaston-by-Ashbourne, Shirley and Yeaveley. On 19 December 1824 Butler wrote thus to

---

[1] further to this see M.R. Austin, 'Religion and Society in Derbyshire during the Industrial Revolution', *DAJ*, Vol XCIII 1973.

John Gardiner, non-resident rector of Brailsford, about the 'old, mean, stone building' of his chapelry of Osmaston-by-Ashbourne:

> In my parochial visitation of the church of Osmaston by Ashbourne last summer I found it in a state of the greatest neglect and decay, particularly the chancel which it would I am sure have given you great pain to see . . . The altar was a rotten table covered with dirt and feathers as if a fowl had been lately picked [plucked] on it . . .

In addition, access to the altar rails was obstructed by appropriated pews.[1] Butler required Gardiner and the Brailsford churchwardens to take the offending pew-holders to the ecclesiastical court in Lichfield if their pews were not removed within six weeks.[2]

When W.A. Shirley (to succeed Butler as archdeacon) became incumbent of Shirley in 1828 he found that 'the church was disfigured by a half-ruinous wooden tower, was green with damp and darkened with cumbrous galleries which were far from sufficient for the population, though they were more than sufficient for the actual congregation'. At Yeaveley the chapel-of-ease was

> so ill kept that on more than one occasion the service was interrupted by the intrusion of cattle, and the snow used to penetrate in winter through the closest fastening of which the crazy windows were capable. There prevailed throughout the parish, as the natural accompaniment of this condition of the externals of religion, a low standard of morals, and one still lower, of cleanliness, order and decency.[3]

Prior to its restoration in 1851, Hathersage parish church was said to be 'in the most despicable order, the "Commandments" are broken, the pavement is damp and dislocated, the monuments are ill kept, and the very whitewash appears of the earliest "Gothic" application.'[4] Earl Sterndale church was in a ruinous condition in 1823, the churches in Church Gresley and Holmesfield 'from being in a ruinous condition have been razed to the ground and new ones built in their stead'. In 1822 a font in a transept of Tideswell parish

---

[1] There were no free seats in this church.
[2] M.R. Austin (ed), *The Church in Derbyshire in 1823–4: The parochial visitation of the Revd Samuel Butler, archdeacon of Derby in the diocese of Lichfield and Coventry* (1972), 135n.
[3] T.Hill, *Letters and Memoir of the late Walter Augustus Shirley DD, Lord Bishop of Sodor and Man* (1849), 124–5.
[4] Cox, *Churches*, ii, 230.

church was 'regularly used by the work people to mix their colours in, when they *beautify* the church with blue and mahogany paint'. It was said in 1824 of this beautiful church that

> indifference and insensibility have suffered the decorations and designations of this fine edifice to fall into decay – a species of destruction fatal in its ultimate effects as the ravages of the Goths and Vandals; the building of such fine churches was a matchless proof of high devotion that is now waxed cold; and their neglect of them is a reproach upon posterity, that ought most sacredly to be avoided.[1]

There is much more evidence from the 18th and early 19th centuries of dilapidation and serious disrepair of churches in Derbyshire, a story which can undoubtedly be told elsewhere.

Yet, together with this evidence of widespread neglect, there was much that was done to repair and extend churches and to build new ones. For example, in the sixty or so years between the early 1770s and the early 1830s (the period covered by the conventionally so-called Industrial Revolution) churches were rebuilt in Little Eaton (in 1791), Smalley (1793), Lullington (1799), Brimington (1808–9), Edale (1812), Elton (1812), Hayfield (1818), Rosliston (1818), Calke (1826), Blackwell (1827), Holmesfield (1827), Dore (1828) and Earl Sterndale (c. 1830), and were substantially rebuilt in Church Gresley (1816–19) and Mellor (1829). Ten new churches were built on new sites. Five of them were Cromford St Mary (1796), Buxton St John (1812), Darley Abbey St Matthew (1819), Ripley All Saints (1821) and Derby St George (erected as a speculative venture by a builder in 1831 and capable of serving either 'as a Music Hall or a Church'). The remaining five were 'Commissioners' churches' provided under the 'Million Act' of 1818 (so styled after the sum initially granted by parliament in thanksgiving for the victory at Waterloo, another half million being added in 1824).

In that year, at a time of rapidly growing population and threatened and actual civil unrest (and thus with a strongly political motive) it was reported to parliament, as part of a national survey, that 16 Derbyshire parishes had populations exceeding 2000 in which the Church of England provided accommodation in its churches for less than half. These were Alfreton, Ashbourne, Belper,

---

[1] M. Sterndale, *Vignettes of Derbyshire* (1824), 59,68,69,73.

Brampton, Chesterfield, Derby St Alkmund, Derby St Peter, Derby St Werburgh, Dronfield, Eckington, Glossop, Heanor, Melbourne, Mellor, Pentrich (which included the township of Ripley) and Wirksworth. Parliamentary grants were, in the event, made available to build the churches in only five parishes on new sites to meet the needs of expanding populations: Belper St Peter, Derby St John, Brampton St Thomas, New Mills St George and Riddings St James. The 1818 'Million Act' under which these churches were built further provided that the cost of their repair should be met from a rate levied in the district in which a church was erected. The building of Derby St John was objected to strongly by nonconformists on this ground for, as one of them said, why should

> one portion of the community be compelled to contribute to the support of an establishment which conscientious feelings alone have induced them to leave, while they are under the necessity of maintaining their own rites and modes of worship without the assistance of the parish or the state.[1]?

Another condition for grants under the 'Million Act' was that 20% of the seats in the new churches must be free. In practice a far higher percentage of free seats was provided; in Belper St Peter, for example, about 66% of the accommodation was free, though just under half of it was in galleries.[2] However, the free sittings in the 'Million' churches measured 2 ft 4 ins from back to back, whereas their appropriated pews were 3 ft from back to back, and were therefore more comfortable![3] The issue of free sittings raised crucial social and theological questions.

'Out of sight and hearing': seats in church for the poor

In one most significant respect the Church of England at this time did little more to meet the needs of a growing population for opportunities for worship than it had in the past. When Archdeacon Butler visited the parishes in his jurisdiction in 1823-4 he found that in 94 churches, or nearly 60%, there were either no, or very few, free seats for the poor. In general, across the county

---

[1] A Nonconformist, *Derby and Chesterfield Reporter*, 17 February 1825.
[2] Pew-renting continued in St Peter's until 1933, though well before this time the renting of pews had largely lost its social cachet and become little more than what *notionally* it had always been – a means of raising income.
[3] PP, 1857–8, ix, 51; Owen Chadwick, *The Victorian Church* (A. and C. Black, 1966), i, 330n.

only some 15% of the pews in churches were free. Those that did exist were placed either 'behind the door' (as at Atlow) or, as at Beighton 'out of sight & hearing' or behind the pulpit in the chancel 'where they cannot hear' as in Dronfield parish church. At Dalbury the poor were segregated by gender on benches at the west end of the church. In the new church at Hayfield (and, sadly, the number of free seats in most of the newly built churches was no more than in the older churches) the poor were placed on a semi-circular bench immediately beneath the pulpit and desk and in front of, and facing, the rented and appropriated pews as an all too clear reminder to the well-to-do that there, but for the grace of God, went they.

The emotions of fear, social prejudice and deep-seated and inchoate anger, if not genetically inherited, are certainly passed down through the generations. We do not have to look far for reasons why today's meritocracy, the descendants of the indigent and labouring poor and the artisans of the 18th and 19th centuries, reject a Church of England that treated their forebears with such disdain on the one hand, and patronising protectiveness on the other. In the 1820s, so Samuel Butler reported, the parish church of Bonsall held 400 people and was well attended. As the only free pew could hold but 12 people and was placed in the south-west gallery, few of the poor could have attended church had they wanted to, or seen or heard much if they did. The incumbent, Robert Greville, was a pluralist and lived in his parish of Edlaston twelve miles away, from which he also served the curacy of Somersall Herbert. His resident curate in Bonsall was the evangelical Henry Sim who was also curate of Parwich. It was probably Sim who objected one day to the presence in his parish of a group of strolling players. One of them, Christopher Thomson, described what happened:

> Our theatre was next removed to Bonsall, until we could fit up a theatre at Matlock. At Bonsall our beginning gave promise of a short, remunerative season; but after two nights' performance the Clergyman put his ban upon us: no unusual thing with us to be stopped by those well-fed and State-paid teachers of the people.[1]

Thomson was wrong to assume that the clergy were 'State-paid', and Henry Sim, with a stipend from his Bonsall curacy of £60 p.a., with surplice fees in

---

[1] Christopher Thomson, *The Autobiography of an Artisan* (London 1847), 222. I am grateful to David Mitchell for this reference.

addition, was not as well-fed as many Derbyshire incumbents. Sims' evangelical zeal to protect the population from the influence of the theatre is paralleled elsewhere in the county. The vicar of Mickleover, the Revd and Hon. Frederick Emmanuel Curzon, objected in the 1820s to musical performances in church, even those of Handel's *Messiah*!

Overall the picture of the Church of England in 18th century Derbyshire is very mixed. We can only state the obvious. In very many parishes the state of the fabric of the parish church in the 18th and early 19th centuries was very poor, certainly by today's standards; that there were exceptions to this general picture; and that, a century later, not only the fabric of the churches, but also the income and social position of the clergy, and, not least, the standard of their pastoral and preaching ministry had greatly improved. Much of this improvement was due to the work of the Commissioners of Queen Anne's Bounty and their successors[1], to local laity raising funds to repair and rebuild churches, to parliamentary grants for church building, and to what nonconformists rightly regarded as the iniquitous imposition of a church rate to maintain parish churches, enforced by law on all ratepayers, Anglican or not, by churchwardens. But, more dramatically, an impetus for improvement in the preaching, teaching and pastoral ministry of the clergy came from another source.

'Publishing the Gospel of peace': John Wesley, Methodism and the Evangelicals

Together with government intervention in the early 19th century to improve clergy incomes and to build churches as a kind of spiritual bulwark against the threat of civil insurrection, there was the undoubted stimulus of a new enthusiasm for religion, an enthusiasm which had disturbed the complacent calm of the 18th century Church of England, not least in Derbyshire.

For much of the 18th century 'enthusiasm' as a word which described evangelical religious zeal was one if not of abuse then certainly of disparagement. As one of several examples we may take the memorial inscription in Trusley parish church to John Freeman, rector between 1770 and 1786. It says of him that not only had he been 'Charitable without

---

[1] See M.R. Austin, 'Queen Anne's Bounty and the poor livings of Derbyshire 1772–1832, *DAJ*, 92, (1972), 78–89.

ostentation, And Chearful without levity' but also 'Pious without enthusiasm.'

The ministry of one man epitomised 'enthusiasm'. This man was John Wesley. Not only did Wesley, against as great an opposition as had greeted George Fox a century earlier, provoke his own Church of England towards reform and renewal, his Methodists also had a catalytic effect on older nonconformity, which, by the second half of the century had largely lost its passion. Wesley's memorial in the City Road chapel in London says of him that

> Regardless of Fatigue, personal Danger, and Disgrace,
> He went out into the highways and hedges
> Calling Sinners to Repentance,
> And publishing the Gospel of Peace.

It was this Gospel that Wesley published for 50 years and across 225000 walked and ridden miles as an itinerant Anglican preacher.

Wesley visited Derbyshire many times. Richard Smalbrooke, bishop of Lichfield and Coventry 1731–1749, roundly condemned Wesley's ministry, apparently for its strict ethical and theological principles. 'Methodism', he said in a Charge in 1746, 'is akin to Romanism'. Despite the rejection of Wesley by their bishop, Wesley names in his *Journal* (together with those who opposed him) several Derbyshire clergymen who received him either grudgingly or sympathetically on his many tours through Derbyshire. William Greaves (vicar of Ockbrook 1734–65) perhaps rather unwillingly allowed Wesley to preach in his parish church on 10 June 1741. In his *Journal* Wesley summed up Greaves' 'doctrine' as 'if you believe, be still. Do not pretend to do good (which you cannot do till you believe); and leave off what you call the means of grace – such as prayer and running to church and sacrament.' We may regard this attitude as fairly general among 18th century Anglican clergy. It accorded with the opinions of Gilbert Mitchell, rector of Breadsall 1700–38. In a sermon in Derby All Saints in 1730 he recognised that the true end of religion is 'to bring men back from their Follies and Superstitions, from their Vices and Irregularities, to a reasonable Service, to a life of Holiness and Virtue.' Yet he made that religion of revelation firmly subservient to the primacy of reason, for

> Natural Religion, or those Notions and Principles which our Reason
> dictates to us; and which the Gospel hath reinforced upon us with the

strongest Arguments and most powerful Motives, are prior to all positive
Institutions whatsoever.[1]

John Baddiley, the perpetual curate of Hayfield, was of a very different kind.
Wesley described him as 'a sort of second Grimshaw'. With Baddiley we are
introduced to the evangelical clergy in Derbyshire at this time, men deeply
influenced by the new revival. William Grimshaw (1708–63), perpetual curate
of Haworth, was, unlike John Wesley, a strong Calvinist yet he warmly
welcomed Methodists into his pulpit and himself later took up itinerant
preaching. Baddiley had been converted to Wesley's enthusiastic Christianity
in 1764, and in October of that year Wesley wrote that Hayfield was 'up in
arms against him already, breathing out slaughter. Notwithstanding he is as
bold as a lion'. Wesley included Baddiley among 'those labourers who are
ministers of the Church of England' who united in agreeing 'in these
essentials': Original Sin, justification by grace through faith, and holiness of
heart and life.

Another 18th century Derbyshire Anglican evangelical was A.B. Greaves,
curate of Stoney Middleton, who had been curate to the great J.W. Fletcher at
Madeley for six years. Another was Thomas Cursham, curate of Ashover. Two
sermons of Cursham's survive. His farewell sermon preached in 1789 on Col.
2:6[2] is a simple evangelical appeal. That we are justified by faith only, he said,
'is a most wholesome doctrine, and very full of comfort.' He reminded his
congregation that 'all our works, unless they are wrought in us by his word
and spirit are sin, death and everlasting condemnation', and he warned his
hearers to beware of 'those false teachers and deceivers who would draw you
from these precious truths by representing them to you as wild and fanatical
notions which have no existence but in the brains of enthusiasts'. Such
enthusiasm was greatly distrusted by many clergy and their patrons. In
Cursham's case his own rector, Lawrence Bourne, was thought to have
drawn up a petition demanding his curate's dismissal. Cursham claimed that
this had

> been handed through the parish from house to house by a Mr M. the
> Rector's agent, and two of his friends, to procure names to it. And in
> order to succeed in this honourable business, the most base and

[1] G. Mitchell, *The Design of Publishing the Gospel, a sermon preach'd at All Saints, in Derby, September
20th 1730*, (1731), v.
[2] 'As ye have received Christ Jesus the Lord, so walk ye in him.'

unjustifiable methods were used – the people were threatened with having their tithes taken in kind &c. By these and such *powerful* arguments, several were induced to sign, though much against their inclinations as they have since acknowledged.[1]

Bourne denounced Cursham's preaching as 'a species of Enthusiasm and Wild Vagaries.' It was for this that the Evangelicals were so opposed, as were the early Methodists in Derbyshire. They answered that what they preached was what the Church of England upheld in its Articles, liturgy and Homilies. John Gardiner, absentee rector of Brailsford, denounced their 'errors and abuses of zeal' in a sermon in 1802. He warned the members of the congregation of his proprietary Octagon Chapel in Bath that on no account were they to allow 'Zeal and Fervour' to influence their opinions 'in regard to Religion' or to determine their judgement 'on articles of faith or practice', for 'Zeal is irregular when it encroaches on the established order of things' and undermines respect for the properly appointed 'spiritual guides'.[2] In that last comment lies the real reason for the opposition to Wesley, his Methodists and the Anglican Evangelicals. It was that their preaching on the absoluteness of divine grace undermined the ecclesiastical authority of the 'spiritual guides' who, in turn, upheld 'the established order of things'. In themselves, theological differences were much less feared than the supposed social and political consequences of those differences. We have evidence of that fear from much earlier in our story.

There were several more courageous evangelical clergy in Derbyshire, all of them curates or in poor benefices, who followed Wesley's example and were inspired by his teaching: John James Dewe, perpetual curate of Parwich and Alsop for several years until his death in 1822; Jonathan Stubbs, curate of Derby St Alkmund from 1798 to 1803; Henry John Maddock, who became curate of Bonsall in 1811; and Andrew Knox, curate of Chesterfield in the 1820s. Rather than spend time here on John Wesley's well recorded itinerant ministry in Derbyshire it has been important to tell of these largely forgotten and faithful men who were influenced by him.

'Outrageous enthusiasm'

Not that Wesley himself had had an untroubled time in Derbyshire. He was

---

[1] T. Cursham, *Constancy in the Faith and Practice of Christianity Recommended and enforced in a Sermon delivered in Ashover Church, Derbyshire* (Sheffield 1789), 6.
[2] J. Gardiner, *Sermons on Various Subjects, preached at the Octagon Chapel, Bath* (1802), 317.

occasionally stoned for his pains, and early Methodists in Derbyshire were often viciously persecuted by mobs encouraged by local Anglican clergy. John Bennett, the itinerant Methodist preacher, told of a clergyman at Monyash who assaulted him while he was preaching[1]. At Eyam the curate, Peter Cunninghame, went round his parish obtaining promises in writing not to hear the Methodists.[2] In a sermon in Chesterfield parish church in April 1756, J. Heywood criticised the Methodists for their 'sullen, severe austerity of conduct and rusticity of manners' as well as for their 'unbounded zeal to propagate their opinions'[3] It was the 'outrageous enthusiasm' of the Methodists which outraged the curate of Edale in 1813 and drove him bitterly to criticise the local Methodist minister, Mr Bird, for 'breaking down the fence between us' and inviting 'all who compose *my* fold, to leap through the gap' and join his.[4] Yet eventually the Anglican evangelicals in Derbyshire were to become as strongly opposed to Methodism as their more orthodox brothers. At a meeting of the Matlock Bath Clerical Society in April 1835 one speaker condemned Methodists as 'our most dangerous enemies' while Walter Augustus Shirley, later to be archdeacon of Derby, said 'the less we have to do with them the better.'[5] By this time opposition to Methodism was ostensibly based on the question of church order sharpened by a dislike of excessive emotionalism but the competitive spirit of the various Methodist denominations and, by this time, their clear numerical success, was perhaps the basic cause.

Undeterred by opposition to their ministry, Wesley, and those who followed his example, continued their witness in the county (though Wesley, not surprisingly for one born in the flat Lincolnshire fens, could not abide what he described as its 'horrid' or 'dreary mountains'!). Just one extract from his *Journal* must represent his ministry here. It is the entry for 5 July 1786:

> Notice was given, without my knowledge, of my preaching at Belpar [sic], seven miles short of Derby. I was nothing glad of this, as it obliged

---

[1] J. Everett, *Wesleyan Methodism in Manchester and its Vicinity* (Manchester 1827), I, 24–5.

[2] J. Everett, *Historical Sketches of Wesleyan Methodism in Sheffield and its Vicinity* (Sheffield 1823), I, 202–3.

[3] J. Heywood, *The Happiness and Duty of Britons under the Present Government; represented in A Sermon occasioned by His Majesty's late Indisposition* (25 April 1756)..

[4] W. Sharpe, *A Letter to Mr W. Bird, An Itinerant Methodist Preacher, in reply to His Remarks on a Sermon by the Revd. W. Sharpe*, (Cambridge 1813), 1, 13.

[5] Arthur Pollard, 'Evangelical Parish Clergy, 1820–1840', *The Church Quarterly Review*, July-September 1958, 392.

me to quit the turnpike road to hobble over a miserable common. The people, gathered from all parts, were waiting; so I went immediately to the Market-place, and standing under a large tree, testified, 'This is life eternal, to know thee, the only true God, and Jesus Christ whom thou hast sent.'

That same day Wesley went to Derby where he found 'the house was thoroughly filled in the evening. As many of the better sort, so called, were there, I explained, what seemed to be more adapted to their circumstances and experience, "This only have I found, that God made men upright; but they have found out many inventions."' John Wesley was then eighty-three years of age.

There is no record that John Wesley preached in Thorpe parish church. In 1766 the rector, Thomas Winder, died. In his will he stipulated that sixpence be given to every poor person attending his funeral, that all debts owing to him be cancelled, and that £20 be distributed to the poor of the parish. He also bequeathed £100 each to the Society for the Propagation of the Gospel, to George Whitefield the Anglican clergyman, Calvinist, and great evangelical preacher – and to John Wesley.[1]

The expansion of Methodism in Derbyshire was to be rapid and widespread during the next 150 years. On 30 March 1851 the attendances at the chapels of six Methodist denominations (Wesleyan Methodist, Wesleyan Methodist Association, Wesleyan Reform, Primitive Methodist, Original Methodist and Methodist New Connexion) exceeded those at Anglican churches by 20%. The colliery village of South Normanton provides a typical example of Methodist expansion. In 1817 the Primitive Methodists converted an old barn into a chapel, building their own meeting place in 1827. In 1845 the first Wesleyan chapel was erected, with the break-away United Methodist Free Church building its own chapel in 1850. The Original Methodist Connexion erected its Zion Chapel in 1857, with a splinter group returning to the original 1817 Primitive Methodist barn to become Free Gospellers in 1867. The United Methodist Free Church erected a chapel in 1879, with the Primitive Methodists building a new chapel in 1881. The Wesleyans erected a new chapel in 1887. This rival chapel-building was in addition to the construction of Methodist school-rooms.[2]

As in other colliery villages Methodist colliery owners and managers

---

[1] E. Higham, 'The ancient parish of Thorpe', *Southwell Diocesan Magazine*, September 1910.
[2] Pamela Stone, *A Village of Considerable Extent*, (n.d.).

encouraged Methodism in South Normanton, and miners were to be found among chapel trustees. Employers favoured Methodism. It encouraged hard work, thrift, honesty and temperance – virtues among the men that made for profitability for their employers.

'*Seam-rent shoes': the witness of Dissent*

We have noticed how Methodism had a catalytic effect not only on the Church of England but also on the older nonconformist churches. The Church of England was ill prepared to meet the needs of an expanding population in 1800, and nonconformist congregations supplied the need.[1]

It is important here, in this Anglican story, to say again how hugely significant a contribution Methodism and old and new Dissent have made to the religious and social history of Derbyshire. Not only were Quakers first so called in Derby, but the Primitive Methodists took as an honour their disparaging nickname 'Ranters' first given them in Belper. Nationally that contribution has been comprehensively analysed[2] and we can do no more than honour it here. There is space to tell only two stories of Derbyshire Dissenters to illustrate the faithfulness of those who refused on grounds of conscience to conform to the state Church, one of a Baptist and the other of a wife and husband who were itinerant Primitive Methodist preachers.

There is the story of Joseph Burrows, General Baptist minister for forty years from 1821, first at Sutton-in-Ashfield and then at Alfreton. He earned his living as a lacemaker. A depression in his industry in the late 1830s compelled him to sell a machine which had cost him £600 for the knock-down price of £120. He then rented another, but when its owner heard that he was a Baptist minister he took it away from him, depriving him of his trade, on the ground that 'one trade is enough for a man to look after'.[3]

Methodism will here be represented by one of its originally more egalitarian secessions, the Primitive Methodists established in 1811. Sarah Kirkland of

---

[1] Between 1801 and 1830, 432 nonconformist meeting houses (294 temporary and 138 permanent) were registered in Derbyshire under the provisions of the Act of Toleration 1689. This compares with a total of 209 meeting houses (158 temporary and 51 permanent) registered between 1689 and 1800. This evidence [based on returns to the Registrar General, PP 1852–3 (156) LXXVIII, 83] must, however, be read with some caution. I am grateful to Dr David L. Wykes for this information.

[2] Notably by Michael R. Watts. For Derbyshire, Gladwyn Turbutt provides an overview, citing original research into the history of nonconformity in Derbyshire by Richard Clark, Margery Tranter, Adrian Henstock, A.M. Johnson, R. Mansfield, and D. Roberts.

[3] ref. in Watts, op cit., 247–8.

Mercaston was converted when she was twenty years old, and, in 1816, became the first woman travelling Primitive Methodist preacher, at a salary of two guineas a quarter. In 1818 she married John Harrison, another Derbyshire-born Primitive Methodist preacher. Michael Watts tells the story of John Harrison.

> By November 1819 Harrison, although only twenty-four, was beginning to suffer the ill-effects of two years of itinerant labours and spent a fortnight at his parents' home at Bradley Park near Hulland in Derbyshire to recuperate. On Monday, 15 November, he left Bradley Park on foot, 'although very unwell', with Hull as his ultimate destination. 'I had caught a bad cold', he recorded in his journal, 'and in addition to this, whilst walking today my shoes came seam-rent, and I have walked several miles wet-shod; so I have added one cold to another.' None the less that night he preached at Belper; the following day he walked eighteen miles to Nottingham; and the day after he walked twenty miles to Newark. 'It rained much, and although it was nearly seven in the evening before I arrived, and I was very wet and fatigued, the friends would have no nay but I must preach.' On Thursday, 18 November, he walked twenty-five miles to Gainsborough and preached at night, and on the following day took the packet-boat for Hull 'but remained very poorly.' That was the last entry in his diary; he died in July 1821 still only twenty-five years of age.[1]

Many more stories like this can be told of Derbyshire nonconformists. For example, George Eliot's description of Methodism on the south-west Derbyshire/Staffordshire border tells of the contribution of nonconformity far more powerfully than can any historian.[2] These accounts place the story of Derbyshire Anglicanism in the proper context of rejection, sacrifice and faithfulness to the Gospel of nonconformists. Yet we must recognise that nonconformity no less than Anglicanism had a strongly political edge. In the

---

[1] Watts, op.cit., 150, citing Herod, *Biographical Sketches*, 387.

[2] In *Adam Bede*, published in 1858. Its opening chapters are set at the turn of the 18th and 19th centuries. The preaching of George Eliot's Methodists was in the sharpest contrast to that of, say, her pluralist incumbent of Broxton, Hayslope and Blythe, Adolphus Irwine, who 'was fonder of church history than of divinity . . . . His mental palate . . . was rather pagan, and found a saviouriness in a quotation from Sophocles or Theocritus that was quite absent from any text in Isaiah or Amos' [J.M. Dent, *Everyman* edition, 1960, 68–9]. At least one of Eliot's clergy names, the Revd Mr Blick [ibid, 57] is authentic. Francis Edward Blick was the non-resident incumbent of Walton-on-Trent with Rosliston 1800–42. His son, Edward, was his curate.

absence of universal male suffrage the only lawful way to express collective opposition to the established order was through nonconformist religious observance. It is often impossible to separate nonconformist religious, and working-class political, radicalism. Among those convicted and executed for their leadership of the abortive Pentrich uprising in 1817, Jeremiah Brandreth claimed to be a Baptist, and Isaac Ludlam was reputed to be the best Methodist lay preacher in the Belper circuit.[1]

[1] Watts, op.cit., 401.

10

'No Ecclesiastical barons': clergy and people, 1824–1884

In its issue for 24 January 1833 the strongly reformist *Derby and Chesterfield Reporter*, having commented on 'the miserable state of Ireland', spread its net wider and took to task the whole 'enormously rich Protestant Establishment' arguing that 'the Church of England is useless and worse than useless to more than half the population of this part of the United Kingdom, and her whole expense ought to be confined to those who retain confidence in her doctrines and respect for her discipline.' It is a comment which introduces us to the period immediately preceding our own; a period in which emerged the most pressing of the problems posed for the mission of today's Church of England.

The *Reporter* expected great things of a newly reformed House of Commons:

> Christianity knows of no Ecclesiastical barons, and the intelligence of the times is about to speak to them through the Reformed House of Commons, and to tell them to lay aside their pomp and vanity, and prepare to be provided for by the people at the exact rate of their estimated usefulness.

This measured outburst was a response to the reaction already voiced against the Irish Church Bill to be presented in Parliament the next month. This Bill proposed to reduce the number of the Irish bishoprics of the united Church of England and Ireland from 22 to 12. This would save £60000. It was a reasonable proposal as Irish dioceses were both small and poor and members in Ireland of the Church of England and Ireland (a single Church created by the Act of Union in 1800) then few in number. Rosingrave Macklin, vicar of Christ Church in Derby 1841-1862, held a living in County Wicklow for many years. While in

Ireland he had been buried up to his neck in a bog by his Roman Catholic parishioners because of his proselytising activities. Dug up in the nick of time Macklin had fled to England and became curate of Derby St Werburgh in 1835. He continued thereafter to receive the income from his Irish benefice.

Opposition to the Bill was to be distilled within weeks in John Keble's sermon on 'National Apostasy' preached before the judges of the Assize in Oxford on 14 July. This sermon was to be taken by John Henry Newman to mark the beginning of the Oxford Movement, an impassioned initiative which represented a reaction against state intervention in Church affairs and 'liberalism' in theology and which sought to return the Church of England both to the supposed simple catholic purity of the early Church and to the high church principles of the Church of the Stuarts. The Oxford Movement, and the anglo-catholic revival to which it gave rise, were to have their devoted and courageous followers in Derby and Derbyshire later in the century.

In a town so strongly liberal and nonconformist as Derby, it was inevitable that the clergy should be unpopular, particularly those who espoused high church principles and the Tory politics to which they were attached in the popular mind. To many people, the clergy of the Church of England represented the political, social and religious privilege which, it had been popularly and fervently hoped, would be swept away by the 1832 Reform Bill. In this they had been bitterly disappointed.

The clergy themselves gave cause for resentment. They were solidly Tory and reactionary in their political allegiance and opposed to any reform which threatened their position and authority. 'The Clergy, Magistrates and Freeholders' in Derby together subscribed to a petition in May 1835 which requested Parliament 'to resist the encroachments now attempted to be made, by the Roman Catholics, upon the United Church of England and Ireland'. For the *Reporter* it would have been better for the clergy to have been occupied in

> petitioning for reform and retrenchment, for the suppression of sinecures both civil and ecclesiastical, for the resumption for the people in two parts of the tithes which the clergy have taken for their own use, and of those enormous sums so unjustly bestowed on ecclesiastical drones.'[1]

---

[1] *Derby and Chesterfield Reporter*, 24 February 1831. The Whig press, especially the *Edinburgh Review* between 1802 and 1829, had long attacked Anglican clergy for their supposed idleness and avariciousness, and the archdeacon of Derby, Samuel Butler, devoted a Charge, *Some late Attacks on the Clergy Considered*, to their defence in 1823.

If this was the Established Church then reformers and nonconformists wanted none of it. These were sentiments with which the archdeacon of Derby, Samuel Butler, privately had some sympathy. In October 1832 he wrote to Edward Burton, regius professor of divinity at Oxford, saying that he wished to see 'Translations abolished, Sinecures abolished, Pluralities greatly restrained, Residence greatly promoted, Small livings increased, Tithes commuted, Scandalous clergy easily removed'. In the same year, he proposed 'a scheme for reform in the Church' which would begin with the sweeping away of the 'whole present body of ecclesiastical laws' for 'the house is too ruinous for repair; we ought to pull it down and build a new one.'[1]

These moderately reformist opinions were not shared by the majority of Butler's parochial clergy. Conscious of their unpopularity, fearful of civil insurrection on the one hand and the supposed threat of a revived Roman Catholic church relieved of its civil disabilities on the other, the clergy felt that the end not only of their privileges or even of the Church of England but also of the English way of life was near. On 15 July 1826 George Paulin Lowther, the rector of Barton Blount and curate of Longford, wrote a letter detailing alterations to Longford church, sealed it in a bottle, and buried it beneath the pulpit. He concluded his letter by saying that he felt 'strongly assured'

> that when these papers see the light it will be under the hierarchy of the Roman Catholic Church which will doubtless gain the ascendancy in proportion as ignorance prevails: and I cannot help predicting the downfall of the English nation, as I fancy I behold in it all the signs of a declining state.

Roman Catholic emancipation came two years later, but the battle for wider and deeper reform was to be continued with increasing ferocity locally throughout most of the 19th century. This was initially focused on the divisive issue of church rates. As we have already noted, these compulsory levies imposed on rate-payers, whether Anglican or not, for the maintenance of parish churches were strongly opposed by nonconformists who had also to maintain their own places of worship. Bitter and very public disputes were fought at annual vestries in the 1830s with often very dubious means being employed by churchwardens to force through the annual rate.[2] Possibly for wider political reasons the bishops resisted the abolition of church rates when

---

[1] S. Butler, *The life and letters of Dr Samuel Butler*, (1896), i, 5–6.
[2] further to this see Austin 1966, 103–113.

this was proposed in 1834 and 1837. Gladstone abolished their compulsory levy in 1868. Such was the highly charged religious and political atmosphere at this time, certainly in expanding urban industrial towns like Derby.

'A considerable exertion'

The nearer we approach our own day more historical material comes to hand and it becomes more detailed. To make the subsequent story manageable in a short book we can look in any depth (and even then only selectively) at the Church of England in only one place in Derbyshire in the 19th century – the county town – drawing on evidence from elsewhere in Derbyshire as we go along. But we must begin with a broad overview of the state of the Church of England in Derbyshire in the years running up to the creation, in 1884, of the diocese of Southwell, of which Derbyshire became a part.

'A considerable exertion' was how Samuel Butler[1] described his archidiaconal visitation of the parishes under his jurisdiction in Derbyshire in the summers of 1823 and 1824. He reported his findings in his Charge in 1825. We have already noticed much that he discovered of the poor physical state of the churches. Some 15% of them were virtually unusable, while the overwhelming majority of the population were excluded from those that were in repair due to pew appropriation by the well-to-do. He had much to say about the discredit that the non-residence of the clergy brought upon the Church yet he implied that given the still very low income of many clergy some pluralism was well-nigh inevitable. Butler noted that 23 incumbents, or 14.5%, received £500 and more per annum while 19, or 11.95%, received £50 or less. This variation made for pluralism and poor standards of pastoral care. As we have noted, he commented unfavourably on the inadequacy and poor quality of many parsonage houses, some 20 of which were 'mere cottages' and 'just capable of accommodating a labourer and his family' and 'quite unfit for a clergyman.'

Butler, also headmaster of Shrewsbury School, had much to say about the Church's provision of schools in Derbyshire and of the need to increase it. He calculated that the Church was educating 11759 children in its schools, though

---

[1] 1774–1839. Headmaster of Shrewsbury School (where Charles Darwin was a pupil), archdeacon of Derby 1821–36, bishop of Lichfield 1836–39. For his political, social and theological opinions see M.R. Austin, *The Church in Derbyshire in 1823–4* (1974), 5–10. He was the grandfather of Samuel Butler, author of *Erewhon* (1873) and the autobiographical *The Way of All Flesh* published posthumously in 1903 in which he details his relationship with his father (incumbent of Langar in Nottinghamshire) and his grandfather, whom he characterised unkindly as 'not the man to trouble himself about his motives'.

29 parishes, with 14000 inhabitants, had no school at all. This must be improved, he said, in an age 'most experimental [and] the most impatient of moral and religious restraint and discipline'. There was a consequent need for the Church 'to stem the torrent of infidelity and licentiousness.' Once again we find here a covert political motive for the promotion of religious belief.

In his 1825 Charge, Butler did not mention three subjects about which his visitation returns provide ample evidence. One was patronage, but he had something to say about this in his 1833 Charge. The other two were church attendance, particularly at holy Communion, and the impact of non-conformity. As to the first we can compare the 1823–4 evidence with that provided in the surviving incomplete set of returns to Bishop Brownlow North's visitation articles in 1772, sixty momentous years earlier. This comparison shows that in the predominantly agricultural areas of the south and west of the county, where the population remained reasonably static, attendance at holy Communion remained equally stable through that sixty years, with many parishes returning virtually identical statistics in 1772 and 1823–4. In the parishes where there had been considerable industrial development, where the population had grown, where the old social patterns had broken down and, not least, where nonconformist activity had been greatest, Anglican attendances at holy Communion declined drastically.[1] In the agricultural parishes with stable populations it seemed to make little difference to church attendance whether the incumbent or his curate were resident or not. In the new industrial villages the residence of the parson seemed of itself to do little to encourage non-churchgoing people to come to church.

Analysis of Butler's visitation returns suggest that four factors influenced Anglican church attendance in Derbyshire in the early 1820s. We can see the effect of three of these – the presence or otherwise of a clergyman living in his parsonage, nonconformist activity, and population change – fairly clearly. The huge importance of a fourth, a sense of alienation from a Church seen to represent, and give Christian warrant to, exclusion, injustice and oppression is far more difficult to estimate, though we can say that unlike their agricultural brothers (or at least such of them as could find a free pew in church), industrial labourers were now beginning to pay scant respect to the church-going habits of

---

[1] for an analysis of the impact of nonconformist activity at this time on Anglican attendances see M. R. Austin, 'Religion and Society in Derbyshire during the Industrial Revolution', *DAJ*, Vol XCIII 1973, 81–3.

their masters.[1] We are still reaping the harvest of that bitter alienation.

'A quiet Conservative vote'

We have already noticed how, throughout our story, politics, social issues and religion were interrelated in what K.G. Feiling has called 'the religious river-bed of party'[2] and we need here to add a very brief note about the political opinions of Derbyshire Anglican clergy in the early 19th century. They have been carefully analysed[3]. Depending on whether or not their patron was the great whig Cavendish family in the north of the county and the lesser landowners whose exercise of patronage the family influenced, most clergy for the previous century and more would, at least privately, have shared the sentiments of Melville Horne Scott, vicar of Ockbrook. In 1868 he noted in his diary that

> it will usually be a clergyman's best plan to give a quiet and silent Conservative vote, as the least obtrusive thing that he can do .... A quiet Conservative vote is the best expression of his gratitude to God for England as she is; England as she is to be the clergyman had better leave to be arranged by persons cleverer and otherwise less solemnly occupied than himself.[4]

We must leave this fascinating question as soon as we have raised it. We should not be surprised that, publicly, most parochial clergymen adopted the political views of those influential laymen upon whom they depended, whether, privately, they agreed with them or not. Almost throughout our story so far the laity had exercised far more local influence than national authority in the Church of England. This was to change in the twentieth century, but whereas in the 1830s in rural parishes this local and deeply conservative influence had rarely been greater, the balance of political and religious influence in an expanding town like Derby was altering radically.

'What big congregations attended that sanctuary'

To take just one of many examples. Within a few years of the 1832 Reform Act

---

[1] It would be quite wrong to assume that pew-renting was the only explanation for the alienation of the poor from the Churches (see K.T. Hoppen, op.cit., 454–5).
[2] K.G. Feiling, *The Second Tory Party 1714–1832* (1938), 187.
[3] Austin 1969, 220–240.
[4] M. Scott, *The Force of Love; memoir of Melville H. Scott* (Derby 1899), 111.

Derby became not only a railway town but a railway centre. The railway came to Derby in 1839. By the 1870s the locomotive and carriage sheds of the Midland Railway Company covered an area as large as the whole of pre-railway Derby. The population increased sharply after 1830, the 1871 census showing that it had more than doubled in 40 years. In addition the principal growth areas were not only away from the town centre but also largely outside the then borough, the population of the township of Litchurch, where the Midland Railway Company had its works, increasing from 516 in 1831 to 25445 by 1901.

The railway brought not only an increase in population, it also inevitably changed the social character of the town with the Liberal industrial and commercial middle-classes prospering while the traditionally Tory and Anglican well-to-do became increasingly outnumbered. Not only did the class structure of the town change; by 1851 half the population over 20 years of age had been born outside the borough, and thus felt little loyalty to the town which came of long residence and family connection. Equally inevitably the rich became richer while the poor congregated in the slums in and around St Michael's parish in conditions which grew worse as their numbers increased. The considerably affluent and the extremely poor lived almost within yards of each other in the centre of the town.

The leaders of the new industry and of the new commercial middle-class were, in the main, men whose instincts were Liberal and nonconformist. Sir James Allport, an early general manager of the Midland Railway Company, was a leading member of the Wesleyan Methodist chapel in London Road. It was recorded that 'the unsympathetic, not to say scornful, used to say what big congregations attended that sanctuary in those days.'[1] Charles Bassett-Vincent was the founder in 1872 of the Amalgamated Society of Railway Servants, the first of the railway trade unions. The initial meetings leading to the creation of the union were held in a room at the Green Dragon inn in St Peter's Street in Derby. Bassett-Vincent wrote in 1902 that Mr Allport (as he was in 1871) was, of all his opponents among officials of the railway companies, 'the most bitter against me.'[2] Bassett-Vincent received the warm support of Anglican clergy elsewhere.

Liberal and philanthropic these men may have been but they were strongly opposed to any working class organisation that threatened their profits. Charles Henry Turner, who succeeded George Hudson, the discredited 'railway king',

---

[1] G.R. Pratt, *Midland Railway Memories* (Derby 1924), 25.
[2] Charles Bassett-Vincent, *An Authentic History of Railway Trade Unionism* (1902), 48.

was also connected with the London Road chapel, towards the building which in 1861 the Midland Railway Company directors gave £100. George Husson, chief of the passenger audit office, was a Methodist local preacher.

This combination of commercial enterprise and nonconformist religion fitted well into Derby's political scene, as indeed it did in Chesterfield as witnessed by the monuments to the Robinsons and other successful industrial families in Elder Yard Chapel.[1] From 1832 to 1885 Derby was generally represented by Liberal and radical MPs sympathetic to nonconformity. The town attracted men of like mind. William Griffiths, one of the 'Three Expelled' reforming 'martyrs' ejected by the Methodist Conference in 1849, and 'a most open advocate of Liberal politics from the pulpit'[2] became minister of the Derby United Methodist Free Church chapel in Beckett Street in 1855, retiring in 1877.

These are just a few of the social factors creating a radically different Derby at this time. A small, new, affluent and very influential commercial middle class, predominately Liberal and reformist in politics, evangelical and nonconformist in religious conviction, fervent in its nationalism, and largely opposed to working-class combination, was making a great deal of money out of railways and the ancillary industries to which they gave rise. The position of these men in the town, and the presence of the very large numbers of those who worked for them, explains much of the story which is to follow.

'The too exclusive appropriation of large pews'

As we have noticed, at the time of the Domesday survey there were six churches in Derby. One subsequently disappeared from the record and for the whole of our story thus far there had been five: All Saints, St Alkmund's, St Michael's, St Werburgh's and St Peter's, only one of which, St Peter's, was still substantially mediaeval. In 1824 these five parishes had supplied Derby's religious needs for centuries but had done nothing to provide for a population that had doubled in size between 1791 and 1821. By 1824 the population had reached over 19000. For this number the Church of England provided 2894 'sittings' in the five parish churches, or room for some 15% of the population – and only for the well-to-do, for of these places only 345 were free, the rest being rented or otherwise

---

[1] I am grateful to David Mitchell for the note about the Elder Yard Chapel monuments.
[2] E.R. Wickham, *Church and People in an Industrial City*, (1957), 123.

appropriated. If Derby's poor had wanted to come to their parish church very few could have done so. They were deliberately excluded, those few who could find a place being accepted at best on sufferance and as an act of marginal charity. But by no means all of the appropriated pews were available. In All Saints and St Werburgh's, for example, the taking of large box pews with up to six seats by one or two people prevented most of the church being used. Pews could be owned by people who rarely, if ever, went to church, used by them as private property and 'subjected to open traffic.'[1] It was possible to find a church in Derby on a Sunday morning with little available accommodation but with comparatively few people in the building, 'the scattered heads showing many void spaces in the high pews.'[2] So the actual accommodation available for the general population was very much less than even these low figures suggest. A bitter and prolonged dispute about pew appropriations at St Werburgh's in 1831 prompted the bishop of Lichfield and Coventry to send commissioners to the parish. In their report they observed that

> the too exclusive appropriation of large pews (in some Churches) to a comparatively small number of persons, and to the manifest deprivation of residents of equal respectability in the same parish has gone very far to alienate the minds of individuals from the Church, and to cause them to seek the more equal accommodation which is readily offered to them in dissenting places of worship.[3]

That is a very revealing comment. It is the 'residents of equal respectability' who are alienated. There is mention of the 'dissenting places of worship' to which 'the respectable' were driven. There is no word here of the deeper alienation of the large numbers of the labouring poor. It was said of the congregation of St Werburgh's at the time that it 'was specially moral and respectable – for it had none of the political element to be found in the principal church, All Saints, and none of the operative element to be found in no church at all.'[4]

Between 1791 and 1831, while the Church of England had done nothing, Dissent had built seven chapels and meetings houses in the town: three Wesleyan and New Connexion Methodist and two Baptist chapels, a New

---

[1] as in St Werburgh's in 1830. See T. Mozley, *To the Honourable and Right Reverend the Lord Bishop of Lichfield and Coventry*, a letter dated 12 March 1831 and published in Derby in 1831.

[2] in All Saints in 1855, letter from 'A Parishioner of All Saints', *Derby Mercury,* 29 November, 1882.

[3] cited in Austin 1966, 16, 190–7.

[4] T. Mozley, *Reminiscences of towns, villages and schools*, (1885), i, 187.

Jerusalem Church building and a Society of Friends' meeting house. These joined a Congregational chapel built in 1784 and the Unitarian chapel, a remarkable centre of truly radical dissent, opened in 1647. In 1824 another Methodist New Connexion chapel was opened. As we have seen, it was not until 1828 that, against opposition, the Church of England provided St John's in St Werburgh's parish.

'Time flies and souls are scattered'

This lack of Anglican initiative was evident more generally ten years later. At a meeting in Derby in December 1834 Samuel Butler stated that 'there is not church-room in the Diocese for 1/7th of the population, nor free sittings for 1/16th of them' and he censured the Church of England for not making provision for the thousands who, he claimed, 'would be gladly received within her walls.' In Derbyshire's towns only 8% of the seats in church were free. In his Charge in 1835 he argued the case for providing galleries in churches. It was quicker and cheaper, he said, to expand provision this way than to erect additional churches. And speed was essential 'since time flies and souls are scattered.' Three years earlier the bishop of Lichfield and Coventry, Henry Ryder (the first evangelical to be made a diocesan bishop in England) had indicated that the position in the diocese as a whole was better, yet, he stated, there was room in the churches for less than 1/3rd of the population and that less than 1/4 of this accommodation was available for the poor.[1] Bishop Ryder went on to note that only a quarter of those who did attend church were communicants. This meant, he said, that only about 2.5% of the population of Derbyshire, Warwickshire, Shropshire and Staffordshire were communicant Anglicans. This was in 1832. It is clear that thousands of people were not prepared to attend Anglican churches *whether or not the Church of England had made provision for them.*

It was evident, by this time, that mere church expansion with the consequent provision of more and better paid clergy, would not *of itself* bring to worship in the parish churches men and women who did not want to come. In 1738 the curate of Rotherfield Greys in Oxfordshire had listed reasons why his parishioners did not attend church: 'want of clothes, Distance from Church, a family of small children, Absence from home &c'[2], each of which, at this distance in time, seem reasonable. Clergy at that time were not convinced.

---

[1] *Christian Observer*, 1832, 735–737, quoted in Owen Chadwick, *The Victorian Church*, (1966), i, 333.
[2] citation in Austin 1969.

They had complained of poor attendance in their churches for many years. Indeed, the 1662 Book of Common Prayer has an Exhortation to be delivered to the 'negligent' who offer 'feigned excuses' for not attending holy Communion. In 1756 William Wheeler, curate of Wingerworth, admonished his parishioners for 'the trifling excuses which often prevent too many from constantly attending at the publick service of the church.'[1] Many clergy were to echo these opinions. Charles Rolfe, rector of South Normanton, published an open letter to his parishioners in January 1833 in which he called attention to the 'awful contempt of God's word and commandment' which had led to 'the lamentable negligence which you have generally manifested in attending the Public Worship of Almighty God'.[2] In 1847 J.A. Fenton of Norton in Derbyshire published a list of reasons offered for non-attendance in his *The Excuses offered for Neglecting Public Worship*: Sunday is a day of rest from 'hard toil'; one can pray as well at home as in church; churchgoers 'are not one wit better' than those who do not attend; lack of clothing 'fit for the house of God'; and the need to care for children.

Among those who declined to attend were the relatively well-to-do for whom rented pews were available and who felt that they needed excuses, trifling or not; excuses which Thomas Cursham said stemmed from 'the desires of the flesh and the mind'[3] and which the evangelical Anthony Auriol Barker of Baslow and Beeley dismissed in 1824 as cloaking 'the most bare-faced contempt [for] God and His holy Ordinances.'[4] Seventy years earlier one perceptive Derbyshire clergyman, G. Baddelley, curate of Melbourne, had suggested another reason for a refusal to attend church. It was, he said, 'because men are ashamed of being thought religious', and noted that 'this false kind of modesty had almost destroyed domestic and social piety.'[5] But these were reasons offered by the well-to-do.

Few of the poor *could* attend, and, apart from the need to go to church to receive support from the endowed charities, fewer still would have attended if they could. Not only were so few seats in church free, but the poor knew that

---

[1] W. Wheeler, *Plain Reasons against Forsaking the Communion of the Church of England to embrace Popery: in a Letter to the Inhabitants of the Parish of Wingerworth, in the County of Derby* (n.d. c. 1756), 27.

[2] Pamela Sharpe, *A Village of Considerable Extent*, (n.d.), 101.

[3] T. Cursham, *Ministerial Reproof and Warning, in a Sermon preached at Ashover Church, June 17th 1787* (Sheffield 1788), 6–7.

[4] A.A. Barker, *Address to his Parishioners* (Bakewell 1824), 2–6.

[5] G. Baddelley, *Sermons on Several Subjects* (1752), 91.

they had no place in a Church where distinctions of status in society were expressed in seating arrangements in churches[1]. Above all, very long week-day working hours made the poor unwilling to attend church on Sundays. A particularly graphic description of the disregard both of the Church of England and nonconformity by the poor is contained in a pamphlet written in the late 1830s or early 1840s. Seemingly unconscious of the reasons for their indifference, their squire, Sir George Crewe of Calke, wrote of the poor in the neighbouring village of Ticknall:

> I much fear that, take all the numbers of anything like regular attendants at our Church, or the two Chapels, the comparison of those numbers with our population would be as startling as it would be small . . . . Let any one walk down the street on a Sabbath-morning just at the hour of attendance upon Divine Service, and see how many are on their road to the place of worship; how evidently neither prepared, nor intending to prepare themselves or their children for such purpose? He will see men and women idly lounging at their doors, or in the streets; boys and girls at play, or setting out in parties to wander in the fields, some in their gardens, or leaning over a pig-sty; and, were he to enter the houses, very many would be found in bed! . . . . I grieve to say that I have seen many, who, at 12 or 1 o'clock in the day stand in their doors, or sit by their firesides in their working dress – their children the same – who appear almost unconscious that it is Sunday.[2]

In 1854, commenting on the 1851 census of religious worship, Horace Mann was to tell of the 'negative, inert indifference' of the mass of the population to the claims of religion – and not merely of the claims of the Church of England. The fundamental reasons for this profound alienation were not understood and addressed then, and the long-term effect of that alienation on attitudes to the Church now are still not fully understood and addressed. We must, however, treat Mann's comments with some reserve. Non-attendance at church by no means implies absence of religious conviction. Henry Kamen says of Europe from 1550 to 1660 that 'the religion of the mass of the people is almost

---

[1] In his return to the 1851 census of religion the minister of the Independent chapel in Ilkeston, Charles Hargreaves, spoke of free sittings carrying 'the badge of poverty'. He had no free seats in his chapel, though the poor were admitted to appropriated pews without charge.

[2] A Friend and Neighbour [Sir George Crewe], *Address to the Poor Inhabitants of Ticknall* (Derby 1846), 9, 11.

inaccessible to the historian'[1] or, for that matter, to the census-taker in the 19th century or the sociologist in the 20th. Analysis of Methodist, Baptist and Congregationalist registers from 1800 to 1837 shows that artisans made up about 75% of membership, though by the mid-century these denominations were becoming more middle class.[2]

'The broad line of demarcation': the Religious Census of 1851

Twenty years after Bishop Ryder drew attention to the low level of communicant attendance in his diocese the government decided to hold a census of religious worship at the time of the national population census of 1851. This was the first, and, so far, the last, census of its kind. It was held on Sunday, 30 March 1851, a Sunday when exceptional attendance would not be expected. Its results were published in 1854 and caused widespread concern in the Church of England and modest satisfaction in Protestant nonconformity. The returns for the Derbyshire registration districts have been analysed and presented by Margery Tranter[3] and those interested in the evidence relating to a particular parish can refer to it easily. All we can do here is to draw some conclusions from this wealth of material.

What surprised the bishops of the Church of England nationally, and Anglican middle-class opinion generally, was not only the strength of support for Protestant nonconformity that the statistics revealed but also, and worse, the degree of apparent irreligion. The returns for Derbyshire illustrated both causes for concern. To take nonconformist attendances first. In the registration districts which lay wholly or substantially in Derbyshire – Shardlow, Derby, Belper, Chesterfield, Bakewell, Chapel-en-le-Frith and Hayfield – there were more nonconformist attendances claimed on census Sunday, 30 March, than at Anglican churches. Michael Watts has estimated the church and the chapel attendances as percentages of population. For Derbyshire as a whole, 16% of the population attended the Church of England's services. The ten Protestant non-conformist denominations that made returns totalled 23.1% of the population. If we add the 1.2% that worshipped in Roman Catholic churches in the county, then non-Anglican churches and chapels attracted a third more worshippers

[1] Henry Kamen, *The Iron Century: Social Change in Europe 1550–1660*, (1976), 279.
[2] Hugh McLeod, *Religion and the Working Class in Nineteenth-Century Britain* (Macmillan 1984), 14.
[3] Margery Tranter et al., *The Derbyshire Returns to the 1851 Religious Census* (Derbyshire Record Society 1995). For a comprehensive statistical analysis of Victorian religion, see K.D.M. Snell and Paul S. Ell, *Rival Jerusalems: The geography of Victorian religion* (CUP 2000).

than did the Church of England on 30 March 1851. In the Belper registration district 30.4% of the population attended nonconformist chapels (principally Baptist 6.1%, Primitive Methodist 6.5%, and Wesleyan Methodist 10.5%) perhaps reflecting the early radical and nonconformist influence of the Strutt family, the principal employers.[1] This compared with the 14.5% that attended the Anglican parish churches and chapels. Only in the Derby registration district were Anglican and nonconformist attendances approximately equal at 18.5% and 18.9%.[2]

These statistics must be interpreted with great care. Expressing worshippers as a percentage of population is very confusing. The census enumerators were able only to record attendances and had no means of determining whether an individual attended church or chapel once, twice or three times on Census Sunday. Horace Mann, the barrister charged with conducting the census, adopted a highly questionable statistical method to make allowance for multiple attendances, and most commentators now reject it. We are left with figures for *total attendances* rather than for *individuals attending*. It may be that nonconformists were more assiduous in attending more than once on Sundays than were Anglicans. In a survey of churches in London in 1902–3 Richard Mudie-Smith calculated that 72% of Anglicans and 58% of nonconformists attended church only once each Sunday.

Sunday 30 March 1851 was not a festival nor did it immediately follow one, though it was Mid-Lent or Mothering Sunday, and some Anglican clergy (together with blaming the weather and accusing nonconformist ministers of boosting attendances by urging their congregations to turn up in force that day) excused low attendances on the ground that adult children were away from home visiting their parents. Anglican attendances would have been much higher at the major festivals, as now, perhaps better reflecting basic Anglican allegiance. Margery Tranter's analysis of the attendance figures gives somewhat different results from that of Michael Watts, but there was no avoiding the fact that on 30 March 1851 there were 30000 more attendances claimed at dissenting chapels in Derbyshire than in Anglican churches.

The Church of England was relatively weak in Derbyshire. Its strength, according to this census, was to be found in a triangle of the country the base

---

[1] though by this time, along with many successful and socially upwardly mobile entrepreneurial families, the Strutts had become Anglican, contributing to the building of Belper St Peter in 1824 and of Christ Church in 1850. The Strutts also donated the land on which Milford Holy Trinity was erected in 1847. I am grateful to E.G. Power for this note.

[2] Michael R. Watts, op.cit., 706–7.

of which stretched from Canterbury to Plymouth with the apex reaching Carlisle. Much of the Midlands lay outside this area, though Derbyshire lay on the edge. Overall, Watts estimates that the church and chapel attendances in Derbyshire on Census Sunday represent 40.5% of the population of the county. The national average was 40.1%.[1]

Anglican middle-class opinion was even more shocked to discover that England was not only not as Anglican as was supposed but (assuming church-going to be a reliable indicator as it did) not as religious. In Derbyshire attendances varied from 47% of the population in the Shardlow registration district to 30.5% in the Chesterfield district. When the statistics were further analysed nationally it became very clear that attendances were lower in the towns than in rural areas; that the larger the town, the lower was the attendance; that in the industrial towns the overall figure for attendance was lower still, and, further, that within the towns and cities attendance declined the poorer the area. Despite their exclusion from rented pews, the attendance of working people was higher in the countryside and in the smaller towns and the villages. It is too easy to say that this was so because squires and employers were near to hand not only to lead by example but to observe the failure of the people to attend (Sir George Crewe's proximity evidently had little effect in Ticknall), though intimidation as well as conviction were factors in working-class attendance in some places.

It would be quite wrong to assume from Mann's report that the poor rejected Christianity. This was clearly not so. Nor is it true that religious worship was completely alien to them. They were married in church, mothers went to the parish church to be 'churched' after the birth of their children, and parents buried their often soon dead sons and daughters in the churchyard. If 40% of the population attended churches and chapels on census Sunday, then many of the working-class must have been there, for it has been conservatively estimated that they constituted four-fifths of the population.[2] Horace Mann and other contemporary observers evidently underestimated working-class piety. In any case church attendance statistics, then as now, are by no means a sure guide to levels of religious conviction. Private belief and attendance at public worship rarely correlate at any point in our story.

---

[1] The methodology and results of the religious census have been much criticised. Other contemporary sources suggest that regular church attendance at this time was only half of this figure [Jose Harris, *Private Lives, Public Spirit: Britain 1870–1914* (Penguin 1993), 153].
[2] Eric Hopkins, *A Social History of the English Working Classes 1815–1845* (Arnold 1979), 82.

'Touching caste': wealth, status and religious practice

Yet the 1851 religious census seemed initially to reveal what the more perceptive of churchmen had realised for several years – that church attendance *in any denomination* was generally a middle-class activity and reflected middle-class attitudes and aspirations. Once again, pew-renting was a symbol of this and we have already noted its importance. By the 1850s even the Primitive Methodists were renting pews in many of their chapels in Derbyshire. Pew-renting, with one remarkable exception, remained in the ancient Anglican parish churches in the county town throughout most of the 19th century. The exception was at St Michael's, and, in 1866, at the new St Andrew's where the incumbent, J.E. Clarke, insisted that the pews should 'be free and unappropriated for ever.'

Opposition to pew-renting was greater when practised by the Church of England than by Dissent, perhaps because the acquisition of wealth, and the uses to which it was put, were viewed differently by nonconformists. Although most historians now deny that Protestantism played any direct role in the development of capitalism in Europe, it seems that to be a member of one of the Protestant nonconformist churches eventually had a positive economic effect. John Wesley had observed that 'we ought not to prevent people from being diligent and frugal; we must exhort all Christians to gain all they can, and save all they can; that is, in effect, to grow rich.'[1] They became more well-to-do as what we would now loosely call the Protestant work ethic took effect. Towards the end of his life Wesley returned to this puzzling problem. He said, in a sermon on the 'Causes of the Inefficacy of Christianity',:

> Does it not seem (and yet it cannot be) that Christianity, true scriptural Christianity, has a tendency to destroy itself? For wherever true Christianity spreads, it must cause diligence and frugality, which, in the natural course of things, must beget riches! and riches beget pride, love of the world and every temper that is destructive of Christianity. Now, if there is no way to prevent this, Christianity is inconsistent with itself, and, of consequence, cannot stand, cannot continue long among any people; since, wherever it generally prevails, it saps its own foundation.[2]

Although many Methodists 'are still deplorably poor', he noted, 'yet many

---

[1] quoted from Southey's *Life of Wesley* by Max Weber in *The Protestant Ethic and the Spirit of Capitalism,* (1921 edition), 175.

[2] *Sermons on Several Occasions,* (London 1866), iii, 277. Sermon preached in Dublin, 2 July 1789.

others, in the space of twenty, thirty, or forty years, are twenty, thirty, yea, a hundred times richer than they were when they first entered the society [that is, Methodism].'[1]

Methodism rarely attracted the poorest of the poor into membership, but the artisans and people in the lower middle class that it *did* appeal to prospered economically, so Wesley himself observed, from the gospel ethic that it preached. It is possible that pew-renting in nonconformist chapels was less questioned and resented than in the Church of England's churches for one main reason. When the Church of England practised it the appropriation of pews was seen as a symbol of privilege and social exclusiveness and, often, of inherited wealth. Henry Mozley was a churchwarden at Derby St Werburgh's at the time of the acrimonious pew dispute in 1830–31. For him, where one sat in church and how much one paid for the pew was a matter 'touching caste', with 'low caste' people, that is 'lower middle people, small tradesmen and clerks', sitting in the nave, while the wealthy sat in their one hundred guinea pews in the galleries.[2] When the Primitive Methodists rented pews in their chapels, quite apart from the economic necessity of the practice, the wealth that it represented was seen as a token of God's favour of a frugal and diligent way of life. Undoubtedly Protestant religion did have a positive material effect. In 1965 Richard Niebuhr was to write that 'the churches of the poor all become middle-class churches sooner or later.'[3] Although you could not buy yourself into heaven, your material wealth on earth might hopefully provide some indication that you were on the way there.

Yet the majority of the population, so it was assumed from the analysis of the 1851 returns, did not worship in any church or chapel. These were the working-classes. Horace Mann noted that 'more especially in cities and large towns it is observable how absolutely insignificant a portion of the congregation is composed of artisans.'

Mann suggested reasons why this was so: the 'social distinction' prevailing in churches; the 'broad line of demarcation' between employer and employee on weekdays inhibiting the church-going of working people on Sundays; the apparent indifference of the churches to the social conditions of the masses; the 'misconceptions of the motives of ministers' which led working people to

---

[1] ibid.

[2] T. Mozley, *Reminiscences of towns, villages and schools* (1885), ii, 80.

[3] H.R. Niebuhr, *The Social Sources of Denominationalism* (Cleveland and New York 1965), 6, 21, in R. Currie, A. Gilbert and L. Horsley, *Churches and Church-goers*, (OUP 1977), 61.

distrust them as representatives of authority; and, very perceptively, the poor and cramped home conditions of so many working people which 'forbids all solitude and all reflection' by which the spiritual life of the middle-classes is sustained. In Mann's opinion the artisan could not grow in grace much as he might want to do so. Poor living and working conditions with long working hours, an inability to sustain the spiritual life, and alienation from the churches were profoundly interrelated.

As we will see, in 1880 the rural dean of Derby had to admit that very few of 'the masses' had been 'reclaimed' by the churches. Mann's note that the absence of working people from the churches was 'more especially' noticeable in the towns is an important caveat. The 1851 religious census statistics did not produce unequivocal evidence of the attitude of working people to *religion* as such. What seems clear is that their failure to attend on Census Sunday was more a rejection of the Churches and less a disinterest in Christianity. It is still an open question whether the first would eventually result in the second. But notions of rejection or alienation were of little practical significance to working people. One basic reason among others for the failure of so many of them to attend church or chapel was expressed by 'Lucy Careful', a child from a poor Derbyshire family, in an improving Sunday school tract in about 1800:

> I never goes to church this fine weather; for father says, it is the only day
> he and mother gets out for a walk; for father is always working at Sir
> William's, or in our own garden, through the week, and till dinner time
> on Sundays; then, when he gets a mouthful of dinner, he cleans himself,
> and takes mother and me a long walk, sometimes to town, where sister
> lives with Squire Martin.[1]

Outside the patronising and improving world of the Sunday School Tract, the reality was much harsher. The exhaustion of six days each of twelve hours labour ill-disposed working people to attend church for several hours on the seventh. For this reason, only the better-off working people sat in the free pews in churches and chapels – and their numbers increased as the years passed.

'The congregations are always full': church attendance, 1851–81

The statistics of church attendance in the four decades after 1851 are very

---

[1] Anon, *Active Benevolence, or, some account of Lucy Careful*, Sunday School Tracts, No 96 (London n.d.). This 'account' was set in Derbyshire.

ambiguous. There is evidence that, nationally, overall church membership fell between 1851 and 1880, to rise again until, by 1910, the combined membership of the Churches was, as a proportion of the adult population, some 3% higher than it had been in 1860.[1]

The Derbyshire evidence points both ways. We have comparative statistics for Anglican attendances in 1851 for Derby and Chesterfield, in 1874 for Derby and in 1881 for Chesterfield. In November 1874, the *Derby Mercury* reported the results of a census carried out by *The Sun* of church attendance in the town. At St Alkmund's, Sunday morning worshippers numbered 600, in the afternoon 200 and in the evening 750. In 1851 the figures for the general congregation (excluding Sunday school children) had been 432, 187 and 475 respectively. At St Werburgh's in November 1874 'the congregations are always full, and on Sunday evenings the church is usually crowded'. At St Michael's the average attendance was 250-300 on Sunday mornings, 50–100 in the afternoons and 350–400 on Sunday evenings. In the smaller building that had existed in 1851 the attendances were 112 in the morning and 132 in the afternoon, with no evening service. In 1874 at St John's there was an average Sunday evening congregation of 1000 despite the fact that 'half the sittings are let at high rates'. On 30 March 1851 the Sunday evening congregation had numbered 375.[2]

In Chesterfield in 1881, as part of an unofficial national survey conducted by local newspapers following discussion at the Church Congress that year, the *Derbyshire Courier* appointed its own enumerators and conducted a comprehensive census of attenders at all 12 places of worship in the town on Sunday 20 November. It adopted the now somewhat discredited statistical formulae employed by Horace Mann in 1851, but the raw data is straightforward. Chesterfield St Mary, with accommodation for 1500, attracted 332 attendances in the morning and 691 in the evening on 20 November. On 30 March 1851 the general congregation had numbered 580 in the morning, 165 in the afternoon and 700 in the evening. The other Anglican church in the town, Holy Trinity, with sittings for 800, had 403 and 468 attendances respectively on that day. The 1851 religious census had recorded adult attendances of 92, 117, and 68 respectively. It should be noted that the *Courier* included the attendance of Sunday School children in its 1881 figures if they were present at services. In 1851 the census enumerators noted them separately. Direct comparisons are therefore difficult, but the data suggests a significant rise in attendance.

---

[1] Jose Harris, op.cit., 154.
[2] 1874 figures from the *Derby Mercury*, 18 November 1874, reprinting information from *The Sun*.

The two Anglican churches were the two best attended churches in the town, closely followed by the Roman Catholic church which accommodated 600 and had 346 morning and 437 evening attendances (though in its table the *Courier* seems to have omitted two earlier morning masses which attracted 143 and 214 worshippers. If this is so, the morning attendances total 703 and give it a greater total attendance that day than at St Mary's.) In total, accommodation in the Roman Catholic church and in the nine nonconformist places of worship in Chesterfield was 4636. In the two Anglican churches there was accommodation for 2300. Ignoring the possible under-recording of attendances at the Roman Catholic church, on 20 November 1881 non-Anglican attendances in Chesterfield were 4457. In the two Church of England churches there were 1894 attendances. Even so, the *Derbyshire Courier*, using Mann's suspect formulae which allowed for those who were unable to attend by reason of age, infirmity or employment, concluded that 38% of Chesterfield's population of 12221 did not attend in the morning of that Sunday, and almost 23% stayed away in the evening, and 'for whose absence there is not reasonable explanation.' Sheer disinclination, for a range of reasons, does not seem to have registered with the editor as a 'reasonable explanation'.[1]

In 1881 C.S. Maill summarised the results of a number of nonconformist censuses taken in 25 English cities. Average church and chapel attendance as a percentage of population, making an allowance for those attending twice, was nearly 38%. Derby ranked twelfth with 28.6%, assuming the accuracy of the figures.[2] In 1851 the combined Anglican and non-conformist attendance figures claimed for Derby, as a percentage of population, was over 37%. The national levels of church attendance were to be maintained until the 1920s, though, in Derbyshire, the Anglican presence, measured as a percentage of population, was to decline. To build towards these levels the churches had embarked on a remarkable programme of expansion. We will consider the Anglican statistics for Derbyshire in the next chapter, but now we will return to the county town.

'Vigour and activity': church expansion in Derby

By 1884 there were 19 Anglican churches in Derby together with a number of

---

[1] *Derbyshire Courier*, 26 November 1881. The report carries full data on all the places of worship in the town together with further statistical summaries.
[2] Owen Chadwick, *The Victorian Church* (A. and C. Black, 1972), ii, 226.

parochial mission rooms. By this time, apart from St Alkmund's and Holy Trinity which retained a high proportion of appropriated sittings, all the seats were free.[1] This expansion witnessed to what the Tory and sympathetic *Derby Mercury*, in January 1885, called the 'vigour and activity' of the Church of England. Its rival the *Derbyshire Advertiser* had been far less sanguine a few years earlier. In July 1878 it had noted 'the spiritual destitution of the new and populous districts . . . on the outskirts of the town'.

The total of Anglican church accommodation in Derby in 1884 was 14527 sittings. The population of the town had grown to 78597 by 1881. The five Derby parishes in 1824 had provided accommodation for 14.9% of the population. In 1884 the 19 Anglican churches provided sittings for 16.9%. Despite a considerable building programme, which included the rebuilding of two dilapidated mediaeval parish churches and the substantial rebuilding of a third, the Church of England only marginally improved its number of sittings per hundred of the population over the whole of a period which saw revolutionary social, political, cultural and technological change, but even to do that was remarkable.

In responding to population growth, Anglican church expansion in Derby in these years was haphazard at best with little or no formal planning or co-operation between parishes. Although the Lichfield Church Extension Society had been established as early as 1835 and, between then and 1885 had contributed to the building of 180 churches and mission halls in Derbyshire, there was no central diocesan planning mechanism as we know it today. In Derby, the centre of attention switched from one part of the town to another as the claims of districts were presented to the public. Given this, the Church of England could do no more than maintain its presence as a percentage of population. By this indicator its presence declined after 1885. Yet the attempt was made and much money raised and spent before it was realised that the task of providing churches and clergy in proportion to population increase[2] *and as a key indicator of the success of its mission* was too formidable – and perhaps, with hindsight, irrelevant or at best unnecessary. And that has implications for our day too.

Much of this church expansion was driven by rivalry. During these years 1824

---

[1] probably due partly to three reasons: to J.E. Clarke's example in declaring St Michael's and St Andrew's (of which he was successively the incumbent) 'free and unappropriated'; to the unfounded argument of those opposed to pew-renting that its abolition would encourage labourers to attend church; and to the establishment of free-will offerings as a means of financing churches.

[2] for the detailed statistics for Derby see Austin 1966, 54–61.

to 1884 the nonconformist Churches in Derby built many chapels. Whereas the Church of England's inability to plan its expansion in the town can be put down largely to parishes failing to co-operate with each other, or even to see the need to plan collectively in the absence of a coherent diocesan policy, the nonconformist churches were rivals of each other for the Protestant conscience. Chapels were built, rebuilt or enlarged and schools established in these sixty years at the rate of two every three years. The Congregationalists completed twelve building schemes, the Baptists completed eight (including four new chapels), the Presbyterian Church of England erected a chapel, the Wesleyan Methodists completed eight schemes, the Primitive Methodists seven, the United Methodist Free Church built a chapel, and the Traffic Street Town Mission and the Corden Street Mission also each built a chapel. The Roman Catholic Church erected St Mary's church designed by Augustus Pugin. This rate of church building was by no means unusual. In the diocese of Lichfield 300 Anglican churches were built or re-opened during John Lonsdale's episcopate from 1843 to 1867, a rate of over twelve a year. This rate of construction inevitably led to subsequent considerable over-provision, and the time came when increasingly empty, and often very large, church buildings themselves provided a disincentive to many who, in any case, had no real commitment to attend them.[1]

These church building initiatives, driven as they often were by denominational rivalry, were often marred by a bitterness scarcely imaginable today. St Mary's Roman Catholic church was built in 1839 in Bridge Street, virtually opposite St Alkmund's. Two years later, owing, so it was reported, to its 'dilapidated and decayed' condition, it was resolved to rebuild St Alkmund's. A contribution of £200 was promised by Edward Strutt, Derby's MP. In March 1844 the building committee made it known that it intended to enlarge the proposed new church by adding a chancel. There was land available for this to have been constructed to the east of the site of the mediaeval church, but the committee announced that the addition would necessitate moving the whole building to the west, re-siting the tower and spire of the new church 10ft 6ins to the west of its previous position. Strutt promptly withdrew his subscription on the ground that the tower of the new St Alkmund's 'would obstruct the principal view of the beautiful Tower of the new Roman Catholic Church' and that the committee's decision, supported as it was by the archdeacon of Derby, 'must be most offensive to the feelings of another congregation of Christians.'

---

[1] K. Theodore Hoppen, *The Mid-Victorian Generation 1846–1886* (Oxford 1998), 433.

'principal view' was from Irongate. Edward Abney, vicar of St Alkmund's, denied that the re-siting had been planned 'to hide the Popish Tower', a phrase which completely undermined his denial. All of this was too much for the *Derby and Chesterfield Reporter*. Its leader-writer dismissed the building committee's new proposal and charged it with committing 'an act of gross and inexcusable bigotry.' There is no doubt that it was. St Alkmund's was rebuilt in its new position, and a century later local people were still calling it 'Spite Tower'. It is a story of which the Church of England in Derby can only feel ashamed and suggests why it was that the building debt on St Alkmund's was not cleared until March 1868. In the mid-20th century the church was demolished to make way for the inner ring road, and the cause of this offence was removed.

'May I go forth and honestly visit': the clergy and their pastoral ministry

The role of the Church of England was not fulfilled merely by building yet more churches. The standard of the pastoral ministry it offered improved greatly as the years passed. Many of the most conscientious clergy realised that they could not exercise their ministry unaided and were compelled to recognise the importance of lay ministry. So, as one of many examples, in 1830 the Derbyshire Ladies Bible Association, founded in 1828 under Anglican patronage, visited 3618 'poor and labouring families', dividing the town into 46 districts and visiting regularly and conscientiously. The Association was concerned exclusively with the poor, as was the Derby Church of England Co-operative Society founded in 1837 to assist the parish clergy in their pastoral care of those 'who are immersed in spiritual blindness, degrading vice, and the most immoral habits [and who] seldom, if ever, come within reach of the preached word . . . ' Several full-time Scripture Readers were employed by the Derby Church of England Scripture Readers and Tract Distribution Society which was formed in 1843. In that year 5955 visits were made 'to the dwellings of the poor'. From the perspective of a later period this might be regarded as little more than slumming, and that merely distributing a tract fell under the condemnation of the Epistle of James[1]. Yet to visit the dreadful slums of St Michael's parish was both daunting and dangerous for anyone not used to

---

[1] 'If a brother or sister be naked, and destitute of daily food, and one of you say unto them, Depart in peace, be ye warmed and filled; notwithstanding ye give them not those things which are needful to the body; what doth it profit' [*James* 2: 15-6 AV].

those conditions, and especially for 'Ladies'. Doing good it may have been, but those who did it clearly believed that they were doing good for a good reason. Not least, the Christian religion enabled these men and women to build a purposeful life for themselves.[1]

With a more overtly evangelistic purpose the Lichfield Evangelist Brotherhood was formed in 1887, after the diocese of Southwell was created. Its members were trained lay evangelists who assisted parish clergy. The founder of the Brotherhood was H.A. Colville. He had been an officer in the Salvation Army and became an anglo-catholic. In 1896 he told the Church Congress that his organisation was evidence of 'a wonderfully increased recognition of lay work in the Church'[2] – and so it was.

In 1838 George Augustus Selwyn had written a pamphlet proposing an even bolder initiative in ministry. 'It seems essential' he wrote, 'to the permanent efficiency of all orders of men that they should be recruited from time to time by well-chosen reinforcements from the ranks below them'. In 1867 Selwyn became bishop of Lichfield having exercised an extraordinary ministry, since 1841, as the first bishop of New Zealand. In New Zealand Bishop Selwyn had taken the opportunity to put his ideas into effect. On the basis of that experience he established in 1870 in the diocese of Lichfield a probationer system of clergy training under which an incumbent recommended a man, directed his studies and employed him in pastoral ministry in his parish. At the end of two years Lichfield Theological College received him for a final year, supporting him by a grant taken from surplus college fees. Several Derby parishes employed these 'lay deacons' as they were called. However, as with similar experiments in the 20th century, this one was not a success. After four years of the scheme no more than 25 lay deacons had been employed throughout the diocese, and of these only 14 were from the diocese.[3]

Lichfield Theological College for the training of clergy had been founded in 1857, against fierce evangelical opposition, by John Lonsdale, the third of five fine pioneering 19th century bishops of Lichfield. In Derby in 1851 this moderate and retiring bishop had also established an institution for training schoolmistresses. He also actively encouraged the training of nurses.

---

[1] Note the same point made about young men in Church organisations in Coventry in 1914, [Kenneth Richardson, quoted in John Stevenson, *British Society 1914–45,* (Penguin 1990), 359–60].

[2] K.S.Inglis, *Churches and the Working Classes in Victorian England* London (1963), 43.

[3] citations in Austin 1966, 64.

Evangelicals accused him of thereby supporting Jesuit seminaries and popish sisterhoods![1]

Inevitably the burden of pastoral ministry fell on the clergy, though the evidence presents a not unimpressive picture of lay participation in ministry, especially in the early decades of the 19th century when, certainly with some of the older clergy, pastoral ministry was at a low ebb. Earlier we told the stories of three 18th century Derbyshire parsons. Here are anecdotes of three Derby clergy of the early 19th century.

In 1882 the high church clergyman Thomas Mozley, whose family home was in Derby, told of three Derby clergy well known to him. Charles Stead Hope was the pluralist incumbent of Derby All Saints 1798–1841 and of St Alkmund's 1801–1841. Hope was, Mozley said, 'always in the presence of his people . . . .He could not walk ten yards without exchanging greetings, or fifty yards without being stopped for a talk.' But as Hope was 'a High Churchman after the fashion of the day and a Tory of course', being mayor of Derby five times and the only Tory in the corporation, Mozley was bound to be sympathetic to him. In 1831 a Derby mob broke all the windows in St Alkmund's vicarage when news arrived of the rejection by the House of Lords of the Reform Bill. Another writer, J. Tilley, writing in the 1880s and from a very different political perspective had a very different opinion. For him Hope was

> Divine, politician, huntsman . . . . How many times he graced the hustings in the Cavendish interest, or how many years he followed the Meynell hounds is of no great moment. There are those living who say that this divine added a picturesque feature to many of the interments at which he officiated by wearing beneath his surplice a coat of scarlet hue, and that he read the burial service in hessian boots with spurs and a skull cap with a velvet peak.

Hope's contemporary at St.Werburgh's was the evangelical Edward Unwin. Mozley had no time for evangelicals for, he said, all they did was declare their message every Sunday: 'they who accepted it were saved; they who did not were damned. That concluded the matter' and relieved the evangelical clergyman of all pastoral duty[2]. So it was with Edward Unwin who, Mozley asserted,

> resided in a pretty villa . . . a good step out of town. I am certain that

---

[1] M.A. Crowther, *Church Embattled: Religious controversy in Mid-Victorian England* (1970), 21.
[2] citation, Austin 1966, 65.

neither I nor anyone else ever saw him in his parish except when he drove
in to take part in the Sunday service . . . . He knew absolutely nothing
about his parishioners.

This tells us no more than how bitter and partisan was the theological atmosphere in the 19th century. John Wakefield, a fierce opponent of Mozley's father,
Henry Mozley, who had been a churchwarden of St Werburgh's at the time of
the divisive pew dispute in the 1830s, had been Unwin's curate. In August 1882
reacting to Thomas Mozley's charge, Wakefield told of Unwin's 'quiet visits of
duty, his religious and other occupations and the extent of his knowledge of the
persons and events of his parish.'

Philip Gell came to the newly built St John's chapel-of-ease to St Werburgh's
in 1829, remaining until 1847. Gell was a pronounced evangelical and he came to
this church, Mozley commented bitterly, because

> as he openly avowed . . . it did not involve baptisms, burials and marriages,
> none of which he could conscientiously perform. Of course, too, in the
> same view of pastoral duty, he had no occasion to enter any house or
> exchange a word with anyone, except in his own theological circle.[1]

Even allowing for Mozley's theological, and Tilley's political, bias the picture
they present of the pastoral ministry exercised in the 1820s and 1830s is not an
attractive one. Mozley was a close friend of John Henry Newman, and
Newman was a frequent visitor to Derby. Thomas and John Mozley married
Newman's sisters Harriet and Jemima. Mozley records that on one occasion
he took Newman to meet Edward Unwin and Philip Gell.

> They were simply surprised to see me, for both regarded me as an
> unconverted heathen. Newman acquitted himself with his usual tact on
> these unpromising occasions. He said the few things he could say under
> the circumstances in a way to make them 'stick', though it was out of the
> question to elicit any sympathy.[2]

---

[1] Gell held that 'water baptism' afforded entry into a visible kingdom (the Church) whereas 'spiritual baptism' effected entry into a spiritual kingdom. 'Except a man have both conditions he cannot enter into the kingdom fully; that is, both spiritually and ostensibly, as he should do so.' *The Scriptural Doctrine of Spiritual Baptism* (London 1851), 7. Gell would therefore have had difficulty with the practice of infant baptism.

[2] Thomas Mozley, *Reminiscences chiefly of Oriel College and the Oxford Movement* (Longman 1882), i, 401. We should treat Mozley's evidence with some care. For one of Newman's biographers, Meriol Trevor, Mozley's reminiscences are 'full of tall stories, inaccuracies and nonsense' [*Newman: Light in Winter* (Macmillan 1962), 615] though this seems a harsh judgement.

As the years passed the situation greatly improved. When David Anderson, incumbent of All Saints for just a year, was appointed to the newly created bishopric of Prince Rupert's Land[1] in 1849 the *Derby Mercury* told, with evident sincerity, of 'his daily visitings throughout his parish; his great attention to the schools, his general earnestness in his sacred office; and his kind bearing towards each of his parishioners.' It was said of Melville Horne Scott, perpetual curate of Derby St Andrews 1872–8, that he visited ten to twenty houses a day, having first prayed that he might 'be led to more thorough visiting . . . . Oh may I go forth and honestly visit, taking the most disagreeable first.'[2]

There is little direct evidence to account for this improvement in pastoral care. In 1854, G.A. Selwyn, on a visit home from New Zealand, said that he had noticed 'a great and visible change' in the Church of England since he left the country in 1841. 'It is now a very rare thing to see a careless clergyman, a neglected parish or a desecrated church.'[3] The determination to improve standards through the implementation of the Church Pluralities Act of 1838 and the Church Discipline Act of 1840 may have had a marginal effect, but this does not explain the change in attitude. The establishment of theological colleges would have had a greater effect, and the example of the evangelicals (Scott called himself 'an honest, simple-minded Evangelical and Protestant churchman') and of second generation Oxford Movement catholicity, of which St Anne's and notably St Luke's in Derby were centres and which other parishes were to become, were clearly significant.

The example and leadership of the diocesan bishop was clearly a factor also, as was the growing sense that the diocese was a community and not merely an administrative convenience. By the 1850s a *Chronicle* for the diocese of Lichfield was being published regularly. It was designed to foster the unity of the diocese but was often the vehicle for theological invective, as was the *Lichfield Diocesan Churchman* in the theologically virulent 1870s. In 1856 the diocese was the first to produce a diocesan calendar.

More important in binding together a huge diocese was Bishop Selwyn's proposal, after he became bishop of Lichfield in 1867, to hold regular synods –

---

[1] in Canada.
[2] M. Scott, op.cit., 128.
[3] G.A. Selwyn, *The Work of Christ in the World; four sermons preached before the University of Cambridge on the four Sundays preceding Advent in the year of Our Lord 1854* (Cambridge 1854), 7, cited in A.D. Gilbert, *Religion and Society in Industrial England; Church, Chapel and Social Change 1740–1917* (Longman 1976), 132.

a pattern he had established successfully in New Zealand – and a practice that had been adopted in other English dioceses. These synods were to be held annually in each archdeaconry with a diocesan synod once every three years. Laymen would be invited. The synods would discuss matters of practical concern and would reach decisions by majority vote, saving only the bishop's veto. Bishop Selwyn held his first synod in June 1868. He visited 40 rural deaneries in the first six months of that year and found clergy enthusiastic for the idea. That first synod discussed issues that the bishop felt were important: education and the provision of church schools, lay co-operation and the training of clergy, and assistance for dioceses overseas. Significantly the synod also addressed the question of the alienated masses.[1] 'Synod' was Selwyn's preferred designation, but they were to become 'conferences', implying that they were to be less occasions for decision and more for discussion, with the diocesan bishop at all times retaining his authority.

Episcopal leadership, the determination to allow clergy and laity at least to consult together, and the desire to make the dioceses more effective units for mission undoubtedly had a marked effect on raising the standard of pastoral ministry. The general raising of professional standards in the civil service, in teaching and in medicine also had an effect. The laity had come to expect more from their clergy. This last point is crucial. K.T. Hoppen argues that the reasons for the extraordinary recovery of the Church of England in the mid-19th century had to do with 'the way in which increasing suburbanization created a growing middle-class demand for the establishment's mixture of social cachet, dignified services, and theological fluidity[2], though, at least in Derby, if the laity were making the last two of these demands they were disappointed.

Yet, as A.D. Gilbert has argued powerfully, another vital change in the social role of the Church of England was the basic factor in raising the standard of ministry offered by the clergy. By the middle of the 19th century (as shrewd observers had realised long before) the Church of England found that it could no longer rest complacently in the assumption that it was the only possible Church for patriotic Englishmen. It now faced competition as the religious census of 1851 had so clearly shown. In many parts of the country, not least in Derby and Derbyshire, it was losing the battle for adherents. The reasons for this were primarily social and political: in Harold Perkin's perceptive phrase, sectarian religion was 'the midwife of class', the vehicle for emancipation from

---

[1] M.A. Crowther, op.cit., 211, 215.
[2] K.Theodore Hoppen, op. cit., 433.

social dependency.[1] More publicly, though far less significantly, the ostensible reasons had to do with differences in theology and church order, and with inter-church rivalries. Yet not the least of the reasons why the Church of England was losing ground to nonconformity was that the worship it offered in its churches was so dull.

'Dull, monotonous and formal': church worship

We know much about Derby's Anglican churches in the 19th century: the times of the Sunday and weekday services, the frequency of, and attendance at, holy Communion, the content of music lists, the subjects preached about, the inadequacy of the provision of baptism, the large numbers of candidates presented for Confirmation and the quality of their preparation, and much else. Particularly in the second half of the century it is clear that the clergy were generally assiduous in their duty. However, as late as the 1860s the standard of public worship was not high even by the criteria of the day. 'Dull, monotonous and formal' was the description of the worship offered in Derby All Saints in November 1859. It was, wrote a correspondent to the *Derby Mercury* and calling himself 'An English Churchman', as if 'the congregation had no part in the sublime and affecting ritual in which they were engaged'.[2]

He was not alone in his criticism. In June 1860 'A Churchman' asked of Derby's churches whether 'anything could be more life-less than the singing in the majority of them'[3], and in December of the same year 'A Musical Churchman' observed that although at St Peter's the musical services 'were very satisfactorily performed . . . the right and capability of the congregation to take part was, and ever has been partially at least, totally ignored', the psalms being the only part of the service in which the congregation could join.[4] The churchwardens at St Peter's came to the same conclusion from a different perspective. Replying to the archdeacon in that same year they complained that the services were 'all intoned or chanted' and said that they were conducted in a manner so distasteful to the parishioners that very few attended the church. However, there was another agenda at St Peter's. Its incumbent, William Hope, was the first of the clergy of the town to become a follower of the

---

[1] Harold Perkin, *The Origins of Modern English Society 1780–1880* (RKP London 1969),196ff.
[2] *Derby Mercury*, 2 November 1859.
[3] ibid., 6 June 1860.
[4] ibid., 19 December 1860.

pioneers of the Oxford Movement.

But congregations did not expect to join in. Answering the archdeacon in 1860 the churchwardens of Holy Trinity stated that 'in the absence of a Parish Clerk the responses are made by the congregation' while E.W. Foley of All Saints wrote to his congregation in 1852 that 'it is often a subject of painful remark that in our celebration of Public Worship there is not a more audible and fervent response.' J.E. Clarke, the remarkable vicar of St Michael's, was more outspoken. In 1862 he accused his congregation 'of the spurious gentility which seems to think it vulgar to speak above a breath, and the listless indifferentism that is too lazy to speak at all.'

In general at this time in the Church of England it seems that the services were attended by numbers of people who took little part in 'the sublime and affecting ritual', and seem to have cared little whether they took part or not. One reason for this was provided in a letter in the *Derby Mercury* in November 1882 from a parishioner of All Saints. He recalled that when he worshipped at All Saints in 1855 the church

> was but partly filled up, the scattered heads showing many void spaces in the high pews. When we stood up the general posture was to lean our elbows on the top of the pew, and, altogether, to take it as easily as possible. Kneeling was the exception and the irreverent 'Half Cock' – half sitting, half kneeling, prevailed.[1]

This virtually all-pervasive non-participation in public worship in the Church of England is one explanation of the expansion of nonconformist places of worship even in a largely nonconformist town.

As time passed, standards of worship in Anglican churches improved. Incumbents pleaded with their congregations to take part in the services. J.E. Clarke held a Congregational Singing Practice each week to such effect that the *Derby Mercury* was able to report in September 1863 that 'the hearty manner in which the responses and musical portion of the service were joined in by the worshippers was something quite refreshing' – refreshing because it was unusual. The influence of the Oxford Movement played a part in this revival of worship. In 1893 it was said that 'Trinity Church may be regarded as almost the only church which has remained practically untouched by the widespread

---

[1] *Derby Mercury,* 29 November 1889. Further citations in Austin 1966, 71ff.

revival of which the Oxford Movement was the precursor' and where 'the black preaching gown still obtains and music is at a minimum.'[1] As only a few of Derby's Anglican churches shared the theological presuppositions of the anglo-catholic revival this shows the extent of its influence.

The Church of England did much more than confine its worship to the conventional times. In 1854 Thomas Scott of St John's began to preach in the open air at the corner of Nun's Street and Brook Street, and in 1858 the assistant curate of Christ Church, G. Carson, began preaching to large congregations at the corner of Abbey Street and Burton Road. Towards the end of the century many parishes were involved in providing 'home missions work' and 'cottage lectures'. As one of many examples, 28 lay preachers were employed in the parish of All Saints each Sunday evening. In 1873 Robert Hey of St Andrew's held daily meetings in nine factories, the Cabmens' Rest, and the Midland Hotel, and for 500 men in the Carriage Works of the Midland Railway Company, together with a weekly service 'in a very warm corner of the retort house' of the town's Gas Works. In 1824 there is little evidence of evangelistic outreach by Derby's Anglican clergy. Fifty years later this responsibility was being taken very seriously indeed, but, as they readily admitted, to no great effect.

'What have we done among the masses?': the Church's social conscience

There is much evidence that the Church of England in Derby had a positive social conscience in the 19th century. Of course this conscience often found expression in ways that we might now regard as patronising and, from our perspective today, it had little grounding in a theology of the Incarnation that embraced the secular world, in fact quite the reverse. We can be grateful for our record nevertheless. To take just a few random examples. In 1825 513 poor children were being educated in Church of England day schools in the town. By 1885 this figure had grown to 8367. From the middle of the century the Church of England was sponsoring night schools for adults, instruction societies and mutual improvement associations, debating societies and reading rooms and libraries, coffee houses and temperance societies, branches of the Happy Home Union and, in three parishes, a British Workman Public House

---

[1] C.J. Payne, *Derby Churches Old and New and Derby's Golgotha* (Derby 1893).

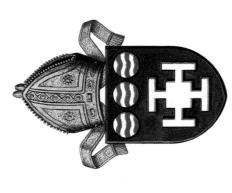

To All and Singular

1 The Grant of Arms to the diocese of Derby, 29 October 1927.

2 Wilne St Chad stone font. This was damaged by fire in 1917. Its date is unknown, but in its undamaged state it was held to be of Saxon origin and possibly formed from the inverted member of a Saxon preaching cross. Date c. 800. Its six panels depict dragons, birds and interlaced knotwork, the theme perhaps being the triumph of Christian faith over paganism.

Norman Chambers

3   Cross-shaft in the churchyard of Hope St Peter. Pre-Norman.

Michael Austin

4 Hermit's cave, Dale [Depedale] Abbey.

Photographed in 1934 for the London, Midland and Scottish Railway Company. British Railways Board.

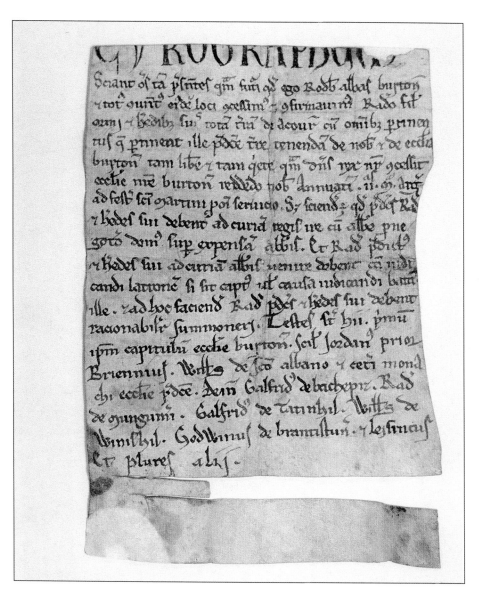

5 A gift by Robert, abbot of Burton and the convent there, to Ralph, son of Ormus, of the whole land of Acovere [Okeover] with all its appurtenances, which the king had granted to the church of Burton, paying annually two marks of silver at the feast of St Martin: the said Ralph and his heirs to attend the king's court at the expense of the abbot and also to attend the abbot's court to judge the punishment of thieves if one should be taken, and trial by battle, although he must have 'reasonable summons'. Witnesses: the chapter itself, Jordan the prior, Briennius, William of St Albans, many of the monks of the church, Geoffrey de Bachepiz, Ralph de Mungumie, Geoffrey de Tatinhul, William de Winishil, Godwin de Brantistun, Leisinais and many others. Date: 1150–1159. *13 cm by 11 cm.*

Derbyshire Record Office/Derby Diocesan Record Office [DDRO] D231 M/T 1.

Photographs of DDRO material by Stuart Whitehead.

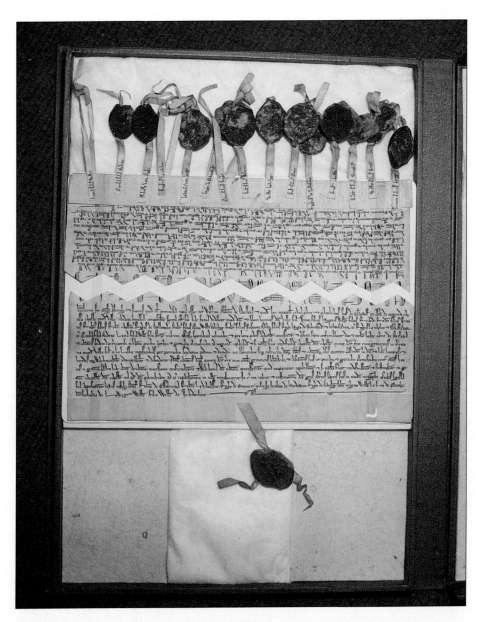

6   An agreement between Abbot Walter and the canons of Darley Abbey and their parishioners of Glapwell concerning the repair of the chancel of the chapel there, c. 1250. These two documents are notable for the fact that both have survived so that the purpose of indenting deeds can clearly be seen. The writing across the indentations was intended to prevent fraud. Each party to a deed had a copy and the two documents had to fit together exactly so that a forgery by a third party would be immediately apparent. They are notable also for the number of seals on the copy sealed by the parishioners, and by the number of women who were involved in the agreement. *Each part 36 cm by 20 cm.*

DDRO D184/1/140 and D187/1/141.

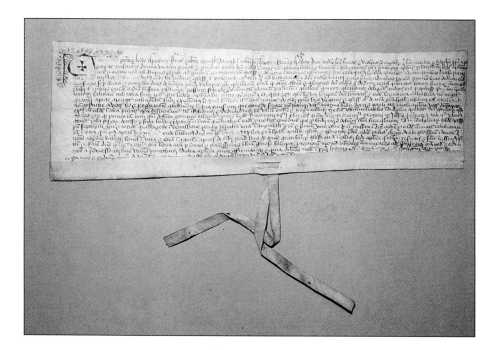

7   An indulgence granted to Henry Bochaw and his wife Joanna in 1480. Some of the illuminated (i.e. coloured) words are the names of popes. The practice of granting indulgences had begun with the remission of an earthly penance or penalty (but later held to have effect after death) arising from sin, even when sacramentally absolved. By the late Middle Ages the granting of indulgences, including their sale by *quaestors or* professional pardoners, had become the gravest of the abuses that led to demands for reform. The office of pardoner was abolished by Pope Pius V in 1567.

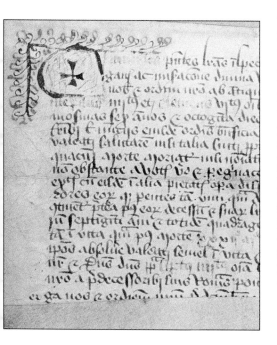

Transcription: 'Brother Robert priest of the house of St Robert near Knaresborough in the diocese of York of the order of the Holy Trinity and Redemption [states in this letter that] . . . the most holy pope Pius II through his spiritual grace has granted to the brothers and sisters of the said order the power to choose a suitable confessor who is able to absolve them, in life as well as at the point of death, of all their sins of which they have repented and confessed . . . and our father and lord Pope Sixtus IV has graciously received all our personal goods and possessions into his protection and he has confirmed the freedoms and privileges granted to us and our order by his predecessors . . . [signed] Henry Bochaw and Joanna his wife'

DDRO D2375 M/204/5. *31 cm by 10 cm*
(excluding seal tag).
Detail: **7a.**

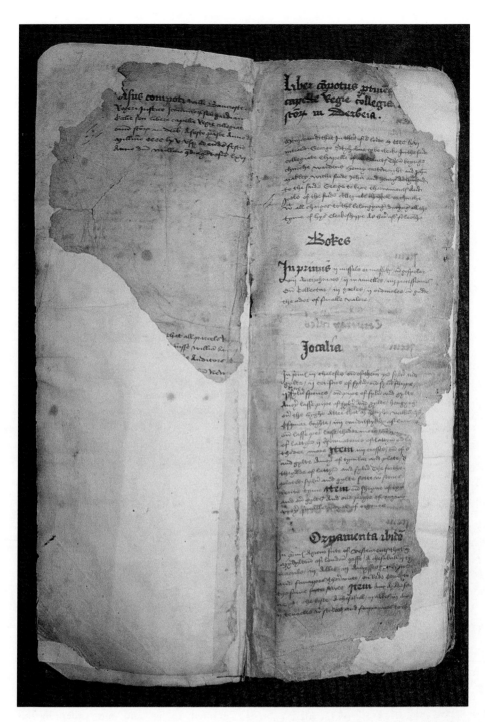

8   Derby All Saints parish meeting book from 1466 including a list of books beginning with '2 missals or massbooks'. *30cm by 40 cm.*

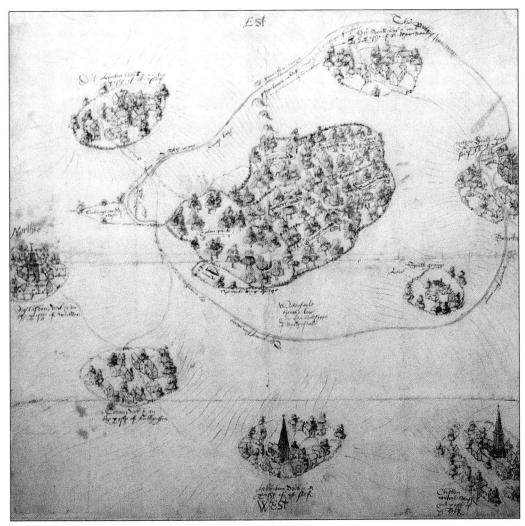

9 A 'processional way' map showing a route through and near villages in and around south Derbyshire and round a wood. The purpose of the procession is unknown but it may possibly have been to bless the trees, and held on the twelfth day after Christmas in the pre-Reformation Church. Early 16th century. The villages [from top left, clockwise] are Linton, Overseal, Netherseal, Seal Grange, Clifton Camperville [Staffordshire], Lullington, Coton in the Elms, and Rosliston. *42 cm by 42 cm.*

DDRO D77/46/1

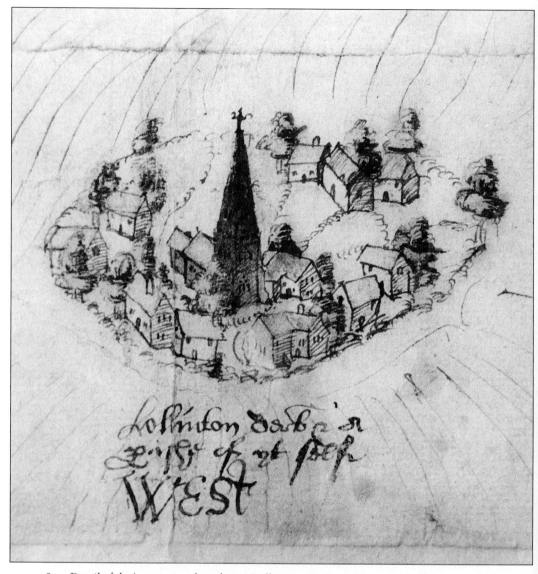

9a Detail of the 'processional way' map: Lullington.

9b Detail of the 'processional way' map: Overseal.

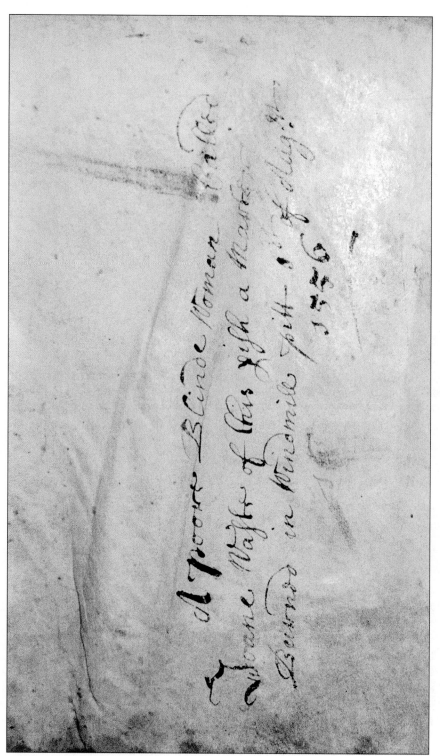

10 The entry, added later, in the first register of baptisms, marriages and burials of Derby All Saints, 1558–1712, recording the death of Joan Waste:

'A Poore Blinde Woman called
Joane Waste of this parish a Marter
Burned in Windmill Pitt 1st of August 1556'

DDRO D3372/1/1

11   Boylestone St John Baptist. In 1644 the church was used as a temporary cage for Royalist prisoners-of-war.

Michael Austin

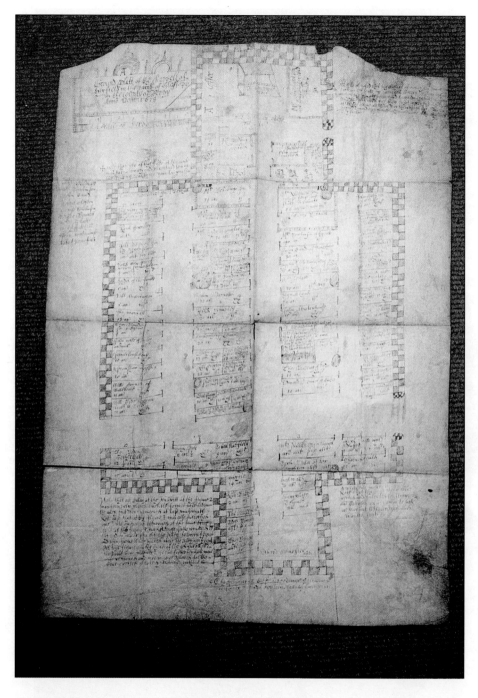

12 Ground and seating plan of 'the Chappell of Heyfield in the parish of Glossop', 1638, with notes on how seats are allocated and inequities of allocation. Hayfield St Matthew dated from 1386. It was rebuilt in 1818. *50 cm by 70 cm.*

DDRO D2426 A/P1 9/1

A

Ground Platt of the chappell of Heyfield in the parish of Glossopp in the County of Derby Anno Domi: 1638

Richard   Silvester

| 1 | 2 | 3 | 4 |

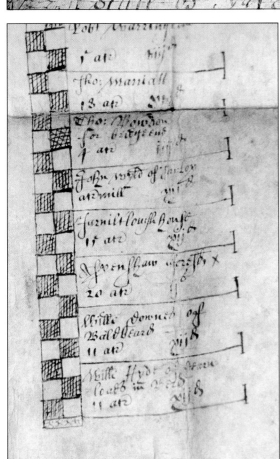

12a Details of the 'Chappell of Heyfield' seating plan.

your Parfonage oʒ Uicarage-houfe , your Almes-houfe and Church-houfe in good reparations: and are they imployed to godly, and their right holy ufes? Is your Church, Chancel, and Chappel decently and comely kept, as well within as without, and the feats well maintained, accoʒding to the 85 Canon, in that behalf pʒobided? Oʒ habe any Patrons oʒ others decayed the Parfonage houfes , oʒ keep a ſtipendiary Pʒieſt oʒ Curate, in place where an incumbent ſhould be poffeffed? Whether is your Church-yard well fenced with walls, rayles, oʒ pales, and by whom: and if not in whcſe default the fame is, and what the defect oʒ fault is? And whether any perfons incroached upon the Gʒound of the Church-yard, oʒ whether any perfon oʒ perfons, habe ufed any thing oʒ place confecrated to holy ufe, pʒophanely oʒ wickedly?

4. Is your Church oʒ Chappel decently paved, and is your Church-yard well and oʒderly kept without abufe? Are the bones of the dead decently interred, oʒ laid up in fome fit place as befeemeth Chʒiſtians? And is the whole confecrated ground kept from Swine, and all other naſtinefs, as becometh the place fo dedicated?

5. Whether habe you the Terrier of all the Gleab-land, Medowes, Gardens, Oʒchards, Houfes, Stocks, Implements, Tenements and poʒtions of Lythes (whether within your Pariſh oʒ without) belonging to your Parfonage oʒ Uicarage, taken by the biew of honeſt men in your faid Pariſh? And whether the faid Terrier be laid up in the Biſhops Regiſtry, and in whofe hands any of them are now? And if you habe no Terrier already made in Parchment, you the Church-wardens and Side-men , together with your Parfon oʒ Uicar, oʒ in his abfence with your Miniſter, are to make diligent inquiry and prefentment of the feberal particulars following, and to make, fubfcribe and fign the faid Terrier as afoʒefaid.

1. How many feveral parcels of Gleab-land do you know, oʒ habe you credibly heard to belong unto your Rectoʒy, Church, Parfonage, Uicaridge, &c. and by what names are they, (oʒ any of them) commonly called and known; And what yearly Rent habe you known, oʒ heard to habe been paid unto the Parfon, Uicar, oʒ to his oʒ their affigns, foʒ ebery, oʒ any of the faid parcels?

2. In whofe occupation are the faid parcels at this pʒefent? How much doth each parcel contain by meafure of the 16 foot pole? How is each parcel Butted on ebery part? And who is to repair the Fences on each fide thereof?

Concerning the Clergy.

1. WHether doth your Parfon, Uicar, oʒ Curate, diſtinctly and reberently fay Dibine Serbice upon Sundayes and Holy-dayes, and othe

13　A page from the articles of enquiry sent out to churchwardens and sidesmen in 1667 by Thomas Brown, vicar of Ashbourne 1660–1669 and archdeacon of Derby. The lay officers were asked whether their parson did 'wear a Surplice' and 'deliver the Bread and Wine to every Communicant severally, and kneeling', and whether he used the 'sign of the Cross in Baptism', and 'whether your minister married any without a Ring'. These questions were designed to reveal Puritan practices among now supposedly conforming parish clergy.

Derby Local Studies Library

14 Trusley, All Saints erected in 1713. The tower has been leaning since well before 1824 when Samuel Butler, archdeacon of Derby, noted that it 'seems sound but leans: no defect however perceptible.' This beautiful church did not meet with the archdeacon's approval. He described it as 'a peculiarly ugly meeting house looking building of brick; built in 1713 in the worst taste of that tasteless period.'

Michael Austin

In the Year 1739 The Parish Church of Kirk Ireton was all new Seated, by the consent of the Parson, Churchwardens, and Parishioners, being Authorised by a Faculty from Lichfield Court — Here followeth an exact Catalogue and Account of all the Seats and Sittings in the said Church, the Persons Names being annexed to whom they at this time belong.

Seats above the Chancel Door		South-side
	Robert Hayne	2 Sittings.
1st Seat	Richd Ryder for Allkins	2 Do
	Saml Walmsley	2 Do
2nd Seat	Joseph Harrison	2 Sittings.
	Robert Webster	All the rest.

Seats over against Chancel Door		South-side
	Paul Yeomans for Wigley	2 Sittings.
	Mr Thos Seacroft for the Hays	1 Do
1st Seat	Jeremiah Ward	2 Do
	Luke Allsop for Steeples & Jackson	2 Do
	Rodger Longdon for Jackson	1 Do

15 A survey of seating arrangements in Kirk Ireton, Holy Trinity, 1739. *22 cm by 35 cm.*
DDRO D2069 A/P1 19/1

16 Samuel Butler, 1774–1839; headmaster of Shrewsbury School, also archdeacon of Derby 1821–1836; bishop of Lichfield 1836–1839. A classical scholar, he published a four-volume edition of Aeschylus (1806–1816).

Derby Local Studies Library

ENGLAND'S GLORY.

THE CONSTITUTION OF 1688,
ON PROTESTANT PRINCIPLES.

BRITONS look to the history of your Country. Whenever **POPERY** found its way into the British Cabinet, England's Glory was always dim'd—our Strength crushed—our Armies beaten—our Fleets destroyed—discord and faction at home—conspiracies and intrigue abroad. All this the effect of **POPISH POWER!!** Be firm and resist!! Save your King— your Constitution! England's Glory.

Hasten to sign the only Petitions **AGAINST** Popery at the New nn—Nag's Head—Clock Room, Market Place---and Wheel Inn.

NEW INN, DERBY, March 5, 1829.   (J. DREWRY and SON, PRINTERS, DERBY.)

17 and 18   Handbills circulated in Derby in 1829 which illustrate the controversy over Roman Catholic emancipation. Under the Roman Catholic Relief Act in that year Roman Catholics were allowed to vote at elections and to sit in parliament. Property restrictions were lifted and most Crown offices were opened to them, the lord chancellorship being the most significant exception.

Derby Local Studies Library

TO THE

INHABITANTS

OF DERBY.

.he following Loyal and truly Christian **PETITION** is now lying for Signature at Mr. Smith's, Ironmonger, Corn Market; & Mr. Cross's Auction Mart, Queen Street, and all lovers of the peace and prosperity of their country are invited to give it their support, as they honour the King, and all who are placed in authority under him.

PETITION.

To the Right Hon. the Lords Spiritual and Temporal of the United Kingdom of Great Britain and Ireland, in Parliament assembled ;

The humble **PETITION** of the Undersigned Magistrates, Bankers, Merchants, Manufacturers, and other Inhabitants of the Borough of Derby ;

SHEWETH,

That your Petitioners very respectfully approach your Right Honourable House, to express their attachment to the Constitution of these Realms, as settled at the Glorious Revolution in 1688, and to the Protestant succession in **the** House of Hanover, as established by the Act of Settlement.

They also beg permission to express their confidence in his Majesty's Government, and their reliance on the wisdom of the Legislature ; and they humbly entreat your Right Hon. House to follow up his Majesty's gracious recommendation to take the whole state of Ireland into your consideration, with a view to the removal of all Laws imposing Civil Disabilities on his Majesty's Roman Catholic Subjects, and to the extension to Catholics of the United Kingdom of all such benefits of the British Constitution as in the wisdom of your Right Hon. House shall not be deemed incompatible with the security of our established Protestant Institutions,

AND YOUR PETITIONERS SHALL EVER PRAY.

PRINTED BY W. & W. PIKE, REPORTER OFFICE, CORN MARKET, DERBY.

In the case of a CHURCH or CHAPEL CONSECRATED or LICENSED since the 1st January, 1800; state

HOW OR BY WHOM ERECTED	COST, how Defrayed
By the Ecclesiastical Commissioners, aided by Voluntary Subscription	By Parliamentary Grant.................. „ Parochial Rate .... „ Private Benefaction, or Subscription, or from other Sources..... 4443.3.0 Total Cost......£ 8000 — or thereabout

V. HOW ENDOWED.	VI. SPACE AVAILABLE FOR PUBLIC WORSHIP
£ .... — Pew Rents .... 136 .... — Fees .... 2 .... — Dues............... permanent } — Easter Offerings ...... ment.... } Other Sources	Free Sittings ....about.... 650 Other Sittings ..about.... 550 Total Sittings... 1200

Estimated Number of Persons attending Divine Service on Sunday, March 30, 1851.				AVERAGE NUMBER OF ATTENDANTS during Months next preceding March 30, 1851. (See Instruction VII.)			
	Morning	Afternoon	Evening		Morning	Afternoon	Evening
General Congregation }	261	158	375	General Congregation }			
Sunday Scholars }	370	275	‹	Sunday Scholars			
Total..	631	433	375	Total...			

REMARKS A large proportion of the persons who attend in the Afternoon & Evening, do not attend more than once a day. The total number of distinct individuals is probably about 900, which is about one-fifth of the popul.ⁿ of the District.

I certify the foregoing to be a true and correct Return to the best of my belief.

IX. ...my hand this 31ˢᵗ day of March 1851.

(Signature) Thomas Arthur Scott, M.A.

(Official Character) Incumbent of the above named Church, S. John's, Derby

(Address by Post) Rev. T. A. Scott S. John's, Derby.

---

19 Part of the return to the religious census of 1851 for Derby St John's by Thomas Arthur Scott, the incumbent. Anticipating the problem of calculating how many of those who went to church on 30 March attended more than once, Scott notes: 'A large proportion of the persons who attend in the Afternoon or Evening do not attend more than once a [Sun]day. The total number of distinct individuals is probably about 900, which is about one-fifth of the populn. of the District.'

Public Record Office HO 129/445/4724/30

20 Derby St Andrew was built in 1866 at the initiative of John Erskine Clarke, vicar of Derby St Michael, to serve 'the Railway end of the town', Clarke himself becoming its first incumbent. This photograph was taken in 1963. The parishes of Derby St Andrew and, Osmaston St Osmund, were united in 1969. St Andrew's was demolished and the area redeveloped. St Andrew's House, a DSS office, was erected on the site of the church.

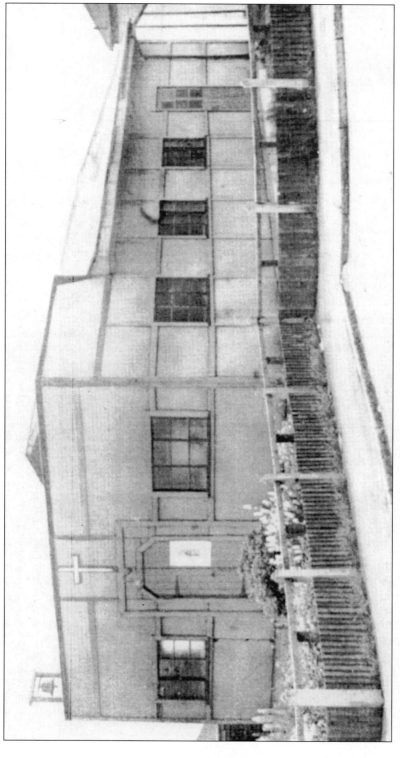

21   The temporary church, erected in 1934, at Frecheville [now in the diocese of Sheffield]. Illustrated in an appeal brochure in 1949, the caption ran: 'What would our forefathers say of this Hut of wood and compressed cardboard, which is all that a model suburb of 6000 has had for a Church these sixteen years?' The building of the permanent church of St Cyprian's was begun in 1950.

'without the drink'. These remarkable initiatives attracted large numbers of men who, as J.E. Clarke of St Michael's said, had soiled hands and blackened faces and who, because of this, found no place in the Derby Mechanics Institute.

Some clergy protested against the appalling living conditions of the indigent poor and the working conditions of those who could find employment (though, in 1838, when an appeal was launched in Derby to buy 'sweeping machines' to replace chimney boys one Baptist minister, William Hawkins, subscribed but no Anglican clergy or congregations). William Wilkinson of St Werburgh's agitated for the implementation of the 1848 public health acts in Derby. In 1855 clergy pressed for the establishment of a cemetery 'at a safe and convenient distance from the town' and in 1859 Richard Curzon, assistant curate of St Peter's, protested at the 'dangerous practice of conveying dead bodies to and from funerals in cabs' as 'this pernicious practice spreads disease.'

The more perceptive clergy diagnosed the economic factors which led to poor public health provision, unemployment, inflation and poverty and were occasionally driven to more direct action. In August 1860 J.E. Clarke of St Michael's chaired a meeting of Derby ribbon weavers called to support those in their trade then on strike in Coventry. The 'accursed thirst for cheapness' had caused the Coventry dispute, Clarke said, and, in a comment that sounds remarkably relevant today, he said how ashamed he was 'of our English ladies giving preference to French goods' and that 'it was unworthy of English salesmen that they should be obliged to put foreign labels on their goods' in order to sell them here.

In addition to these initiatives the clergy encouraged the working-classes to adopt the Victorian middle-class virtue of self-help. Provident societies, clothing clubs, sick and funeral aid societies, Friend-in-Need Work Societies and Penny Banks were established in several parishes.

There is detailed evidence of many similar enterprises. Although there were many obvious gaps in the Church of England's practical social service, given the Church's conservatism and its prevailing theology of poverty which reduced personal (and national) misfortune to a question of personal ethics, this evidence shows that much was done for the poor. Yet it is not surprising that the rural dean of Derby, Edward Abney of St Alkmund's, should say in 1880 that

> philanthropic efforts seemed to have failed with adults . . . . We had the

clergy, scripture readers, district visitors, lay deacons and bible women, and they are most useful persons, but what had they done among the masses? Where were the men who had been reclaimed? Here one and there another.[1]

One reason was that though the Church of England might try to aid the poor, it could not now be an artisan church. It has not been so for centuries. The Church of England was seen by working people of the day as a middle-class agency dispensing charity to them but not being a church for them. In addition the masses could read of clergy and influential laymen giving themselves much more readily to theological controversy than to debate about economic and social conditions, still less to genuine identification with the life and expectations of the poor. Meetings to object bitterly to, say, Roman Catholic emancipation in the early years, and, in the 1870s and 1880s, to ritualistic practices in Anglican churches in Derby, were much better attended and more fully reported than meetings to discuss the relief of poverty. Public discussions about the supposedly corrupting theologies of Strauss and Renan, or 'The New Testament Law of Marriage and Divorce not opposed to the Divorce Act of 1857' or Holyoake's *The Logic of Death*[2], or the defence of the 'Mosaic account of Creation' or 'the terrible false doctrines of Dr Colenso', or meetings of the Midland Prophetical Investigation Society, to take but a very few examples at random, occupied and excited the clergy far more than the implementation of the public health acts, or agitation to remove the slums, or consideration of the economics of poor relief.

It was this Church of England in the county, with its long history as an archdeaconry in the diocese of Lichfield, that was, in 1884, spot-welded to Lincoln's archdeaconry of Nottingham to form the new diocese of Southwell.

---

[1] quotation from a speech at a meeting to commemorate the 100th anniversary of the founding of Sunday schools, *Derby Mercury*, 14 July, 1880.
[2] In 1854. Class 10 of the secularist Owenites met in Derby between 1856 and 1859.

11

'In times of doubts and questionings': the early years of the diocese of Southwell, 1884–1917

The last decades of the 19th century were a time of great change both in the *role* of religion in social life, and also in its *character*. The configuration of belief, that is, what people believed and how (or not) those beliefs and values influenced their lives, was being transformed. Politically, the battle lines between Liberal nonconformity and a Conservative Church of England were by no means as sharply drawn as they had been. Nonconformists had long opposed the political and social privileges that membership of the Church of England afforded, but now, too, many Anglicans were asserting the independence of the Church from the state. As Jose Harris puts it, 'the relationship between politics and religion was becoming much more complex, individualized and indeterminate; the symmetry of belief, self-interest and political ideology was nothing like as strong as it had been a generation before.'[1]

Patterns of belief were changing too. What an individual believed began to be detached from active membership of a Church in an evolution described by sociologists as the privatisation of religion. Yet the Churches continued to compete with each other as vigorously as ever, not only in church building but also over issues of social welfare provision, most notably in education, such that the state had reluctantly to act, as Jose Harris observes, as an impartial umpire and to establish public policies which were overtly neutral. Taken together these developments led inevitably to the increasing marginalisation of the Churches.

---

[1] *Private Lives, Public Spirit: Britain 1870–1914* (Penguin 1994), 167.

For the Church of England this period thus marks the beginning of another stage in the disassembling of the symbiotic relationship between Church and state. The notion that the Church of England was the Church of the whole nation – that England was a uniconfessional state – had never possessed much reality. By the 1900s, the history of the Church had long since ceased to be the history of the state. The legal framework, if not the social assumptions, of the Church of England's role as the established Church were, as they still are, very much in place, but by the first World War the role of the Church of England as the spiritual guardian of England's soul had been much diminished, and it had become one Church – and indeed one voluntary organisation – among others.

From this point on our story inevitably reflects this profound shift in the place of the Church of England in the national life. Just as the Church became much more efficient as an organisation, and its clergy better trained and more professional than they had ever been, so its influence, and its numbers, began to wane. It was just at the beginning of this period of great change that the diocese of Southwell was established.

The pattern of a renewed Anglican pastoral ministry established in the second half of the 19th century, and which we have considered using Derby as an example, continued into the first quarter of the 20th. But it was a ministry in transition. As one example: in Edwardian Derbyshire there were gentry clergy whose forebears had been incumbents of the same parish for generations and who were connected to other long established land and property owning families in the county. One of them was Canon Edmund Carr, vicar of Holbrooke, of Holbrooke Hall and Boscobel in Staffordshire, inheriting both properties from his cousin, Sir Thomas William Evans of Allestree Hall. His mother was Ellen, daughter of William Evans of Darley Abbey and aunt of Sir William. William Evans had been High Sheriff of Derbyshire in 1829 and was an MP for the county for 16 years. Sir William was High Sheriff in 1872 and was MP for the South Derbyshire constituency. The Carrs had come to Derbyshire in the 17th century, and in 1768 Anthony Carr became vicar of Alfreton. The family was connected by marriage to the Gells of Hopton. Canon Carr had married three times, finally to Mary, daughter of William Leeke who had carried the colours of the 52nd Foot at Waterloo, and been vicar of Holbrooke.
    This family history illustrates a personal identification of parish clergy with landed families which we have noted earlier in our story but which was now

rapidly passing. Increasing industrialisation and rapid population growth, not least in Derbyshire and Nottinghamshire, caused profound social and cultural changes. This had inevitable consequences for the Church and its ordained ministry. Church and clergy were under scrutiny. Diocesan bishops, as they had done only rarely in previous centuries, had now personally to manage their dioceses. They now feature much more in our story than they have hitherto: what follows is inevitably, in part, an account of their leadership.

Reviving Thomas Cranmer's proposal of 1540, Bishop Selwyn of Lichfield had, in 1877, pressed for the division of his huge diocese. It had then a population of over one and half million. Of all men it was expected that Selwyn, who had travelled across the North and South Islands when he was bishop of New Zealand, 'fording and swimming rivers, sailing along uninhabited coasts'[1] would be undaunted by the diocese of Lichfield. In 1933 Egbert Hacking, archdeacon of Newark, said of Bishop Selwyn:

> Physically the Bishop seemed strong enough to perform any enterprise any human being could do. Mentally and spiritually he seemed to stand above his fellows. Sixty years ago I saw him bring into order one of the most violent Church Congress Meetings ever held, in which ecclesiastical strife seemed likely to end in physical violence.[2]

Yet even this extraordinary man could not carry through his proposal to separate Derbyshire from his diocese. Speaking at the diocesan conference held in Derby on 27 September 1877 he said that he had recently appealed for £50000 from the diocese to meet a similar contribution from the diocese of Lincoln. This would allow Derbyshire to be detached from the diocese of Lichfield and Nottinghamshire from Lincoln to form, and endow, a new diocese. 'To this day' he said, 'I have not received a shilling'.

'That distant and wild country'

The parishes of the dioceses of Lichfield and Lincoln raised some of the necessary endowment capital, and public appeals promoted at large meetings

---

[1] S.L. Ollard, G. Crosse, M.F. Bond, *A Dictionary of English Church History* (1948) 563.
[2] E. Hacking, 'Jubilee of the Diocese: Recollections and reflections of the Foundation and earliest days of the diocese'; a paper given to the Newark and District Clerical Society and the Gedling Ruri-Decanal Conference, December 1933, *Southwell Diocesan Magazine,* January 1934, 6.

attended by distinguished people raised more. A Derbyshire land-owner, A.J. Beresford Hope MP[1], was assiduous in attending and speaking at these. On 22 October 1879 he addressed a gathering in the Guildhall in Lichfield. He argued that the formation of the diocese of Southwell was but the first stage in the creation of a separate diocese for Derbyshire, with its cathedral and dean in Derby – 'for Tideswell or Ashborne, fine as are their churches, cannot lay claim to be a Cathedral town'. A week later, on 30 October, Beresford Hope addressed 'a numerous and distinguished company' in the Masonic Hall in Lincoln. Coming, he said, 'from the depths of Derbyshire, from that distant and wild country' he lamented that, on the creation of the new diocese of Southwell, 'the county of Derbyshire will be divorced from its spiritual alliance with that other county, with which for two thirds of the Christian age it has been allied – not to become itself a spiritual unit but to be transferred to a strange county, to another and a new Bishopric.' For Derbyshire, he said, this was a great sacrifice and one which Nottinghamshire was not making, for its incorporation into the diocese of Lincoln was of recent origin.

George Augustus Selwyn died in 1878. He was succeeded by William Dalrymple Maclagan, who was to be translated to York in 1891. In his first Charge in 1880 Maclagan noted that 13 parishes in his diocese had populations of more than 10000, 24 with populations in excess of 7000, and 77 with populations of 4000 and more. For these parishes the number of clergy was 'quite inadequate to the necessities of the population as regards their efficient pastoral care' and he supported the proposal to form the new diocese. Many Derbyshire clergy and congregations did not agree with him.

'Entrusted with a great office': George Ridding

Egbert Hacking had become rector of Eyam in 1885 and knew Derbyshire opinion well. There was then, he said, 'literally no general wish for separation from Lichfield', though some Derby incumbents strongly supported the scheme, Hacking noting particularly Edward Abney of St Alkmund's, James Chancellor of St John's, Alfred Olivier[2] of St.Thomas's, R.J. Knight of All

---

[1] Alexander James Beresford Hope (1820–87) MP for Stoke 1865–68, and for the University of Cambridge from 1868 to his death. A devout Anglican, and a great benefactor, he had secured the passing of a Cathedrals Act in 1873 which allowed for the re-endowment of canonries. He wrote, amongst much else, *The English Cathedral of the Nineteenth Century* (1861).

[2] He built, and became the first incumbent of, both Derby St James and Derby St Thomas. He was the great-uncle of Laurence Olivier.

Saints, C.H. Molineux of St James's, and Robert Hey of St Andrew's. Christopher Wordsworth, bishop of Lincoln, was also strongly in favour of the proposal. The population of Nottinghamshire was 392000 and growing rapidly, as it was in Derbyshire, from the development of coal-mining and ancillary industries. But clerical and lay support was generally lukewarm. Hacking noted in his diary for 30 June 1883: 'Meeting today in London in favour of the Southwell Bishopric Fund. Speeches were good, especially that of the archbishop of Canterbury, but the sum raised was not very large.'

The unease felt in both counties to the proposal was well-founded. Some of the new dioceses formed by amalgamations were successful but Southwell much less so. Owen Chadwick understates the case when he observes that 'Derbyshire did not easily marry Nottinghamshire'[1]. Any one who has served as a priest in both counties will know that the topography of each creates a character and people ill-matched to the other. It was for this reason at least that it was so difficult to raise the necessary finance. The Bishoprics Act of 1878, passed to make for the greater efficiency of the Church of England's mission, required that no new diocese could be formed unless sufficient capital was raised to provide a specified annual income.

In the counties of Derbyshire and Nottinghamshire discontent centred as early as 1877 on the strongly argued claim that the bishop of the new diocese should have his seat in Nottingham. The small town of Southwell with its great Minster was chosen to the disappointment of the large city of Nottingham with its civic church of St Mary's. Derbyshire clergy and laity were strongly opposed to both. The choice of Southwell made parts of Derbyshire at least as remote from the see town as Lichfield had been. Discontent not merely with the choice of see town but with the prospect of amalgamation itself was expressed in the subscription lists for the new diocese. A capital sum of £100000 was required to establish the new diocese. Church people in Staffordshire, Shropshire and Lincolnshire contributed £40000 at a stage in the fund-raising when Nottinghamshire and Derbyshire together could find only £18181. The truth was that 'there was no longing in Derbyshire to join Notts and no acute desire in Notts to join Derbyshire in making up the new Diocese of Southwell.'[2]

Almost on the eve of the formation of the new diocese £15000 was still needed. The bishop of Lincoln accepted personal liability for this shortfall and, at his death in 1885, it formed a charge on his estate. The debt was not cleared until

---

[1] Owen Chadwick, *The Victorian Church,* ii, 346, n.2.
[2] Hacking, op. cit., 7.

1889. The first bishop of Southwell, George Ridding, made a personal contribution of £3600. Following his example, 500 additional contributions came from individuals and parishes at a time when, Hacking records, the Derbyshire Peak District Church Fund alone raised over £2500, and the Dore and Chinley Navvy Mission about £500 each year, for their own work, and when many other Derbyshire church schemes had been started and financed. The money to endow the new diocese had been available. The will to contribute it had not.

Another problem to plague bishops of Southwell, as Edwyn Hoskyns, the second bishop, was to note in 1917, was the issue of patronage. Patronage of Derbyshire benefices held by the bishops of Lichfield and Lincoln came to the bishop of Southwell, but no provision had been made for a similar transfer of patronage of several Derbyshire parishes held by the bishops of Ripon and Manchester. This was to cause both difficulty and resentment.

There were two further causes for episcopal concern. Lichfield and Lincoln cathedrals possessed well-endowed residentiary canonries, with further endowments capable of ensuring the maintenance of the cathedral's services 'through a well paid Dean and other officers who held post with assured incomes' said Hacking. 'It seemed equitable that some of this income should, on the division of the Dioceses, accrue to the daughter See' for the maintenance of cathedral worship in Southwell. Bishop Ridding argued the case for years with the deans and chapters of both ancient cathedrals but with no success. In 1841 Southwell Minster had been deprived of its prebendal properties, in part to the benefit of the new dioceses of Manchester and Ripon. W.E. Gladstone had opposed this, arguing, as Egbert Hacking put it, that 'the Southwell prebendal funds might well be needed some day for the judicious benefit of that immediate neighbourhood which they had served, though not always in a wise way, since the reign of Henry VIII.' So it turned out. It was Gladstone who was to recommend that the headmaster of Winchester College, George Ridding, become the first bishop of Southwell on the formation of the diocese in 1884.

Not the least of the new bishop's difficulties was deciding where to live. The town of Southwell wanted him to live there. Nottingham wanted him there, and Derbyshire Anglicans suggested that he live in Derby. Somebody said that the bishop had better live in London than Southwell! Eventually Bishop Ridding was offered Sir John Robinson's house at Thurgaton near Southwell as a temporary home at a very low rent. He lived there until his death in 1904.

The difficulty of creating one diocese from two disparate counties prompted

Bishop Ridding, in his Charge in 1887, to himself propose Beresford Hope's radical solution:

> One question cannot fail to be suggesting itself to you. If county Sees are felt to present the ideal scale, were it not well that even now these counties should begin their destiny.

He clearly foresaw the need for further subdivision. In Nottingham on 15 October 1889 he made the issue a personal one:

> I have said before that I would gladly resign feelings and income for such a proper arrangement if it lay with me to do so and if the counties showed any wish for it. I should like nothing better myself than to be the first to begin such a scheme of subdivision. But it has been determined to be an unpractical question, and there are other things to be done.[1]

A subsequent formal proposal to create a separate diocese for Derbyshire was opposed, Hacking noted, at a diocesan conference held in Derby, but by 1911, seven years into Bishop Hoskyns' episcopate, the need for further subdivision had become clear. The population of the diocese had grown by almost 14% from 1,136582 to 1,317292 in ten years. The combined populations of the two Derbyshire archdeaconries of Chesterfield and Derby had increased by 12% from 627702 to 712736. The rate of church expansion had increased since 1884; mission churches had been established and new church schools built. This had required much of Bishop Ridding. In 1887 alone he presided or preached at 200 services, attended 74 meetings and functions and made 176 parish visits. During his episcopate at least 60 new churches and 21 district missions were built in the new diocese, 193 churches restored (118 completely or with considerable enlargements, and 75 following major repairs) and clergy appointed to serve them.[2]

'Losing the spring out of the year': the parishes

What did George Ridding find when he visited his parishes in Derbyshire? In 1884[3] there were 339 parochial clergy serving 345 parish churches, chapels-of-ease and mission rooms in the county. These buildings contained room for 116423 people. The majority of this accommodation was free though

---

[1] Hacking, op. cit., 8.
[2] Undelivered *Charge* 1904, quoted in Laura Ridding, *George Ridding* (Arnold 1908), 184.
[3] statistical information derived from editions of the annual *Southwell Diocesan Church Calendar*.

substantial pew-appropriation remained. In 80 churches and chapels-of-ease only some 45% of the pews were free and available to the poor. The worst examples were Ashbourne St John which had total accommodation for 650 but free pews for only 120, or 18.5%, and Chapel-en-le-Frith which could seat 900 but had free pews for only 80 – a mere 9%. The Census of 1881 had recorded an archdeaconry population of 471700. For this the Church of England provided places in church for 25% but with free seats for only 21%.

George Ridding found that so large were parishes in the north-west of the county that it was impossible for many of the people to attend church even had they wanted to, though there was ample room for them. In 1884 the parish of Derwent Woodlands[1] covered 25000 acres or 39 square miles and had a population of 395. The parish church of SS James and John could have accommodated over 64% of the population. There were four baptisms that year, and the incumbent, William Mills, presented no Confirmation candidates. The parish had a day school which could have accommodated 80 children, but there were only 35 on the books. The parish of Earl Sterndale was even larger. It covered 33000 acres, or over 51 square miles. Its parish church of St Michael and All Angels could have accommodated a third of the population of 600. The incumbent, George Robertson, baptised 11 children in 1884, but again presented no candidates to the bishop for Confirmation. This was hardly surprising, though not to have a Confirmation class, the bishop said, was like 'losing the spring out of the year.'[2]

In the Derbyshire parishes as a whole the Church of England in 1884 was educating 46363 children in 209 day schools. In areas of rapid population growth these schools were grossly over-crowded. Staveley had church school accommodation for 1661 children but there were 1933 on the books. Swadlincote school had places for 141 with 184 attending, and Swanwick for 408 with 507 attending. In farming communities there was spare room. Taddington had a church school which could accommodate 200 with only 70 children attending, while 270 children went to Tideswell church school which could have accommodated 718.

In addition, the Sunday schools, committed to teach 'useful knowledge' to children who could not attend a day school, also attracted high numbers. In

---

[1] This was originally a chapelry coextensive with the township of Derwent in the parish of Hathersage. It became a separate parish in 1871 having added to it much of the township of Hope Woodlands from the parish of Hope. It was united with Bamford in 1943. The church was flooded when the Ladybower reservoir was formed.

[2] Laura Ridding, op. cit., 200.

1884, in the archdeaconry of Derby, 38817 children went to school of Sundays. No less than 1420 attending the school at Derby St James in a poor and rapidly growing area of the county town, with 629 attending in Staveley, and 1000 at Whitfield. Older children and adults attended Bible classes in considerable numbers. Tibshelf had a Bible class with 250 on the books, Derby All Saints 225, Riddings 100, and at Holbrooke a rather surprising 109, but there the incumbent was the 'squarson' Canon Edmund Carr of Holbrooke Hall who no doubt exercised a benign but powerful influence.

Historians of the Church of England have tended to ignore the extraordinary contribution it inadvertently made through its schools to working-class emancipation in the 19th century. It taught the children of the poor to read in order that they might study the Bible. The evangelical Daniel Wilson argued that the purpose of such an education was to

> lay in the children's minds the foundation of obedience to their governors in Church and State, [and to] to make them contented with the station which providence has appointed to them in the world.[1]

In fact of course, as working-class leaders were to say repeatedly and with gratitude, to be taught to read the Bible was to be introduced not only to its politically 'highly incendiary' passages, as Eric Hobsbawm has described them, but to be equipped to read and learn from the secularist and socialist tracts. More generally, the contribution the Church of England made to social reform in the 19th century through its educational provision was extraordinary. By 1861 76% of the nation's children were being educated in Anglican primary schools, and the Church was providing almost 70% of teacher training places in its colleges.

'He has no servant': the clergy

For this unintentionally subversive activity the clergy were far from well paid. In 1884 the highest benefice income in the county, £800, was enjoyed by the rector of Whitwell, while the lowest went to the curate-in-charge of All Saints, Matlock Bath who received £35. Stipends were to improve but did not keep pace with inflation. By 1914 the income at Matlock Bath had risen to £211[2] though

---

[1] quoted in *The Poor Child's Friend* edited by R. Simpson [curate of Derby St Peter], No VII, July 1825, iv–v.

[2] As a comparison with other professions, in 1909 a non-resident public school master could expect to earn £300 a year after 10 years' service. A bank manager might be earning £600 in 1897 [John Stevenson, *British Society 1914–45* (Penguin 1990), 33.]

this was 'less Pension to former Vicar'. In his notebook the bishop recorded one of his first parish visits, to a hamlet of no more than a hundred people:

> The Church is a regular barn, divided by partition from the chancel, which is empty except for the Communion-table and church rubbish – deal seats like kitchen chairs, etc.- stove put away, not used. The Glebe house is a two-roomed cottage. A dear old Rector, aged seventy-seven, a student, seems very happy. He has no servant: a farmer's wife 'does' for him. He tells me that once a week he has a hot dinner, and keeps it in a cupboard, and it lasts the rest of the week.[1]

The income of this living was £70 p.a. By 1905, 40 of the 80 poorest benefices had been augmented by funds raised within the diocese. After visiting poor parish clergy in north Derbyshire the bishop said that 'people do not realise, I am sure, how hopelessly depressing such endurance is when years go on with no prospect.'[2] In 1889 he established a fund of £5000 to augment poor livings in the Peak District. He listed 13 parishes of which, by the following year, eight had been augmented (albeit modestly). 'Special appropriated gifts' went to the remaining five. This was the situation after 175 years of the augmentation of poor benefices by Queen Anne's Bounty.

The sheer weight of numbers to whom the clergy had a duty to minister was due, of course, to the increasing exploitation of the Nottinghamshire and Derbyshire coalfield and the development of ancillary industries. Take the parish of Tibshelf, where coal had been mined since the Tudors. In 1823, according to archdeacon Butler's visitation returns, Tibshelf church could hold 450, with free seats for 20, for a population of 711. By 1884 the pews could accommodate only 224 with free seats for 45, but by now the Colliery School Mission had been erected with seats for 400, all of which were free. The population now stood at 2244. In 1817 there had been a 'subscription school' with a 'very dilapidated school house' attended by 42 children although, it was noted, 'during the winter months they are somewhat increased' when children were not employed on the land. In 1818 this school, with 'a few small schools' in Tibshelf contained about 100 children.[3] In 1884 the church school in Tibshelf had accommodation for 650 children with 626 on the books. In 1823 there had

---

[1] Laura Ridding, ibid., 185–6. Not to have a servant would be regarded as a sign of genteel poverty. The going rate for a live-in maid in London in the years before 1914 was £10 or £12 a year [Stevenson, ibid.].
[2] ibid., 187.
[3] M.R. Austin, *The Church in Derbyshire in 1823–4; The parochial visitation of the Rev Samuel Butler, archdeacon of Derby in the diocese of Lichfield and Coventry* (1974), 169 n4.

been no Sunday school in the village. In 1884 the Sunday school was attended by 362 children with 250 others (presumably young adults) in the Bible class. This was a remarkable response by the Church of England, and one repeated elsewhere.

'The perplexities of variety': the diocese

Confronted with a situation very different to the one that had faced him as headmaster of a great public school, Bishop Ridding conducted a primary visitation of his diocese in 1888. In his very closely argued and lengthy Charge[1] subsequently delivered in eight centres in the diocese (five in Derbyshire) the bishop commented on the answers to his visitation questionnaire and drew conclusions from them. Twelve Derbyshire churches were in need of major restoration. Eleven were listed: Barlborough, Bradley, Chesterfield St Mary and All Saints, Codnor, Derby St Peter, Earl Sterndale, Hayfield, Mugginton, Sawley, South Wingfield and Taddington. Of the others, only 89 churches possessed lightning conductors, 25 were not insured, 66 lacked terriers (records of the property of a church), only 139 kept registers in a fire-proof safe, 119 failed to display tables of fees, 197 did not display tables of affinity (the list of relatives prohibited from marrying each other) and 111 did not possess preachers' books (listing the dates on which sermons had been preached, with the signature of the preacher). Churchwardens had not been formally admitted to office in 79 parishes, the significance of this being that these parishes lacked elected laymen with legal authority to act for them.

Bishop Ridding passed from these important practical matters of parish administration to speak at length on the pressing ecclesiastical matters of the day: the Tithe Rent Charge Bill and the Clergy Discipline Bill then before Parliament. But for today's readers of his Charge the most significant section had to do with ecumenical matters – 'our relationship to Nonconformity, and the difficulties arising from it.' Here Bishop Ridding was both acute and sensitive. While spelling out clearly the limits of co-operation (it would be inappropriate, he said, for an Anglican clergyman to take part in services 'constructed in opposition to the Church of which he is a Minister, and in Buildings erected simply to promote that opposition') he urged his clergy to work with all those united in a good cause 'as citizens of a great brotherhood',

---

[1] published in full in the *Southwell Diocesan Magazine,* June 1888.

remembering always why schisms had occurred historically. He observed that while these divisions have by no means always been the fault of the Church of England, they had been created 'when the ever recurring spirit of rigid uniformity rises against the perplexities of variety.'

This raised the question of patronage. Bishop Ridding reminded his clergy and churchwardens 'that the times when the lay people imposed rigid uniformity were the times when too tight fetters cramped some with apathy, and galled others into rebellion; the two causes of schism.' He continued:

> It may be well, when men desire to enfeeble the Church's men, and to bring the Clergy under close lay control, to remember that the times when the Clergy 'were passing rich on forty pounds a year', and had to dance attendance upon Patrons, and serve as great men's chaplains, were the times when the Church had least spiritual power against vice, and good men craved most a spiritual system free from bonds of state control.

This was a very perceptive comment. It was also courageous in the heated and competitive ecclesiastical atmosphere of the 1880s.

'To stimulate, not to supersede': the bishop

Bishop Ridding's ministry as first bishop of Southwell is fully recorded and there is no need here to do other than briefly to draw attention to three aspects of his ministry relevant to our time: his defence of the distinctiveness of the Church of England, his social concern, and his spirituality.

Bishop Ridding was a teacher and fully exercised that episcopal ministry. He was concerned, first, to defend the distinctive position of the Church of England, both in its continuity with the early Church and also in its relationship with the state. This central issue of Anglican identity was particularly significant at the time, as the Church of England strove to maintain its numerical superiority in English Christianity, but it was one with which Derbyshire's bishops before and since have had to engage.

In a very lengthy and detailed analysis of *The Continuity of the Church of England,* given to his diocesan conference in Derby in 1886, he argued that 'the Church of England has never separated from any one' and went on to dispose of six 'delusions' about the Church's evolution and its relationship to the civil power, delusions which, he believed, hindered its mission to the nation. These were the delusions that 'the Church of England was ever Roman'; that 'the

Church of England seceded or separated from Rome'; that 'the Church of England was a different Church after the Reformation from before it'; that 'King, Queen, or Parliament, either reformed the Church or ordered that the Pope should no longer be her head' (it was the Church who determined this, in Ridding's view); that 'the recognition of the Royal Supremacy meant or means any Spiritual Headship' over the Church; and that 'Parliament settled the Church of England, or even that the Church is subject to Parliament.' In 1927 the bishop of Southwell, Bernard Heywood was also to argue for the historical continuity of the Church of England. His position was bitterly ridiculed by the *Nottingham and Midland Catholic News.*

Richard Hurd, bishop of Coventry and Lichfield, had defended the Church of England's unique position, but much more briefly and with great elegance, in his first Charge to his clergy in 1775–6. He affirmed the Church's 'Creeds and Confessions' as based upon scripture and necessary for the continuity, unity and catholicity of the Church, and then continued:

> Thus the case stands, before the State gives a preference to any particular Church. Thenceforth, indeed, the State concurs with the Church to enforce one common Confession, by confirming the emoluments, which it provides for the encouragement of Religion, to the peculiar doctrines of the favoured Church. This the State does, in equity towards that religious society with which it is now so closely connected: it does it, too, in prudence and good policy; because it conceives its own true interests to be concerned in maintaining those peculiar doctrines.

Thus was the continuity of the Church of England with the earliest Church, and its formal and legal role in English life, defended in Derbyshire, as it was defended, and accepted (at least by Anglicans) elsewhere. As Edward Royle neatly puts it, the 'acceptance of the Church was implicit in acceptance of the social order, and the social order itself was constructed upon the religious sanctions administered through the Established Church.'[1] This symbiotic relationship of the Church of England and the state was already under threat.

In another lengthy and related paper, on *Some considerations on The Holy Communion,* which formed his Charge to his clergy in 1893, Bishop Ridding set out the classic Anglican theological position on the eucharist[2]. By addressing these crucial historical and theological questions, Anglican bishops

---

[1] Edward Royle, *Modern Britain; A social history 1750-1997,*(Arnold 1997), 330.
[2] Laura Ridding, op.cit., 346–50.

from the seventeenth to the early twentieth centuries sought to offer a well-argued *apologia* for the distinctiveness and historical integrity of the Church of England.

Bishop Ridding was concerned too for the wider social life of his diocese. He attempted to conciliate in the South Derbyshire coal strike in 1886, and in a lock-out of Nottingham lace-workers in 1889. He took part in the promotion of the Factory Legislation Amendment Bill in 1895 and the Workmen's Compensation Bill in 1897, and he strongly promoted the Church's own diocesan social provision.[1] He attempted to play an active conciliatory role during 'the great Coal War' which lasted from 28 July to 18 November 1893. One hundred parishes in Derbyshire and Nottinghamshire were directly involved in the dispute. Ridding took an even-handed position seeking to achieve reconciliation during the lock-out. On 10 September he addressed a well attended meeting of miners in Holy Trinity, Ilkeston, and, two nights later, spoke to 3000 miners in Bulwell market place. He made clear his support not only for the families of the striking miners but also for workers in industries which depended upon mining but who did not receive strike pay. On 10 October he moved a resolution at his diocesan conference which expressed 'deep sympathy with the sufferings resulting . . . from the stoppage of the coal trade and the consequent stoppage of so many industries dependent upon it.' He commended the clergy of mining parishes 'who had said little and done what they could' and noted that 'if any of their people doubted the sympathy of the clergy before, they cannot doubt it now.'[2] To a contemporary ear that may sound like wishful thinking, but the bishop was to note that in those 100 parishes, over 190000 people, of whom 75000 were women and children, received aid for periods varying from five weeks to three months at the hands of joint relief committees. In 60 pit villages the clergy alone, or with others, distributed relief, and in two-thirds of these villages they chaired the relief committees at the request of the miners.[3]

Bishop Ridding often invited the clergy of Derbyshire and Nottinghamshire to quiet days at his home at Thurgaton Priory. For them, as men 'entrusted with a great office', he wrote *A Litany of Remembrance,* notable for its deep spirituality, its perceptive self-awareness and its beauty, and framed for those

---

[1] ibid., 248, 269.

[2] ibid., 267.

[3] George Ridding, 'Some Reflections on the Recent Stoppage in the Coal Trade as affecting the Diocese', *Southwell Diocesan Magazine,* December 1893, and see Laura Ridding, op. cit., 266–7.

'times of doubts and questionings' about which he prayed and through which the Church was passing.

Though of different temperament, his goodness and faithfulness made him a spiritual brother of his great contemporary and neighbour, Bishop King of Lincoln. In all that he did as bishop, he said, his aim was 'to stimulate, not to supersede.' Like that of his immediate predecessors as bishops for Derbyshire, Henry Ryder, Samuel Butler, James Bowstead, John Lonsdale and George Augustus Selwyn, his ministry was in sharp contrast to that of many of his, and their, predecessors. We can underestimate the extent to which the contemporary Church of England in Derbyshire has been the outgrowth of the faithfulness, example and leadership of its 19th century bishops.[1]

Bishop Ridding was assisted in Derbyshire by E.A. Were. In a description that could be applied to each of the assistant bishops and suffragan bishops of Derby in the years that followed, he was said to be a man 'of broad sympathies and ever patient industry'. E.A. Were had been invited to be a canon and chancellor of the new cathedral of Southwell, but was soon made suffragan bishop of Derby. He was to combine this post with that of archdeacon of Derby (which, until October 1910, covered the whole county) and, to provide his income, the incumbency of Derby St Werburgh.

'A manly example of the athletic cleric': Edwyn Hoskyns

In one of those glossy local productions in which the Edwardian gentry loved to see their names and photographs, Sir Edwyn Hoskyns, made second bishop of Southwell on George Ridding's death in 1904, was so described.[2] He was much more than this, though his suffragan bishop in Derbyshire, C.T. Abraham, later recalled 'that sturdy figure, hardy and strong, built up and disciplined on the river at Cambridge and by all manly sport.'[3] Sir Edwyn Hoskyns was the fourth son of the Revd Sir John Leigh Hoskyns Bt, who was rector of Aston Tyrrold in Berkshire for 60 years. Edwyn Hoskyns had been ordained in 1874 to a title in Welwyn. He served a further curacy at Quebec Chapel in west London before becoming, successively, incumbent of parishes in Notting Hill and in Stepney. In 1895, he became vicar of Bolton, and in 1901 rector of

---

[1] Much of the credit for the revival of episcopal ministry in the late 19th century must go to Lord Palmerston, who appointed 19 diocesan bishops during his premiership. See Nigel Scotland, 'Good and Proper Men': Lord Palmerston and the Bench of Bishops (James Clarke, 2000).

[2] Derbyshire and Some Neighbouring Records (n.d.).

[3] C.T. Abraham, a memoir in Southwell Diocesan Magazine, March 1934, 51.

Burnley. In the same year he was made suffragan bishop of Burnley.

When he became bishop of Southwell in 1904 he had therefore had an extensive pastoral experience which enabled him to comment vigorously on social issues. Taking the year 1910 alone he firmly opposed the current operation of the Poor Law, and tried to resist the removal of parental rights over religious education in elementary schools. In his letters to his clergy he frequently returned to the question of marriage and the family. In October 1908 he called attention to 'the pain and grief' caused by unemployment. For many clergy in urban parishes, he said,

> the vision of the unemployed becomes a nightmare . . . . We cannot wait
> for, or entirely depend upon, laws or mechanisms. We have to deal now
> and at this moment with the sufferers from a civilization which we
> cannot call Christian.

The suffering of the unemployed moved Bishop Hoskyns deeply throughout his ministry. In November 1923 he inveighed again against the 'terrible burden' of the unemployed, for whom there was 'little hope and no security.'

Bishop Hoskyns was also outspoken about other matters. In February 1918 he acknowledged receipt of 'many protests' on the appointment of the Dean of Durham, Hensley Henson, to be bishop of Hereford. Henson's nomination, the first by Lloyd George, had created a storm. He was, to use the language of the day, a noted theological modernist. Hoskyns wrote that

> The protests are abundantly reasonable, for until Dr Henson recanted,
> any readers of his works were justified in thinking that he not only spoke
> for the doubter, but himself had lost faith in the most fundamental
> Christian doctrines. This he asserts now to be an unfair interpretation,
> and we must accept his word, though he is alone to blame for the arousing
> of deep suspicion.

Hensley Henson returned to Durham as its bishop in 1920.

Church and people in 1913

In his administration of his diocese Bishop Hoskyns was energetic, decisive and outspoken. In 1910 he created additional archdeaconries in the north of both counties: of Chesterfield for north Derbyshire and of Newark for north Nottinghamshire. He conducted major parochial visitations of his diocese.

Between 1908 and 1911 he personally visited all 520 parishes in the diocese at the rate of about eight parishes each month. He reported on deanery visitations conducted between 1911 and 1915 in the *Southwell Diocesan Magazine*. There is space for only four representative examples from Derbyshire, but they give a clear picture of the Church of England in the county on the eve of the first World War.

In the May 1911 edition the bishop noted his visitation of the Glossop rural deanery. It had a population of 'above 40000' (in fact 38662 in 1911), with Anglican church accommodation for 7500. There were 14 clergy in the parishes. The communicant attendance on Easter Day 1910 was 2291 or some 6% of the population. Calling for more clergy to be appointed to the parishes of Glossop, Dinting, Whitfield and New Mills the bishop remarked that 'in no place in England does it take a vicar two and a half hours by train to reach the other side of his parish.' He was blunt in his criticisms. Though at Whitfield and Mellor there was 'marked advance', he lamented that 'in more than one parish the Church of England has been far too slow in taking up the work, whilst in others the Church is living down ancient scandals.' The bishop appealed to the clergy to take account of the influx of a new and permanent population into the deanery from Manchester, and to provide forms of worship attractive to the many weekend trippers into the area.

In June 1911 he visited the Ashbourne deanery. He noted there that the farming industry was in decline: 'That which governs the whole life and work of your people is milk' yet the number of farm labourers was small and declining such that 'your young people all leave the villages, the girls for service, the boys for other farms or for our colonies[1].' In this deanery 23 clergy cared for a population of 10900 and the Church of England provided accommodation in its churches for 5400. There had been 1414 communicants in Easter Day in 1911, or 13% of the population, twice as high as in the Glossop rural deanery a year earlier.

In September 1912 Bishop Hoskyns noted in his report of his visitation of the Buxton deanery that the farming industry was depressed and 'the young people get away soon after school age, and the population is decreasing, save where the quarries and mine works give employment'. Housing in the deanery was poor.

---

[1] It has been estimated that there was a net loss of population of 750000 due to emigration in the years 1901–10 alone, with even higher levels in the years immediately before the first World War [Stevenson, op.cit., 146–7].

There was 'gross overcrowding', often with no proper bedroom accommodation. Under such conditions 'ordinary decency becomes impossible.' In these difficult social and economic conditions the 24 Anglican clergy cared for a population of 29300. Accommodation in the Church of England's churches and chapels was 8200 sittings, Easter communicants that year came to 2560, or just under 8.75% of the population.

In April 1914 the bishop told of his visit to the Melbourne deanery. Its population of 16015 in 13 parishes was served by 16 Anglican churches able to accommodate 4476 people (or 28% of the population), and by 13 clergy. There had been 1265 communicants on Easter Day that year (or 8% of the population). The bishop noted that nearly 50% (an exaggeration) of the population lived in the two parishes of Boulton and Alvaston yet there had been no increase in the number of clergy serving those parishes. Anglican church accommodation in Chellaston, he said, was inadequate and should be doubled. Elvaston vicarage was unsuitable and too far from the church, and he noted that the church school building in Findern had been condemned. Ticknall church was being restored, but the numbers in the church school there had fallen from 206 to 116 reflecting a 'most marked' decrease in the numbers of children in the deanery as a whole. To his astonishment, the bishop declared, what was for him one of the most beautiful churches in the world – Melbourne parish church – was grossly under-insured.

The statistics provided to the bishop from these four representative deaneries are revealing. Their population totalled 96000. The ratio of clergy to population varied very widely from one for every 474 people in Ashbourne deanery, to one for every 2762 in Glossop deanery. Church accommodation provided by the Church of England varied very widely also. Nearly 50% of the population could have attended church in the Ashbourne deanery but only 19% able to do so in the Glossop deanery. Easter Day communicants as a percentage of population matched the ratios of clergy and church accommodation to people, with 13% of the population attending on Easter Day in Ashbourne deanery, and only 5.9% in Glossop. However, in all four deaneries roughly the same percentage of the available church accommodation was filled with Easter Day communicants: Glossop 31%, Buxton 31%, Ashbourne 26% and Melbourne 28%, though interestingly the Anglicans in Buxton and Glossop seemed somewhat more faithful on Easter Day than those in the two deaneries further south which, together, had a better clergy staffing ratio.

An obvious conclusion had been drawn well before 1927 when the diocese of

Derby was created. There was simply too much Anglican church accommodation for those who wished to attend, even on the great Church festivals. This was beginning to become plain by the eve of the first World War. In addition, fewer clergy were serving a much larger population. By 1927 the population of the county had doubled since 1882 but the number of parochial clergy had fallen by 29, as the suffragan bishop of Derby, C.T. Abraham, noted. It had become difficult, he said, both to find assistant curates and also to maintain clergy stipends. Many parishes had been united since the diocese of Southwell had been created.[1] By the eve of the first World War a period of extraordinary church growth had come to an end. It is worth reviewing here what had been achieved.

Church growth 1851–1913

Between 1881 and 1913 the population of the parishes in the Derbyshire archdeaconries grew by a third from 471700 to 712736[2]. To meet this increase the Church of England alone increased its provision of sittings from 116423 to 131973, or 13%. On the eve of the first World War the Church of England had 443 churches, chapels-of-ease and mission rooms in Derbyshire. Of these nearly 54% had been newly built, rebuilt, substantially enlarged or otherwise provided in the 63 years from 1850 to 1913, increasing the church accommodation it provided by 46.9%. Many churches had been re-ordered to provide more sittings. Within this overall provision the Church of England had opened 154 mission churches, mission rooms and Church Army halls in areas of major population growth. In 1913 these churches and missions were served by 380 clergy.

This expansion had not been achieved easily or even without opposition. To give one example: In 1845 Goodwin Purcell was asked by Bishop John Lonsdale to become incumbent of the new parish of Charlesworth which had been carved out of the large parish of Glossop, the parish church being four miles from the majority of the people. There had been no Anglican chapelry in Charlesworth since the Restoration, so Purcell hired a room which, he was later to say, was 'soon filled to overflowing.' This incurred the opposition of the nonconformist clergy in the area. Purcell later recorded that 'stones were frequently thrown at me, curses grew louder and deeper, and more insults were commonly offered.'

---

[1] C.T. Abraham, 'Derbyshire Clergy 1882–1927', *Southwell Diocesan Magazine*, February 1927.
[2] Statistical and other data in this section are taken from annual editions of *Southwell Diocesan Church Calendar*. Dates of churches *etc* are of their consecration.

He survived this and raised the money to build a church by touring the country pleading for funds. Bishop Lonsdale consecrated St John the Evangelist, Charlesworth on 9 October 1849, notwithstanding the opposition of the Independent minister, Robert Wilson, who, inheriting a building which had replaced the former Anglican chapel of St Margaret, 'declared that the bishop only came to rob the people, and that he himself was the Bishop of Charlesworth'!

In 1849 the vicar of Glossop, Christopher Howe, died. He had been incumbent for 56 years and had supported Purcell. The new incumbent, Alexander Thomas Grist Manson, immediately disputed Purcell's right to receive the Easter offering of the people, and pressed him for non-payment of tithes. He took Purcell to the magistrates court where he disputed the legal existence of Charlesworth as a parish. Purcell won the case but only after he had produced his letters of orders (proving his ordination), the bishop's licence of his appointment to the parish, and an attested copy of the conse-cration deed of the church![1] To be opposed by Charlesworth nonconformists in these disputatious times was one thing, to be bitterly challenged by the vicar of Glossop was quite another.

Purcell continued undaunted in his parish, frequently facing opposition. During the long recession in the cotton industry in the 1860s he uncovered corruption among members of the local Cotton Distress and Relief Committee, later noting that under threat of starvation some unemployed men 'had to sign a submission charging themselves with crimes of which they were not guilty.'[2]

Many of the mission churches built by the Church of England in these years were substantial, the Colliery School Mission Room in Tibshelf, as we have noted, provided 400 sittings in 1884, more than in the parish church. The speed of their provision was remarkable. At Clay Cross the parish church of St Bartholomew was built in 1852, with the mission churches of Handley St Mark, Danesmoor St Barnabas, and Stretton St James following in 1871, 1883 and 1899. At Norton Woodseats, St Paul's, erected in 1877, was soon joined by Derbyshire Lane Mission Room, and St Chad's, built in 1912, by Broxholme Mission Room. In Ilkeston the 13th century parish church of St Mary's was

---

[1] G. Purcell, *Church Management in the Present Day* (D. Woodhead, Glossop, 1874), 9, 14, 15, 52–3, 59–61.
[2] ibid., 112.

joined in 1887 by Holy Trinity, and in 1911 by the church of St John the Evangelist. The Larklands Mission was provided in 1908. St Bartholomew's, Hallam Fields was built in 1896, with a stipend for a clergyman provided by the Stanton Iron Works Co. The Bridge Mission attached to St John's followed in 1912. In Bolsover, the 11th century St Mary's was served by an incumbent and two assistant curates who conducted worship in the parish church and in the five mission rooms and churches that had doubled Anglican provision in the parish since 1884. In 1912 these five missions taught 931 children in their Sunday schools compared to 377 in the parish church. The parish of Staveley had its 14th century parish church of St John Baptist, a chapel-of-ease at Handley opened in 1838, and the mission church of St Andrew, Barrow Hill in 1894. The chapel-of-ease of St Peter, Woodthorpe was built in 1632 and the Speedwell mission room, the Seymour mission room, the Mastin Moor mission room and Poolsbrook St Alban's mission church were provided in 1891, 1888, 1914 and 1894 respectively. Together, these eight churches provided Anglican accommodation for 2610 for a parish population of 12018 in 1911, up from 9363 in 1901.

There are many examples like these. Yet such was the speed and concentration of population growth in the county, particularly in the north, that *with fewer churches the Church of England provided more accommodation in 1884 as a percentage of population than in 1911.* In 1884 the Church of England provided places in its churches for 25% of the population. By 1911 this had reduced to 18.5%. Church expansion and increased numbers of clergy had not kept pace with population growth despite great faithfulness, great effort, episcopal leadership of a high order and much expenditure of money. The nonconformist denominations were also providing numerous chapels as we have seen. The combined effect of population growth outpacing Anglican provision of churches and clergy, competition from nonconformity, and (and this was perhaps the most important factor but impossible yet to quantify) a slowly growing indifference to organised religion by all sections of the population, had just begun to show by the eve of the first World War. In 1910 Bishop Hoskyns had called attention to this indifference, and worse, when he spoke of 'the ranks of the indifferent or hostile' which he believed the provision of more churches and clergy would combat.[1]

---

[1] in a pastoral letter quoted in Turbutt, 1583. For an account of the response of the Churches in the south of the county at this time see William Bates, 'The Church's Mission in South Derbyshire and North West Leicestershire 1901–1911', unpublished University of Leicester MA thesis, 1997.

By 1927 the Church of England in Derbyshire could accommodate an estimated 17.4% of the population in its churches had the people wished to come. The numbers in its Sunday schools had declined by 12% since 1914, and although baptisms correlated very closely to the birth rate nationally from the 1880s certainly until the 1960s, this suggests as much custom and social pressure (and, frankly, a measure of superstition) as conviction. Similarly the number of Confirmation candidates in this period correlate closely with the baptism returns 14 or 15 years earlier.[1] We will consider this and other statistical evidence later but the Derbyshire evidence confirms Maurice Halbwachs' contention that 'the expansion of religious communities' results 'most often from trends and movements affecting the entire population.'[2] The religion of the Incarnation has nothing to fear from this, but the implications for the Church's understanding of its mission and ministry, particularly when church expansion becomes church closure, can be disturbing. But we must return to 1914.

The Church and the first World War

The central years of Bishop Hoskyns' long episcopate were dominated by the first World War. He encouraged the clergy to take their ministry to soldiers and their families very seriously. In September 1914 he visited local Territorial regiments training in Bedfordshire and Norfolk. On 1 November 1914, in a moving letter, he bade farewell to the Territorial regiments from Nottinghamshire and Derbyshire embarking for France: the Sherwood Foresters, the Sherwood Rangers, the South Notts Hussars and the Derbyshire Yeomanry.

In November 1915, the bishop reported to his diocesan conference that 20 diocesan clergy were serving as chaplains, a number which was to grow to 26 by August 1916, with four other diocesan clergy serving as combatants. Together with other diocesan bishops, Bishop Hoskyns did not encourage his clergy to volunteer, for

> It is imperative that our younger Clergy should stick to their posts, unless specially released for Chaplain's work. Whilst laymen can do Army

---

[1] Robert Currie, Alan Gilbert, Lee Horsley, *Churches and Churchgoers; Patterns of Church growth in the British Isles since 1700*, (Oxford 1977), 47, 51.
[2] quoted in Currie, et al, ibid., 46.

Service Corps or canteen work, no one can take their place in the spiritual campaign in our cities and colliery villages.[1]

Many of his clergy felt otherwise. Of the 26 clergy serving as chaplains in August 1916 there were 18 assistant curates, six incumbents and one priest from the Society of the Sacred Mission[2] at Kelham in Nottinghamshire, together with the domestic chaplain of Lord Saville of Rufford Abbey. The majority of those who had been (and remained) parish clergy came from the industrial towns. Of the ten chaplains who had served in Derbyshire parishes two had been curates together at Derby St Thomas, and others had served in Ilkeston at St John's and at Holy Trinity, and at Heanor, Derby St James, Chesterfield, North Wingfield, Winster and Turnditch. J.P. Hales, the assistant diocesan inspector of schools was awarded the DSO, and A.C.F. Freeman, assistant curate of Ilkeston St John, the MM, both in 1917. Of the four clergy who had volunteered as combatants two had served in Derbyshire. A.L. Rose, another curate of Ilkeston Holy Trinity, served with the Notts and Derbys Reserve 1914–16, and J.C. Carter, an assistant master at Repton School, served from 1914–19 with the Royal Berkshires.

In January 1916 the *Southwell Diocesan Magazine*, which was circulated to the clergy, listed the names of 178 sons and brothers of diocesan clergy who were serving with the armed forces, and for the remainder of the war few months passed without a sad note of a clergy family bereft, or of a Reader killed in action.

Inevitably in Bishop Hoskyns' pastoral letters in the *Southwell Diocesan Magazine* between 1914 and 1918 there are frequent references to the war, its implications for priestly ministry, and calls for the prayers of the congregations. It was the parishes from which young men, some only boys, went to war that supported them most directly, as the remarkable story of the priest and people of Derby St Michael between 1914 and 1919 shows.[3] But not only that parish. In April 1918 Bishop Hoskyns noted that he had received a petition from a colliery village asking that he should not remove their parish priest for chaplaincy duties as he was in touch with 350 'boys at the front'. He told of another parish priest who sent over 500 letters every two weeks to young servicemen, and who received 25 to 30 letters daily from them expressing

---

[1] 'Supply of Clergy', *Southwell Diocesan Magazine*, March 1916.
[2] a religious community founded by H.H. Kelly in 1891 in order to provide free training for ordination (initially for work overseas) 'with no half-baked gentility.'
[3] further to this see M.R. Austin (ed), *Almost Like a Dream* (Merton Priory Press 1999).

gratitude for the ministry offered to their families.[1] There were many other clergy and congregations showing the same pastoral care.

By January 1918, though still concerned that the parishes should be adequately staffed, Bishop Hoskyns had been compelled to respond to an urgent appeal for chaplains. He had nominated 30 more clergy for instant or future appointment, and noted that this would bring the list of chaplains from the diocese to 85, out of about 190 diocesan clergy of military age. This required, he said, that many parishes would have to be content with only one service each Sunday, and that laymen, other than lay Readers, should be prepared to read morning and evening prayer and, if necessary, read an authorised sermon as was 'a common custom in the colonies.' This 'temporary expedient' might turn out for the Church's good for 'our good and godly laymen may rise to a keener sense of their priesthood in the Church.'[2] This 'temporary expediency', and somewhat grudgingly rediscovered theology of ministry, were to be significant.

Bishop Hoskyns greeted the armistice with the conviction that God had triumphed, for 'thus was God justified, and all those doubts which found expression during the War were scattered. The God of Righteousness and Justice had revealed Himself, and the great soul of the nation responded to His call'[3]- but at what dreadful cost.

---

[1] Report in the *Nottingham Guardian* reprinted in the *Southwell Diocesan Magazine*, May 1918.
[2] *Southwell Diocesan Magazine,* February 1918.
[3] ibid., December 1918.

12

'They shall not return to us': the years 1917–1927

On 30 October 1917, just a week before the Third Battle of Ypres ended, the battle called Passchendaele, the *Derby Daily Telegraph* carried its usual daily coverage of the war on this and other fronts. In France there had been artillery exchanges at Chavignon and Pargny, and Nancy had again been bombed. In Belgium the river Meuse was once more the scene of heavy shelling. German forces had advanced but had been counter-attacked and driven back. Belgian troops had attacked enemy positions north and south of Dixmunde and captured 50 prisoners. On the Russian front there had been heavy enemy bombardment in the Skuti region. Italy's military situation, and its cabinet, were in crisis. In the Balkans brisk artillery fire was reported on the Macedonian and Dobrudja fronts. It was even reported that Brazil had declared war on Germany, and that the cost of the war to the Austrian economy was 'unbearable.' The newspaper's daily roll of honour listed the names of four officers of the Sherwood Foresters who had been killed, together with those of no less than 22 other local men, members of other corps and regiments, who had been killed or wounded or were missing or had been taken prisoner in recent days. In another report it was acknowledged that 'these were dark hours' for the Allies.

'Passengers on the ship'

In adjoining columns on the same page, and in the sharpest of contrasts, the newspaper carried an account of the Southwell Diocesan Conference which had been held a day or so earlier in the Albert Hall in Derby. The debate in the morning session was on a proposal for a greater measure of self-government for the Church of England. The background to this discussion was the 1916 *Report on the Relations between Church and State*. This report was to be followed in 1919 by the so-called 'Enabling Act', that is, the Church of England Assembly (Powers) Act, the provisions of which closely followed the recommendations of the 1916 report and which was to authorise the Church of England 'to deliberate on all matters concerning the Church of England and to make provision thereof.'

There is no doubt at all that this modest reform was brought about by the war, though it was far from being as fundamental a change as some had wished. Army chaplains, and a considerable number of parochial clergy and laity, recognised that the Church of England needed radical reform. Public perception of the Church of England had inevitably been deeply affected by the war.[1] Confidence in the Church of England as the guardian of the nation's moral conscience had, for very many, been undermined by the readiness with which its bishops (as had Edwyn Hoskyns) had greeted the outbreak of the war, and had celebrated its ending, as a crusade for God and his righteousness. Soldiers had asked whether God was honoured by so much appalling slaughter.[2]

In face of this what could the Church of England do? At least, many believed, it could listen to its own people and allow them a role in its government. In March of that same year, 1917, a small group of influential clergy and laymen, including William Temple and Dick Sheppard, met to discuss how reform in the Church of England could be carried forward. These meetings resulted in the 'Life and Liberty' movement, the aim of which was 'to win for the Church the liberty essential to fullness of life'. It made radical proposals: the equalisation of clerical stipends, the ending of the parish system, and the establishment of a volunteer force of mission priests to re-evangelise England. In 1917 its Council reported that many returning army chaplains were 'almost in despair' at the failure of the Church to respond adequately to the challenge it faced in the modern world.

The Life and Liberty movement reflected in the Church of England the recognition of the need for widespread social reform and post-war reconstruction. The war had revealed major shortcomings in the education

---

[1] For a cogent analysis see Alan Wilkinson, *The Church of England and the First World War* (SCM edition 1996), especially chapter 10.

[2] see, for example, Sapper Caleb Fletcher's letter in June 1915, in M.R. Austin (ed), *Almost Like a Dream*, (1999), 17–18.

system, in welfare provision, in fiscal policy, in the status of women, and in other areas of social life. The experience of managing the war had shown governments what could be achieved in a short time by resolute intervention. Above all, ordinary people now knew that they could influence national policy. To a degree, therefore, the leaders of Life and Liberty were pushing at a half-open door. Yet by 1920 their more exciting and far-reaching proposals had been rejected, save only their plea for a greater degree of self-government for the Church of England.

The 1916 report had itself proposed fundamental changes in Church government, and, by now, the need for change was recognised, though many feared that reform of the Church's franchise would lead to disestablishment. While, in the event, the legislated changes were much more conservative than those hoped for by the Life and Liberty movement, for many outside the Church it seemed that the Church of England had responded to criticism of its role in the war by resort to trivialities. Yet the modest reforms which were to extend the Church's franchise were far-reaching.

At the meeting of his diocesan conference in October 1917 the bishop of Southwell was outspoken on the issue. Calling for greater involvement of the laity in the government of the Church, he said that 'laymen in the past have been ecclesiastical paupers – passengers on the ship instead of members of the crew'. This was a proverbial preaching to the now already half-converted. The vicar of Derby St James, Herbert Ham (later to become vicar of All Saints and the first provost of Derby), argued that 'working men' (what the bishop had earlier called 'Labour') were now accustomed to a degree of self-government and 'the Church would never win them back, or retain them, by a system which refused them a real voice and influence in the conduct of affairs.' This was met with applause, the *Derby Daily Telegraph* reported. The Revd W.H. Green (Derby All Saints) was also in favour of a much wider franchise for the Church of England. This should be, he argued, 'a baptismal franchise' though he tempered his enthusiasm by adding the caveat: 'together with a declaration that the elector belonged to the Church of England and no other.' The resolution to support the extension of the Church of England's franchise was carried unanimously.

'For the greater effectiveness of the Church'

The debate in the afternoon of the conference concerned the proposed division of the diocese to create a diocese for Derbyshire.[1] As we have seen, this move had been suggested within a year or so of the formation of the diocese of Southwell in 1884. It had then received little support from Derbyshire clergy and laity. But the world had been turned upside down since. Bishop Hoskyns proposed 'That, for the greater effectiveness of the Church in this diocese, it is expedient that preparatory steps should be taken for the formation of a diocese for each of the counties of Nottinghamshire and Derbyshire.' He pulled few punches. The *Derby Daily Telegraph* summarised his argument like this:

> Recalling the events which led to the formation of the present diocese in 1884, the Bishop pointed out that no regard was had to such important matters as finance and patronage, and the extraordinary position was created that the Bishop of Manchester had in his gift 16 livings in [this] diocese, which was the seventh largest in the kingdom. He had always felt as if his hands were tied behind his back when he tried to cope with the situation. He had endeavoured to do his best, but the task was one which no man could perform (Hear, hear.) He might be reminded of the existence of a suffragan bishop, but no suffragan bishop met the need. The bishop must have jurisdiction and freedom for initiative, which could not be secured under the system of appointing a suffragan. The questions he wished to place before the conference were whether they believed that the principle of a diocese of two hundred and fifty parishes was correct – the number laid down as a standard by the Archbishops' Committee was 300 – whether the principle of division should be in county areas, and whether it would be for the effectiveness of the Church that a new diocese should be formed.
>
> If the feeling was in favour of the proposal he would do all he could to make it feasible and to carry it out. There was no case in England in which the formation of a new diocese was so easy, because there were no geographical or historical complications, and he could conceive no difficulty if they set their faces towards the goal (Hear, hear.) Preparatory steps would include the setting up of a collegiate church in Derbyshire, and of a consultative body, which he would suggest should consist of seven members of the [Southwell] Cathedral Chapter, 15

---

[1] An Archbishop's Committee, formed to consider the needs of the larger dioceses, reported in 1915 in favour of the division of the diocese of Southwell at the earliest possible time.

clergy elected in rural deaneries, and 48 laity belonging to the conference
and elected in rural deaneries, with power to co-opt ten others. The sole
objective in view would be the greater effectiveness of the Church's work.

The archdeacon of Derby, E.S. Noakes, seconded the proposal. He said that
only ten English dioceses were larger in area than Southwell. More to the
point, he noted, the population of Derbyshire and Nottinghamshire had
totalled 853000 in 1884 but had grown to 1,320000 by 1917. With the
populations of the two counties being approximately equal this meant that the
population of each was now nearly as great as that of the whole diocese of
Southwell in 1884. The population increase alone was greater than the
populations of nine English dioceses.

The debate then took a perhaps inevitable turn to issues of territorial (and
even tribal and class) rights and identity. Archdeacon Crosse of Chesterfield
advanced the claim of Chesterfield parish church as the cathedral of the new
diocese 'in a racy speech', the *Derby Daily Telegraph* reported, 'which was
frequently interrupted by cries of dissent.' With the morning debate clearly
in his mind he argued that there was truth in the confession that the Church
was not in touch with 'the labouring and industrial classes' and was
associated more with 'the better classes and the landed gentry.' Now, he
said, there was a chance in Derbyshire to make the Church of England the
Church of the labouring classes and of commercial and industrial enterprise
in the county.

Changing the ground of his argument to no less sensitive territory,
Archdeacon Crosse, the *Derby Daily Telegraph* reported, said that in the
north of the county

> they were going to have nothing to do with the putrid, narrow stream of
> party spirit at which wild asses quenched their thirst. (Laughter.) If it was
> suggested to make the collegiate church [and therefore the new
> cathedral] one that was in the gift of a narrow party society[1], the north
> would down tools over the job straight away.

He believed it would be to the great advantage of the county for the
conference to decide forthwith that it was going to have the centre of the
diocese 'right in the middle of the industrial works.' To this there was both

---

[1] a reference to Derby All Saints, then in the patronage of the evangelical Simeon's Trustees.

applause and rival cries of 'Derby'. Archdeacon Crosse said that he would not say where that centre should be, to which there was more laughter, but that

> all he knew was that where he lived he was in day to day contact with the leaders of all the industrial and commercial enterprises of the county, and that all the great Labour meetings were held there. Owing to the rectitude of its great leaders Chesterfield stood out as the centre – (cries of "No") – where there had been no strike during the war (Loud laughter.) He claimed that Chesterfield Church was the most beautiful in the county.

Before W.H. Green could put in a claim for Derby All Saints as the new cathedral the bishop of Southwell ruled that the question should be confined to the principle and that the question of the new cathedral be left for further consideration. An amendment proposed by Mr. W.H. Edmunds of Chesterfield that the proposal be submitted to parish and ruridecanal conferences as a preliminary to its further consideration was defeated by an overwhelming majority. The resolution was carried.

It has been important to set out the debate as the local Press reported it. The length and detail of the report, even in a broadsheet like the *Derby Daily Telegraph,* suggests an interest in church affairs not matched eighty-five years later.

There were therefore four principal arguments for the division of the diocese of Southwell: the financial and patronage problems bequeathed to the diocese on its formation in 1884 which inhibited the bishop in the exercise of his jurisdiction and hindered freedom of initiative; the geographical area of the diocese, a problem seen as more important than the number of its parishes and which the appointment of a suffragan bishop did little to ease; the ease, geographically, with which a new diocese for Derbyshire could be formed; and the virtual doubling of the population of Derbyshire and Nottinghamshire since the 1880s.

This last point alone would have carried the argument. As Archdeacon Crosse implied it was not merely population growth that made Southwell so unwieldy a diocese, but rather the very considerable additional industrialisation in the north of the county consequent on the rapid development of the Nottinghamshire – Derbyshire coalfield. The social contours of the county had changed. But it was one thing for the Church of England to adjust its administrative boundaries to take note of this; it was another, as Archdeacon Crosse implied, for it to change its own social contours also.

It took ten years following that overwhelming vote at the Southwell diocesan conference in 1917 for the resolution to take effect. It took that time to address consequential legal and patronage issues and for Bishop Hoskyns to raise the funds to make the establishment of the new diocese possible.

The decision about the see town (and therefore the name of the new diocese) and the cathedral was soon made. Derby, and its 'Great Church' of All Saints, had an overwhelming claim. The issue of the patronage of All Saints (the right to appoint the provost) was resolved in 1919 by the bishop of Southwell, who was patron of Derby St Werburgh, exchanging with Simeon's Trustees who held All Saints. This caused consternation in the parish and congregation of St Werburgh's whose future incumbents would be evangelicals. Party strife was far from dead.

The day-to-day responsibility for bringing the proposal to fruition was given to Canon Francis John Adams, vicar of St Peter's Mansfield from 1910, and then, from 1918, of Elvaston. He became secretary of the Division of the Diocese Fund in 1923, the year when the Diocese of Southwell [Division] Measure was passed.

The financial target set for the whole diocese to enable the new diocese of Derby to be created was £120000. Of this, £75000 was earmarked for the endowment of the bishop's stipend, £4000 for his residence, £1000 for legal and parliamentary expenses, and £40000 to endow the cathedral chapters in the two dioceses. This latter requirement was eventually, and ill-advisedly, dropped from the Measure. Under a provision of the Measure, patronage of Derbyshire parishes formerly in the hands of the canons of Southwell and transferred to the bishops of Ripon and Manchester in 1840 was returned, while under another provision a temporary arrangement enabled the suffragan bishop of Derby to be paid until the new diocese was formerly inaugurated.

By the beginning of 1923 the sum raised was about £7000, but Canon Adams had increased this to £27000 by the year's end. By the time that Derby All Saints was hallowed as the cathedral of the new diocese the fund stood at £73811 of which the parishes of the diocese of Southwell had raised £51000 (with £29000 from Derbyshire) with the remainder coming from personal donations. The Ecclesiastical Commissioners made a grant of £6000, their first ever grant for the founding of a new diocese under recently passed legislation. Canon Adams was to become the first secretary of the Derby Diocesan Board of Finance.

'The Church has become hypochondriac'

The end of the war in November 1918 brought high hopes. The promise that this country could be made fit for the returning heroes to live in was widely accepted. This conviction, based on little more than a sense of relief that the war was over at last, rapidly and inevitably turned to disappointment and then to disillusion. The political and economic realities were such that the promise could not be delivered. In November 1918 it would have seemed inconceivable that within a few years very many of those heroes, wearing their medals, would be selling matches from the gutters of city streets. In 1917 a grieving father, Rudyard Kipling, had bitterly attacked those who had led so many young men to their deaths:

> They shall not return to us, the resolute, the young,
> The eager and whole-hearted whom we gave:
> But the men who left them thriftily to die in their own dung,
> Shall they come with years and honour to the grave?[1]

There seemed no honour for those they led who had survived, and who were now begging in the streets.

What of the wider Church? The story of English Christianity in these years and for much of the period of the history of the diocese of Derby has been fully and perceptively told by Adrian Hastings in his *A History of English Christianity 1920–1985*. What is important here is to catch a glimpse of the Church and the way it was seen to be relating to the world locally at the time that the diocese was being formed. For that we turn again to the local newspapers. What follows is highly selective. It serves merely to give some idea of how the Churches locally, and Christianity generally, were perceived.

Did those men of Kipling's poem – the resolute, the young, the eager and whole-hearted – that were not slaughtered and that did return to Blighty return to the Church? If some did, it was said, it was no thanks to the Churches. On 24 April 1918 in a report headed 'Soldiers and Religion: The

---

[1] from *Mesopotamia 1917.*

wrong way to save the Church' the *Derby Daily Telegraph* covered the annual assembly in Manchester of the Baptist Union. The new president, the Revd J.E. Roberts, told the assembly that though for the Church to attempt to stop the war with an uplifted hand, as a London policeman stops the traffic, was useless, the Church had indeed failed the nation for she had not built up barriers strong enough to restrain the war spirit. We were now, he said, paying for this failure, for

> Tommy's invective about the churches was hair-raising in its directness and its shattering simplicity. It was worse than bombing. One dominant fact emerged. The churches as the mouthpiece of organised religion had given an altogether too narrow an interpretation to religion.

He continued:

> It is perfectly clear that any definition of religion is inadequate and misleading which claims people as religious because they go to church and repeat creeds and sing hymns, though they are selfish and proud and grasping, but which denies religion to men who are brave and kind and self-sacrificing because they swear and drink or because they spend Sunday in a different way from us. The men of Britain are ripe for a real religion.

He then offered a reason for this mis-definition. The Churches had defined Christianity in terms sponsored by their own self-centredness and self-interest:

> We have become the victims of the idea that the way to save the Church is to coddle it. The Church has become hypochondriac. It is always feeling its own pulse, consulting statistical charts, putting out its tongue in front of a looking glass, dosing itself with the drugs of religious quacks, and coddling itself within its closed buildings by the fires of self-satisfaction, when it ought to have found its health out in the open air of the world, hard at work building the city of God.

Coincidentally, the newspaper carried alongside this account reports of the death of Manfred von Richthofen, the most celebrated air ace of the First World War; of the shooting to death of a British prisoner-of-war in a closed guard room in the POW camp at Chemnitz; of the publication of a booklet, *Everybody's Guide to Rations*, issued because of 'the bewildering number of food orders'; of the sinking of a German submarine by depth charges; of a session of the Chesterfield Borough Military Tribunal which had sat for three hours 'without getting a single man for the army'; and the daily, and still lengthy, list of local men killed, missing and wounded in action. Taken together, Roberts' invective and the war reports make a very powerful point.

That was the world in which the Church was set. J.E. Roberts's forthright reaction to what he saw as the Church's inability to engage with that world was both socially perceptive and theologically acute. Locally, the response of the Churches to the world was good-hearted but naive. Early in November 1919 a 'Forward Campaign' was initiated at Normanton Road Congregational Church. The Revd Tolefree Parr said that

> it was in the nature of men and women to seek Christ . . . . Some sought satisfaction in earthly Christs – money, pleasure, art, music, great ideals and human love – none of which satisfied the soul of man. Nothing lower than the spiritual could satisfy a spiritual being, and nothing less than God could satisfy the children of God.

A few days earlier, at a time when English Methodism was moving slowly towards the unity that it achieved in 1932, the United Methodist Church of Derby was addressed by the president of the Methodist Conference, the Revd John Moore. He too was concerned that the greatest problem of church life was what he called 'coddling saints' but his response was altogether more ingenuous than that of J.E. Roberts. 'Religion', John Moore said, 'must be the basis of the reconstruction of man. Men must be told the old, old, story and they would respond', an unqualified assertion greeted with applause. Reactions like these, while perhaps asserting fundamental truths, were far too vague and imprecise and lacking in theological sharpness, social awareness and practical application to win hearts and minds in the immediate aftermath of the bloodiest war in history.

'Certain facts of history' and the call for Christian unity

One sign of hope was the impetus that the first World War gave to the movement for Christian unity. As Methodists sought to unite, so a wider ecumenical movement appeared to be gathering some momentum. It seemed that the war had convinced many that what the Churches could not do separately, as J.E. Roberts had said, in restraining the war spirit, they must try to do together in contributing to the peace. Their divisions called into question the peace and unity that they had prayed for and that all craved.

In a very significant initiative, the 1920 Lambeth Conference called for Christian unity in its *Appeal to all Christian People.* A representative meeting of the Free Churches in Derbyshire met in Bakewell in November of that year. It discussed the proposals for reunion set out by the Lambeth Conference. The Bakewell discussion was remarkable both for its generosity of spirit and the integrity of its conclusions. While 'rejoicing in the spirit that breathes through the appeal issued by the bishops' and with them deploring the divisions of Christian people, the final resolution of the meeting criticised the vagueness of the Lambeth proposals; the 'largeness' of the episcopal claim 'considered in the light of certain facts of history'; the Lambeth requirement of re-ordination of nonconformist ministers as a precondition for unity, given 'the scale and fruits of non-episcopal ministries'; and the difficulty of uniting churches 'the very existence [of which] is in some sense a protest against the injustice and hurtfulness of the State tie.' This remarkable resolution concluded by calling on Derbyshire's Free Churches to 'consider well what lengths of sacrifice, short of surrender of principle, they will go in the interests of the reunion suggested.' Many of the key social and theological issues inhibiting Christian unity are set out there. They still wait to be resolved.

'Two relentless conditions': theology and social issues

As the first World War gave an impetus to a reform of the government of the Church of England, and to the movement for Christian unity, so it awakened the Churches to a greater awareness of their social responsibilities.

In 1918 the Derby United Christian Council, representing most of the Derby churches, had been formed 'to work for closer fellowship and co-operation in the work of the kingdom of God.' In October 1924 the Council's chairman, the Revd Thomas Rook, minister of Victoria Street Congregational Church, referred to several initiatives undertaken by the Council since 1918: a moral purity campaign in 1921, the establishing of Industrial Christian Fellowships in 1922 and a visit by Cambridge student missioners in 1923. In 1924 the Council had passed a resolution designed to strengthen the Mayor of Derby's attempt to solve the town's housing problem and had arranged a series of lectures on housing, unemployment, education and international peace – subjects arising from the 1924 Conference on Christian Politics, Economics and Citizenship (COPEC) presided over by William Temple.

Canon E.S. Woods, vicar of Holy Trinity, Cambridge, then preached at the Council's annual service in All Saints. He showed social awareness and a consequent theological sharpness. We have to face the fact, the *Derby Daily Telegraph* reported him saying,

> that the great supernatural life, which is God's intent for every personality, had to be lived out inescapably under two relentless conditions – that it was housed in a human body, and that it was never isolated but always in a group .... At a thousand points, man's life was conditioned by his bodily, physical conditions. How could a man be a satisfactory Christian if he was continuously unemployed and lived in a slum. It was no good to say that the spirit of God triumphed over matter. It was true in a certain sense, but they had to admit that the full growth of personality under those conditions was impossible.

That was a simple statement of the social consequences of accepting the religion of the Incarnation. It was thoroughly biblical. Yet, given all that was written and spoken by Christian social thinkers in these years, the Christian response to social need, locally as nationally, seems so modest. The religion of the affluent can be deaf to the cries of the poor.

But rifts in wider society were too profound to be bridged by comment, even shrewd Christian comment. By 1922 the hopes of so many that the end of the war would bring a better world had been disappointed. The *Derby Daily Telegraph* for 28 October published an article by John Scott Lidgett, a Wesleyan Methodist minister, editor of the *Methodist Times* and regarded by many as the greatest Methodist since Wesley. This moved Christian comment on the economic depression and industrial struggles that had beset Britain from social awareness and theological insight to prophetic declaration. In a long piece headed 'The Hope for the Young' Scott Lidgett shattered the illusion of peace. He argued that the war had come only to its official close in 1918. Since then

> we have had ample opportunity to see that war sows not peace and prosperity but more war; that those who fought together against an alien foe may later in the bitter struggle for existence fight against each other for the right to live as each understands it.

Scott Lidgett pleaded that national policies be put in place that assured lasting prosperity for the young: 'We must see to it that they reap the blessings of peace as we have reaped the sufferings of war.' The post-war struggle between employers and workers 'to live as each understands it' was to culminate in the General Strike which lasted from 4–12 May 1926. This was a response to the lock-out of the miners, a bitter conflict which began on 1 May and was to last until 19 November, and in which the men of the Nottinghamshire and Derbyshire coalfield were deeply involved.

Scott Lidgett was not a lone prophetic voice of course. Many within the Church of England echoed his call for political and social action, yet the Churches could do little more than fulfil their duty to be pastoral and prophetic. Effective social change results from socially acceptable political action. Direct intervention by the Churches in social affairs often has results which are at best equivocal. After the General Strike ended, a group of bishops and leading nonconformists, led by the bishop of Lichfield, J.A. Kempthorne[1], and including William Temple[2], attempted mediation during the continuing miners' strike. The group's proposals for the practical implementation of the Report of the Royal Commission on the Coalmining Industry, which had been published earlier in the year, were rejected by the government, the coal-owners and by the miners' county associations, though, initially, the miners' leaders nationally had accepted them. The group was bitterly criticised for seeming to side with the miners. Though it is debatable whether this intervention in fact prolonged the dispute (it was argued at the time that the miners continued their action because they believed that the Churches supported them), the secretary of the Derbyshire miners, Frank Hall, had no doubt that the proposals of the Kempthorne group would have been carried in Derbyshire.[3] The Churches' attempt at mediation thus came to nothing.

Locally, the public response of the Churches to this deep industrial unrest was muted. On 13 May 1926, at the conclusion of the General Strike, the *Derby Daily Telegraph* published a statement from the Anglican clergy and nonconformist ministers in Derby, signed on their behalf by John Bell and Herbert Ham, chairman and vice-chairman of the Derby United Christian Council. It thanked God for 'the country's deliverance from a grave danger.' While calling for mutual forbearance and understanding and 'a just and

---

[1] chairman of the Christian Social Union, 1911–1920.
[2] the bishop of Manchester and a former headmaster of Repton School (1910–14). He was to become archbishop of York and then of Canterbury.
[3] Report in the *Derbyshire Times*, 7 August 1926.

righteous settlement' of the dispute there was no word of concern in the statement[1] for the cause of the striking workers, not least for the miners whose lock-out had precipitated the General Strike and who were refusing to return to very substantial wage cuts and longer hours – and nor was there from the bishop. Soon after coming to the diocese, the bishop of Southwell, Bernard Heywood, wrote to his clergy in the June issue of the *Southwell Diocesan Magazine.* He observed that the General Strike had been called off on the last Rogation Day of the year, implying that it was an answer to prayer. He could not demonstrate this, he said, but 'faith can trace what is incapable of logical proof.'

The end of the General Strike brought no deliverance for Derbyshire's miners. The same edition of the paper reported Frank Varley, MP for Mansfield and the leader of the Nottinghamshire and Derbyshire miners, describing it as 'a dreadful debacle' and denouncing the TUC for its 'abject surrender'. Local Derbyshire congregations in mining areas supported the striking miners and their families, as they had done in the pit strikes in the late 19th century[2], but the response of the majority of Anglican church leaders was marked more by relief that the General Strike was over than concern for the economic conditions which had led to it and which had still to be addressed.

There were exceptions. On 4 November 1926, two weeks before the miners' strike ended with their defeat, the Southwell Diocesan Conference met in the Temperance Hall in Derby. The afternoon session, on 'The Church and Industrial Disputes', was addressed by Bishop Kempthorne. He admitted that the attempt of his group to bring a solution to the long coal dispute had failed, but, he said, their sole desire had been to make peace. That was the duty of bishops. Hinting at the opposition he and his group had faced, he said: 'We failed, but I do not make any promise that we will not be naughty again . . . . We mean to do our best to work out the principles of the kingdom of God in every part of our common life.'[3] The work of living the religion of the Incarnation could not have been better put.

These are but a few examples of the response of the local Churches to the social and political legacy of the first World War in the decade before the creation of

[1] published in the June issue of the *Southwell Diocesan Magazine.*
[2] Granville Stone, *Strike Action at Swanwick Colliery during the Nineteenth Century* (Derbyshire Record Office, n.d.), 14, 16, 17. See also the call for collections to be taken in places of worship and sent to the District Committees of Relief in the *Southwell Diocesan Magazine* for July 1926.
[3] Report from the *Derbyshire Advertiser* in the *Southwell Diocesan Magazine,* December 1926.

the diocese of Derby in 1927. Much more could be said, not least of the clergy of the Church of England locally in these years. Geoffrey Hare Clayton became vicar of Chesterfield in 1921. Though some bishops condemned what Hensley Henson of Durham called 'Anglo-Catholick lawlessness' in these years, Clayton, rigidly lawful, almost immediately dispensed with matins in Chesterfield parish church on Sundays and replaced it with a choral eucharist with vestments and incense. Clayton was to become a resolute but controversial archbishop of Capetown. In 1917 Alfred Walter Frank Blunt had moved from the parish of Carrington in Nottingham to became vicar of Derby St Werburgh. He was a member of the provisional chapter of Derby Cathedral which formally elected the first diocesan bishop in 1927. Later, as bishop of Bradford, Blunt, in a sermon, questioned the morality of Edward VIII's liaison with Mrs Wallis Simpson. This was picked up by the *Yorkshire Post.* The other national papers broke the silence they had maintained hitherto, and so began the public debate which led eventually to the abdication. There were very many more in these years, by no means all of them clergy, who served the Church in Derbyshire, in high office or very quietly, with deep devotion.

'A not inconsiderable pastoral revolution': the new dioceses

In 1876 a meeting of influential clergy and laypeople meeting in London resolved that the 'spiritual necessities' of the nation required 'a well organised scheme for the increase of the Home Episcopate'. Disraeli was persuaded and his Home Secretary, Richard Assheton Cross, carried through legislation (principally the Bishoprics Act 1878) creating the new dioceses of Truro and St.Albans (both in 1877), Liverpool (1880), Newcastle-on-Tyne (1882), Southwell (1884), and Wakefield (1888). These were followed by Sheffield (1914), Coventry (1918) and Bradford (1919). Similarly the creation by parliament of the Church Assembly in 1919 allowed for the creation of a further five new sees to allow, so it was hoped, the evangelistic and pastoral responsibilities of the Church of England to be better fulfilled. These were to be the last new dioceses to be created in England. They were Blackburn and Leicester in 1926, and Derby, Guildford and Portsmouth in 1927.

Fourteen new dioceses had been created in fifty years, ten of them in the north and the midlands, not, as Adrian Hastings points out, regions where the Church of England was strong. That they were created within a period of fifty years is 'one expression of the not inconsiderable pastoral revolution that the Church of England had been carrying through in an unrevolutionary way.'[1] Hastings suggests that this initiative is evidence that Anglican influence may actually have been increasing in the north central region during this period.

The Measure by which the new diocese of Derby was formed was passed in 1924 and it was constituted by Order in Council in July 1927. The diocese was to be in the province of Canterbury.[2] In the following month Dr Edmund Courtenay Pearce was appointed the first bishop of the new diocese. When the appointment was announced, the bishop of Southwell noted that it was rare to have as a diocesan bishop one who had been both a vice-chancellor of a university and mayor of a borough.[3] The new diocese was composed of the archdeaconries of Derby and Chesterfield and had a population of some 770000. Its constitution was to be ratified by the Privy Council on 7 May 1928 and published in full in the *London Gazette* the next day.

The suffragan bishop of Derby, Bishop Abraham, necessarily had to leave. He became rector of Astbury in Cheshire. Charles Thomas Abraham had spent his entire ministry in the dioceses of Lichfield and Southwell. He became vicar of Bakewell in 1897 and suffragan bishop of Derby in 1909, holding both posts concurrently until 1918. In noting his departure from the diocese the *Derby Daily Telegraph,* in a generally warm tribute that nevertheless somewhat damned the departing bishop with faint praise, said of him that 'in the ecclesiastical sphere he held opinions that were not universally endorsed' yet 'without laying claim to great gifts of scholarship and eloquence' he was 'infinitely human'. This somewhat equivocal tribute concluded: 'we could better have spared a better man.' Bishop Abraham must have spent a few minutes determining whether this was a tribute or not!

The Derbyshire section of the Southwell diocesan conference met for the last time in September 1927. Theological controversies that had raged for many years, even many centuries, raged then as they do today. In that same month in the wider Church, to dash the hopes with which the decade had begun, Christian unity seemed as far away as ever. 'The Deposited Book', the

---

[1] Hastings, op.cit., 194.

[2] In 1935 the diocese of Southwell was returned to the province of York from whence it had been transferred in 1837.

[3] Pearce had been assistant curate of St James, Muswell Hill 1899–1900, vicar of St Benedict, Cambridge 1900–6, a Cambridge town councillor in 1915 and mayor in 1917. He was elected a Cambridge county councillor in 1919 and served as its chairman in 1927. He was Master of Corpus Christi College 1914–1927, and vice chancellor of the University 1921–1927.

fruit of at least seven years of revision of the Book of Common Prayer (prompted by pastoral considerations) was accepted by Convocation and Church Assembly in 1927. An evangelical protest at what was regarded as the Catholic direction of this conservative revision was signed by 30000 people. The Federal Council of the Evangelical Free Churches of England was reported, in the *Derby Daily Telegraph* for 21 September, to have expressed 'grave concern ... in regard to the reservation of the sacramental elements of the Lord's Supper, especially in view of the abuses which are at present so widely prevalent within the Church of England' and which to evangelicals the revised prayer book appeared to countenance. It was an issue which the new bishop of Derby was to confront.

The diocese thus came to its birth in controversial times. A month later the paper reported the public denunciation by Canon Bullock-Webster of St Paul's Cathedral of the bishop of Birmingham, E.W. Barnes, for preaching 'gorilla sermons'[1]. There is evidence here of that narrowness of vision which condemns both religious imagination and scientific enquiry, a narrowness by no means confined to the Church of England. The *Nottingham and Midland Catholic News* for 15 October 1927 launched a bitter attack on Ernest Barnes. A Jesuit priest, Henry Day, cited his opinions on both evolutionary theory and the Real Presence as 'an open confession of the doctrinal bankruptcy of the Established Church.' In the same issue, published a week before the hallowing of Derby cathedral, a leader writer commented on an Anglican conference in Suffolk. The bishop of Southwell, Bernard Heywood, was bitterly attacked for a contribution to the conference in which, in what Anglicans today would regard as a straightforward argument, he defended the historical catholicity of the Church of England. The Reformation, Bishop Heywood argued, was 'not less a political than a religious reformation' and that, in excommunicating Elizabeth, the Pope 'had himself determined the great schism'. This was too much for The *Nottingham and Midland Catholic News*. In a leader headlined 'The Origin of English Protestantism. Gas Escape at Ipswich' it condemned this 'cowardly and malicious piece of episcopal pepper-throwing' by a bishop attempting 'to bolster up That Heresy-Shattered, Schism-Be-smattered, Chaotic Ecclesiastical Wreckage known as the Church of England.' This was

---

[1] referring to E.W. Barnes' unequivocal support for theories of biological evolution, still, at that time, a matter of theological controversy. He was also a strong opponent of the doctrine of transubstantiation. He argued against the second by recourse to the first. Ernest William Barnes D.Sc, F.R.S., was a mathematician, a scientist and a theologian. His book *Scientific Theory and Religion* (1933) made a very significant contribution to the science/religion debate.

the climate of the times, and we may be grateful that the passing of the years has brought a cooling of the theological temperature and a warming of ecumenical relationships.

Bishop Hoskyns, who had brought the new diocese almost to its birth, had died in 1925. On 28 October 1927 the parish church of Derby All Saints was hallowed as the cathedral of the new diocese by his successor, Bishop Bernard Heywood. This was one of the few acts of his brief episcopal ministry in Southwell. The provisional chapter of the new cathedral was then able formally to elect the bishop of the new diocese. It was said that there was 'but a score of the general public' present in the cathedral for the election.

The *Derby and Chesterfield Reporter* fully covered the hallowing of the new cathedral and the enthronement of Edmund Courtenay Pearce as the first diocesan bishop of Derby, its correspondent noting that

> one thing was very evident both during the service and afterwards. The church is by no means adequate to such processional ceremonies. It is not spacious enough, nor is the architectural plan of the east end at all convenient.[1]

In his enthronement sermon Bishop Pearce very readily admitted that he 'had lived for forty years within the walls of a Cambridge College, and that the administration of the life of the Church had been for him largely a sealed book.' It was an ignorance, he said, that was inevitable but not culpable and that he would soon repair. He concluded by quoting from the diary of Elizabeth's first archbishop of Canterbury, Matthew Parker:

> On the 17th of December, in the year 1559, I was consecrated Archbishop of Canterbury; alas, alas, O Lord God, for what times hast Thou kept me. Now am I come into deep waters, and the flood hath overwhelmed me. O Lord, I am oppressed; answer for me and strengthen me with Thy free spirit; give me of thy sure mercies.

With that same anxious confidence the first diocesan bishop of Derby began his ministry, and the new diocese began its life.

It did so in an extraordinary year. In science, Werner Heisenberg propounded

---

[1] 4. 11. 1927. Nor was it until Ronald Beddoes, provost of Derby, so boldly, imaginatively and against some opposition put in place the extensions, completed in 1972, to Sebastian Comper's sensitive design.

the 'uncertainty principle' in quantum physics. In the air Charles Lindbergh flew from New York to Paris in 37 hours. In archaeology Leonard Woolley began his momentous excavation of Ur of Chaldea, the home of Abraham. In philosophy Sigmund Freud published his *The Future of an Illusion* hoping to put religion to flight, and Martin Heidegger his *Being and Time* which few understood but which was to have a profound influence, not least on theology. In politics Adolf Hitler produced the second volume of *Mein Kampf*; in the bookshops Henry Williamson's *Tarka the Otter* was on sale; and in the dance halls the slow fox-trot became something of a craze.

In the first year of the new diocese the voting age for women was reduced from 30 to 21; Alexander Fleming discovered penicillin; and John Logie Baird transmitted television images across the Atlantic. Max Ravel composed *Bolero* in 1928, and Kurt Weil and Bertolt Brecht's *The Threepenny Opera* was first performed. Within months, in May 1929, the first British election under universal adult suffrage was held with the Labour Party returning most members to the House of Commons, but without achieving a majority. In October came the Wall Street Crash and the beginning of the Great Depression which lasted for years. The world became a smaller place, social change more rapid and intense, economic life more unstable, and international politics more dangerous.

13

'As varied a scene as any could wish for': the early years of the diocese of Derby, 1928–1936

'What the parishes are doing'

Extracts from parish magazines in each edition of the *See of Derby Diocesan Magazine* in the early years suggest that the parishes were doing what they had done for very many years, and that the creation of the new diocese had little immediate effect on them. In August 1930 it was reported that the vicar of Chesterfield Christ Church, writing 'at considerable length' in his parish magazine on the question of Sunday games, had argued that 'they were unnecessary, harmful to the Church and the community, and that there was no demand for them'; that the Cathedral had produced a variant of Kipling's *If* adapted for Girl Guides; that the vicar of Littleover had drawn the attention of his congregation to a 2d booklet by H.B. Vaisey, the chancellor of the diocese, on *The Writing of Epitaphs;* that the Band of Hope at Somercotes was to have its annual outing to Rhyl on 5 August; that the July issue of the North Wingfield parish magazine had 'some challenging remarks' on the issues to be discussed at the Lambeth Conference; that at Hallam Fields a Belgian family who had lived in Barrow-on-Trent during the first World War had presented an oak crucifix to the church as a thank offering; that Church Broughton was the latest country parish church in the diocese to create a Children's Corner; that at Kirk Langley a recreation field for children had been put at their disposal by the rector; that the chancel of Wirksworth parish church, under repair for five years, had been reopened by the bishop on 23 June; that open-air mission services were now being held after Evensong every Sunday at St Mark's Mission Church in the parish of Brampton . . . and much else. Modest though this activity seems, all the main concerns of the Church are reflected here: worship, thanksgiving, mission, maintenance, education, social responsibility, and a concern for the wider church. Such was, and is, parish life, the heart of the life of the Church.

Serving the parishes: diocesan organisation

It was to encourage and support this patient, every-day and unpretentious parish ministry that the new diocese had been created in 1927. It had, and still has, no other purpose.

The first secretary of the diocesan Board of Finance, and therefore effectively the first diocesan secretary, was Canon Francis John Adams. He had spent his whole ministry in the diocese of Southwell, being ordained to a curacy in Holbrook and then serving as assistant curate at Derby St Thomas. He became incumbent successively of Sutton-in-Ashfield, Mansfield St Peter, and Elvaston, which last incumbency he held with his new post. As we have noted, much of the practical work of creating the new diocese had fallen to him. He died in 1930. His successor was Harold Boorman, vicar of Derby St Luke, who was to serve until 1962. Both F.J. Adams and Harold Boorman were described by their contemporaries as 'indomitable' and the diocese owes them, and their successors, much.

The progress in establishing a central diocesan organisation can be traced in the *See of Derby Magazine* and in the minutes of the diocesan conference. At the first diocesan conference, held in the Temperance Hall in Derby on 23 February 1928, the bishop regretted that the members would have 'to talk so much about finance' and there was the first of repeated requests to the parishes to 'expedite the sending in of their quotas'! These were unfortunate but inevitable observations. In an appeal in 1931 the bishop was to remind the diocese that it had started work with no balance in hand and in fact had begun its financial existence with an overdraft.

The bishop regretted also that there was as yet no Church House in Derby to send quota payments to, 'and where the Finance Board and other Societies could have their offices and where perhaps a corner could be found' in which he could hold interviews. He had no permanent address and lodged, first, in the diocesan retreat house in Ambergate, and then in the Judges' Lodgings in St

Mary's Gate in Derby ('except, of course, during the Assizes') before eventually moving to Breadsall Mount.

Already there was a shortage of money to achieve everything that the enthusiasts for one cause or another, or even the bishop, wanted to achieve. At this first diocesan conference Bishop Pearce noted that providing a Church House 'was more vital than the beautifying of the Cathedral' and that 'though he admired the type of architecture of All Saints . . . we ought not to prejudge a future generation which might like to follow the example of Liverpool and build a Cathedral of its own'! (He was soon to revise this opinion). Eventually, in the summer of 1929, the diocesan offices found a home at 3, The College, in Derby, the money to purchase the building being raised by a mortgage and the sale of debentures and not by appeal to the parishes and the public.

Very soon a pattern of key diocesan boards and committees was established: finance, education, dilapidations, church extension, overseas missions, ordination candidates, clergy pensions, and, with an eye to good communications, Magazine and Calendar, and reports were prepared by each for the annual diocesan conferences. In this the new diocese was helped by the failure fully to effect a practical union of the two counties and archdeaconries of Nottingham and Derby into one diocese after 1884 and that the old archdeaconry of Derby in the former diocese of Southwell had always retained, virtually, its own accounting systems, education committee and church extension society from the Lichfield days.

The chancellor of the diocese, H.B. Vaisey, regularly reminded the clergy and churchwardens of their legal responsibilities, through the *See of Derby Magazine*. In January 1928 he asked that no work requiring a faculty should be ordered or contracted before a faculty had actually been granted – a plea to be repeated by successive archdeacons, diocesan registrars and chancellors. In September he explained the Tithe (Administration of Trusts) Measure 1928. In February 1929 he explained at length the Benefices (Patronage) Measure; in May he warned that churchwardens who had not been formally admitted to office could be liable for assault if attempting to 'expel a "brawler" or other disorderly person' from the church, but could do so with impunity if they had been; and in July he expanded at length on the importance of publishing banns of marriage. In March 1930 Chancellor Vaisey explained in detail the application of the Adoption of Children Act 1926 as it affected clergy who were asked to solemnise the marriage of an adopted person who was under the age of 21. Prosaic as this may seem, it was, and is, central to the Church of

England's mission that its basis in English law should be clearly recognised and respected. The Church/State relationship has not yet been disassembled.

In these ways the central organisation of the new diocese supported and encouraged the clergy and the parishes as they worshipped, preached the Gospel, and engaged with, and ministered to, the society of which they were a part and in which they were set. They were soon to be subjected to episcopal scrutiny.

The varied scene: the bishop's visitation, 1929

In April 1929, less than two years after his appointment as bishop of Derby, Edward Courtenay Pearce carried out a primary visitation. He circulated articles of enquiry, and, on the basis of the replies, delivered his first visitation Charge to his diocese. The diocese comprised, he said, 260 parishes with 724000 people in a geographical area of 650000 acres which was virtually the same as that of the administrative county of Derbyshire. He said that

> In few dioceses are there such varied commercial interests: all up the Erewash valley, and again in the south-west, on the Leicestershire border, are the coal mines; in the north are the limestone quarries and kilns; in the Glossop district are the cotton and paper mills; there are some sporadic lead-mines with temporary phases of activity; in the south and west are agricultural districts, mostly given up to milk-production; in Derby we have the works of the L.M.S, and of the Rolls-Royce Company, with Celanese close by; and in Matlock, Buxton and Dovedale are holiday resorts. From north to south the Diocese is 56 miles long, with Derby almost at the southern extremity; north-wards it comes within about four miles of Sheffield, and with appreciable nearness to Manchester; and any Sunday you can meet from these big cities hundreds of young people, boys and girls, sometimes so dressed alike that it is difficult to distinguish the sexes, tramping over the moors and through the Hope valley. That is roughly the scene of our labours; it is as varied a scene as any could wish for.

Openly referring to recent enmities the bishop noted that the creation of the new diocese meant that 'a greater concentration of energy and a more helpful supervision of the parishes' was possible than before: 'Nottinghamshire and Derbyshire were not quite so mutually exclusive as the Jews and the

Samaritans, but county patriotisms did not run well in harness and Derbyshire, quite naturally, did not appreciate being run from Nottingham.'

Bishop Pearce listed the immediate tasks to be faced: among what he called 'desiderata' he noted the provision of 'an adequate business home for the Diocese'. This was soon achieved. Another concerned the cathedral. He hoped to establish a choir school and provide a verger's house, together, he hoped, with 'a rest room for the Clergy and their families, where they could get lunch and tea and feel that they had a place of their own'. He planned, too, to establish two endowed canonries in the cathedral to which could be appointed men who would undertake a full-time diocesan ministry. These objectives were to take many years to achieve. In a major appeal he was to make in 1931 to meet 'ultimate needs' in the diocese, the bishop asked for £40000 to provide an extended chancel for the cathedral; to erect a choir school and to build a new organ; and to pay off the £1000 of debt that still remained four years after the modest improvement to Derby All Saints undertaken in 1927. He hoped that an additional £20000 could be raised to endow the two full-time canonries he wanted 'for the more efficient working of the Diocese.' The bishop was to acknowledge then that discontent with the choice of Derby All Saints as the cathedral still lingered but he hoped that 'there will in time grow up a feeling of satisfaction about keeping All Saints' as the Cathedral, and also that it is worth spending a good deal of money upon it to make it really worthy as the Mother Church of the Diocese.'[1]

But these were relatively marginal items. In his 1929 Charge, after these 'desiderata', Bishop Pearce listed the immediate and essential tasks facing the new diocese as these: the provision of churches and clergy for new centres of population with a consequent reorganisation of parish boundaries; the recruitment and training of clergy; the Christian education of children and adults; worship, especially in the light of the revision of the Prayer Book; and clergy stipends and pensions. Every one of these, directly or indirectly, touched on the concerns of the parishes that we noted earlier. Bishop Pearce had much to say about each.

'The prime duty': the provision of churches

'The prime duty of the Church is to minister to the people, and to provide the

---

[1] Appeal made at the diocesan conference, 21 April 1931, reported in the *See of Derby Magazine*, June 1931.

means of doing so as conveniently as possible' said the bishop. He listed areas in and around Derby alone where more churches and clergy were needed: the Nottingham Road end of the parish of Chaddesden, and the new Corporation housing on the Uttoxeter Road (which he described as those 'colonies of subsidy houses' in a kind of 'No Man's Land . . . where St Luke's, Mickleover and Mackworth join'). In addition, 'Allenton calls aloud for help.' He repeated Bishop Hoskyn's lament in 1915: 'I could spend £50000 upon Derby tomorrow, without wasting a penny upon luxuries.' St Bartholomew's, built near to the Rolls Royce works, was 'the only contribution that has been made to meet the problem' and that church was burdened with a large debt 'which ought to have been liquidated before consecration.' And then there was Chesterfield, where 'the building of St Augustine's Church is long overdue.' In 1931 the bishop was to indicate other places where churches and clergy were urgently needed.

'A serious lack of men': the recruitment of clergy

A second and related essential task was the recruitment and training of clergy. The bishop noted one 'appalling fact' – that one parish clergyman has to attempt alone 'to deal with a population of from 10000 to 15000'. In a county that, forty years previously, had been served by 327 Anglican clergy, there were now 293 clergy, though the population had more than doubled. He was to return to the issue of clergy recruitment two years later.

The Church of England's annual *Official Year Book* for the 1930s shows how relatively under-provided with clergy the new diocese was. For example, in 1937 the home counties' diocese of St Albans, with a population 20% less than that of the diocese of Derby, was served by 15% more parochial clergy in 18% more parishes. Its Easter communicants were 12% higher in 1935 and represented 8.3% of its population, compared with 5.8% in the diocese of Derby.

The difficulty of clergy recruitment was primarily the result of the ever present problem of finance, but was made worse by the inefficiency with which their recruitment and deployment was hampered, in Bishop Pearce's opinion, by the acquisition of patronage by party trusts. This was, he said, 'a most unhealthy sign that there should be before us the possible perpetuation of extreme views in both directions in our midst.' He was concerned that only some 62 of the 260 benefices in the diocese were in the gift of the bishop.

'A most vital problem': Church day schools

The third immediate task facing the diocese had to do with education. In his address to his first diocesan conference Bishop Pearce had commented on the importance of the church schools in the diocese. He returned to the theme here with the longest section of his Charge being devoted to it. What kind of religious education should be given in state schools? Was the Church/State dual system working well? (On the whole, yes). Should the Church have right of entry into state schools to give denominational education to Church children? (No, the NUT would never support it). How is it that a great number of Church schools have been either closed or transferred to state control? (Partly for educational and partly for financial reasons). The bishop was glad that the standard of education was rising, with a government policy (Board of Education Circular 1397) which would reduce class sizes in senior schools to 40 and in elementary schools to 50. This would entail the Church in much expense because it would require the re-modelling of the accommodation in many of its schools.

'Stopping the leakage': Sunday schools and adult education

A fourth priority facing the new diocese was to provide Sunday schools of quality; to stem the loss of young people from church worship after Confirmation; to promote adult Christian education through the Church Tutorial Class movement (which was based on the methods and organisation of the Workers' Educational Association); and 'to restore the educative power of the home.'

'The chain of worship': church services and state control

Bishop Pearce turned next to the worship of the Church, a fifth and fundamental priority. He noted that though in many churches Morning and Evening Prayer were said daily there were obviously some in which this was not so. There were still churches where there was no regular celebration of holy Communion on Sundays. He warned against 'sudden changes and innovations in services, for which [the people] had not been prepared and for which they need to be educated.' In particular – and here he was clearly commenting on anglo-catholic practice – he was concerned that in some parishes at the choral eucharist the invitation, confession and absolution were deliberately omitted, and there was no communion for the congregation.

Bishop Pearce then again addressed an issue that was absorbing much of the Church's energy at the time. He noted that much use was being made in the diocese of the newly revised Prayer Book. This had been approved by Church Assembly with large majorities in July 1927 (and previously by large majorities in the Convocations of Canterbury and York) and also by the House of Lords, but had been rejected by the Commons in December 1927. A second Church Assembly Measure proposing the use of an amended revised Prayer Book, designed to meet Protestant objections, was rejected by the Commons by a somewhat larger majority in June 1928. However, the so-called 'Deposited Book' (so named because it had been deposited with the Clerk of the Parliaments in June 1927) was published with the clear statement that its publication 'does not directly or indirectly imply that it can be regarded as authorized for use in churches.' It was to be widely used.

In his Charge Bishop Pearce addressed the key issue of theological contention in the debate about the revised Prayer Book. He said that the reservation of the sacrament in one kind only (that is, the consecrated bread or Host reserved for purposes of adoration and not primarily for the communion of the sick) would never meet with his approval (though in this he was not to be consistent). The proposed revision of the Prayer Book allowed for continuous reservation of consecrated bread *and wine* for the purpose of communion for the sick. This was being interpreted by the more extreme anglo-catholic clergy as implying permission to promote the adoration of Christ in the sacrament (and this, for their evangelical opponents, was explicit Romanism), even though the House of Bishops, in 1926, had specifically declared against services with this object. Clearly this was an issue for some diocesan clergy and congregations at the time. It is impossible to know for how many, though there was a daily celebration of holy Communion in 20 churches in Derbyshire in 1928[1] and opposition to a strict episcopal line would probably have come from among these parishes.

The final defeat by the House of Commons of the Prayer Book measure in June 1928 caused much concern. It touched on a basic issue. Can a secular Parliament determine the doctrines of the established Church as enshrined in its Prayer Book? In September 1928 the *See of Derby Diocesan Magazine*

---

[1] *Church of England Year Book*, 1930, 379. Compare this with the 10 parishes with daily celebrations in the diocese of Blackburn which had much the same number of incumbents as in Derbyshire at this time.

published a statement, 'of ... grave and weighty importance', made to the Church Assembly by the now very elderly archbishop of Canterbury, Randall Davidson, on 2 July:

> It is a fundamental principle that the Church – that is, the Bishops together with the Clergy and the Laity – must in the last resort, when its mind has been fully ascertained, retain its inalienable right, in loyalty to our Lord and Saviour Jesus Christ, to formulate its Faith in Him, and to arrange the expression of that Holy Faith in its forms of worship.

By late 1928 the debate about the revised Prayer Book had become well-nigh exhausting. It focused on two contentious issues, one constitutional and ecclesiological, namely, the relationship of Church and state, and one theological and pastoral, the question of continuous reservation. A lengthy discussion at the diocesan conference on 6 November had ended with the carrying unanimously of the all-inclusive resolution: 'That the Conference is prepared to trust the bishop to rule the Diocese.'! In January of that year, again noting that the revised book 'offered no sanction to services in relation to the Reserved Sacrament', Bishop Pearce had asked: 'Is it too much to hope that in this Diocese we shall be law-abiding?' Almost two years later the bishop once again asked all clergy and parochial church councils 'to keep within the limits of the 1928 Book' but, with some asperity, added that

> it is high time that the Church gave up discussing the Prayer Book and devoted itself to its proper work, the reclaiming of humanity and the teaching of the principles of faith. The energy that has been put into the discussion of the relations of Church and State might well now be diverted to a more profitable purpose.[1]

Bishop Pearce acknowledged that some parishes would refuse to accept these limits. He said, 'I shall regret it, but will not refuse to visit them' for that would be behaviour 'partaking of the nature of an ostrich.'[2] If beneficed clergy elected to disregard their bishop in this matter they could do so with relative freedom. Bishop Pearce's successors were to be faced with the same difficulty.

So was adjourned, for a while, the debate about the relationship of the Church of England to the state, a relationship enshrined in the laws to several of which the first chancellor of the diocese continually drew the attention of the

---

[1] *See of Derby Magazine*, October 1929.
[2] Diocesan conference 29 October 1929: *Minutes*.

clergy, and whose mutual benefits had drawn from Bishop Hurd of Lichfield and Coventry such frankness and eloquence in 1775. It is an often troubled relationship which has occasionally engaged Hurd's successors in Derbyshire to the present day.

'£300 a year': the incomes of the clergy

In his 1929 Charge the bishop turned finally to the problem that had beset Derbyshire clergy for hundreds of years and to which he and his successors were to return again – the low level of clergy stipends. Tithe was still being collected in kind by some incumbents and the bishop counselled against this. The Tithe Acts now required that the collection in kind should cease with the vacation of benefices where this was still the practice. That the bishop should devote a long paragraph to this shows that income from tithe, which could vary considerably from year to year, was still a vexed issue in 1929. Bishop Pearce hoped that all benefice incomes would be raised above the then minimum of £300 a year.[1] This was little enough given that the cost of living had risen by 60% since 1918, but it was roughly equivalent to the income of a bank clerk. Two years later Bishop Pearce was to call for a annual minimum benefice income of at least £400.

With final comments about clergy pensions (a 3% p.a. compulsory contribution was not too excessive, he said) and the working of that 'most onerous piece of legislation' the Dilapidations Measure, the bishop of Derby ended his first Charge. Seventy-three years later it provides us with a clear picture of the priorities of the new diocese.

The Church's agenda

The themes raised by George Ridding, Edwyn Hoskyns and Edward Courtenay Pearce in their visitation Charges to Derbyshire congregations and clergy, namely: Christian worship; the call to mission and church extension; the recruitment, maintenance and deployment of the clergy; the wider social responsibility of the Church; the alliance of Church and state; the relationship with other

---

[1] In 1913/14 the national average annual income of the clergy was £206, and that of managers £200. By 1922/4 these averages had risen to £332 and £480 respectively. In 1935/7 they were £370 and £440. The average annual income of a bank clerk in 1935 was £368 [John Burnett, *A History of the Cost of Living* (Penguin 1969), 298–9].

Christian Churches; and the education and ministry of the whole people of God, comprised the agenda of the Church of England in Derbyshire as it did elsewhere. It was to do so from that day to this, though with differing emphases as the years passed. Each one of these themes was the concern of the parishes, as we have seen, and each occupied a central committee in the new diocese.

The first diocesan conference in March 1928 received committee reports on Rescue and Prevention, Clergy Pensions, Ordination Candidates, Dilapidations, Overseas Missions, Church Extension, Magazine and Calendar, and Division of the Diocese. Apart from the last, the functions of each of these first committees remain the predominate concerns of the central committees and boards of the diocese, now re-focused and re-named to meet radically changed circumstances: Social Responsibility, Ministry, Mission and Unity, the Parsonages Committee, and the Pastoral Committee. These, together with the diocesan Boards of Finance and of Education, and the diocesan Advisory Committee for the Care of Churches – key committees from the beginning – are the principal central committees of the diocese today. Circumstances have changed, but the agenda is the same. There is space only to illustrate this from the first years of the life of the diocese and to indicate the direction of future developments in six key areas.

'For Maintenance and Extension': finance

So were labelled the two divisions in Duplex envelopes for weekly offerings by worshippers, the virtues of which were described in the *See of Derby Magazine* for April 1928. It had been recognised long before this date that if worshippers could be persuaded to set aside their offerings each week, even when they could not attend church, it would have a beneficial effect on the Church's finances. 'For Maintenance' and 'For Extension' (that is, for church building, and for mission and evangelism) form a good definition of the work of the Diocesan Board of Finance (the 'DBF') which was established in March 1928, reaching its full complement of 60 members in June. The function of the Board in 1928 was, as its successor was described by its secretary in 1977, to be 'the executive and financial arm of the Diocese.'

In encouraging and supporting the parishes and clergy, the central organisation of the diocese, very modest indeed in 1928, needed money to function. Few issues of the *See of Derby Magazine* lacked a financial report, or an encouragement to its readers to persuade more people to give more money.

In December 1929 it pointed out that if the 72000 people on the electoral rolls of the parishes were to give one half-penny a week 'the whole needs of the diocese could be met.' There were regular pleas for quotas to be paid early and in full. Quotas – frequently a contentious subject then as now – were the subject of an article by John E. Dallimore in the diocesan magazine in September 1928. He set out the formula by which they were assessed by the DBF:

> The method of arriving at the ruridecanal quotas is to take the population, communicants, and total amounts spent in a given year on Church expenses in each rural deanery and discover what are the percentages of the Diocesan totals under this heading. For instance, we will suppose that the population of a rural deanery is 46000. Easter communicants 2200, and Church expenses £2000, whilst the Diocesan figures are respectively 724000, 48000 and £43200. The ruridecanal percentages are 6.35, 4.58 and 4.63. The average of these is now taken giving 5.19, and this is the figure governing the R.D. apportionment. On a diocesan quota of £7000, this deanery would therefore be asked to contribute £363. This amount has now to be distributed amongst the various parishes of the rural deanery; and in this there is no fixed rule.[1]

Leaving to one side the formula, that there was 'no fixed rule' gave much scope for dissension as rural deans soon discovered. In that year the total diocesan budget amounted to £7743 which was reduced by estimated receipts, including subscriptions and donations of £750, to £6808. This sum was raised by the parishes through their quotas. The diocesan contribution to the Church of England's central finances through the Church Assembly Fund was £2398, or 31% of the gross figure. Seventy years later, in 1998, the gross diocesan expenditure budget was £5,283,318. Of this, £3,444,009 or 65%, was financed from Parish Share (the 'quota'). The diocesan contribution to central Church funds was £231,570, or 4.4% of the total budget. Although the 1928 and 1998 figures are not strictly comparable (the basis on which they are produced is very different now), the extraordinary rise in expenditure to finance the Church's basic ministry since 1928, and the income from the parishes to meet it, far outstripped inflation. It witnesses to the commitment of church people, far fewer in number than in 1928, to sustain the Church's ministry to the wider community.

---

[1] Successive methods of assessment of the quota/parish share were to be remain controversial until the 1990s when a more objective basis, related to national census data, was adopted.

Late in 1929 the bishop wrote to parochial church councils about the importance of the quota and urging them to take this responsibility seriously. His letter, he remarked in the diocesan *Magazine* in January 1929, had 'brought in some strange answers . . . . One Council said frankly that it declined to support the Central Fund [the Church Assembly Fund], and thereby confessed that it had not accepted the doctrine of the unity of the Church.' He continued: 'Such a confession shows that there is much yet to be done in educating the Diocese.'

The responsibilities of the DBF now include setting and paying clergy stipends following decisions by the diocesan Synod (the much strengthened successor of the old diocesan Conference), fixing and collecting the parish share (the 'quota'), and the management of church property including glebe lands and, since 1974, parsonages. It is a limited company.

'Unwisdom, mis-guidance or mis-direction': social concerns

The Derby Diocesan Association for Rescue and Preventative Work was set up in 1928. Its aim was to co-ordinate the work of affiliated groups in the diocese. It had 'rescue homes' in Bass Street and in Gerard Street in Derby, and workers based in Derby, Chesterfield and Ilkeston. The St Margaret's Training Home for Girls in Bass Street had been established 75 years previously. It was an institution for the benefit of girls 'who, for one cause or another (un-wisdom, mis-guidance or mis-direction) need to be befriended and put again in the right way', so said an appeal for funds in the diocesan magazine in April 1928. The work of the home was set out in the Derby diocesan *Kalendar* for the same year. It was to 'technically train' the 'inmates' in 'laundry-work, cooking, needlework, and other things which qualify them for domestic service.' There was room there for 22 'inmates'. It continued its essential work for very many years. It was later to be owned and staffed by the Church Army as a home for girls who were cared for there for one year.

The radical change in the attitude of the Church of England to social issues is illustrated by the changes of focus and therefore of title of this first Diocesan Association for Rescue and Preventative Work with its very narrow, however important, object. In 1932 it changed its name to the Derby Diocesan Council for Moral Welfare and in 1960 to the Diocesan Council for Social Work. In 1974 it became the Diocesan Council for Social Responsibility. The objects of the Council, as set out in the 1970s are basically 'to encourage the Church to become aware of the social implications of the Gospel and thus to foster a spirit of caring and service', and, based on that fundamental theology, 'to promote effective co-operation in meeting the needs of individuals and the community as a whole', and to be proactive in identifying areas of concern where independent action by the Church might be appropriate.

This wider concern was well illustrated in the early years of the diocese. In March 1928 the *See of Derby Magazine* carried a lengthy review by 'R.F.L.' of the radical COPEC report *Rural Life.* The review tells graphically of the ending of one way of rural life in Derbyshire and the beginning of another, and implies, rather than states, the implications of this transition for the rural Church of England. The report had noted, as the reviewer said, that

> in the exodus from the country to the town, it is the enterprising and the most vigorous who uproot themselves and seek employment in the cities, or, happier still, respond to the call of the uncultivated tracts of waste dominions overseas. The result of this fact on our rural villages has to be pondered over to be realised.

The reviewer drew attention to the many changes taking place in the countryside. The old squirarchy (the 'paternally-minded squire and his lady') was disappearing, as was 'the Hall . . . taken over for some public institution', or passing into the hands of

> some magnate who has accumulated money in the town but does not understand country ways or the management of the bought estate, nor yet again enter into the feelings of the peasantry. And country-folk, loyal indeed to old traditions, and to "the gentry" . . . are very discerning, and even resentful when mere wealth is flaunted as a sign of superiority. In many ways the ties which once retained the labourer and his family upon the soil have been weakened, and the country suffers.

The implications of these social changes for the rural Church of England were becoming increasingly clear, as were their effects on the rural economy. In sentiments very similar to those still being voiced, 'R.L.F.' wrote that 'my heart has ached . . . to see the little village shops go under, when a branch of the adjacent town "Co-op" with capital at its back has opened.' If the 'enterprising and the most vigorous' were leaving the countryside, and the village shops were under threat, could the village church school and the parish church remain untouched? The question was unasked but implicit.

The answer for individual farmers, 'R.L.F.' suggested, was that they 'ought by combination ... to get into nearer touch with their actual customers.' The answer for their industry, so the COPEC report radically recommended and which 'R.L.F' supported, was the state ownership of land so that

> the farmer will have fair opportunity of achieving success in all cases, and not only as now on the few well-equipped estates. The landlord's duties will be taken over by the State ... [to provide] up-to-date equipment, improved buildings and a well-drained soil.'

Not only was the rural economy changing. The early years of the diocese were years of the most profound economic depression suffered by industrial nations for over a century. Harsh deflationary measures slashed production in the major staple industries and created widespread unemployment among manual workers. Coal output, on which much of the economy of Derbyshire depended, fell by 20% between 1929 and 1931. In the same issue, the *See of Derby Magazine* began a correspondence column. F.W. Elliott used the establishing of a branch of the Church of England Men's Society in Derby as a pretext for asking some very sharply focused theological questions. Pleading that the Society, and therefore the wider Church, should pay far greater attention than it did to 'the economic side of everyday life' he asked why it was that well over one million people applied for Poor Law relief in 1927; why miners' wages were lower than the 1913 level; whether usury was a sin or not; and whether credit could be considered a material possession and who should control it. F.W. Elliott posed a series of theological rhetorical questions and came to a fundamental conclusion: 'Is it possible to apply Christian principles to industry?' he asked. 'Is the well-being of the nation a religious question? If it is, this is part of the Church's work.' These questions were to be asked again and again, and realistic answers were to require some uneasy ethical compromises.

Much of the Church's inability to pay informed attention to these questions, Elliott argued, was because, as a Church,

> we are greatly handicapped by the inability of the majority of the Clergy to understand properly the economic life of the nation, and I see no way to remedy this, if our Clergy are to be specially trained for their ministry; but is there not a ministry of the laity as well? .... What a force ... a combination of the two ministries would be.

That theologically obvious and essential combination has yet to be fully effected. He concluded: 'Has the Church no use for men over 25 years of age? . . . .I know such men are difficult to handle, and perhaps that is why so many of our Clergy leave them severely alone, and it may be a reason why 85% of our population is outside the pale of organized Christianity.'

The inability of the clergy fully to engage with social issues was taken up by an anonymous layman writing in the diocesan magazine in August 1931. He called attention (as Bishop Hoskyns had done, repeatedly, in the early 1920s) to 'the demoralising effects of the widespread evil of unemployment.' An enquiry is needed, he said, 'and it is the layman's job to undertake this rather than the clergy, who are not, as a rule, equipped in this respect.' He added that if a 'Ministry of the Laity' should ever bear fruit 'it will be on the economic side that the main duties will lie.'

In July 1929 one solution to the problem of a clergy ignorant of industry was discussed in Derby, though its focus was less on their ignorance and rather more on the shortage of their numbers. Canon Blunt chaired a meeting in All Saints Church House on 4 July which considered 'the proposal to ordain Laymen of approved character and spirituality to administer the Sacraments on Sundays while continuing their ordinary avocations during the week.' The subsequent widespread and greatly valued provision of what were then called 'Voluntary Clergy' (and now non-stipendiary, or self-supporting, ministers) tended more to serve the shortage than to repair the ignorance, with the emphasis inevitably falling on Sunday priestly duty than on priestly presence in the secular work-place.[1]

These perceptive comments from Derbyshire laymen helped eventually to widen the focus of the Church's social concern in the parishes from 'Rescue and Prevention' to a much broader conception of its social responsibility. But in one significant area the Church had taken its social reponsibility very seriously for a century and more – in its provision of schools and teachers.

'To help necessitous schools': education

We have noticed that though the Church of England's provision of day and Sunday schools had been by no means wholly disinterested, it had a profound

---

[1] Further to this significant development see Patrick Vaughan, *Non-Stipendiary Ministry in the Church of England; the history of the development of an idea* (San Franciso, Mellin Research University Press, 1990) and James M. M. Francis and Leslie J. Francis (eds) *Tentmaking: Perspectives on Self-Supporting Ministry* (Gracewing, 1998).

and, eventually, socially beneficial effect. To be educating in the county, in 1884, more than 40000 children in 209 church day schools was an extraordinary and often ignored achievement. The list of files relating to the Derby Diocesan Board of Education in the Derby Diocesan Record Office runs to 16 pages[1], and a comprehensive history of the Board's work would be of book length. We can here only pay tribute to the parishes, the day and Sunday schools and their teachers, the members and officers of the Board who have carried out what successive diocesan bishops regarded as a central task of the Church, and sketch in the broad historical outline.

The Church of England in Derbyshire, as elsewhere, had its reasons, disinterested and open-hearted as well as sharply and narrowly social and political, for promoting the education of the poor, and several agencies were established to further it, of which the principal was the Lichfield Diocesan Educational Society, formed in 1839. Derbyshire parishes contributed to the establishment and maintenance of a training school for schoolmasters in Lichfield. Soon after this a diocesan commercial or middle school was erected in Derby. The parish schools in the county used up most of the funds available in Derbyshire for educational purposes but an appeal in 1845 enabled the Derbyshire committee to offer a small payment to promising pupils to be retained as monitors; to employ an organising master for the National Society[2]; to offer grants to schools for equipment and books; to assemble teachers during harvest holidays for in-service training by the National Society, and to grant exhibitions of £5 to a few entrants to the Lichfield training school. The Derbyshire Church Day School Association, whose functions were taken over by the diocese in the 1960s, existed to raise money 'to help necessitous Schools by grants and by loans free of interest' and, at least by 1928, to provide funds for prospective male student teachers. The Derbyshire Bible Examination, founded in 1872 in memory of Philip Gell of Derby St John's, whom we have met before, was another venture dedicated to education, though admittedly with a rather narrow focus.

A training school for females was established by Bishop John Lonsdale in Derby in 1851. Known originally as the 'Training Institution for Females' it had a distinguished history as a centre for training teachers. It became the

---

[1] Document reference numbers D4825/

[2] 'The National Society for the Education of the Poor in the Principles of the Established Church' was formed in 1811. With the British and Foreign Schools Society, established in 1807, which was in the main a nonconformist body, the National Society was the principal agency in promoting popular education in England and Wales until the creation of Board Schools by the government in 1870.

Diocesan Training College, and then Bishop Lonsdale College. After two amalgamations and further changes of name, it finally became a constituent part of the new University of Derby. In 1928 the then Diocesan Training College advertised for students. Those from the dioceses of Southwell, Lichfield and Derby who were confirmed members of the Church of England would pay a fee of £70, while other students would pay £75. This fee covered 'tuition, board, lodging, washing and medical attendance for the two year's course, and subscriptions to the Sport and Magazine Fund.' There were to be very considerable changes in the ensuing seventy years.

Under the Education Act of 1870 HM inspectors were not allowed to examine children in their knowledge of the Bible and the Book of Common Prayer. In Derbyshire it was believed that religious education would be neglected as a result and it was decided to appoint a diocesan inspector, to examine pupil teachers and monitors in religious knowledge, to award prizes to pupils, and to provide finance for school buildings and furnishings so that church schools could avoid being transferred to School Boards due to lack of funding. However, this system was not wholly welcomed, some schools objecting to paying money towards the maintenance of a diocesan schools inspector.

But the system seems to have worked, and very many schools in the county continued to be supported by the Church of England. On the eve of the founding of the diocese of Derby, the Diocesan Visitor of Church Day Schools, the Revd Norman Louch, was able to report that in 1925 he had visited (that is, inspected) 134 Derbyshire schools, that a number of parochial clergy had formally visited 30 additional schools, and that teachers from 30 other schools had met in conference with him. He hoped that the Derby Church Day School Sunday Fund, from collections in churches taken on 22 November 1925, would receive at least the average sum for previous years, £246.

Throughout the 19th century and well into the 20th the Church of England Sunday Schools also had inspectors or 'Visitors'. By 1925 a training programme for teachers had been established, and summer schools for teachers were held, as were residential week-end courses for Sunday school superintendents. By this year a Sunday School Headquarters had been set up, a Sunday School touring caravan was travelling around Derbyshire, and Childrens' Missions had been promoted 'with efforts to reach parents.' This was a considerable achievement against a background of steadily falling numbers in Sunday schools nationally.

In the seventy years that followed, fundamental changes in national education policy, and the shortage of finance available to the Church of England, have changed the nature of what, then as now, is known as the 'dual system' of Church/State education. In 1999 the Derby Diocesan Board of Education had statutory responsibility for 30 aided schools, two grant maintained schools, and 40 controlled schools[1], as well as being accountable to the diocesan Synod for the policies and work of the diocesan religious education, lay development, youth and childrens' advisers.

'The good estate of the Church': new churches

In his primary visitation Charge in May 1929 Bishop Pearce had drawn attention to the new housing areas where churches and clergy were needed. Since 1913, and not merely due to the effect of the first World War, the building of new churches in Derbyshire had almost ceased. The attempt to keep pace with the growth of the population had not been sustained since the turn of the century. Yet the Church of England had, and has, a responsibility to provide what the *BCP* calls the 'means of grace', so that the people may have the 'hope of glory'.

In a financial appeal in 1931, based upon a survey of 'the ultimate needs of the diocese', Bishop Pearce made his first priority, as it had been in his Charge in 1929, the provision of churches for new areas of population. He once again listed the places that he had noted in 1929, and added others: in Derby, the Nottingham Road in St Paul's parish where 'for some time there has been an intention to build a new Church of St Mark somewhere there'; in Sandiacre, where the parish church, 'a thing of beauty', was too small and too remote from the population and where another church was needed 'among the people'; in Allenton, 'now a great residential district' in the parish of Alvaston; in the area of the Uttoxeter Road where the parishes of Derby St Luke's, Mickleover and Mackworth met; in Normanton; in Chesterfield; in the parish of Brampton St Thomas 'with over 14000 people' and which 'cries out for help'; in Newbold where the existing parish church 'is very small and not well situated for the growing population'; in the deanery of Bolsover where 'Shirebrook Church ought to be completed, and [where] at least two mission halls are needed; in Staveley, at Hollingwood where 'the Staveley Company has generously given a site and farm buildings, and the Diocese must back this

---

[1] For the definitions of 'aided' and 'controlled' church schools see the *Glossary*.

generous gift by adapting the buildings for church purposes'; and in Pinxton, where the church needed to be entirely rebuilt. The debt on Derby St Bartholomew's had still not been paid off. For this building programme the bishop appealed for £168000.

It took many years to provide churches for these places and subsequent new housing areas, but it was done and it is appropriate to list what was achieved here. This list includes New Whittington St Barnabas (1927), Draycott St Mary's Mission Church (1928), Frecheville St Cyprian (temporary church 1934, permanent church 1951), Derby St Mark (1937), Loscoe St Luke (1938, cost met by Mr J.J.A. Woolley), Allenton and Shelton Lock St Edmund (1939), Brampton St Mark (1939), Marlpool All Saints (rebuilt 1950), Earl Sterndale (rebuilt 1952), Mackworth St Francis (1954), Basegreen St Peter (1955), Allestree St Nicholas (1958), Hemsworth St John (1960), Holmesdale St Philip (1962), Boulton St Mary (extended 1963), Dunston Church House (1963), Greenhill St Peter (1964), Loundsley Green Church of the Ascension (1964), Wingerworth All Saints (an extension making virtually a new church 1964), Stapenhill Immanuel (1965), Mapperley Holy Trinity (1966), Gamesley Bishop Allen Church and Community Centre (1970), Gosforth Valley St Andrew (1973), Sinfin Moor (new parish 1976), Mickleover St John (1978), Sinfin St Stephen (1981), Inkersall St Columba (1982), Temple Normanton St James the Apostle (1986), Cotmanhay and Shipley Christ Church (rebuilt 1988), Blagreaves St Andrew (new parish 1989), Oakwood (LEP 1993), and Holmewood St Alban (rebuilt 2000).

This is an incomplete but impressive list and witnesses again to great energy and self-sacrifice by church people. If the Church of England could not keep pace with population growth *per se* (as Bishop Pearce still hoped), it could follow where council housing authorities and speculative developers led and provide churches for new centres of population. One example of this was the building of Draycott St Mary in the parish of Wilne. It was dedicated on 14 January 1928. In reporting this the *See of Derby Magazine* noted that the vicarage and 95% of the population of 2500 were in Draycott 'a good mile across open country away from the Church at Wilne.' There were other places like that.

'Men of education and culture': the clergy

The selection, training, deployment and support of clergy is a primary responsibility of a diocesan bishop. Every incumbent receives the 'cure of souls' (that is, the care for the spiritual, emotional and physical well-being of each one of her or his parishioners) directly and personally from the bishop, who shares that 'cure' with the incumbent.

Additional churches required additional clergy, but recruitment was low in the 1930s. The laity were asking for a greater share in the appointment of clergy to parishes, but, Bishop Pearce said in 1931, if numbers seeking ordination did not increase, 'far from having any choice, you will be begging anyone to come and minister to you.' The reason for low recruitment, in his view, was low stipends. Bishop Pearce frankly admitted that men would seek to serve God outside the ordained ministry if clergy remained as poor they were. He asked, 'Is it possible for a man to give that whole-hearted devotion to the ministry which is essential, if half his energies are spent upon anxieties about his family budget.' This, for Derbyshire, was a very familiar plea. In 1929 he had asked for a minimum stipend of £300. By 1931 the gross incomes of half the benefices were under £400 p.a., a figure reduced considerably by pension contributions, dilapidations' assessments and rates. 'Is the remainder really adequate for the man of the type of education and culture that you look for in the Vicarage?' asked the bishop candidly. He urged that all benefice incomes be raised to at least £400 p.a. To do this would require a further £75000 of capital.

The clergy were not averse to speaking for themselves on this matter. In 1926, Howard Dobson of Clay Cross, who had been a proctor, or elected representative, of Derbyshire clergy in the Canterbury Convocation, argued for the formation of a Parsons' Union which could subsidise the expenses of proctors ready to agitate for the better provision of pensions for the clergy. He was disturbed that 195 proctors from the province of Canterbury had not voted for the final approval of the recent clergy Pensions' Measure. He said

> Whatever reasons prompted this wholesale abstention, it is difficult to include among them a hearty desire to look after the interests of their fellow clergy. I hope it is not offensive to suggest that possibly many of these total abstainers were men so richly blessed with this world's goods that a mere three per cent off their stipends wasn't worth the missing of a match at Lord's or some other attractive entertainment.[1]

Bishops had, in the past, frequently drawn attention to the low level of clergy

---

[1] See *of Derby Magazine*, September 1926.

incomes, and they were to continue to do so. Low levels of income could compromise pastoral care. That could not be said in the 1930s, unless Bishop Pearce was correct when he seemed to imply that only men of relatively poor education and 'culture' would be attracted to a poorly paid profession, and that they would compromise standards. Yet modest education and social background could, and did, make parish clergy much more accessible to their parishioners. There were other reasons why pastoral care could be compromised, as an anonymous contributor to the diocesan magazine observed in November 1929. Committees and conferences, he wrote, keep clergy from their primary work: 'Parsons are less seen in their parishes than they were; they know their people less than their predecessors knew them. Many men in large parishes must be profoundly ignorant of their parishioners.'[1]

'Reunion is in the air': mission and unity

The ecumenical movement, that is, the movement for the recovery of the unity of the Christian Churches, was never off the Anglican agenda. A critical moment was reached in May 1919 when a representative interdenominational conference was held in Tranquebar in an attempt to bring unity to the Protestant Churches in South India. The *Appeal to all Christian People*, issued by the bishops attending the Lambeth Conference the following year, raised hopes. A joint committee was established, drawn from the Anglican and Methodist churches in South India together with the South India United Church (itself a union of the Presbyterian, Congregational and Dutch Reformed Churches). Eventually, after much controversy, the Church of South India was inaugurated on 27 September 1947.

The Lambeth Conference in 1930 was to encourage this initiative, and the prospect that Anglican dioceses in South India might formally be brought into union with other churches engaged attention in the months leading up to the Conference. In September 1929 Prebendary W. G. Clark-Maxwell, rector of St Leonard's, Bridgnorth, addressed the Heanor ruri-decanal conference on the subject.[2] He concentrated on a crucial issue, one which had beset unity negotiations for years. It was the question of the episcopal re-ordination of nonconformist ministers as an Anglican precondition for union with the Free Churches. We have noted that the Derbyshire Free Churches had baulked at

---

[1] 'Reflections of a Parson', *See of Derby Magazine,* November 1929.
[2] reported in the *See of Derby Magazine*, October 1929.

this requirement when they found it in the *Appeal* issued by the 1920 Lambeth Conference.

At this stage in the South India negotiations it had been suggested that for 30 years the ministers of the participating Churches in the South India scheme should be allowed to exercise their ministry in parity with each other. Clark-Maxwell met the issue head on.

> There is obviously no special virtue in the term of 30 years; if the thing is wrong, it will not be put right by the lapse of time. Therefore, the question that we have to face is this: Is it, or is it not, unlawful for a Christian minister not episcopally ordained, to exercise the functions of the Christian priesthood, especially in the celebration of the Holy Communion? And conversely, is it, or is it not, permissible for us as members of a Church standing in the Catholic tradition to receive such ministrations at their hands?

He then launched into a lengthy discussion of precisely what 'lawful' meant, relying heavily on Thomas Aquinas and a consensus of Roman Catholic theologians. From this analysis Clark-Maxwell reached the conclusion that, on the question of ordination, the Church could suspend her rules in order not to be contrary to the mind of Christ. But, he asked, if we were to ignore the requirement to re-ordain, why bother with ordination at all? Indeed,

> why not throw open our pulpits to all and sundry, welcome to our altars the ministers of any and every denomination, sweeping [away] all regulations as to the necessity of ordination, confirmation, or even baptism, and make reunion a reality by the simple process of abolishing everything that is destructive?

Clark-Maxwell's answer was, firstly, that no one has the right to act independently of the whole Church; secondly, that reunion on the basis proposed would not be reunion at all, for 'no one can secure it by sacrificing what he believes to be true'; and, thirdly, that the time for reunion has not yet come, for 'we must not only desire it, but desire also to be shown wherein we are wrong, and be prepared to give up our most cherished beliefs and practices, if we are wrong.'

Virtually identical arguments were, much later, to be advanced by those opposed to the ordination of women to the priesthood. In 1947 nearly 40000 Anglicans in the Nandyal district of South India refused to join the newly inaugurated Church. In another near parallel to the issue of women's ordination, a state of 'limited intercommunion' has, since 1955, existed between the Church of South India and the Church of England. It seems that Clark-Maxwell's very guarded reception of the South India proposals would have found support from the bishop of Derby, who was not regarded as a supporter of the ecumenical movement by its enthusiasts.

'The hospitable roof'

There was much else to engage the parishes in the first years of the new diocese. Supporting them, quietly and unpretentiously, were two communities of Sisters in the county. The Southwell diocesan retreat house in Ambergate, Oakhurst, (which was to serve both Southwell and Derby dioceses) was acquired in 1924. By 1926 it was being managed by deaconesses from the East London Community of Deaconesses led by Sister Mary. In its first year the house attracted 350 people who used it for long or short retreats. The former rectory of Morley was to become the diocesan retreat and conference house in 1960.

The Community of St Lawrence[1] had been established in Norwich in 1874 by E.A. Hillyard, rector of the parish of St Lawrence. Its first community house was in Willow Lane, Norwich, but in 1877 the community moved to Belper when E.A. Hillyard became vicar of Christ Church. Bishop Selwyn professed the superior of the community and two sisters in his chapel in Lichfield in July 1877. They followed a rule similar to that of the community of St Margaret, East Grinstead. The community eventually occupied a house in Belper, erecting an 'iron chapel' in the garden and opening a small school and an orphanage. The sisters also nursed the sick in their own homes, one sister dying of typhoid fever as a consequence. Several sisters were trained and certified as midwives. The community's school was eventually closed and two wards for incurable patients were established at the convent. In 1930 the community was also working in mission houses in Norwich and in the parishes of Ilkeston Holy Trinity and Derby St Anne. It continued its work in Belper until 2001, when it moved to Southwell.

The Community of The Holy Name, another Anglican community of Sisters, moved its Mother house from Malvern Link to Oakwood, Derby, in

---

[1] now spelt 'St Laurence'.

1990. There are seven branch houses of the Community in England and one in South Africa. The Sisters, like those of the Community of St Laurence, are dedicated to a life of prayer and service. The diocese of Derby has gained greatly from the ministry of these communities.

By 1928 the Community of St Laurence had, for several years, provided a rest home for clergy in two houses in Montpellier Terrace on the South Cliff in Scarborough. Clergy and their families, it was said in 1930, could testify 'to the benefit they received in Scarborough under the hospitable roof of the Clergy Rest.' One can imagine the sepia photographs of the South Cliff. They would tell of a very different age.

But times were changing. Edmund Courtenay Pearce died in 1935. The bishop of Durham, Hensley Henson said of him, in a letter to the archbishop of Canterbury, Cosmo Gordon Lang, that his death 'has removed a very useful member of the Bench [of bishops], not great, or attractive, or particularly interesting, but always sane, sensible and serviceable.'[1] The archbishop's own judgment was rather more generous. Bishop Pearce, he said, was a man 'of singularly clear and sane judgment,[and] firm principles, a sincere and wholly unaffected piety, and [with] a very real sympathy with the clergy in their work.'[2]

He was succeeded by Alfred Edward John Rawlinson, who was to be bishop of Derby for the next twenty-four years. Like his predecessor, A.E.J. Rawlinson was an academic of distinction and a very perceptive and courageous theologian. He had been Student and tutor of Christ Church Oxford, and, before his appointment, archdeacon of Auckland in the diocese of Durham. It was to be said by F.A. Iremonger, the biographer of their close friend William Temple, that Rawlinson was one of the acutest theologians among Temple's contemporaries.[3] Michael Ramsey, once a boy at Repton School and to become archbishop of Canterbury, held Rawlinson's scholarship in high regard, while having a low opinion of that of much of the rest of the bench of bishops. It is said that the future archbishop told a friend in the early 1950s that 'If you walked from Humber to Severn and dodged Derby, you would not find a bishop who can read or write.'[4] Amongst much else, A.E.J. Rawlinson had published, in 1925, a pioneering commentary on St Mark's Gospel which still

---

[1] cited in Robert Dell, *Honest Thinker; John Rawlinson 1884–1960* (1998), 135.
[2] Derby Diocesan Conference *Minutes*, 12 November 1935.
[3] F.A. Iremonger, *William Temple, Archbishop of Canterbury,* (OUP 1948), 609.
[4] Owen Chadwick, *Michael Ramsey, A Life,* (SCM edition 1998), 76. This comment seems as unfair as it is unkind. The route could take you through Nottinghamshire. If so, you would need also to 'dodge' the scholarly and apostolic bishop of Southwell, Frank Russell Barry!

ranks among the best of its *genre*. His predecessor had been a parish priest for eight years but, like his two immediate successors, each a scholar and teacher, the new bishop had had little personal parish experience, apart from a year as priest-in-charge of St John the Evangelist, Wilton Road, in London, 1917–18. However, for much of his episcopate Bishop Rawlinson was supported by two archdeacons, T. Dilworth Harrison, vicar and archdeacon of Chesterfield, 1934–1963, and, in the latter years, by Jack Richardson, archdeacon of Derby, 1952–1973. With Ronald Beddoes, provost from 1953 to 1980 these men, renowned figures in the recent history of the diocese, with other senior clergy, including assistant bishops who were parish clergy in the diocese, more than compensated for the bishop's lack of parish experience. In the event, the next two decades were to call from Bishop Rawlinson what he could best offer to the Church – prophetic and theological insights of penetrating depth.[1]

---

[1] See Robert Dell's concise and shrewd biography of A.E.J. Rawlinson, *Honest Thinker, John Rawlinson 1884–1960, Theologian, Bishop, Ecumenist* (1998). Much of what is readily available there of Bishop Rawlinson's life and writings, and of his time as bishop of Derby, is not repeated here for reasons of space. What is included here is, generally, not found in Robert Dell's book.

14

'Hard-pressed times': 1936–1959

Bishop Rawlinson came to a diocese that would, during his episcopate, see, first, a fall and then a modest rise in the numbers claiming church-going allegiance to the Church of England. This trend was to continue until the early Sixties when a rapid decline began. As, from this point in the story, numbers become increasingly important, it is helpful here to gather together some comparative statistics. They provide the unavoidable backdrop against which the remaining story must be set.

If, as Maurice Halbwachs says, the expansion of religious communities results most often from trends and movements affecting the entire population, *so too does their contraction.* In 1965 the provost of Derby, Ronald Beddoes, noted the fact that between 1928 and 1959 the population of the diocese had increased by 17% while the number of Confirmation candidates had fallen by 34%. He said:

> On the perimeter [of the wider society] the parochial system ticks over efficiently. *This does not depend on the talents or virtues of the clergy. Success or failure is written into the situation.*[1]

The fundamental change in the relationship of people generally to religious institutions, shown in rapidly declining church attendances after the mid-Sixties, inevitably resulted in the closure of churches, and in radical proposals to change the patterns of recruitment and deployment of the clergy. As to church closure, there had been 171 chapels-of-ease, mission churches and mission rooms in Derbyshire's Anglican parishes in 1928. In 1997 this number had been reduced by over 60% to 66. More significantly, some large parish

---

[1] R.A. Beddoes, 'Facing the Facts of Change', *DDN,* June 1965. Italics mine.

churches, serving small congregations in urban parishes with declining populations, had been closed and demolished, or sold, or their use changed. The church expansion of the last half of the 19th century to meet the needs of a rapidly growing population in new urban areas, had, a hundred years later, become contraction in what had now become areas first of social and economic depression and then of redevelopment. In no case did the Church of England leave these areas, but the form its presence took changed markedly.

Although the Church of England continued to provide churches, parsonages and church halls for areas of new housing development, a still growing population had become largely indifferent to the spiritual provision made for it by the Church of England, and, of course, by the other Churches. Together with them, the Church of England is demographically dependent on the wider community.[1] The theological implications of this obvious truth for the religion of the Incarnation are profound, as is its impact on the psychological and spiritual well-being of clergy and congregations.

Numbers: the pattern of growth and decline

In the 1930s the Church of England counted everyone connected to it who did anything in its parishes, together with every penny that was contributed. For 1936, the year that A.E.J. Rawlinson became bishop of Derby, we know not only the number of the incumbents (244) and assistant curates (82) in the diocese, the number of infant baptisms (7947) and Easter Day and additional Easter week communicants the previous year (44742 and 2016 respectively), the number of sittings in its churches and mission rooms (120266) together with the pattern of frequency of celebrations of holy Communion, the number of children in its Sunday schools (40428) and in its youth and adult organisations (11720), but also how many churchwardens and sidesmen there were (4297), the number of licensed Readers (96), Sunday school teachers (3602), paid and voluntary lay district visitors (4 and 1426 respectively) and even the numbers of paid and voluntary organists (313 and 126), choristers (464 and 6838) and bell-ringers (414 and 579 respectively). In 1936 there were 71809 qualified electors on Anglican parish electoral rolls from a population, at the 1931 Census, of 768970, suggesting that about 9% of the population of the county claimed a tangible association with the Church of England in Derbyshire.

---

[1] Robert Currie, Alan Gilbert, Lee Horsley, op. cit., 46.

The Church of England collected few statistics between 1941 and 1947. In 1948 it restricted itself (together with its customary mass of financial information) to recording the number of infant baptisms (with 10525 in Derbyshire, a 32.5% increase on the 1936 figure reflecting the post-war growth in the birth rate); Easter Day and additional Easter week communicants (in 1947 35068 and 2299 respectively, a fall of 20% from 1936); and qualified electors on church electoral rolls (at 56607 a fall of over 21% from 1936). In 1948 2621 candidates were presented to the bishop for Confirmation, a fall of just over 25% from the 1937 figure of 3507.

These statistics suggest that the effect of the second World War had been to remove at least 20% of the adult membership of the Church of England in Derbyshire. It may well be that this 20% represented what had previously been the peripheral membership of the Church. For example, Easter Day communicants included, together with those who worshipped each week, very many who did so only once or twice a year on the great Church festivals. In 1937 Bishop Rawlinson spoke of those who paid the Church the 'lip service of distant loyalty.' These would have included those who attended only on these rare but significant occasions. The number of Easter Day communicants was to decline very markedly from the early Sixties. The distantly loyal had by then become the virtually indifferent.

There was to be a recovery in the numbers attending church in the diocese in the years immediately after 1948, reflecting the national trend. By 1950, Easter day communicants in the diocese had risen marginally to 35873 and the numbers on electoral rolls to 57454. By 1958 there had been further increases to 39775 and 57920 respectively. Confirmation figures were to be back at the 1928 level by 1962 (3686 and 3627 respectively).

Statistics from the parishes in the Bolsover and Glossop rural deaneries provide a clear picture of church attendance in these years[1]. In 1952 average Sunday communicants at the nine churches in the Glossop deanery numbered 408 (of which New Mills alone contributed 200), or about 1% of the population[2]. There were 427 communicants on an average Sunday at the ten churches in the Bolsover deanery, or 0.77% of the population.

From the early 1960s, in Derbyshire as nationally, there has been a steady decline in all numerical indices and a very rapid decline in some. In 1958 *Easter Day communicants* in the diocese had numbered 39775, but ten years later they

---

[1] Derby Diocesan Record Office, data files 1952, D4987/5/1 (Bolsover) and D4987/5/2 (Glossop).
[2] based on the 1931 census, given with the returns.

were down to 32433 (a loss of just over 18%). By 1973 the number had dropped to 29937, by 1978 to 24395 and by 1997 to 21100.

Infant baptisms in the diocese fell from 10525 in 1948 to 9326 in 1953 and 8144 in 1958. They rose to 8800 in 1968 but fell back to 6634 in 1973, to 4400 in 1989 and to 3420 in 1997 (but in both those last two years the baptisms of all children under 12 years had been included).

Membership of parochial *electoral rolls* show a similar decline from 56609 in 1948 to 21300 in 1997, though, to a degree, this fall was due to attempts between those years to produce electoral rolls which included only those who genuinely wished to play a part in the life and government of the Church.

Critically, the number of those presented to the bishop for *Confirmation* in the diocese fell overall from 3686 in 1929 to 617 in 1997, a decline of no less than 83.25%. As a percentage of population, they represented 0.5% in 1929 and 0.06% in 1997. Given that the numbers confirmed in the diocese after 1948 had recovered to the 1928 level by 1962, this 83% decline had taken place in the 35 years since then.[1] Nationally, the decline from 1960 to 1997 was 79.2%.[2] It is a critical decline, because by the rite of Confirmation men and women are admitted to communicant membership of the Church of England, and, from the age of 17, are eligible to hold elected office. In part this decline can be explained by the absence of those who, a generation earlier, would have been confirmed principally because it was expected of them. This is no longer so. As with the other indices of decline that we have considered, it may be that the loss is that of the once distantly loyal.[3]

But if this is so, what has caused this loss? Crucial factors have influenced membership of the Churches, among them the privatisation of religion; the disinclination of many to join traditional participatory voluntary organisations in recent decades; and, though this is impossible to quantify though one feels it in the air, a general scepticism that any *institutionalised* world-view, be it religious, scientific or political, holds the answers to the fundamental questions of life and death. Adrian Hastings speaks of 'a crisis of

---

[1] Despite this decline, in every year in Derbyshire since the late 1920s the number of females confirmed has been greater than the number of males, usually within the 60%/40% range. This phenomenon had been commented on by Charles Abraham, suffragan bishop of Derby, in 1926. For a discussion of the question 'Why is it that Women are more Religious than Men?' see Grace Davie, *Religion in Britain since 1945* (Blackwell 1994), 118–121.

[2] *The Official Year Book of the Church of England* (all years) and *Church Statistics* 1997, 24.

[3] Another factor influencing Confirmation statistics since the late 1990s has been admission to holy Communion before Confirmation. This is at the bishop's discretion.

relevance (or capability for sheer survival) of long-standing patterns of thought and institutions of all sorts in a time of intense, and rather self-conscious, modernization.'[1]

This may offer some explanation for these indices of decline, but very small comfort. *Weekly church attendances*, representing the Church's core allegiance[2], also declined, certainly from the mid-Sixties. No reliable national or diocesan statistics for weekly church attendance exist for the whole period since 1927, but at least by the 1970s a decline in this key indicator had become very evident. Between 1979 and 1998[3] Anglican Sunday church attendances nationally fell by 41%, with similar falls for the older, so called main-stream, Churches (the Methodists by 39%, the United Reformed Church by 36%, and the Roman Catholic Church by 38%. Only the Baptists more or less held their own with a decline of 4%). In the east Midlands economic region, comprising the counties of Derbyshire, Nottinghamshire, Lincolnshire, Leicestershire and Northamptonshire, the overall decline in Anglican Sunday attendances was, at 40%, near the national average. In 1998 the national percentage of Anglicans who attended church at least once a week was 46% with 39% in the east Midlands region. Both nationally and regionally this was a considerably lower figure than for the other main Christian denominations. In addition, the Church of England's 'market share' of Church allegiance, measured by weekly Sunday attendances, also fell, both nationally and in the region, by 5% between 1979 and 1998.

Do these statistics mean that the Church of England is in decline? By the statistical indicators which point to the serious and rapid loss of which, in other Churches, is formally called 'membership', it clearly is. This is evident from every index by which comparisons with the past can reliably be made. To summarise: although a slow numerical decline had been noticeable in one or two indices well before 1927 (particularly, as we have seen earlier, in the falling numbers of children attending Anglican, and other, Sunday schools), the British Churches enjoyed their highest ever level of membership, nearly six million, in the year the diocese of Derby was founded. Numbers held up during the 1930s but, apart from the significant but temporary increases in some indices during

---

[1] Hastings, op. cit., 580–1.

[2] though in all periods many more people than those regularly attending services had occasional contact with the Church.

[3] Statistics from *UK Christian Handbook Religious Trends No 2, 2000/01*, (Christian Research, 1999).

the 1950s and early 1960s, from then all the indicators have pointed downwards. The Derbyshire evidence mirrors the national picture, allowing for regional variations.

Overall, between 1960 and 1985 it could be said that 'the Church of England as a going concern was effectively reduced to not much more than half its previous size.'[1] That is the raw data. It can be interpreted in several ways, but no amount of special pleading can soften its impact.

'The Church and the Challenge of Today': the bishop's visitation 1937

Yet the strength and spiritual vitality of the Church has never been measured merely by the numbers admitting to allegiance to it, or even attending its services. Dietrich Bonhoeffer had taught that the Church is most free when it is poor, few in number and imprisoned for the Gospel, and most enslaved when it is powerful, rich, and identified with those in power. This is, of course, not to claim that the Church of England is either poor and imprisoned or rich and powerful, but it serves to remind us of an important truth. The Church is in the world, and it lives with the consequences.

Bishop Rawlinson conducted a primary visitation in 1937. His Charge (typically, for him, of book length) was published under the title *The Church and the Challenge of Today*.[2] The title indicated that the Church must always be fully engaged with the world in which it is set. Rawlinson had earlier told his diocesan conference that the theme of his Charge would be evangelism, the Church's first task, he said. Though many would claim that the Church's first responsibility was to worship God, the bishop was asserting here no more than that the Church had a fundamental responsibility to preach the Gospel.

The Church, Bishop Rawlinson argued, undertakes its work of evangelism in a society the fundamental attitudes of which have been shaped by the discoveries of science. His argument ran like this: the way men and women think about the world, and therefore about what is fundamentally true, had been radically changed by the physical sciences. The idea of the supernatural, and, as he was to repeat in 1943, the ability to grasp spiritual values, had been seriously undermined. Rawlinson was by no means denying the importance of scientific method, still less the truths it had revealed, but he did question

---

[1] Adrian Hastings, op. cit., 603.
[2] Longman 1937.

whether empiricism could encompass the whole truth. He believed that the dominant influence of science, which had changed the way men and women look at the world, had led Christian preachers to depend more on exhortations to good works (the practical value of which could be demonstrated) and to rely less on the Gospel of God's grace and his forgiving love (which were not empirically verifiable). In a striking phrase in his seminal commentary on St Mark's Gospel, published in 1925, Rawlinson had observed that: 'As compared with other forms of religion current in the Graeco-Roman world, Christianity was distinguished by its doctrine of forgiveness. "The Son of Man has power to forgive sins" was the Church's great characteristic word.'[1] It was a truth central to the bishop's own faith and he reasserted it in his Charge in 1937.

This gospel was being proclaimed in a British society which seemed to be deaf to it. Rawlinson spoke of 'a widespread and modish prejudice against anything as old-fashioned as Christianity', and, in that memorable phrase, of 'the lip-service of distant loyalty' which had replaced discipleship and which necessarily hampered the Church's work of evangelism. In a perceptive chapter on 'Opportunities and Difficulties' he attempted to explain the reason for the scepticism of the late 1930s:

> Great wars, such as the world conflict which afflicted mankind less than a generation ago, do not produce harvests of happiness, nor do they leave legacies behind them of spiritual well-being . . . . A great war not only has the effect of carrying off prematurely the flower of a generation of manhood; it leaves also the souls of the survivors bruised, and their nerves jangled, and their spirit sceptical, disillusioned, and weary . . . . There is apt to be a casting away . . . of restraints: a calling in question of previously accepted conventions and creeds: a manifest coarsening of spiritual fibres.[2]

He hoped that the mood was changing and that 'the moment has come for a return movement of spiritual recovery.' Although it is important, he wrote, for the Church to co-operate with civil and voluntary organisations in promoting the well-being of society, the Church's fundamental task is to proclaim the good news of God's grace. This involves translating the gospel into a language that people can understand and which tells of truths that they can see engage with their day-to-day lives.

---

[1] A.E.J. Rawlinson, *The Gospel according to St Mark*, (Methuen 1925), 23.
[2] A.E.J. Rawlinson, *The Church and the Challenge of Today*, 25–6.

This task was the responsibility of the clergy. While recognising that they were few in number in the places where they were most needed, Rawlinson had only a modest opinion of them. He said that 'in the judgment of shrewd and not unfriendly observers, the type and quality of the rank and file of our clergy today does not in every respect compare favourably with the type and quality of their predecessors a generation ago.' It was hardly a remark from their new bishop which was likely to win friends among the clergy seated in front of him. It was an example either of his forthright courage, or of his occasional lack of tact and sensitivity, both of which were to mark his episcopate. Yet he had a point. As he said in his Charge, the proclamation of the Gospel of Christian truth in today's world required much careful and sustained study.

Turning then to other equally practical areas of pastoral ministry, Rawlinson urged the laity to undertake parish visiting, and affirmed the pastoral opportunities offered by the 'Occasional Offices' – baptisms, weddings and funerals. As Bishop Hoskyns had done before the first World War he urged the clergy in the Peak District to encourage the many that came to the area for recreation to come to worship also.

Somewhat controversially, the bishop recommended that opportunities for private confession and absolution be made available in parishes. This raised the related and still somewhat fraught issue of the 1928 Revised Prayer Book. Rawlinson reaffirmed that 'the use of strange Missals, devoid of any ecclesiastical sanction other than that of self-appointed compilers, is not authorised', and neither was 'the public recitation of the "Hail Mary."' He noted that there was continuous reservation of the eucharistic elements in only 22 parishes in the diocese (probably including the 20 parishes in the diocese having a daily celebration of holy Communion that we noted in the 1930 Church of England *Year Book*). As his predecessor had done, the bishop forbade any form of worship before the reserved sacrament, though, as Robert Dell notes, he discovered that Bishop Pearce had allowed devotional practices contrary to regulations agreed collectively by the bishops of the Church of England.[1] Several clergy refused to surrender to the new bishop's demands in this regard.[2]

These observations on the parochial ministry of the clergy, expected as they were from any new bishop, nevertheless display a somewhat less assured touch

[1] Robert Dell, op. cit., 153.
[2] ibid., 154.

than that of his predecessor, who had considerably more experience as a parish priest. What Bishop Rawlinson had, to a degree greater than most bishops at the time, was a sharp and practical perception of the political world founded on a critical and liberal Christian orthodoxy.

'The international sky is dark': the Church and politics

With his first presidential address to the diocesan conference on 9 May 1936 A.E.J. Rawlinson was to offer the first of a series of measured comments on international affairs that were to continue for the next 23 years. He observed that:

> the international sky is dark . . . the League of Nations has been shown to be impotent to restrain the ambitions of a European dictator. The pledge solemnly taken by Italy . . . to abstain from the use of poisonous gases in war, has been treated, like other pledges, as a scrap of paper.[1]

He was referring to the war in Abyssinia which had ended, ten days earlier, with the formal annexation of the country. The Council of the League had denounced Italy as the aggressor on 7 October 1935, five days after it had invaded Abyssinia. The 'European dictator' was, of course, the fascist Benito Mussolini. A 'scrap of paper', another pledge to be dishonoured, was to be waved by Neville Chamberlain on his return from meeting another European fascist dictator three years later.

At the next diocesan conference, Rawlinson continued his outspoken criticism of Italian aggression in Abyssinia. He then turned to the third fascist leader in Europe, commenting on 'the continuing tragedy of Spain' and praying that 'Franco and his friends', whom he rightly believed were likely to be victorious in the Spanish civil war, 'may be given grace to be restrained and merciful in the hour of their victory.' This was an early comment on what was to be a bitter conflict. Franco and his *fascisti* had led the army revolt in July 1936 which began the civil war.

A.E.J. Rawlinson was strongly anti-fascist at a time when many were sympathetic to fascism, or at least were ready to accept an accommodation with it. He was no pacifist and believed that aggression must be confronted. As the international sky became blacker, he was to say repeatedly that though he

---

[1] Derby diocesan conference minutes, 19 May 1936.

honoured pacifists he believed them to be wrong. Yet he believed also that no theological *carte blanche* existed which allowed Christians to go to war in any circumstances. At the same diocesan conference in October 1936 he cited the Latin text of Article XXXVII of the Church of England's *Articles of Religion*. In the English version the Article declares it lawful for 'Christian men, at the commandment of the Magistrate, to wear weapons, and to serve in wars'. The Latin text, Rawlinson pointed out, has *justa bella administrare* which allowed Christians to bear weapons only in *righteous* wars. He continued:

> I believe the pacifist position to be mistaken; but I believe, nevertheless, that it is one of those errors which, in however mistaken a form, yet represents the affirmation of an eternal truth – even the supreme truth of the Gospel: the affirmation . . . that God is love, and that He desires good, and not evil, for His children.[1]

He here encapsulates the ever-present dilemma facing the religion of the Incarnation: how to live fully in the world yet not be dominated and controlled by it.

In a detailed and incisive political analysis offered to his diocesan conference in October 1938, Rawlinson spoke of the crisis facing Czechoslovakia. He trusted that 'the German dictator' had 'sustained a shock' from the international condemnation of his policy to annex Sudetenland. In a comment prominently reported in the *Derbyshire Times*, the *Derbyshire Advertiser* and the *Derby Evening Telegraph*, he said:

> There is some hope that a further deterioration of world politics in the direction of a despairing acquiescence in the abandonment of the moral principle, and of a reversion to the so-called law of the jungle might be averted.

At the time such an outcome was less a possibility than a hope, and in this, as in his hope that Franco might be restrained and merciful, Rawlinson was to be disappointed. Guernica had been destroyed in April 1937, and Czechoslovakia was to be dismembered in March 1939. At this conference, for the first time, the bishop had spoken directly about the possibility of war. He warned the clergy that 'no ordained man ought in any circumstances to serve in a combatant

---

[1] ibid., 20 October 1936.

capacity' or ought even to accept service as 'air wardens'. In his view their primary responsibility as priests would be compromised by either role.

At the next diocesan conference, on 15 May 1939, Rawlinson condemned what he described as 'the wicked assumption that war is inevitable', saying that he did not believe that it was.[1] At the time his hope was probably justified, but as the weeks passed he must have known that the chances of avoiding war were becoming ever more remote. On 3 September France and Britain declared war on Germany, following Germany's invasion of Poland and the annexation of Danzig.

Throughout the second World War the bishop continued to confront the parishes and the clergy of his diocese with the moral dilemmas created by total war, refusing to take refuge in the spurious comfort of simplistic Christian platitudes. For example, in May 1940 he condemned 'the naked exhibition of power politics in action, and the course of continuous military aggression upon small neighbouring States upon which the rulers of Germany have embarked.' Such a display, he said, 'was unhappily not uncharacteristic of modern German ambition, which from the days of Frederick the Great onwards [had] launched a succession of aggressive wars in Europe.' In the face of this what hope was there other than the Christian hope?:

> In the last resort only the Christian spirit can bring real peace to the nations, [yet] the maintenance, under the conditions of war, of the Christian spirit and temper is not easy – it is desperately hard.[2]

That comment would have met with general approval. It took considerably more courage to take a view opposed to popular opinion. In May 1941, disturbed by Press demands for vengeance following the bombing of British cities by the *Luftwaffe*, notably the destruction of Coventry and its cathedral the previous month, Rawlinson said: 'I for one should very greatly regret it if a time were ever to come when our airmen were asked, in the name of retaliation, to indulge in Germany in raids, terroristic in nature, against admittedly non-military objectives.'[3] Dresden was to be needlessly destroyed on 13–14 February 1945 by Allied air forces at the insistence of the Soviet Union. About 150000 people perished, mainly refugees fleeing from the Soviet armies.

---

[1] *Derbyshire Advertiser*, 19 May 1939. Newspaper references hereafter are to reports of diocesan conferences, unless otherwise indicated.
[2] *Derby Evening Telegraph*, 7 May 1940.
[3] *Derbyshire Advertiser*, 16 May 1941.

Similarly, in May 1942, when the direction of the war on all fronts was going very much against the western allies, Rawlinson objected to the adoption of emergency powers by the government. A stand must be made against the doctrine which regarded children as state property, he said, 'to be recruited and organized, whether as cannon-fodder or as potential factory-fodder, but in any case to be disciplined, drilled, and conditioned in uniform moulds' for 'State controls can be tyrannous, and the excessive regimentation of society by bureaucrats can be a menace alike to freedom and to initiative.' He was to express almost identical sentiments in May 1951. He argued then that freedom and democracy were facing a formidable challenge. Our civilisation, he said, had become 'dessicated, de-spiritualized, robbed of its essential soul. Men became factory fodder, cannon-fodder, or material for commissars to manipulate in the mass.'[1] Although 'commissar' related primarily to the Soviet system, it was clear that Rawlinson was applying the term more widely, and was perhaps scarcely concealing his own political position: in this country Labour governments had been in power since 1945.

As had some other political observers since the early 1930s, Bishop Rawlinson had seen clearly from which direction the next threat to world peace was coming. George VI, on the 25th anniversary, on 21 February 1943, of the formation of the Soviet Red Army, announced the presentation of a sword of honour to Stalingrad. A few months later, at a time in the second World War when pro-Soviet feeling was running high, Rawlinson told his diocesan conference that 'the government of Russia had been, and still was, totalitarian with its own dark record of cruelty, and [had] an avowed hostility ... to all forms of belief in God.'[2] Although he thought, then, that the Soviet threat might be lifting, by May 1948 he had realised that, once again, his hopes for world peace had been dashed. The final decision between peace and war, rests, he said, with 'the handful of half-frightened, half-blustering men who control the Kremlin .... The effective frontiers of Russia have been advanced half across Europe.' A halt must be called, and he believed that it should be possible to achieve this short of war. However, he believed that the recent signing of the treaty between Britain, France, Belgium, the Netherlands and Luxembourg[3] indicated that the Western powers were contemplating the

---

[1] *Derby Evening Telegraph,* 12 May 1942 and 30 May 1951.
[2] ibid., 1 October 1943.
[3] The Brussels Treaty, signed on 17 March 1948, for a fifty year alliance against armed attack in Europe and providing for mutual social, military and economic co-operation.

possibility of a third world war. 'This is a dreadful commentary on the wickedness of man', he said.[1]

When Allied victory seemed to be assured the bishop reminded his diocese that 'the responsibilities of victory will be immeasurable . . . [and] the transition from totalitarian war to peace [will] be gradual, difficult and slow.' The 'postwar problems', he reminded the clergy,

> would include those who had married during the war and had no experience of settled family life. There might be a child the father had never seen, who had lived in the homes of others and had never known a home of his own. There would be those who had been unfaithful to their marriage vows and whose future would be jeopardised; there would be those who returned, suffering from wounds and loss of faculties, to face an invalid life.[2]

No sooner had the war in Western Europe been won than the consequences of victory in the East, achieved at a terrible cost, had to be faced. On 6 August 1945 the United States had dropped an atomic bomb on Hiroshima. A second atomic weapon destroyed Nagasaki three days later. Bishop Rawlinson did not refer directly to these events at the diocesan conference in Buxton in September, though he was to have much to say when the nuclear arms race got under way and weapons of much greater power had been developed. On this occasion he made a more general point. As the *High Peak News* reported him:

> The disinterested pursuit of truth [by scientists] has a noble passion which theologians and others could learn and which could be of service to God. Yet it was true that the results of scientific discovery could be exploited for evil, and it was becoming a commonplace to say that man's capacity of control over the forces of nature was in danger of outrunning his capacity of control over himself.[3]

By May 1954 world nuclear conflict had come near. The Soviet Union and the western allies had each developed nuclear devices which dwarfed in destructive power those dropped on Japanese cities a decade earlier. Bishop Rawlinson addressed his diocesan conference on the moral problem posed by the

---

[1] *Derby Evening Telegraph*, 11 May 1948.
[2] ibid., 29 September 1944.
[3] *High Peak News*, 6 October 1945.

development of the hydrogen bomb. He condemned its manufacture, but, he said,

> I am afraid my puny voice will not be likely either to penetrate the
> recesses of the Kremlin or to exercise influence there. The future of
> planet Earth is not, in these days, likely to be determined primarily by
> the opinions, desires or policies of Englishmen, or even, necessarily, of
> Americans.

Yet, arguing a position which was later to be taken in public debate by senior
diocesan staff when, in 1962, the matter was again raised, he did not regard
nuclear arms as different in kind from any other weapons, and therefore their
use should not be made subject to the application of different moral criteria:

> The strictly religious and moral problems raised by the simultaneous
> destruction of whole territories and the accompanying loss of a very
> large number of human lives are not very different from the problems
> raised by a single act of destructive violence (the explosion, for example,
> of an ordinary bomb), or the loss of a single human life by violence,
> whether in war or peace.[1]

When the issue was next debated at the Derby diocesan conference, this line of
argument was vigorously and skilfully – though fruitlessly – opposed from the
floor.

The next major international questions which engaged Bishop Rawlinson's
attention were the futile Hungarian revolution in 1956, the Israeli/Egyptian war
in the same year, and the South African government's *apartheid* policy. He did
not develop the critiques that he had applied in earlier years. He was now 71,
and did little more than condemn military aggression and call for prayer,
though he denounced racism vigorously. The South African government's
policy, he said in October 1956, could lead to 'the most horrible racial war'.

In the uncharacteristic absence of full engagement with these issues by their
bishop, others now provided it. In December 1956, the editor of the *DDN*, W.L.
Chivers, vicar of Darley Abbey, offered a sustained theological critique of the
situations in Cyprus, Egypt and Hungary. Referring particularly to the crisis in
the Middle East, he concluded:

> Christians may well find that it is their duty to represent again and again
> that means should always be moulded by ends and never justified by

---

[1] *Derbyshire Advertiser*, 28 May 1954.

> them. This is the lesson of the Third Temptation in the Wilderness[1]. It
> may be better, in the last analysis, for Britain to retain her integrity and
> lose her oil – for man does not live by oil alone – and to raise her standard
> of morals even if it means lowering her standard of living.

This was well and courageously said, and one or two clergy cancelled their
parish subscriptions to the *DDN* as a result!

These are some examples of the way in which a diocesan bishop of Rawlinson's
breadth of view was able to set the mundane concerns of a modest diocese firmly
in an international context, and to encourage others to do so too. The
congregation of a parish church in a remote Derbyshire village had its place in
the world. While Rawlinson was their bishop Derbyshire Anglicans found that
their Church provided no easy refuge from the responsibilities, and the horrors,
of the world. Quite the opposite. Although he did not show quite the same sure-
footedness when he was commenting on domestic politics, and avoided some
important questions completely (for example, he appears to have made no
public comment on the abdication of Edward VIII and the controversy that
precipitated it) Rawlinson saw it as a primary duty of a bishop fully to engage
with the world, speaking prophetically to it in judgement, and, in turn,
interpreting it theologically to the Church. In exercising this primary
episcopal ministry he encouraged his diocese repeatedly to focus closely on
social affairs. It is convenient here to show how other items on the wider social
agenda were addressed during these years.

'The imperilled freedom of human personality': social concerns

The perceptive and focused contributions to social questions made by Anglican
laymen in the diocese in the early 1930s seem not to have been matched by them
for a generation. Perhaps because the clergy were beginning increasingly to be
recruited from those sections of society with first-hand knowledge of the
commercial and industrial economy – or at least were aware of its importance
and were sensitive to it – they later began themselves to make theological and
ethical connections between the world and their faith.[2] At the diocesan
conference in October 1938 a debate on 'The imperilled freedom of human

---

[1] Matthew 4:8–10. It is the second temptation in Luke 4:6–8.

[2] As one of many examples, but 30 years later and the only one relating directly to industry, see M.R.
Austin, 'Industry and Christian responsibility', *DDN*, December 1964.

personality' was opened by the provost, Philip Micklem. In a protest that was to be made repeatedly, he said that 'we no longer live in village compartments . . . the whole of life has become departmentalized'. This 'departmentalization' was 'a consequence of the loss of Parliamentary control and the substitution of a host of controls by boards and other bodies who made ordinances not subject to any form of control.'[1] Bishop Rawlinson, with his repeated references to children being used as cannon- and factory-fodder was to argue similarly. These were years when the need to protect democratic freedoms was felt acutely.

J.H. Oldham was one of the most remarkable of the 20th century's Christian leaders. He was secretary of the International Missionary Council, but his influence was felt far more widely than the ecumenical movement of which he was the undisputed leader. He became the Churches' leading social thinker in the 1920s and for two more decades. Adrian Hastings says of him that he was 'the international ecclesiastical statesman in comparison with whom almost every bishop appeared immeasurably provincial in outlook.'[2] *Almost* every bishop, but not A.E.J. Rawlinson, who, in April 1940, asked this deaf Presbyterian layman to address his diocesan conference. Speaking on 'The Church in relation to the War' during the darkest days of the second World War (British forces were to begin their withdrawal from Dunkirk on 29 May), a war which was to continue for four more years, Oldham characteristically looked far beyond the immediate crisis and called upon his hearers to prepare for the struggles of the peace. The attempt to install a dictatorship of the Left, he warned, would be countered by an attempt to establish a tyranny of the Right. Freedom founded on democracy would be at a premium for, he feared, democracy did not hold a strong appeal for the young.[3] This seems so obvious an observation now, but it was far-sighted in 1940 when attention was directed to more immediate dangers.

Debates and episcopal pronouncements on social and political questions were not always to reach this level. So, for example, in May 1939 the bishop's wife Mildred (held in much affection in the diocese but to become increasingly eccentric as the years passed) opened a debate at the diocesan conference on 'The Modern Challenge to Christian Morality'. She based her criticism of that modern challenge on an observation made to her by 'a well-known magistrate' who had said that his court was filled as a result of the growing number of young

---

[1] *Derby Evening Telegraph*, 26 October 1938.
[2] Hastings, op.cit., 95.
[3] *Derby Evening Telegraph*, 1 May 1940.

girls living away from home 'in business hostels without friends'; the acquisition by young people 'of knowledge with regard to contraceptives'; – and pillion-riding![1] In 1937 a debate on 'The observance of Sunday from the point of view of the younger generation'[2] promised much, but it seems that no young people were present to take part. The discussion was led by A.G. Hardie, chaplain of Repton School, who was perhaps not fully in touch with the views of young adults in Ilkeston or Bolsover.

Questions of marriage, the family, and personal morality were frequently discussed at the diocesan conference, more so than any other social topic. The 'modern challenge' to Christian ethics which had been on the agenda in May 1939 and criticised by Mildred Rawlinson, had resulted in the 'terribly relaxed standards of marriage and family life' and the 'appalling' divorce statistics which so shocked her husband a decade later.[3] But a balanced critique was not offered by the mere voicing of criticisms. By contrast, in 1956, the provost of Derby, Ronald Beddoes, who was chairman of the diocesan Mother and Baby Home in Vernon Street in Derby, addressed the diocesan conference on unmarried motherhood. While recognising that it is 'one of the great moral problems of our age' (as it did appear to be then), he told the conference that whereas 'there was a time when the girls in our home were spoken of as bad girls ... they are now representative of a large number of people', implying that merely to castigate them would be to call into question the sexual mores of many of the young adult children of the members of the conference.[4] Canon Tony Chesterman, a diocesan General Synod representative, was to make a similar observation, but much more overtly, in a telling contribution to a Synod debate on cohabitation in July 1992.

In 1959, in another comment on the then current state of marriage and the family, Bishop Rawlinson observed that it was wrong to marry with no intention of having children. This seems to have provoked no adverse reaction. On remarriage in church after divorce Rawlinson stood firmly behind the Act of Convocation which had laid down that clergy should not allow the use of the marriage service for anyone with a former partner still living.[5] Yet on the issue of homosexuality he was somewhat more liberal. Reflecting on the report of the

---

[1] Diocesan conference *Minutes*, 15 May 1939.
[2] ibid., 9 March 1937.
[3] *Derby Evening Telegraph*, 14 May 1946.
[4] *Derbyshire Advertiser*, 18 May 1956.
[5] *Derby Evening Telegraph*, 8 November 1959.

Departmental Committee on Homosexual Offences and Prostitution (the Wolfendon Report) in 1957 he supported 'with some hesitation' the committee's proposals that homosexual behaviour between consenting adults in private should no longer be a criminal offence. He believed homosexual conduct to be sinful but, he said, he could not regard homosexuality as a disease or an illness 'with the implication either of irresponsibility or diminished responsibility . . . . It is not a disease: it is a particular propensity, a type of temperament.'[1] In the climate of the time that was a courageous, and ethically sharp, position to take.

On other social questions the bishop took a conservative line. In 1956, when the suggestion was made to launch Premium Bonds, he said that it would have been better that the Chancellor's proposal had not been made, for this was a 'socially harmful experiment' and was 'a kind of official endorsement by the State of the gambling propensity.'[2] It was an experiment that was to become a scarcely noticed product of the savings industry. A national lottery was to become a much clearer state endorsement of 'the gambling propensity'.

There were many other social questions which engaged the attention of church people in the diocese. In 1955 Bishop Rawlinson criticised the 'continued indulgence in large-scale strikes, paralysing the economic life of the country for prolonged periods', for it must 'in the long run, failing a remedy, tear our society to pieces.'[3] In the late 1950s Bill Chivers raised a number of significant social issues in the *DDN,* in the absence of comment from his bishop. For example, in June 1957, in a leader on Christian responsibility in local government, he said that 'the Christian will constantly seek to modify both private enterprise and social planning by consideration for the person, to insist that people are more important than the party-line, and [that] individual need comes before administrative convenience.'[4] In February 1959 he criticised the Church Commissioners for allegedly speculating in aluminium shares. Bill Chivers was to continue to ask sharply focused questions and to propose often controversial, but always clearly considered, answers.

'We are very, very POOR': church schools

A central feature of the engagement of the Church of England with wider

---

[1] ibid., 20 October 1957.
[2] *Derbyshire Advertiser,* 18 May 1956.
[3] *DDN* July 1955.
[4] *DDN* June 1957.

society in these years was its still very considerable responsibility for education, and especially primary education.

Under the terms of the 1936 Education Act it was open to the managers of schools in the voluntary sector, mainly those belonging to the Church of England, to submit proposals to local education authorities for the enlargement or improvement of schools. If a LEA approved the proposal it was empowered to make a grant not exceeding three-quarters of the total cost. This was a significant departure and established the still very important formal relationship between the Church of England and LEAs. Bishop Rawlinson noted and welcomed this development at the diocesan conference on 9 March 1937. And well he might, because the financial, and therefore the physical, condition of many church schools was very unsatisfactory. The tranche of education legislation that was to follow, especially the 1944 Act, was to determine the nature of the Church/State partnership and the extent to which the Church's schools could retain a degree of independence from state control. There is here no space to review this relationship as it affected Derbyshire's church schools, but one snapshot of these schools survives to illustrate how vital that relationship was to become.

In 1940 the diocesan Board of Education sent a brief questionnaire to each of its day schools asking for such information as: the number of children on the school roll ('excluding evacuees'); the population of the parish; the regular school income; the method of meeting routine repairs; the amount spent on repairs and improvements since 1931; religious instruction other than given by the staff; where the trust deeds were kept; – and asking also for 'Any other information.'

The questionnaires returned[1] indicate that in 1940 the Church of England was providing at least 15270 places in 153 schools in 146 parishes, mostly in small rural communities. Fifty-five parishes, or 38%, had schools with less than 50 pupils, and 23, or 16%, with fewer than 31. The managers (almost always chaired by the incumbent) scrimped and saved as best they could, meeting routine repairs from church collections, sales of work, rental income, whist drives, dances, 'entertainments' and jumble sales. At Edlaston the incumbent, G.E. Raven, reported that the parish could not afford to provide wash basins in the school, though water had at last been laid on – by pump from a nearby spring! There were 44 children on the roll from a population of 180. At

---

[1] Derby Diocesan Record Office, Matlock, D4825/19/1 and D4825/19/2.

Hognaston there were no Prayer Books in a school with 45 pupils, the incumbent, J.D. Shemilt, noting: 'Reason appears to be friction on behalf of Non-Conformists.' The rector of Longford, H. Bennett, reported that in his widely scattered parish 'Church Teaching does not make Churchgoers when they have 2 or 3 miles to come! I have my doubts whether the maintenance of a Church School is worth the constant strain of raising the necessary funds for an antiquated building.' The school roll there was 64. In the parish of Stoney Middleton, with a school with 68 pupils and a population of 530, it was noted that 'being entirely without accommodation for parochial organisations we lose the vast majority of the children when they leave school', while at Youlgreave (school roll 180, population 1250) the incumbent wrote: 'Our income has been so little and our expenses so great that [the] Foundation Managers once or twice felt we should give the School up. Income (regular) insufficient to pay regular annual expenses which amount to £12.' The incumbent of Ilkeston Holy Trinity, F.R. Money, wrote:

> The staff has a fine record as teachers. They are Church folk, but all live outside and far beyond my parish. This is the only Church School in the old borough of Ilkeston. It is old and inconvenient. About 50% of the scholars are Non-Conformists. I enjoy teaching them, but the end is near!! We are very, very POOR.

His school, with 197 children under seven years of age, served a population of 9000. With this degree of real financial need it is little wonder that many managers of church schools were ready to close their schools and transfer the children to the state sector, or at least to surrender management control of their schools to the LEA.

In 1956 the attempt to maintain the financial independence of church schools was called into question by Bishop Rawlinson. He told the diocesan conference: 'I do not myself propose to do anything in support of the further raising of funds for church schools . . . . Our proper policy ought to be, not to compete with the State in the building of schools, but to concentrate on the Church training colleges and to flood the schools, both of those of the nation and those of the Church, with church teachers.'[1] Yet the diocese was clearly exercising its educational responsibility very effectively. Four years earlier, Canon R.W. Stopford, secretary of the National Society and later to become bishop of

---

[1] *Derbyshire Advertiser,* 2 November 1956.

London, had told the conference that the diocese was a model in its educational provision, and paid a warm tribute to H.S. O'Neill, the diocesan director of education.[1]

But Rawlinson's point was soundly, if controversially, made. The Church's teacher training colleges were beginning a period of major expansion. In 1953 Miss H.K. Hawkins, principal of the Diocesan[2] Training College since 1927, retired. She had very much set the tone of the college. Under its next principal, Amy Sephton, the college expanded rapidly, taking advantage of state funding. In July 1956 it had 200 women students taught by a staff of 21. By 1961 it had erected a campus on a new site on Uttoxeter New Road in Mickleover while continuing to use the 1851 buildings and residential accommodation. The expanded college, now mixed, would virtually double the number of students. The cost of the new buildings in Mickleover was £392000 of which the Ministry of Education provided 75%. When the tenders for the original 'Training Institution for Females', designed by Henry I. Stevens, had been returned in 1850, the lowest was for £4617 12s, from John and Geo. Lilley of Measham.

'With father's blessing and nothing else': finance

The legacy of poorly maintained school buildings was but one of the financial problems of the diocese of Derby. As in Bishop Pearce's time, so in Bishop Rawlinson's the need at least to maintain and, very gradually, to raise clergy incomes; to provide new churches in new housing areas; to maintain the diocesan contribution to central Church funds; and to service the committees and boards of the diocese, was a continual strain. At his first diocesan conference Rawlinson had been 'frankly dismayed by the present state of affairs.' Fifty per cent of the parishes were not meeting their full quota commitments, which were, in any case, 'very modest', and the bishop was driven to compare his new diocese very unfavourably with the diocese of Durham, where he had served as an archdeacon. Durham was 'economically striken', he said, but its poor parishes struggled and succeeded 'as a matter of honour' to pay quotas even when the majority of their adult populations were on the dole. He forebore to add that Durham was an ancient and relatively wealthy diocese.

We have noted that the diocese of Derby began with an over-draft. Jack

---

[1] *Derby Evening Telegraph*, 21 October 1952.
[2] that is, of the three dioceses of Lichfield, Southwell and Derby.

Richardson, archdeacon of Derby, reminded the diocesan conference in May 1955 that it had started life 'very much like a modern young couple today – with father's blessing and nothing else.'[1] By that time the diocese was virtually bankrupt, with cuts of 25% being made to grants voted by the diocesan conference to the work of its committees and boards because insufficient revenue was coming in from the parishes. By October 1957 the diocese was the only one in England which was not meeting its financial obligation to ordination training.[2] Yet the financial tide had already turned. In March of that year only 13 parishes, or 5%, had made no quota payments, while 174, or 79%, had paid in full or in excess.[3] The quota returns, by May 1961, were the best for fourteen years.[4] This turnaround had been achieved by raising the profile of parish giving, by stewardship campaigns, and perhaps not least by Bill Chivers who took to naming and shaming non-paying and under-paying parishes in the *DDN*, together with the names of their incumbents and the excuses offered by their churchwardens!

The financial improvement was not achieved without controversy. A heated discussion at the diocesan conference in October 1950, following a deficit in 1949 of £1700, had ended with the conference agreeing to fix parish quotas as the average of the sums raised in the previous three years by individual parishes for their expenses. An amendment that each parish should give 'such sum as it deems fit' was defeated. It was, said J.F. Young, vicar of Turnditch, 'a splendid idea to which the diocese was not yet educated.'[5] Two years earlier, Canon S.L. Caiger had objected to the allocation of £3293 to central Church funds (an increase of 500% since 1934) using the frequently deployed argument that central Church staff were overpaid and that there was, in any case, 'much wasteful and unnecessary expenditure.' In May 1952 the archdeacon of Derby, H.E. Fitzherbert, had resigned after nine years in post 'in which the work of the Church has been increasingly hampered by economic and other difficulties.'[6] The diocesan Board of Finance was roundly taken to task during the diocesan conference in October 1953. Bill Chivers, vicar of Darley Abbey, moved that the estimates for 1954 be referred back to the DBF 'in view of the neglect of the Board of Finance to take adequate steps to make known the financial needs of

---

[1] *Derby Evening Telegraph*, 18 May 1955.
[2] ibid., 20 October 1957.
[3] *DDN,* March 1957.
[4] *Derbyshire Advertiser*, 2 June 1961.
[5] ibid., 20 October 1950.
[6] *Derbyshire Advertiser,* 30 May 1952.

the diocese in terms the parishes can understand.'[1] The motion was withdrawn but the point was taken.

It should be said here that although the diocesan finances improved in the short term, they were to face a major crisis in the mid-1980s. That there has been a very considerable improvement since says much both for episcopal leadership, especially that of Bishop Dawes, bishop of Derby, 1988–75, (who, as one who knew the situation well has noted, in his 'gritty and downbeat way' tackled the problem quickly and decisively) and, above all, for the faithfulness of Derbyshire Anglicans. There are far fewer of them now than there were in 1927, but the proportion of those who then professed allegiance but who offered no more than 'the lip service of distant loyalty' is also far less now. Sunday church-going then was, for many, what it had been for the barrister Hubert Langton in P.D. James' *A Certain Justice*, namely 'a formal affirmation of a received set of values' which had become little more than 'a pointless exercise designed to give shape to the week.'[2] People do not give sacrificially to a religion that provides them with no more than a calendar.

'Through the eyes of those outside': evangelism

But the Church *did* offer much more than shape to the week, though its ability to do so effectively required it to be open to radical change, and the Church of England did not take to radical change readily. The diocese celebrated its 25th anniversary in 1952. In the February *DDN*, a Bolsover sidesman, G.F. Altoft, suggested a theme for the jubilee year: 'Every member gain a member.' The idea was taken up by the assistant bishop and provost, R.S.M. O'Ferrall. The aim that year, he said rather hopefully, should be 'to win Derbyshire for Christ.' In the next month's edition another layman, Michael Lazenby, responded that

> we must first view the Church and the Churches through the eyes of those 'outside': this is a great need, requiring earnest concentration. Only thus can we understand their difficulties and expect to help them to adjust their values.

Today that sounds somewhat patronising but he had made a crucial point. Not only would such a policy require 'earnest concentration', it would demand a

---

[1] ibid., 30 October 1953.
[2] Penguin 1998, 57.

radically new theological approach which undermined the complacency of the established ways in which the Gospel and its proclamation had been understood. This radical insight was provided by the deeply biblical so-called 'secular Christianity' of, among others, Ronald Gregor Smith, extending and applying Dietrich Bonhoeffer's insights. It was a theology which spoke powerfully to only a relatively few clergy, among them the most hard-pressed. New ideas were often met at best with incomprehension and entrenchment – and not merely new *theological* ideas.

'*As it was in the beginning*': pastoral organisation

By the early 1950s it had become clear that although church attendances were rising, the Church of England could not maintain its supposedly ideal pattern of an incumbent resident in every separate parish. Although it was an ideal that had perhaps never been achieved (the populations of many parishes had always been too small), most church people felt that they had a right to have their own incumbent. Low clergy recruitment made this impossible, but even had the number of candidates for ordination improved, any increase in incumbents' stipends, however modest, meant that the Church could not afford to appoint them, and there would need to be more 'joint livings'[1]. But there was another consideration. One parson for each parish was not only impossible in practice but unsustainable in theological principle, for it gave credence to the notion that Christian ministry was for the clergy alone, and that the Church could not exist in the absence of a priest.

In the light of the practical considerations (it is often these which drive theology) the diocesan Pastoral Reorganisation Committee was established in 1950, following the passing, by Church Assembly, of the Pastoral Reorganisation Measure in 1949. Under strict safeguards, the Measure allowed for the uniting of two or more benefices, the altering of parish boundaries, and the holding of two or more benefices in plurality. It was to be superseded by successive Measures during the following 35 years. Although Bishop Rawlinson was strongly in favour of the new legislation, some senior diocesan clergy expressed disquiet. Canon S.L. Caiger, the vicar of Wirksworth, felt that the Measure was 'drastic and epoch-making' and that the safeguards were not

---

[1] Bishop Rawlinson, diocesan conference April 1947, *Derbyshire Advertiser*, 25 April 1947.

strict enough. If the Measure was to be implemented, he argued, every rural deanery must be represented on the diocesan pastoral reorganisation committee.[1]

The function of the committee was to consider the reorganisation of the parochial structure of the diocese in the light of the limited powers granted under the 1949 Measure. To this effect, in the early 1950s it conducted a series of surveys of the rural deaneries and formulated proposals for change. As S.L. Caiger's response indicates, these proposals were frequently met with considerable resistance. For example, in 1951 surveys were made of the rural deaneries of Longford, Duffield and Ashbourne and proposals made for amalgamations of parishes. These involved one union of four benefices; seven unions each of three benefices; two unions each of two benefices; and one scheme for a new plural holding of benefices. The chairman of the diocesan pastoral reorganisation committee was a layman, S.J. Bartle. Having put these proposals to the parishes involved, he reported to the diocesan conference that it appeared that their clergy and laity

> had taken to themselves a new article of faith. It has nothing to do with the three main creeds, but has some affinity with the *Gloria*. So far as Pastoral Re-organization is concerned, it is "As it was in the beginning, is now and ever shall be."[2]

Other deameries had been far more ready to embrace change. On the basis of the figures quoted earlier the Bolsover ruri-decanal conference had itself recommended a quite radical pattern of amalgamations of parishes and re-deployment of clergy.

By 1955 rationalisation, if not reorganisation, was well under way. In that year Canon Geoffrey Busby, vicar of Wirksworth, became rural dean of Wirksworth. He held two-fifths of the benefices in his rural deanery.[3] The committee was superseded in April 1969 with the coming into force of the Pastoral Measure 1968. Up to then any major scheme for pastoral reorganisation required legislation, but under the Measure (superseded by the Pastoral Measure 1983) the diocese, through its Pastoral Committee, was able to create new parishes, alter existing ones and declare churches redundant by following a statutory process which involved consulting all interested parties

---

[1] *Derby Evening Telegraph*, 23 November 1949.
[2] *Derbyshire Advertiser,* I June 1951.
[3] *DDN* February 1955.

and obtaining the necessary authority from the diocesan bishop, the Church Commissioners or, as appropriate, the Crown.

Failure to rationalise, and therefore to deploy clergy effectively, led to anomalies. In 1953–4 600 services were taken in the diocese 'without proper consent' (that is, of the 'ordinary', usually the bishop), in some cases by laymen who were not licensed Readers. This may seem of marginal importance in the context of eternity, but there are good reasons for requiring permission to conduct worship by those not licenced to do so, and, for a Church of England established by law, lawlessness, however notional, causes bishops and archdeacons some agitation.

'The fantastically clericalist manner': the nature and maintenance of ministry

Throughout this period concern was often expressed at the Church's failure to recruit sufficient numbers of clergy. In fact ordinations to the stipendiary diaconate in the diocese each year remained remarkably consistent between 1929 and 1979, generally, with very few exceptions, within the band 7–10. The war years produced very few ordinations, with none at all in 1942, and there were exceptionally high numbers in the early 1960s, with 15 deacons ordained in 1961 and 12 in 1962 and in 1967. Ordinations to the non-stipendiary ordained ministry began in 1980, and women were first ordained to the diaconate in 1987 and to the priesthood in 1994. Even so (with very low numbers in one or two years) ordinations remained generally within the same band well into the 1990s, although in later years a quota system was applied nationally to dioceses.

The level of clergy stipends has been a far from insignificant sub-theme of this social history, and we need to add a brief note about it in this period. In 1947, 40% of the benefices in the diocese had a gross income of less than £450 a year. This, for Bishop Rawlinson, was 'a minimum living wage.' He said to his diocesan conference in April 1947 that 'what has become quite clear is that the days when the lay members of the Church of England could normally expect to hope to be provided with a parish priest free of charge . . . and without any need to contribute to clerical stipends, have gone by.' By 1953 minimum clergy stipends for incumbents were set at £550 of which the Church Commissioners provided £50. The clergy were provided with a house free of rates and repairs (or 'dilapidations'). However, in 1954 the stipends of 192 benefices in the diocese fell below this figure. Of the £28500 required to reach the new minimum,

£25305 would have to come from parish quota payments.[1]

The condition of parsonage houses improved greatly as the years passed, but from a low base. A report from the DBF to the diocesan conference in May 1940 noted the very poor condition of some parsonages, a condition 'almost unbelievable in the 20th century.' In many there was 'most primitive sanitation', 'inadequate water supplies', and 'a lack of lighting facilities.'

The prospect of supporting their families on poor stipends in large and ill-maintained parsonages did not recommend the parochial ministry to men in the 1940s and 1950s, and, though many willingly committed themselves to this ministry, the bishops were rightly concerned to improve the income and living conditions of the clergy. But this added to the costs of maintaining the ordained ministry and reduced the numbers that could be employed.

Of course, low clergy recruitment could not be blamed solely, or even mainly, on poor housing and low incomes. At his first diocesan conference in November 1959, Bishop Rawlinson's successor, Geoffrey Allen, formerly principal of Ripon Hall theological college, commented on the 'very serious' shortage of clergy. He said:

> Like the days when Our Lord walked the earth, the present is an age of intense yearning after the consolation of religion, but of intellectual doubt scarcely less intense. Hence many temperamentally religious men are shy of taking up religion as a profession, and some at least, who had they lived in the later years of the nineteenth century, would almost certainly have accepted Orders without a single mental reservation, confess that they find it an impossible task today to bring their intellectual beliefs within the four corners of a precisely-worded creed.[2]

He went on to imply that this fact alone should bring the Church to a deeper understanding of the nature of ministry: 'God is lifting us out of a false passivity on the side of the laity, and a corresponding error, an equally false clericalism on the side of the clergy.' His predecessor had gone further. A decade earlier Bishop Rawlinson had inveighed against 'the fantastically clericalist manner in which the Church of England is administered that such spiritual matters as the administration of the sacraments are discussed in the Convocations [rather] than in the Church Assembly'[3] in which lay representatives had a voice and a

[1] *The Church in Derbyshire: Report of the Bishop's Finance Commission 1954.*
[2] *Derbyshire Advertiser*, 13 November 1959.
[3] *Derby Evening Telegraph*, 10 May 1950.

vote. The low level of recruitment to the ordained ministry, as with falling church attendance figures and Confirmation numbers, was evidence, as Ron Beddoes so shrewdly noted, that the success or failure of the Church was written into the general social situation. The Church of England was beginning, in the 1950s, slowly and unwillingly, to recognise this truth, though rarely was it articulated publicly. It was to be very different in the 1960s as we will see.

'The religious compromise': the parishes

Yet parish life continued relatively unmoved by these considerations. Pastoral ministry touches people's lives at moments of deep significance for them, and men and women gather together in church congregations for spiritual, temperamental, psychological and social reasons which defy easy analysis, but from which, at the very least, much good flows. Bill Chivers, as editor of the *DDN,* received 70 parish magazines every month. On reading them, he wrote in 1959,

> one suddenly realises the vast amount of individual and corporate service being given simply, unaffectedly and unostentatiously, all over the diocese .... [The] regular weekly and monthly routine which these modest magazines record is a symbol of the spiritual level of the Church's parishes which is often higher and more sincere than administrators are sometimes aware.[1]

But parish life makes for much variety. In February Bill Chivers published an article from 'a professional man' whose work had brought him to Derby. He searched for a church to attend:

> In my wanderings between Melbourne on one side and Ilkeston on the other, I've enjoyed partaking in the simplicity and dignity of a "plain" service beautifully read; have been well and truly incensed; have stood and listened (feeling rather an eavesdropper than a participant) as clear voices have soared heavenwards; have ducked when the whole organ seemed to have been thrown at me; have been welcomed into the family; and have been completely ignored.

---

[1] *Derby Diocesan News,* March 1959.

This experience, he said, illustrated the truth of a sentence he had once learnt parrot-fashion in school: 'Elizabeth achieved a religious compromise on a wide and comprehensive scale.' Those two quotations from the *DDN* describe the Church of England as it was in Derbyshire nearly fifty years ago – and as it largely still is. But much was changing in the Church.

Contraction and expansion: religious decline?

By 1936 only £34000 had been raised towards Bishop Pearce's appeal for £250000 for new churches made six years earlier. The building of Derby St Mark's had been started. A conventional district (the first stage in the creation of a new parish) had been formed to serve the private housing development of Frecheville. The appeal fund had paid half the cost of providing a site for a church, vicarage and parish hall in Normanton-by-Derby, had contributed to a new Sunday school in Boulton to serve the needs of Allenton, and had met part of the cost of providing a site for an additional church in Brampton, to be dedicated to St Mark. It had also provided a site for a mission hall in Mackworth, 'erected to deal with the results of a Corporation slum clearance scheme.' Then came war, and the programme of church expansion was not continued until 1945.

In that year Bishop Rawlinson launched a ten year plan 'to proclaim the Gospel, teach the faith, and make Christian disciples.' He appealed for £175000 of which £40000 was to be earmarked for the cathedral, £27000 for post-war needs in the diocese generally, and, of importance for this bishop, £5000 'towards Christian regeneration in Europe.' Bishop Pearce's appeal for £250000 had never approached its target, and neither did Bishop Rawlinson's, but much was done. By 1949 eight new building projects had been started. As one example, Frecheville, in an outlying part of the parish of Beighton, had come into existence in 1934 as a privately financed housing development of 1500 homes. The majority of those who lived there came from, and worked in, nearby Sheffield. A temporary church, accommodating 100, was opened in December 1934. It was still in use, slightly enlarged, in 1949. By then, it was said, 'its compressed cardboard walls are now very rotten, and it has always been draughty in winter and horribly stuffy in summer.' A photograph of this church shows it to be what it was – a cardboard box. Little wonder that it was said that 'apart from its practical inconveniences it compares very unfavourably in appearance with other public buildings on the estate which already possesses a permanent Methodist chapel and a lavishly-equipped community centre.'[1]

Frecheville became legally separated from Beighton in 1943 and part of the endowment of the suppressed parish of Derwent, now submerged beneath the Ladybower reservoir, was transferred to the new benefice of Frecheville St Cyprian. Compensation of £20000 was paid for the now submerged Derwent church and this was diverted to the erection of a new church and vicarage for Frecheville. These were designed by J.Harold Gibbons and building began in 1951 at a cost of £23000. By 1960 it could be said that St Cyprian's Frecheville had been completed, a vicarage built, a curate's house acquired, and a lay parish worker appointed and paid for all within the 16 years incumbency of its vicar, Paul Tuckwell. The parish was transferred to the diocese of Sheffield in 1974.

The closing of now redundant mission halls and churches, and the building of churches and parsonages in new housing areas took place at a time, immediately following the second World War, when church attendance figures were increasing. In 1955 a study of Derby was published which included estimates of religious allegiance.[2] Bill Chivers reviewed it in the *DDN* in August. The Church of England was credited with the allegiance of 73% of the population of the city, the Methodists with 11%, the Roman Catholics with 7%, and other nonconformists with 7%, while 2% of the population professed no denomination. Seven per cent of those professing to be members of the Church of England were once-a-week worshippers compared with 51% of Roman Catholics and 23% of nonconformists. It was claimed that 55% of Derby's children attended Sunday school (though Bill Chivers doubted this, believing the figure to be nearer 35%). Twenty-five per cent of the parents of these children did not attend church (implying that 75% did). Today these figures seem almost unbelievably high, such has been the attrition since. Fifty-five per cent of these parents never read the Bible and 53% did not even possess a copy. By contrast these figures now seem very low. It is impossible to know how reliable these estimates are, though the survey seems to have been undertaken on a sound basis. Assuming their accuracy, and given the rise in church attendance figures since 1948, the Church of England had reason to be confident in the 1950s. This confidence led to a renewed hope for Christian unity by some, and, for others, to a determination to maintain denominational identity.

---

[1] Appeal brochure, Ten Year Plan 1949.
[2] T. Cauter and J.S. Downham, *The Communication of Ideas: a study of Contemporary Influences on Urban Life* (1955).

'The intolerable burdens of sinful divisions': Christian unity

The diocesan conference in October 1938 debated Christian reunion. Bishop Rawlinson invited the Revd E.K.C. Hamilton, secretary of the Fellowship of Reunion to open the discussion. He said: 'We Anglicans do manage to bear the intolerable burdens of sinful divisions with something very near equanimity . . . [and] we forget how they positively shock the outside world.' The Fellowship had apparently not always been welcomed by the diocesan bishop. Robert Dell records that when speculation about Bishop Pearce's successor was rife, Canon Tissington Tatlow, in a letter to Cosmo Gordon Lang, then archbishop of Canterbury, pleaded for the appointment of a bishop less opposed to the ecumenical movement. Writing from The Hayes conference centre in Swanwick he claimed that the Fellowship would not come to Swanwick again until 'Derby is ruled over ecclesiastically by an ecumenically minded bishop.'[1] Rawlinson was certainly ecumenically minded, but during the debate in 1938 he warned, with justification, that the issue of Christian unity was very difficult and would take generations of hard study and prayer to solve.[2] He brought hard-headed realism to the on-going debate about Christian unity and, unlike many others committed to it, would never allow that lasting reunion could be attained by ignoring the causes of division.

For the whole of Rawlinson's episcopate, as it had been for that of his predecessor, the focus of attempts to bring unity to the Churches was South India. In July 1943 he said of the proposed scheme for a United Church of South India that 'I think it fair to say that it contains one or two provisions which, as they stand, could be accepted by Church people only with considerable reluctance and with some hesitation', though, while acknowledging that there were risks in the scheme, he believed that there were also great possibilities.[3]

During the 1948 Lambeth Conference Bishop Rawlinson had been chairman of the sub-committee considering the South India scheme, inaugurated the previous year. In November he took Christian unity as the theme of his address to the diocesan conference meeting in Ilkeston. He referred to the division of opinion about the South India proposals within S.P.G[4], the principal Anglican missionary society in southern India. That, under the

---

[1] Robert Dell, op.cit., 138.
[2] *Derbyshire Advertiser,* 26 October 1938.
[3] *Derby Diocesan Leaflet,* July 1943.
[4] *Society for the Propagation of the Gospel.*

proposals, some bishops and clergy of the new C.S.I. would not be episcopally ordained had divided the Society. It was the issue which, from the Anglican side, was to destroy the scheme for Anglican-Methodist reunion in 1969. On the question of wider Christian unity, Rawlinson was hopeful. He said that one of the most impressive results of modern biblical study was the realisation that the central theme of the Old and New Testaments was

> the theme not simply of God, but of God and His people; that, as God is one, so also His people is one; that the idea of a plurality of disunited and implicitly rival religious societies, all and each of them claiming to represent Christ and His cause in the world, is in complete contrast to the teaching and outlook of Scripture; that, on the contrary, our Lord means His disciples to be one, in the unity of the Holy Spirit.[1]

Ten years later Rawlinson was to condemn the 'smug insensitiveness to the flat contradiction between what the New Testament understands by the Church and the miserable facts of today [its disunity] is (alas!) still far to common; and the Gospel is hindered thereby.'[2]

The issue of Christian unity, of course, is the issue of the Church, its nature and its purpose. Above all, it speaks directly to the Church's understanding of the nature of the God it worships and the Gospel it proclaims. Bishop Rawlinson saw this very clearly. The inadequacy, as perceived by many, of the Church's understanding of itself, its Gospel and its God was to become the Church's major challenge in the extraordinary decade that now followed.

---

[1] *The Pioneer*, 5 November 1948.
[2] *DDN,* January 1958.

15

'The Missionary Fellowship': The Sixties

A young priest coming to his first incumbency in an inner-city parish in Derby in 1960 could be both frightened and excited by what he found and what he had to do. The post-war increase in those claiming some kind of allegiance to the Church of England was coming to an end, but it had only been a modest increase, and, in the inner city, dedicated but small congregations worshipped their God and served their communities as they struggled to maintain churches built in the 19th century to accommodate congregations many times as large.

As the early 1960s saw, for the Churches, the end of the improvement in numbers and the beginning of the decline, so, too, they were years either of a destructive questioning by theologians of theological certitudes, or of the most exciting and far-reaching theological explorations of the 20th century, depending on one's point of view. It was said then, and is still said now, that the two were closely connected, namely that church attendance declined because a radical, questioning theology was rejected by people who wanted from the Churches (whether they belonged to them or not) nothing less than religious certainty. Loss of certainty, the argument went, inevitably led to loss of faith and loss of people.

It would be foolish to refuse to see any connection between the two, and there is no doubt that some theologians, particularly those with little experience of parish ministry, allowed their excitement at the positive ideas with which they were engaging to dull their judgement as to the negative impact their radicalism was having. And much of this so-called new theology was, when expounded by its less skilled teachers, somewhat muddled, as the bishop of Derby, by now Geoffrey Allen, pointed out. At the diocesan conference in May 1966 he spoke of

> the rather muddled language about the secular society and a religionless Christianity[1]. I do not believe for one moment that we can do without religion in its true and proper sense, the bond between the human heart and the love and truth of God made known in Christ.

Yet, he continued,

> much that we call religion is better called religiosity. We spend so much time discussing very minor matters of religious observance completely irrelevant for the need of the world. If that is religion, then let us have religionless Christianity. But of course it is not. The Church is called to stand for the Old Testament virtues of justice and righteousness, and the New Testament virtues of forgiveness and service.[2]

The negative impact that the theological mini-revolution had on some was outweighed by the positive impact that it had on others. Not untypical was the reaction to *Honest to God*. Bishop John Robinson's book was trailed in an article in *The Observer* in March 1963 with the title 'Our Image of God must Go'. Nearly a million copies of the book were sold in less than three years. Within a few weeks of its publication the chief executive of a major engineering company in Derby had read the book and had told the young incumbent (who had not) how exciting he had found it.

It is clear that the Churches' numerical losses in the late Sixties had much less to do with radical theology (which was more a response to decline than its cause) than with the 'crisis of relevance' of long-standing institutions that we have noted. Its effect on religious institutions is usually characterised as 'secularisation', a word employed in a variety of ways (some unhelpfully) to interpret the decline of religion not merely in terms of church membership or attendance but also its loss of influence in significant areas of social life – in education, for example, or in the determination of ethical standards.

---

[1] This phrase was Dietrich Bonhoeffer's. In prison in Germany before his execution by the SS in 1945, he had written that 'we are proceeding towards a time of no religion at all: men as they are now simply cannot be religious any more', so, he asked, 'What is a religionless Christianity?' [*Letters and Papers from Prison* (SCM 1953), 122–3]. By this he meant that, in the modern world, men and women were no longer concerned with the state of their own souls or the arguments for the existence and nature of a God beyond their world, with which traditional Christianity had been concerned. Shorn of that now rejected metaphysics, what must Christianity become and what form must it take?

[2] *DDN*, July 1966. Bonhoeffer's theology was very much in accord with this view.

Just as this period of great change began, the diocese of Derby was given a new bishop. A.E.J. Rawlinson retired in 1959. Geoffrey Francis Allen succeeded him. He was already a bishop, having been bishop in Egypt from 1947 to 1952 following service in China and three years as archdeacon of Birmingham. Following his years in Egypt he had become principal of Ripon Hall, then the leading liberal theological college in the Church of England. Although, like both his immediate predecessor and his successor, he had limited parish experience, he had a shy sensitivity, wisdom, a capacity for administration, a gentle sense of humour, considerable (if understated) learning, and a deep personal commitment to the world-wide Church. He also had a wife, Madeline, who, with Betsy Richardson, wife of the archdeacon of Derby, was to care deeply if unobtrusively for the families of the clergy. When Bishop Allen retired ten years later not only had the religious map of Britain changed, as Adrian Hastings suggests, but significant topographical features of the religious landscape had been considerably eroded.

'To see clearly, to act efficiently': the bishop's visitation 1962

As his two predecessors had done, Geoffrey Allen conducted a primary visitation of his diocese early in his episcopate, sending articles of enquiry to the clergy and churchwardens. The visitation was held in 1962. Its purpose, he wrote, was 'to make a survey of the state of church life in the diocese, and to encourage a sense of responsibility for the outgoing work of the Church in mission and evangelism.'[1] The visitation was followed by the bishop's Charge.

Compared with Bishop Rawlinson's substantial book-length Charge in 1937, Bishop Allen's was published as a much more modest booklet of 33 pages with three chapters: The Worship of the Church, The Work of the Church, and a list of financial priorities entitled Counting the Cost. The purpose of the visitation, he said, quoting Pius XII, was 'to see clearly in order to act efficiently.' Modest though it was, the bishop's survey provides a shrewd and perceptive account of the diocese just at the moment when the tide turned, the numerical decline began, and when searching questions were being raised about the nature of Christian ministry.

---

[1] Geoffrey Allen, *Survey of a Diocese: The Bishop of Derby's Primary Visitation* (1962), conflated from addresses given at three centres on 10, 11, and 12 May 1962, and the presidential address at the diocesan conference on 6 June 1962.

Geoffrey Allen came to a diocese so varied, he said, that it found it difficult to establish a sense of community. Many of its parishes looked outside the diocese for their nearest towns and cities: Sheffield, Mansfield, Burton-on-Trent, Stockport and Manchester.[1] This had been so for many years, but the pressure on Derbyshire to provide new housing developments clustering near these conurbations was increasing. For example, we have noted that during A.E.J. Rawlinson's episcopate the Sheffield over-spill into north-east Derbyshire created major housing areas which looked to Sheffield for employment, shopping and recreation but to the diocese of Derby for the provision of Anglican churches and clergy. Bishop Allen noticed that one in five of the parishes had its postal town outside the diocese. He added: 'As [the diocese] embraces a great variety in these different ways, so also . . . [it] embraces the variety of churchmanship to which we are accustomed in the Church of England', and which the anonymous 'professional man' had encountered between Melbourne and Ilkeston three years earlier.

In his *Survey of a Diocese* Bishop Allen spoke firstly of what the returned articles of enquiry told him of the worship of the Church in this widely diverse diocese. He noted the development of a parish holy Communion service as the principal act of Sunday worship at the main morning service time in parishes of all traditions in the diocese. Out of 39 parishes with populations of over 10000, 23 had a Parish Communion every Sunday; out of 40 parishes with between 5000 and 10000 people, 24 had a Parish Communion; for parishes between 1000 and 5000, less than half had the service; while out of 62 parishes with a population under 1000 only 13 reported a weekly Parish Communion, with another eight having the service once a month. This witnessed, he said, 'partly [to] the greater conservatism in village congregations and their dislike of change, and partly [to] the necessity in many villages to let times of service fit in with milking hours' (though one wonders to what extent the last factor was an issue even forty years ago).

Geoffrey Allen, as had his two predecessors, was concerned that, liturgically, the diocese should be law-abiding and he was glad to find that 'with very rare exceptions' it was. Forty-four parishes used the so-called interim rite, a modestly anglo-catholic practice countenanced by the Upper, but not the Lower, House of Convocation. It was an illegal rite, strictly speaking. That forty-four parishes used it may suggest that the diocese had become marginally

---

[1] In 1975 the *Derbyshire Structure Plan* noted that 12% of the work-force commuted out of the county.

more inclined to moderate Catholic practice in its worship than it had been a generation earlier.

Having a eucharist as the principal Sunday service posed two problems, the bishop noted. These were that regular worshippers now rarely heard the Old Testament read and expounded[1], and that sermons at this service were invariably brief and therefore, the bishop felt keenly, quite inadequate. He suggested that clergy should also take note of modern adult education techniques and experiment with question and answer sessions and a with time for informal discussion after the service. It is doubtful whether many clergy took their bishop's advice in this matter. The expository sermon, however brief, was much regarded by Anglican clergy.

Bishop Allen was, he said, concerned to discover that in 75 of the parishes, or over 25%, there was no weekday service of Morning and Evening Prayer. He made much of this. Bishop Pearce had made a similar observation a generation earlier, though it seems that the practice had declined since his day. This question touched as much on the personal devotional disciplines of the parish priest as it did on the public performance of worship. Some felt that if people did not come to the weekday daily Offices why say them at all? But, Bishop Allen observed to his clergy, 'as compared with other professions we are very little subject to supervision in our work; it is the more important that we are strict in self-discipline, and regular attendance at our place of worship is an act of such self-discipline.'[2]

But however disciplined the clergy and however faithful in the exercise of their ministry and however much, the bishop observed, they might regret that more people do not come to worship in their churches, 'we have got to start further back, realizing that vast numbers in England today would not know what to do if they came.' This raised the next issue.

If worship is the Church's first work, mission is its second.

> The congregation which remains a little closed circle, living for itself and its needs, either has not truly come face to face with Christ in worship or else is living in deliberate disobedience to his commands. The church that truly worships must by its worship become the missionary fellowship.

---

[1] as they did at Morning and Evening Prayer. The two readings at holy Communion in the Book of Common Prayer are, with very few exceptions, both taken from the New Testament. This was to change as alternative forms of holy Communion came to be authorised during the next four decades.
[2] ibid., 8.

But to what effect? Already the statistical writing was appearing on the Church's walls. Having studied the visitation returns the bishop divided the parishes into four groups: those with populations of under 1000, of 1000 to 5000, or 5000 to 10000, and of over 10000.

> In the villages under 1000, out of every hundred on an average 13 or 14 come to Easter Communion, and 5 or 6 attend worship on other Sundays. The figures get progressively smaller as the parishes get larger, with 4.8% for Easter and 3.3% on an ordinary Sunday in parishes from 1000 to 5000, and 3.3% and 2.4% in parishes from 5000 to 10000. In the vast urban and new housing parishes only 2 in 100 come to Easter Communion, and less that 2 in 100 attend worship on an average Sunday. In every group only half as many men attend worship as women; and I suspect that at many services the proportion is smaller.[1]

As pertinent were the replies to the bishop's question about what proportion of the population were either regular Anglican worshippers or occasional worshippers, members of other denominations, or 'out of living touch with any Christian Communion.' As to the last category, in the villages 20-50% were out of touch with the Churches. In parishes with over 10000, the estimate was generally 80-90%. These figures might be considerably higher today, but the reasons for the loss of contact they revealed would be the same. Was it, the bishop asked, the result of open hostility or of apathy to the work of the Church? In answer the clergy reported widespread apathy but little hostility. In his Charge Bishop Allen suggested that hostility at least indicates some interest, but 'where people are politely bored, the Church has ceased to count for anything in their lives.'[2] Indifference is a stage of separation from the Church well beyond that of amiable tolerance.[3] It is a mark of de-Christianisation.

Bishop Allen suggested that the statistics indicated that in England as a whole 'the average number of Easter communicants is high where the proportion of clergy to population is high and low where it is low.' His conclusion was that one reason for 'our weakness is clearly the shortage of the ordained and whole-time ministry,'[4] particularly in the large urban and suburban parishes. This was

---

[1] ibid., 15. This was better than the gender differentiation of candidates for Confirmation.
[2] ibid.
[3] For an important series of studies on this topic, see *Indifference to Religion*, Concilium, May 1983.
[4] Geoffery Allen, op. cit., 17.

the conclusion that each of his two predecessors had come to, and his successor was also to emphasise. Although each of the three bishops recognised the value of the ministry of the laity, and that, as Bishop Allen said, 'clergy and laity must together work out new patterns for the pastoral work of the parish', for them a principal answer to the Church of England's 'weakness' was more clergy. Yet the case for this was far from proved. A similar proportion of clergy to people in the large town parishes as in the country parishes would not ensure that the percentage of the population attending church in the large urban parishes would radically improve and match that in the rural villages. As we have noted, the proportion of clergy to population had little effect on Easter communicants in four deaneries in Derbyshire in 1912–13. The 1851 census of religion had shown not only that the heartland of Anglican allegiance was the south and east, but also that it was strongest in rural rather than urban parishes, and so it had continued. The reason why fewer people came to church in the east Midlands' counties (than, say, in the two home counties in the diocese of St Albans) and why fewer clergy were recruited from them and attracted to them, was the same. It had little to do with proportion of clergy to population and much more to do with social context. A key lesson to be drawn from the Church's history is that its acceptance or rejection is written into each social situation.

This was to be further suggested by anecdotal evidence later in the Sixties. The leader in the *DDN* in January 1965 commented on a recent article in *The Observer* by the rector of Woolwich, Nicholas Stacey. For four and a half years, he and his team of very well educated Oxbridge graduate curates, praying for two hours a day and visiting for six, had only succeeded in increasing the congregation attending the parish church from 50 to 100, with most of this increase coming from outside the parish. During this period candidates for Confirmation had fallen to 11. Stacey had come to the conclusion that traditional patterns of pastoral ministry had failed. He and his assistant curates were now to take secular employment, and to visit and counsel their parishioners in the evenings. The editor of the *DDN*, Ben Roberts, vicar of Heanor, asked for comments. None were offered.

Bishop Allen fully recognised the over-riding significance of the social context. He spoke in his Charge of 'the need to see the relevance for the Church of underlying secular patterns of community.'[1] He had asked the

---

[1] ibid., 22.

clergy about parish evangelistic missions. The answers convinced him that they had little effect. The fifty parishes which had had some form of parish mission in recent years reported that they had not been effective in reaching those outside the Church. Nor was the Church successful in keeping those who *had* come into contact with it. Bishop Allen noted that out of every 100 of the population in England, 66 had been baptised, 24 confirmed but only 6 remained as communicants even once a year at Easter.

The reason for this, he argued, was that far too many young men and women entered the secular world as adults with an immature and inadequate understanding of the Christian faith. This being so the answer must be better religious education. Of course – but the parish clergy knew this, and many of them were already providing it, but, once again, social factors tended to vitiate the impact that the most skilled and dedicated parish priest could make. Five years earlier, and writing as an experienced parish priest, Bill Chivers had identified four stages in the progressive pattern of drift away from church attendance by young people after Confirmation: (i) after they left primary school, when children 'put away childish things', and going to church is seen by many of them as one of those childish things; (ii) the period immediately after leaving school, when 'the lure of non-Church-going contemporaries is too strong'; (iii) the period of what was then still called courtship, when 'in a Church and non-Church alliance, the former has the scales heavily weighed against it'; and (iv) after marriage, 'when children are born and freedom for a time is reduced.'[1]

So was the 'secular pattern of community' to blame for loss of faith? The bishop asked the clergy and churchwardens what they felt were the main areas of 'moral weakness' in society. The replies included such words and phrases as materialism, the affluent society and wasteful spending, acquisitiveness, football pools, hire purchase and gambling and much else. The bishop was not convinced that this list was wholly negative. The situation, he said, needed very careful assessment. He pointed out that 'the affluent society is something for which we have striven, and that in itself is good and not bad' and offered a much more sophisticated analysis, concluding that 'the price of affluence is work well done in co-operation for the common good.'[2] The implication was that rather than merely criticise secularity as moral weakness, the clergy should be attempting actively to harness its positive forces.

---

[1] *DDN*, February 1957.
[2] Geoffrey Allen, op. cit., 25

Here we must leave Geoffrey Allen's analysis. The Sixties were to test whether the Church had a theology of the Kingdom of God broad and generous enough for it to engage critically but co-operatively with secular agencies for the common good.

'Order and liberty in continuous revision': social concerns

The engagement of the Church of England with secular agencies (of which its commitment to education was, and is, a principal and undervalued example) did not inhibit it from offering the wider society a considered critique. At the diocesan conference in November 1959 Geoffrey Allen called for 'a toning-up of discipline in entertainments, clubs and advertizements, which relied for their appeal on exciting erotic emotions.' Lest that seem to be no more than mere censure, he added this: 'In a healthy society order and liberty must be held in continuous revision and each needs the other.'[1] For Geoffrey Allen, one of the tasks of the Church was to promote, and contribute to, the analysis that that 'continuous revision' implied. For example, twelve months later he condemned the influence of 'that first cousin of political power, a condescending benevolence . . . in our attitude towards other races'. As a former bishop in Egypt he was referring to the Church of England presuming 'to exercise author-ity over the emerging life of the Church in other lands', but as the bishop of Derby he was also deeply aware of incipient racial prejudice in this country, perhaps not least in the Church.

Yet the bishop was far from alone in his concern that social issues be addressed. He was as much echoing the deeply felt convictions of some as he was educating the consciences of others. Leaders in the *DDN* in the early Sixties, for example, condemned anti-Semitism as 'offensively unChristian'; *apartheid* in South Africa as 'a challenge to fundamental religious belief about the nature of man and of all men, in the manner of their living together'; gambling as 'an irresponsible use of our time and our money . . . in looking for adventure and rewards in life in the wrong place,'; and 'the alarming failure of the World Refugee Appeal in Derbyshire to make an impact.'[2] There were many other social issues which received attention in episcopal letters, at diocesan and deanery conferences and in the *DDN*: the inappropriate prolongation of life of the terminally ill; the appeal to self-interest in election addresses; the role of

---

[1] *Derby Evening Telegraph*, 19 November 1960.
[2] *DDN*, February, May, January, March 1960.

MPs; the treatment of immigrants; the need for better industrial relations; trade, industry and Christian responsibility; stock market investment; the aftercare of patients discharged from psychiatric hospitals; Third World poverty; capital punishment; homelessness; nuclear weapons, and much else.

Occasionally, a serious political event was treated with an appropriately light touch. In October 1963 the 14th Earl of Home renounced his peerage on his appointment as prime minister. The much respected R.W.T. Moore, rector of Newbold, wrote in his parish magazine: 'Lord Home is an Episcopalian. If we must have a Scots Prime Minister this is the best kind to have.'[1]

There is no doubt that the sense that the Church had of its responsibility to the wider society in which it was set – a responsibility both to seek to influence public opinion before political decisions were made, and to stand against them if, once made, they were held to be unjust – came increasingly into focus in the 1950s and 1960s. Of course the Church's voice was puny, as Rawlinson had said (and it was to become even less regarded as the years passed), but the still, small voice has its own remarkable resonance.

Two major issues of conscience in the first half of the decade show how the Church of England in Derbyshire reacted to social questions. The first concerned nuclear weapons. The United States detonated the first fusion device in May 1951. The Soviet Union followed in August 1953 and Great Britain in May 1957. Public opinion about the consequences of these tests was sharply divided, not least in the diocese. A voluntary moratorium on nuclear tests collapsed following the Cuban missile crisis, and the public debate continued strongly until Harold Macmillan's administration was able to negotiate the Partial Test Ban Treaty, to which the three nuclear powers were signatories, in 1963.

At the diocesan conference in June 1962, Bill Chivers proposed a resolution which condemned nuclear weapons. They were, it said, 'a misuse of the very substance of creation, and the devastation which they cause is a denial of the principles of the Kingdom of God.' The resolution was seconded by Albert Batsleer, the vicar of Glossop. It was opposed by the archdeacon of Derby, Jack Richardson, who employed the argument advanced by Bishop Rawlinson in May 1954. 'Weapons', he said, 'were a matter of degree'. Therefore, to be consistent, opponents of nuclear arms would need to take a pacifist position

---

[1] ibid., February 1964.

and reject all weapons. This was a position he respected but could not adopt. V.R. Nickalls, the vicar of Norbury, agreed, though he was content merely to say that if the government believed that the nation should possess nuclear weapons we should accept them on that ground alone. It might be supposed that this response scarcely revealed the Church of England at its most prophetic! At the conclusion of the debate the conference agreed not to put the motion to the vote.

The arguments against the development of nuclear weapons had been powerfully and extensively deployed before the conference met in June. In March, Bill Chivers had written in the *DDN* about the evils of nuclear warfare, and had argued, then and in response to subsequent correspondents critical of his position, that it was ridiculous to suppose that civil defence preparations for the impact of a nuclear bomb could possibly be effective. There would be nothing and nobody left.[1] Shortly before, Albert Batsleer, with 17 clergy and ministers in and around Glossop, wrote a measured letter to the *Glossop Chronicle* asking what possible 'commensurate benefit' could justify the 'widespread and immense devastation' and consequential long-term suffering that would be the result of a nuclear war.[2] The debate in the diocese on this issue continued for months.

A second issue of conscience arose following the conviction of Ian Brady and Myra Hindley, the Moors Murderers. On 9 November 1965 the Act abolishing the death penalty for murder came into force in Great Britain. The issue had been the subject of passionate debate since Sidney Silverman had introduced an abolition bill into the House of Commons in December the previous year. The conviction of Brady and Hindley for the serial murders of children in 1966 inevitably brought calls to reinstate capital punishment. In the *DDN* for November that year Ben Roberts expressed his strong opposition to reinstatement, noting the 'doubtful deterrent value' of hanging. He went on to quote an ex-governor of Pentonville prison who had said that executions had produced in him 'an acute sense of profound shame' and that 'there must be something wrong with a law which has the effect of lessening the self-respect of those whose duty it is to carry it out.' These arguments were abruptly dismissed by Roy Upton, the evangelical vicar of Derby St Chad. In the December issue of the *DDN* he rebuked Ben Roberts for his abolitionist stand. Upton argued that the death penalty, and all 'retributionary rights of society

---

[1] ibid., March 1962.
[2] reprinted, ibid.

against offenders' found warrant in the Bible, citing Gen. 9:6 and Rom. 13:4, and claiming that 'the Christian who takes the Bible seriously has a strong case against the subjective reasoning of the abolitionist.' Roberts replied: 'Does Mr Upton not "censor" clear commands [in the Bible] not to eat blood (Gen. 9:4), and not to stone parent-cursers, adulterers, homosexuals etc (Lev. 20). What about "let him that is without sin amongst you cast the first stone."'[1] The argument between Upton and Roberts was less about the merits of the cases for or against capital punishment in a modern society and much more about the authority and interpretation of Scripture in the modern Church. That debate was to become more vociferous as the years passed.

As parishes tackled these intractable issues so their perspectives were widened. Bishop Allen encouraged them strongly. For example, in February 1965 he asked each parish to consider whether its worship was designed to meet the needs of its own congregation 'or whether we are in fact primarily concerned . . . to show the love of God . . . throughout the whole community of the parish' and thus to move from being a closed society concerned exclusively with its own life to being an open fellowship fully engaged with and in the wider community.[2]

But how was the Church, through its worship, 'to show the love of God' to the wider community? It was urged strongly that church services had to reflect the ways in which people in the middle of the 20th century thought, and to employ the words they used. Thus liturgical revision came very much to be on the Church's agenda in the Sixties. In 1962 Geoffrey Allen set out his own three principles for Prayer Book revision. Our worship, he said, must be in keeping with the teaching of the Scriptures; it must be truly *common* prayer, that is people should be able to find a church service which was recognisably the same anywhere in the Church of England; and our worship 'must express the praise and prayer of the people in the present world in the language of our own day.'[3] That last principle has been the most difficult to embody in practice. But as the Church attempted to fulfil this mission to be alive to the world in all its diversity it had to ask itself whether it was equipped for the task. Once again, the clergy were to be the focus of attention.

---

[1] *DDN*, December 1966.
[2] ibid., March 1965.
[3] ibid., May 1962.

'In the light of changing circumstances': the clergy and the Paul Report

In July 1960 Church Assembly instructed the Church of England's Central Advisory Council for the Ministry 'to consider, in the light of changing circumstances, the system of payment and deployment of the clergy, and to make recommendations.' The Council asked a sociologist, Leslie Paul, to make a fact-finding enquiry and to submit a report. This was published in January 1964 as *The Deployment and Payment of the Clergy.* Leslie Paul made 62 principal recommendations of which two were the most radical and controversial though not the most immediately practical. Recommendation 8 proposed that, as it became vacant, an incumbent's freehold should become a ten-year leasehold. This recommendation was designed to make the deployment of the clergy more efficient. Paul wrote:

> It is not really possible to maintain the clergy today as though they were minor eighteenth-century landed gentry. What to some is a guarantee of their freedom is to others a prison from which they can neither be pushed out nor climb out. They can be left there in loneliness and frustration.[1]

Recommendation 42 proposed the replacement of the traditional system of private patronage, by which incumbents were appointed, by regional staffing and appointments boards. Paul argued that

> patronage by private individuals, by colleges, [and] by religious patronage trusts defies any justification except the pragmatic one that men might be found this way and in no other. It is the oddest principle indeed that compels a college to offer livings to its members: and an irrationality which does the Church moral harm if a patronage society or religious trust owns advowsons and uses them to determine parochial appointments of the colour of churchmanship it approves.[2]

These were far-reaching proposals. Although these two recommendations were not fully implemented (though bishops discovered ways by which some of the more obstinate barriers to deployment could be circumvented) some of Paul's recommendations did find their way into legislation in the 1970s.

---

[1] *The Deployment and Payment of the Clergy* (1964), 172.
[2] ibid., 196.

Unfortunately the value of the report was somewhat undermined by Paul's over-estimation of the number of men likely to be ordained by the end of the decade. He believed the number in 1971 would be 831. In fact it was 393. Rather than rise steadily by 22% to Paul's estimated figure, it was to fall by nearly 40%. Adrian Hastings says:

> There is something rather pathetic, indeed a little ludicrous, about the Church turning for the first time, in the new age of efficiency, to lay sociology to obtain a thoroughly professional view of what it should be doing with its priests and how many it should have, and being so grotesquely misled.[1]

That is a most unfair judgement. The statistical projections were based upon assumptions that were seriously amiss, but many of the recommendations in the report were sound and did not rely upon these projections, ranging as they did from the formation of lay pastorates to the adequate professional support of the clergy, and from the rationalisation of clergy stipends nationwide to the making of economies by simplifying the 'labyrinthine financial operations of the dioceses and the [Church] Commissioners.' These have largely been implemented, and other recommendations were included in the Pastoral Measure 1968, and in subsequent legislation.

When the report was published, the bishop and many of the clergy in the diocese immediately recognised its value. Geoffrey Allen was in general agreement with it believing that 'the Church must weigh [it] very seriously and would ignore it at its peril.'[2] D.B. Webb, vicar of Langley Mill, feared that the report *would* be ignored. He said,

> Our attempts to adapt ourselves to the 20th century have been feeble beyond belief . . . informed and sympathetic people outside the Church find our behaviour beyond comprehension . . . . The work of God has been paralysed by an attitude of mind which only a Dr Parkinson[3] could adequately describe. Sloth and timidity have been described as caution and even wisdom. Instead of vision and leadership we have had procrastination and ineptitude. Bishops and proctors have spent hours discussing the dress of clergy at divine service and [have] ignored the

---

[1] Hastings, op.cit., 535.
[2] *DDN,* March 1964.
[3] Cyril Northcote Parkinson, brilliant political economist, and author of *Parkinson's Law* et.al.

failure of the Church to commend either itself or the Gospel. If the Paul Report goes the way of other documents, then it will be up to individual clergy to consider whether, under God, they should not leave the parochial ministry and seek spheres where their efforts will be less hampered by the irrelevance of the system they perpetuate.[1]

Other clergy were equally strongly supportive of the report's proposals, if a little more restrained in expression. Arthur Robertson, vicar of Ilkeston St Mary, wrote in his parish magazine:

> In Ilkeston we have [a population of] about 35000, eight Anglican priests and eight places of worship, none of which can boast a regular half-full building. They all have their own frantic efforts to raise money to ensure their own survival, with the great task of extending the world church pushed down the agenda. If the Church of England is going to mean anything more than a convention, radical and far-reaching changes will have to come. How long are we going to delay?

However, George Seamer, the conservative evangelical vicar of Normanton-by-Derby, felt that the report 'misses the root of the trouble and would only exchange the old problems for new ones. If put into operation, there would be little room for Evangelicals in the Church of England, or Anglo-Catholics. The Church would become an Episcopal sect.' He was referring to the proposal to abolish private patronage trusts in favour of regional diocesan boards of patronage. Several trusts had been established in the 19th century to purchase rights of presentation to benefices so that evangelical clergy could obtain preferment. Another criticism came from F.J.H. Lisemore, vicar of Ashbourne St Oswald, who believed that the Paul Report gave a false impression. It suggested that everything could be put right by putting in place an interlocking series of reforms. But, he asked, 'will Regional [patronage] Boards, a Staff College, a Central Statistical Register, and the abolition of freehold raise the influence of the Church in the country as a whole?' He doubted it, though he acknowledged that many of the report's proposals were bound to be accepted.[2]

---

[1] *DDN*, March 1964.
[2] parish magazine comments reprinted in the *DDN*, April 1964.

'The policy of ecclesiastical re-organisation': new churches for new areas

While these far-reaching debates about social issues, the role of the Church in society and the reform of the Church's own structures were continuing, the Church of England in Derbyshire pursued its policy of building churches in areas of new housing. We have noted that at least 22 churches were built or enlarged after 1950, with nine new churches being erected in the Sixties alone. This policy touched on each of the three areas of debate. New housing areas raised issues of social policy. As one of several examples, the Mackworth estate had been developed as a result of slum clearance in Derby. The religious role that the Church saw itself as fulfilling required that it should provide churches and clergy to serve these new communities. Its social role required it to provide community facilities for them (so far as it could). Mackworth St Francis had been designed as a dual-purpose building serving both as a church and as a community facility.

To service these roles in a rapidly changing social context required a radical reform of the way the Church governed itself, managed its human and material resources and, by no means least, of the way that it worshipped. As to the last, the 1960s and 1970s were years of liturgical experiment leading to the *Alternative Service Book* in 1980 and to *Common Worship* in 2000. The process of the reform of the Church's system of government led to the Synodical Government Measure 1969 which was so fundamental a change that it was less an alteration and reform and much more the creation of a more or less entirely new system of government,[1] while the reform of the parish system was aided by new powers taken under the Pastoral Measures of 1968 and 1983.

No one issue prompted this process of rapid reform and the consequent raft of legislation. Yet, had the Church of England, *as the established church*, not gone with the people to the new housing estates to offer there 'the means of grace and the hope of glory' it would indeed have become no more than an episcopal sect concerned only with the gathered and exclusive few, the maintenance of its own traditions, and little else.

At least once in the 1960s the policy of providing churches and clergy for new housing areas was publicly challenged in the diocese. In 1967 Canon Paul

---

[1] K.M. MacMorran, E. Garth Moore, T.J. Briden, *A Handbook for Churchwardens and Parochial Church Councillors* (Mowbray 1994), 7.

Miller, a residentiary canon of Derby Cathedral, wrote in the Cathedral *Notes and Comments*:

> The present policy of ecclesiastical re-organisation is to concentrate on the new dormitory suburbs. This is understandable but unprophetic. Present day suburbs consist of thousands of small houses where families live out the principle that an Englishman's home is his Castle. The life lived in them is in fact a very pale and fanciful reflection of the 'gracious living' of the stately home, but without the responsibilities which once went with it. The new churches in the suburbs are enjoying a certain success, but it is questionable whether the quality and depth of their life is very deep.[1]

This comment seemed to some to convey a sense of exclusivity and social superiority. Was the spiritual life of the new churches on the housing estates shallow compared with that of the old churches in the villages of the landed estates? The following month Paul Miller was taken to task by David Cherry. Church life in the new housing estate in which he had lived was, he said, 'vigorous, joyful and Christ-like.' Paul Miller's article was, for him, a denial of Christian charity and he rebuked the editor of the *DDN* for reprinting it. But Paul Miller represented a point of view that was, and is, possibly quite widespread. Implicitly, it raised again the question of the Church of England's heartland, its 'constituency' as the sociologists say, its natural home.

This same question may covertly have influenced the issue of church unity. For some in the Church of England, behind the overt faith and order issues that separated the Churches, there lurked the questions: Will the Church of England's unique contribution to English life be compromised by union with other Churches? Do we belong together socially and culturally? Is our constituency their constituency? Is the disunity of the Churches at root a question of social class?

'A divided witness is a crippling handicap': Anglicans and Methodists

In the 1960s and early 1970s the question of organic Church unity in England was engaged when a specific unity proposal was made, and, at least for several decades, answered.

---

[1] reprinted in *DDN*, October 1967.

Since the late 1940s the Anglican and Methodist Churches had been discussing the possibility of union. In 1946 the archbishop of Canterbury, Geoffrey Fisher, had invited the Free Churches to 'take episcopacy into their own system' not, however, as a precondition of full union (which he opposed) but as a necessary step towards intercommunion between the Churches. In fact the Anglican-Methodist proposals, when they were published in 1963, were for 'union in one church.' Geoffrey Allen was clearly in favour of the proposals succeeding. He told his diocesan conference in May 1964 that 'more and more we are discovering in this century that the mission and unity of the Church belong together .... a divided witness is a crippling handicap'[1] and, at the following conference, that the unity talks must be forwarded 'with urgency and determination.'[2] As the moment for decision came closer, matters of supposed principle became sharply defined, and anomalies revealed. Bishop Allen pleaded that Anglicans not prejudge the outcome, for

> within the fellowship of the Church and for the sake of Christian unity
> we must all accept some points about which we are hesitant, because
> these points may seem of particular importance to some other members
> of the Church .... In Christ's eyes it may well seem a far greater wrong
> that we should cling to our present divisions rather than that we should
> accept something a little new and unusual for the sake of healing them.[3]

The first stage of the reunion scheme was to be initiated by a Service of Reconciliation during which the ministries of Anglican priests and Methodist ministers would be 'reconciled', that is, fully and unconditionally accepted by the other. No words would be said. Hands would be laid on the heads of priests and ministers by Anglican bishops and Methodist superintendent ministers in silence.

Matters of theological principle collected around what this meant. In May 1964 the *DDN* ran an article by Rupert Davies, a leading Methodist theologian. He pointed out that the Service of Reconciliation did not constitute the re-ordination or even the *conditional* ordination of either Anglican or Methodist clergy but was meant (i) to extend the authority of Methodist ministers into the Church of England and *vice versa*, (ii) to pray for the gifts of the Holy Spirit for each body of clergy, and (iii) to share with the

---

[1] *Derby Evening Telegraph*, 27 May 1964.
[2] ibid., 31 October 1964.
[3] ibid., 28 October 1967.

ministry of each Church the spiritual heritage of the other. This would be symbolised by the silence in which the laying-on of hands would be carried out, for, Davies wrote, 'God knows what, if anything, is defective in either ministry; we ask him to supply what we need . . .'[1]

As the moment for decision came closer, there had been much ecumenical sharing in the diocese. The Frecheville *Torch*, its parish magazine, regularly devoted two of its 16 pages to Methodist news; churches in Ilkeston were manning an ecumenical bookstall at the weekly market in the town; Methodists and Congregationalists had joined Anglicans in St Oswald's in Ashbourne to hear a lecture by Alan Richardson, professor of Christian theology in Nottingham University; at Greenhill Anglicans had worshipped with their Congregationalist neighbours, and the local Methodists met with the Anglican parochial church council for Bible study and discussion; in Heanor, Anglicans and Methodists had cooperated in a joint visiting programme, while at Moor Ends, 40 Anglicans and Methodists had enrolled as 'Good Neighbours' to offer support to the five hundred families in the village.[2] All that may sound very prosaic, but, given the history of these Churches, these were deeply significant encounters.

In May 1968 the editor of the *DDN*, Ben Roberts, echoing the bishop, expressed the hopes of many when, on the publication of the final report of the joint commission on Anglican-Methodist reunion, he wrote: 'We dare not wait until all risks and anomalies are eliminated before tackling the greater anomaly of our disunity . . . ' Two meetings were held in the diocese in July, one at the Methodist Cliff College, and the other at the Anglican Bishop Lonsdale College. Speaking at Cliff College, another leading Methodist, Harold Roberts, said, 'I tremble to think what it could mean for the future of Christian unity as a whole if we reject this scheme.' In November, Geoffrey Allen, at the conclusion of a well-balanced and comprehensive article about the reunion scheme in the *DDN*, wrote: 'Anomalies there may be: but before we reject some plan of union on that account, we must be very sure that they are not far outweighed by the great, existing anomaly of a divided Church.'[3]

The two Churches had agreed that a 75% majority in favour of the Stage One proposals (that is, the reconciliation of ministries) by the two legislative bodies, the Methodist Conference, and the two Convocations of Canterbury and York

---

[1] *DDN*, May 1964.
[2] ibid., June, July, October, 1964.
[3] ibid., September, November 1968.

meeting together, would be required for progress towards full union could proceed. At the local level the Anglican diocesan conferences would express a view first. The Methodist district synods would wait to confirm any decision by the Methodist Conference. In March 1969 the Derby diocesan conference voted. The clergy voted 109 for the proposals with 51 against. Five did not vote, and no less than 126 clergy, entitled to vote, were absent. The laity voted 127 in favour, 41 against, with four present but not voting. There were 199 laity entitled to vote but who were absent. This gave an affirmative vote for the clergy of 66% and of 73.8% for the laity, very close to the national average of 65% and 77%. The diocesan vote thus averaged 69.9%, a strongly affirmative result, but well below the 75% majority required in the two national legislative bodies.

What was disturbing was that 43.25% of the clergy members and 53.6% of lay members of the Derby diocesan conference failed to vote. This was only just exceeded by the clergy and laity of the diocese of York, and by Exeter's laity. The national average for absenteeism at diocesan conference votes on this crucial issue was 22.9% and 27.4% respectively.

The two Convocations met on 8 July. The majority in favour of the scheme was 69%, again well short of the required 75%. The Methodist Conference, meeting the same day, voted in favour of the Stage One proposals by 78%, easily meeting the required majority. An alliance of anglo-catholics and evangelicals in the two Convocations, led by the bishop of Willesden (later bishop of London) Graham Leonard, defeated the scheme. The anglo-catholics did not regard the Service of Reconciliation as an episcopal ordination of Methodists, while the evangelicals, who believed themselves to be on a par with Methodist ministers already, felt that the Service called Methodist ordinations into question.

On 7 May 1970 the Methodist Nottingham and Derby District Synod voted on the provisional legislation relating to the Stage One proposal for reunion passed overwhelmingly by the Methodist Conference the previous year. Those voting in favour were 182, with 89 against and with one neutral vote, giving a majority of 66.9%. Thus neither the Anglicans nor the Methodists locally reached the required 75%.

In 1972, when the reunion scheme again came before what had now become the diocesan synod, it again failed to pass by the required majority, with 61.2% of the clergy members voting in favour, and 71.8% of the laity, slightly less than the majorities in 1969. The bishop, Cyril Bowles, voted against the proposals.

Absenteeism, at 35% and 21.6% respectively, was at least an improvement on 1969.

After the earlier vote the *Ashbourne Parish News* stated the obvious: the two wings of the Church of England had come together simply to prevent the proposals succeeding. The *Normanton Link* revealed the reason for evangelical opposition: 'the basis of reconciliation does less than full honour to the ministry in the Lord's name committed to the Methodist clergy' – yet the Methodists themselves had been overwhelmingly in favour of what Anglican evangelicals felt dishonoured them!

The story of the attempt to unite the Anglican and Methodist Churches may seem irrelevant in a social history, yet, as bishops of Derby pointed out, the Churches could hardly seek to promote social unity if they could not achieve unity themselves. Ron Beddoes characteristically set the vote, and many of the other internal issues which had absorbed the Church of England in the Sixties, into a wider context in the Cathedral *Notes and Comments*:

> If we cannot renew and revitalise Christian belief, our preoccupation with reorganisation is no more than a paddling in the ecclesiastical shallows, a mere mending of the nets and a repair of the boat, without the intention or capacity to launch out into the deep.

Some preoccupation had been necessary. The changing times demanded it. In June 1966 Ingram Cleasby, the archdeacon of Chesterfield and a self-confessed traditionalist, had said:

> Without some . . . radical reappraisal of what the Church is trying to do and how it is to do it under the conditions of a rapidly changing society, it is hard to believe that the Church can survive for much longer except as a quaint archaic institution destined to join the Dinosaurs in the mud of past history.

That was said in the mid-Sixties. By the end of the decade Ingram Cleasby's plea for radical reappraisal had become the introspective preoccupation of which Ron Beddoes despaired. The excitement of the Sixties had already cooled. It was to be followed by reaction.

16

'A difficult and perplexing time': 1970–2000

The episcopates of the diocesan bishops of Derby have coincided with fairly distinct periods in the religious history of much of the 20th century. A.E.J. Rawlinson was bishop during the period immediately before, during and after the second World War, a time of numerical decline and post-war revival. Geoffrey Allen was bishop during the so-called 'secular Sixties'. Cyril Bowles was bishop during the 1970s and 1980s; a time which saw what Grace Davie has called 'the re-emergence of the sacred' and which was, for the Church of England, a period of reaction, consolidation and reform. The last decade of the 20th century saw the development of a process almost of the redistribution, certainly of the reformulation, of the sense of the sacred. Peter Dawes was bishop of Derby from 1988 to 1995, and Jonathan Bailey succeeded him. In every case, came the moment came the man, for in each of these periods a bishop of Derby was appointed whose spirituality, personal style, theological stance, leadership abilities and professional skills equipped him for the task he faced. The much criticised method by which diocesan bishops are appointed in the Church of England has served the diocese of Derby remarkably well.

So it did with the appointment of Cyril William Johnston Bowles as bishop of Derby in 1969. Apart from a brief curacy in Barking, and, immediately before coming to Derby, six years as archdeacon of Swindon, Cyril Bowles had spent his ministry in a Cambridge theological college, becoming successively chaplain, vice-principal and principal of Ridley Hall. Like his two immediate predecessors he had little experience as a parish priest, but he brought to the diocese skills of analysis and of conciliation, gentleness of spirit, a sharp intellect, an innate conservatism and, as the first evangelical bishop of Derby, a quiet confidence in his theological position. These were attributes in its bishop which the diocese needed as the Sixties came to an end.

The sermon at Cyril Bowles' ordination as bishop in Westminster Abbey was preached by Professor C.F.D. Moule, one of the finest New Testament scholars of his day. He said:

> It may be said that there has never been a more difficult and perplexing time for organised Christianity; but I dare to believe that there has never been a time when the deep-rooted Christian life of the Beatitudes has more chance to make itself felt.

That was remarkably perceptive and far-sighted, for the Beatitudes[1] enshrine not dogma (most emphatically not that) but the most fundamental Judaeo-Christian religious orientation, an orientation which was finding, but rarely acknowledging, fresh expression during these years.

In 1994 Grace Davie described the last decades of the 20th century as 'a crucial moment in the religious history of this country.' They were years, in Davie's refrain, of 'believing without belonging' in which 'both traditional institutions and traditional certainties struggle, in secular as well as religious life.'[2] Yet they were also years in which those 'intimations of immortality', those, seemingly, almost (perhaps actual) instinctive perceptions of the sacred, began to be embodied in words and forms very different from, indeed often alien to, those sacred words and sacramental forms central to the older Churches, and indeed often of Christianity itself.

The year of Cyril Bowles' ordination as bishop was also the year when, if the distinction is sensible, the 'modern' Church of England became the 'contemporary' Church of England very familiar to its present members. During his episcopate the Church of England passed a tranche of reforming legislation. It took to itself a radically reformed system of government (by the Synodical Government Measure 1969). Years of liturgical experiment led to the Church of England (Worship and Doctrine Measure) 1974 and to the *Alternative Service Book* of 1980. Fresh powers were given to the dioceses, under the Pastoral Measures of 1968 and, particularly, of 1983, to enable pastoral reorganisation to be undertaken more speedily and efficiently.

---

[1] Matt. 5: 3–10, though note also the verses following.
[2] Grace Davie, *Religion in Britain since 1945* (Blackwell 1994), 190. We will briefly consider this and related themes in the Postscript.

Additional powers and responsibilities were given to parochial church councils in 1969. Quite radical reforms of the patronage system were put in place by the Patronage (Benefices) Measure 1986. Non-residential ordination courses were greatly extended during these years, and non-stipendiary clergy ordained in the diocese in 1980. Although the first women were ordained to the priesthood in the Church of England only in 1994 the General Synod had, in 1975, accepted that there were no fundamental objections to the priesting of women. Bishop Bowles was very much in favour. By no means least, the final failure to achieve a sufficient majority of those qualified to vote in the Church of England on the Anglican-Methodist unity scheme, and, a decade later, on the Covenanting for Unity proposals, meant that new ways had to be found, at the grass-roots, to move forward the need and the desire for Christian unity. All of this created the post-1970 Church of England. Its very contemporaneity makes that only certain science, hind-sight, impossible to apply. What follows is, therefore, less a detailed analysis and more a brief comment on the diocese in these years. We will consider, briefly and selectively, just three themes: the Church's social responsibility, the parishes and their ministry, and the quest for Christian unity. The end of the story of each of these is by no means clear, and so the section headings are presented as questions.

A secular colouring?

Edward Royle suggests a reason why the theologically liberal Churches have declined, numerically, faster than the conservative and evangelical Churches, and while many charismatic and fundamentalist sects have grown. He says:

> The Churches now exist in an increasingly secular environment, taking their colour from it. Religion in the traditional sense of the quest for the supernatural or transcendental seems to have little part in the activities of many Churches, especially in the liberal Protestant tradition, which appears preoccupied with secular social welfare issues or mere instrumental survival.[1]

That is a less than generous judgement, though a casual glance at the history of the Church of England since 1970 seems to confirm it. On the one hand the Church appeared to react to the challenge to its survival by undertaking the

---

[1] Edward Royle, *Modern Britain: A Social History 1750-1997* (Arnold 1997), 345.

programme of structural and liturgical reform which we have outlined, while, on the other, there seemed to be no social issue which was not seen by the Church as its business.

Royle was not the first to have concluded that, for the main-stream Protestant Churches, a concern for secular relevance had replaced its vision of heaven. In 1978 a BBC radio lecturer was reported in the Press as regretting that

> the whole emphasis of contemporary Christianity eschews traditional doctrinal priorities and is about applications .... The contemporary debate about world resources, over-population, pollution or nuclear catastrophe is according to the analysis of secular thinkers, although the Churches tag along, offering a religious gloss to precisely the same ideas.

In commenting on this, Cyril Bowles had some sympathy with this criticism, yet, he pointed out, 'God speaks through circumstances and not merely through Christians. The consciences of many who do not claim to be Christians are enlightened, and truth can be learned from them about the application of Christian faith.'[1] This was an important theological corrective, seemingly lost on Edward Royle. It was the bishop's ability both to hold to a strong, unequivocal and conservative Christian faith and also to embrace a broad view of the nature of truth which enabled him to apply this necessary corrective. This combination of conviction and openness was again evident when, in 1984, he greeted the appointment of David Jenkins as bishop of Durham. David Jenkins had made comments (commonplace in theological discussion for at least one hundred years) about the Empty Tomb being an inadequate proof of the resurrection of Jesus, which were met with considerable opposition – not least from evangelicals. Cyril Bowles defended him strongly, adding: 'We have no proof either in religion or in our relationships with one another in daily life. We do have certainty as our faith is tested by the facts and found to be trustworthy.'

These were not only difficult and perplexing years for the Church of England. The 1970s was a decade of economic, and therefore political, volatility which saw, amongst much else, oil prices quadrupling in 1973, the imposition of a three-day working week in 1974, repeated strikes in key industries, and the 'winter of discontent' in 1978-9. By 1983 unemployment matched that of the

---

[1] *DDN,* December, 1978.

slump of 1929. That there were five governments in office between 1970 and 1979 reflected this instability. Man had landed on the moon for the first time in 1969, and many wondered why that could be achieved while domestic economic stability could not.

Little wonder, then, that social issues arose which demanded comment by Churches which, because they profess a religion of the Incarnation, are deeply committed to the secular world. In 1974 the diocese created a Board for Social Responsibility under a new constitution, and appointed staff to serve it. In 1972 an industrial adviser to the bishop was appointed. Part-time industrial chaplaincies were established, and, in 1980, an industrial committee with local groups working in five areas in the county to foster industrial mission on an ecumenical basis. In these years, the following social concerns were at least commented upon in the diocese, either in diocesan synod, or in letters from the bishop, or in articles in the *DDN,* and, where possible, action taken, however insignificant that action might have seemed to be: capital punishment; remarriage in church after divorce; Enoch Powell and racial justice; euthanasia; abortion; the closed-shop; the Immigration Bill in 1971; alcoholism; poverty; the Brant Report; unemployment; homelessness; prisoners of conscience; mental health; the financial collapse and nationalisation of Rolls Royce in 1971, and much else.

These issues touched individuals personally and deeply. As one example, in 1981, Stephen Verney, the suffragan bishop of Repton and a charismatic and much loved figure in the diocese, married a divorcee. At the time this inevitably became something of a national *cause celebre.* Bishop Verney subsequently wrote a typically sensitive article for the *DDN*. Rightly considering that his marriage required neither explanation nor apology, and addressing the wider question, he noted that marriage is both difficult and creative, and that within it 'we build up our homes on the good news of repentance and forgiveness'.[1] This good news, of course, had much wider social relevance and urgency.

As in the Sixties, so now, many of these issues were politically very controversial. For example, there would have been many in the diocese who would not have supported increases in child benefit and unemployment benefit and the removal of inequalities in housing subsidies, which were the short-term goals of the ecumenical pressure-group, *Church Action on Poverty*

---

[1] ibid., August, 1981.

which Ann Morisy, of the diocesan Board of Social Responsibility, argued for in the *DDN*. This was in September 1982, when, in the last months of Margaret Thatcher's first administration, unemployment was rising rapidly. There were many similar issues in which staff members of the Board took a firm and, some in the parishes undoubtedly thought, a politically left-wing line.

There were issues that seem not to have been discussed: for example, in the 1960s, the Cuban crisis and the liberalisation of censorship, and, in the 1970s, the Vietnam war. It is impossible to think that, had he been the bishop, A.E.J. Rawlinson would not have had much to say about Vietnam in 1974 or the destruction of the Berlin Wall and the re-unification of Germany in 1989. Nevertheless, that so many social issues were brought to the attention of church people in the diocese *as matters of urgent Christian concern*, by no means least by Cyril Bowles, is of considerable significance. In fact, more of these questions were raised in the reactionary 1970s than in the radical 1960s.

One of many instances of the way in which social issues were approached by Bishop Bowles in the these years, and potentially the most controversial, had to do with the relationship of Church and state and the position the Church should take on politically sensitive questions. In 1971 the report was published of the last commission on Church and state, chaired by Owen Chadwick. In reviewing this, Cyril Bowles wrote:

> Are we being too exclusively world-affirming or too fanatically world-renouncing? Are we sacrificing the divine life of the Church or retreating from our duty in the relationship of sinful human society? Is it possible to have a conscience so insensitive that protest against wrong becomes impossible or one that is so ridden by guilt that life loses its joy? To have no distinction between Church and State and to have no relationship with the State may both be easy ways of escaping from the creative tension in which we ought to live.[1]

This comment is not only very typical of Bishop Bowles' approach to controversial issues (contrasting several points of view such that one is occasionally not sure which position he himself had adopted) but also poses the Christian dilemma succinctly. Christians may be in the world but not of it, but the wisdom to distinguish between 'in' and 'not of' is difficult to achieve. A practical example of the dilemma created by the Church/State relationship was

---

[1] ibid., February, 1971.

the strike by members of ASLEF and the NUM in 1974. The 1973 oil crisis coincided with a major dispute over miners' pay. An overtime ban by miners, railwaymen and electricians led to the imposition of the three-day week by Edward Heath's administration. The miners called a strike and were supported by the railwaymen. It was a dispute which was only resolved when Heath called a general election in March, was defeated, and the second Wilson administration was formed. The Church had to react in some way. Bishop Bowles, having condemned 'the absurdity of maintaining a major industry by overtime' continued:

> The Church officially should not identify itself with government policies which are inevitably based in part on wrong ideas and past mistakes, nor should it identify itself with an opposition which easily deceives itself over the arguments it uses to try to achieve power. Still less should the Church identify itself with groups of quiet and subtle agitators which use outward devotion to the cause of removing injustices as a cover for overthrowing our system of parliamentary government and such social justice and trust of one another as we have achieved.[1]

What Cyril Bowles seemed to some to be suggesting was a kind of Christian quietism combined with a conservative affirmation of the political status quo. Could any diocesan bishop of the established Church, wishing to avoid unnecessary controversy, say other than this? Yet what *does* it say? This is exactly the dilemma he had outlined so well in 1971.

In March 1979, commenting on the strike by hospital and local authority workers during what was described as the 'winter of discontent', the bishop took a firmer line. He said that a Christian view of strikes must be that 'however desirable it is that the right to strike should be secured, a strike for higher wages can only be justified if the poverty of the strikers is extreme and the strike does not produce sufferings for others.'[2] But, it would have been argued, what is the point of striking unless it compels action to ameliorate working conditions? The threat of the damage a strike can cause serves to induce just this. Bishop Bowles' comment revealed his innate conservatism, a stance shared by many in the diocese, but one which, because it was stated with such care and in a way which in no way inhibited the expression of contrary views, created a climate in which controversial social issues could be

---

[1] ibid., February, 1974.
[2] ibid., March, 1979.

freely discussed. In fact, he fully acknowledged that 'Christians, including clergymen, cannot avoid being political, because we need the framework of political activity to enable us together to love our neighbours as ourselves.'[1] Yet 'being political' inevitably involved taking a political position, for him as for those who differed from him.

The best example of Cyril Bowles' social and theological conservatism meeting a radical political agenda head-on, though certainly not deliberately so, was provided just before his retirement in 1987. In April, Tony Benn, the well-known and much respected left-wing Labour MP for Chesterfield wrote an article for the *DDN*. In it he said that

> The Church of England has sometimes been seen, in the past, as upholding the natural orders of society, and providing spiritual support for the status quo leaving the bishops and clergy to appeal to the rich to be kind and to the poor to be patient, in the expectation that all injustices would be put right in the next world.

Yet,

> the social message of Jesus has never been completely obscured by ritual, mystery, or the temptation to escape from social responsibility by the pursuit of personal salvation, and over the centuries it has always retained its cutting edge, exposing injustice and calling upon people to work for a better 'here and now'.

For Tony Benn the cutting edge of the Church of England's social witness could only be kept sharp by the Church's disestablishment, and by bringing 'some democracy to its own internal affairs.'

This was not a direct challenge to the bishop of course, and the next month, in reviewing the Church of England's major report, *Faith in the City*[2], Cyril Bowles did not respond as if it was, yet he placed his own view firmly and finally on record:

> The worst deprivation of all is spiritual poverty. Those who are rightly related to God have in them the Holy Spirit who enables them to transform any kind of deprivation.[3]

---

[1] ibid., June, 1983.

[2] This drew attention to social deprivation in urban areas, and was to result in a very considerable, and on-going, financial commitment by the Church of England to social projects in its inner-city parishes.

[3] ibid., May, 1987.

We have noted that this theology had been sharply called into question in Derby by E.S. Woods, in the aftermath of the first World War. Bishop Bowles' reliance on the power of personal salvation to overcome adverse social and economic conditions is very much the opposite of Benn's political theology. The theological corrective that Cyril Bowles had offered in 1978, that is, the recognition that the consciences of many who do not claim to be Christians are enlightened and can teach the Church much, is perhaps not so evident here.

Undertakers facing bankruptcy?

Cyril Bowles' generous and open conservatism undoubtedly chimed with the opinions of very many in the parishes, particularly in the countryside. As essentially agricultural communities, these parishes had changed little since before the first World War. We have noted that when Edwyn Hoskyns had visited the Ashbourne deanery in 1911 he observed that 'that which governs the whole life and work of your people is milk'. It was still of major importance in 1968 when the rural dean noted that the current outbreak of foot-and-mouth disease was the worst for many years, with Brailsford church, in the fields, being closed as a result.[1] However, there had been significant changes in the Church's organisation and ministry in these rural parishes. For example, in 1911 twenty-three parish clergy were working in the Ashbourne deanery, serving a population of 10900. In 1968 twelve clergy served a population of 12000, nearly half of which lived in Ashbourne itself. Again, when Bishop Hoskyns visited the rural deanery of Melbourne in 1914 he noted that nearly 50% of the population of the deanery lived in two parishes, Boulton and Alvaston, on the outskirts of Derby. In 1968, the expansion of Derby was such that W.G. Cook, the rural dean, wrote that 'it might seem difficult to find a reason for this Deanery. Four major parishes are soon to be engulfed by Derby Borough and should logically become part of Derby Deanery.'[2] Social and demographic change compelled the Church to change, not merely in its structures and organisation.

Given its profound sense of continuity with the past, but facing the need to change, the Church of England is inherently, and some would say properly, cautious. Its cautiousness means that it has taken to inevitable change rather

---

[1] ibid., February, 1968.
[2] ibid., March 1968.

slowly. This was frustrating for some. In 1973, David Shaw, vicar of Swadlincote Emmanuel, wrote in his parish magazine that 'compared to the enthusiasm of a programme like "Burke Special"[1], the average church service often looks like a group of undertakers facing bankruptcy.'[2] Nearly ten years later, a team of four members of the Church of North India, visiting the diocese for several weeks on a *Partners in Mission* programme, commented less graphically but with equal emphasis on what they had found. The parishes, its report said, were too much attached to 'old prayer books' and to church buildings. The congregations were too inward looking and concerned more for themselves than for others. There were few in the 18–35 age group attending services; indeed, 'the Church looks like a creche and/or a home for the old.' In fact, the young would not be attracted because 'most of your worship services are based on a very obsolete view of the universe and are therefore not contemporary enough to attract youth.'[3] If it did not attract the young, then what of the future?

'Worthy, dull and respectable?'

This raised again a critical issue rarely raised publicly in the diocese: drastically falling church attendances. Was the attitude noted by the *PIM* team causing church attendances to decline so rapidly? Certainly, as we have noted, not of itself. Nor would evangelism reverse the trend. Philip Crowe, rector of Breadsall, wrote in 1980 that 'there is no guarantee that faithful evangelism will bring results; and certainly no divine assurance that buildings erected to serve the needs of a community 100 years ago will be filled again today by faithful preaching of the Gospel.'[4]

There was no avoiding the implications of decline in church attendance. However, the statistics rarely indicated a straight-line decline, and this underlines the care which must be taken in interpreting them. In January 1985 Bishop Bowles noted that in the six years 1978–84 usual Sunday attendances in the diocese (not including those adults who came seldom, or only at the major Christian festivals) had increased by 9.2%. Thirteen deaneries making returns had reported an increase. In three there had been a reduction, but 'these three included very difficult missionary areas' the bishop said. The total number

---

[1] a television science series.
[2] ibid., February, 1973.
[3] ibid., July, 1982.
[4] ibid., July, 1980.

normally attending Sunday worship in the diocese in 1978 was 12860, and, in 1984, 14049. Yet these figures indicated a temporary reversal of a trend. In the previous five years not only had Anglican adult attendances in Derbyshire declined by 3.8% but had done so more rapidly than in any other county in England apart from Devon (-6.5%) and Cornwall (-4.8%).[1]

Coincidentally, in 1975 Cyril Bowles had asked the critical question, 'Why are the churches empty?' His answer was primarily theological. It was because of blindness to the truth and the attractiveness of sin, an opinion which echoed that of Thomas Cursham in 1787. The bishop acknowledged that there were 'stubborn facts' from the past which were offered as explanations:

> . . . it has never been a churchgoing area, or the villages are still enjoying the freedom from the squire, or still following his example, or his prosperous successor is staying away, or there is a kind of racial memory of the Church being on the side of exploitation and injustice.

Equally stubborn facts in the present situation inhibiting church attendance might be, the bishop noted, the existence of one social group predominating in a parish, or resentment at 'natural' lay leadership, or the existence of an elderly population producing an inevitably ageing congregation.[2] While acknowledging the strength of these explanations, Cyril Bowles clearly believed that his primary theological reasons carried most weight yet they did not match the sophisticated sociological and theological analyses undertaken on this issue in the Sixties.

There were other reactions to decline. In November 1976 the diocesan synod discussed 'the ministry of every member of the Church.' Bob Dell, archdeacon of Derby, argued that 'lay people can and should be encouraged to undertake spiritual and pastoral ministries.' This encouragement was somewhat undermined when a lay member of the synod noted that the resolution to this effect had been both proposed and seconded by clergymen! Cyril Bowles initially handled the issue of lay ministry with less than his usual skill. In June 1974 he asked lay people to consider their ministry: 'It may be [in] fuller service or greater giving. It may be to offer for ordination, to be a missionary, a monk or a nun. It may be to join the Readers.'[3] There was little theology of the ministry of the whole people of God there.

---

[1] M.R. Austin, 'Prospects for us', *DDN*, February 1981.
[2] *DDN*, October, 1975.
[3] ibid., June, 1974.

The development of lay ministry, or, better, collaborative ministry, was to progress rapidly in the coming years, with the appointment of lay training advisers and a parish development officer. These appointments embodied a strong initiative, often against the flow of parish opinion, to revolutionise what many committed Anglicans had assumed ministry to be, that is, the service of the clergy alone. In this, the diocese of Derby was to take a significant lead in the late 1990s with its *A Better Way* initiative. In relation to these developments, it is appropriate here to acknowledge the increasingly important ministry of lay Readers in the diocese throughout its history. It was to become indispensible. In 1929 there had been 119 licensed Readers and 314 parochial clergy in the diocese. In the late 1990s there were 277 Readers, considerably more than the number of stipendiary parochial clergy at 185.[1]

Challenging the slow pace of institutional change there were, in the early Seventies, the first indications of the growing significance of the charismatic movement. An article in the *DDN* in June 1974 by David Hughes, the assistant curate of St Thomas, Crooks, Sheffield, a leading centre of the movement, was answered by Alfred Ennis, rector of Stanton-by-Bridge and Swarkestone, and the first exchanges were made, at least in Derbyshire, in the theological dispute between those who welcomed the uninhibited enthusiasm of the charismatics with their emphasis on healing, speaking with tongues and the immediacy of the graces and gifts of the Holy Spirit, and those who believed them to be wrong in their theology of baptism, in their lack of intellectual rigour and in their seemingly scant respect for church order.

Another challenge to the *status quo* of the Church in the Sixties and early Seventies was the growing significance of the movement for the ordination of women to the priesthood. Two articles in the *DDN,* in July and August 1971, advocating their ordination were followed by strong support by Cyril Bowles in November. Citing St Paul's statement that 'in Christ there is no such thing as male and female'[2] the bishop argued that this passage 'would be given effective expression if it were at least possible for women to be ordained as priests and consecrated as bishops.' The first was achieved in 1994. In contending for the priesting of women Cyril Bowles was probably challenging the conservative presuppositions of many in the parishes at that time. Norah Oakley, his redoubtable adviser for what was then called 'women's work', was strongly opposed, deploying what were to become very familiar arguments against

---

[1] figures for 1929 and 1997 respectively.
[2] Galatians 3:28.

those of Philippa Robinson, headmistress of St Elphin's School, Darley Dale, who wished to be ordained.[1] The *DDN* published more articles in favour than against. In September 1977 the bishop roundly declared: 'Seeing the grace of God at work in the women of our diocese can we forbid the laying-on of hands to make some of them priests?' In May 1984 the diocesan synod passed a resolution urging General Synod to introduce legislation leading to the ordination of women to the priesthood. It was opposed by Bryan Hackney, then the bishop's industrial adviser. He said that many other priests opposed to the resolution had been afraid to speak. They were soon to set their fears aside. Following legislation, women were made deacon in the diocese in 1987, and, in 1994, 17 women were ordained to the priesthood at two centres: the cathedral, and Tideswell parish church.

A further development, and an apparently radical one, in the rapidly changing pattern of ministry in the Church was the establishment of non-residential ordination training courses, and the ordination of men (initially) to a non-stipendiary and, notionally, secular work-based, ministry. The Lambeth Conference in 1930 had given somewhat lukewarm encouragement to what were then called 'voluntary clergy.' In 1968 the Anglican report *A Supporting Ministry* led to the selection and training of non-stipendiary clergy. The East Midlands Joint Ordination Training Scheme, now the East Midlands Ministry Training Course, an ecumenical training venture, was established in 1973 with Canon David Wilcox, a residentiary canon of Derby Cathedral, as its first warden, and Alan Rodgers of the University of Nottingham's department of adult education, where the course was based, as its first director of studies. Its Anglican students were drawn from the dioceses of Derby, Southwell, Lincoln and Leicester.

The first students from the course were ordained to the non-stipendiary ministry in 1976. In 1978 Cyril Bowles argued that the very fact of men being ordained to a self-supporting ministry would link the secular to the spiritual. In 1983 he believed that 'the bringing together of people who spend their lives on the frontiers where there is most challenge to Christian convictions could well show more clearly the ways in which the Church's missionary task should be discharged in the coming years.'[2] In fact by this time, nationally, the requirements of the parishes had largely conditioned the way the non-

---

[1] *DDN*, March 1975.
[2] Patrick Vaughan (ed), *Training for Diversity of Ministry* (University of Nottingham Department of Adult Education, 1983), 8.

stipendiary ministers interpreted their ministry. Some students from the non-residential courses were now being ordained to the stipendiary ministry, and the ministry of the non-stipendiaries tended to be restricted to Sunday duty. There were few who were free to work constructively and successfully with the theology and practice of an ordained ministry focused primarily in the secular work-place. The Church failed them signifantly in this respect. They tended to be seen more as stop-gaps or substitutes for, or assistants to, the stipendiary parochial ministry (though some were later to be appointed priests in charge of parishes) than pioneers of priestly ministry in a wholly secular environment.

In these and many other ways the diocese attempted to dispose of the picture it seemed to present to outsiders of a worthy, dull, respectable, and somewhat out-of-touch institution. 'Worthy, dull and respectable' were epithets applied in 1978 to the recently changed format and style of the *DDN*. Remarking on this (and apparently regretting the changes) Cyril Bowles pointed out that its previous format and style had been criticised as 'unworthy, bright and not respectable because it did not present a particular staid form of the Anglican tradition.'[1] The Church of England had never met everybody's expectations, but, in the years to the end of the century, it set in train an impressive process of reform. To be staid implies that the Church was sober, composed, steady and sedate. The first three epithets might apply, but sedate the Church of England in Derbyshire was not.

Low clergy recruitment, the inevitable financial constraints, but, above all, the need to manage the Church's resources and deploy its clergy as effectively as possible, led the diocese to take full advantage of the powers conferred by successive Pastoral Measures. Pastoral reorganisation was high on the agenda in these years. Many benefices were united, some parishes amalgamated, a few churches declared redundant, and, throughout the diocese, Group and Team ministries established and pluralities formed, together, as we will see, with the creation of Local Ecumenical Partnerships. To illustrate the scale of this re-organisation, there were, by 1999, some 38 united benefices in the diocese comprising together about 110 separate parishes. The parishes in a united benefice retain their autonomy, but have one incumbent. For example, in 1999 the united benefice of Wirksworth, Alderwasley, Bonsall, Bradbourne and

---

[1] *DDN*, January, 1978.

Brassington, Carsington, Idrigehay, Kirk Ireton and Middleton was also a Team Ministry and was served by three clergy: a team rector, a team vicar and an assistant curate. In 1913 these eight separate benefices had been served by nine clergy: seven incumbents, a curate-in-charge and an assistant curate. In 1913 the eight parishes of Boylestone, Church Broughton, Dalbury, Longford, Long Lane, Radbourne, Sutton on the Hill, and Trusley were served by seven incumbents. In 1999 they comprised a united benefice served by one.

The Church of England in Derbyshire was served by 380 clergy in 1913, almost all of them in parochial ministry. By 1997 there were 192 full-time stipendiary clergy, 185 of them in the parishes with the remaining seven in specialist roles in support of the parochial ministry. These latter included two diocesan directors of ordinands (holding this portfolio in addition to parochial posts), an adult education adviser, a parish development adviser, and an adviser for the in-service training of the clergy. There were, in addition, the industrial chaplains and those working with deaf people. There were clergy working as school, university, hospital and prison chaplains, with others undertaking similar roles. With one or two exceptions these last were not diocesan staff paid by the Church Commissioners. Much of this specialist ministry was pioneering work, and it had to win its way.

The diocese of Derby (together with every other diocese) had thus, by the end of the 20th century, undertaken a quite radical programme of pastoral re-organisation to meet changing circumstances; had provided professional support for the work of ministry in the parishes; and had devoted resources to the engagement of the Church with and for the wider community, through its (mainly part-time) advisers for social responsibility, its race relations officer, its interfaith adviser, tourism officer and rural advisers and its education and youth advisers. In addition, by the 1990s the diocese was engaging with the rapidly changing religious scene through the work of an adviser for new religious movements. Pastoral care and counselling was undertaken on a fully professional basis, as was the ministry of the diocesan consultant on the paranormal (an increasingly important role). The diocesan ecumenical officers were working in partnership with other Christian Churches in Derbyshire. The Derby Asian Christian Ministry Partnership had become a formal Local Ecumenical Partnership, as had industrial mission in the county. This is an impressive record, but the Church of England was by no means working alone.

The death of denominations?

In June 1977 the Anglican, Baptist, Methodist and United Reformed Churches in Derbyshire inaugurated a formal partnership with the Church of North India. This partnership, Cyril Bowles said, underlines that 'we are no longer strangers and foreigners, as Church and Chapel largely were in 1927.'[1] Six years earlier he had remarked that 'the denominations must die to themselves if they are to live in a united Church.'[2] We have noted the failure, on two occasions, of Anglican votes on the Anglican-Methodist reunion proposals to reach the required 75% majority. Yet two-thirds of the Church's electorate had been in favour, and this encouraged local ecumenical initiatives. If reunion, even intercommunion, was, thus far, impossible, much work could still be done by the Churches in partnership with each other.

In 1970 Derbyshire's first 'Area of Ecumenical Experiment' was established in the new housing area of Sinfin Moor. These local ecumenical 'experiments' were to become 'projects' and then formal 'partnerships', sponsored, from 1987, by the Derbyshire Ecumenical Council (now Churches Together in Derbyshire). The changes of designation indicated a rapidly growing trust and desire for close and more permanent cooperation between the participating Churches. In 1987 Mrs Terry Garley, secretary of the diocesan Board for Mission and Unity, became the ecumenical officer for the counties of Derbyshire and Nottinghamshire. She was funded by nine participating Churches, including the dioceses of Derby and Southwell. Some local initiatives came to nothing, but by 2000 more than a dozen Local Ecumenical Partnerships had been established, with 'single congregation' partnerships in Dronfield, Langley Mill, Sinfin Moor, Oakwood, Overseal, and The Haven (Littleover).

However, though Church and Chapel had long overcome their mutual antipathy and rivalry, by the end of the century their organic union, even the more limited goal of intercommunion[3], seemed as far from achievement as ever. Churches Together in Derbyshire, the principal ecumenical body in the county, was committed, as was its national parent, to the unity of the

---

[1] ibid., June, 1977. The partnership was to be furthered by diocesan visits to and from the Church of North India in the 1980s and 1990s.

[2] ibid., January, 1971.

[3] It would be claimed that, as the eucharist is the sacrament which celebrates unity, intercommunion, that is, a sharing in the eucharist before the organic unity of the Church is achieved, is at least a misnomer.

participating Churches and to 'deepening . . . their communion with Christ and with one another.'

These Churches included the Roman Catholic diocese of Nottingham. In 1969 the Anglican-Roman Catholic International Commission, ARCIC, had been established. It was to produce a series of reports on central theological issues, each of which showed a considerable level of agreement between the two Churches. Cyril Bowles commented on each report as it was published. Agreement on Ministry and Ordination, in 1974, was, he said, 'wide', and followed the 'remarkable' level of agreement on the doctrine of the eucharist, in 1972. Subsequent ARCIC reports on even more contentious issues led to a real hope that unity between the Anglican and Roman Catholic Churches was not as remote, even as unthinkable, as it had seemed.

The union of those non-Roman Churches in England that were separated less by issues of dogma than by church order had seemed a more realistic possibility, despite the failure of the Anglican-Methodist proposals in 1969 and 1972. In May 1978 the diocesan synod approved ten propositions on Christian unity referred to the dioceses by General Synod. In that year a five month ecumenical mission, *Jesus Call '78*, had been undertaken in the diocese by the Church of England and the Methodist, Baptist and United Reformed Churches. It was reported that events had taken place in 35–45% of local areas in the county, and 'new action' initiated in 15–25%. This statistical vagueness suggests that what was achieved was difficult to quantify, though perhaps achievement was less important than the aspiration and co-operation of the Churches.

In March 1980 a major report, *Towards Visible Unity: Proposals for a Covenant,* was published. Since the bishops at the 1920 Lambeth Conference had called for a restoration of fellowship between the Churches there had been, as Cyril Bowles noted, a fundamental change of attitude, and many attempts had been made to achieve unity. Some had succeeded. The Churches of South India and of North India had been established. The United Reformed Church, a union of the Congregational Church in England and Wales and the Presbyterian Church of England, had been created in 1972. *Towards Visible Unity* proposed that the Church of England, Methodist, Moravian and United Reformed Churches enter into a Covenant. This would be inaugurated by a solemn service which would include an act of reconciliation and of 'covenanting together' in the ordination of presbyters (a less contentious word than 'priests' for nonconformists) and bishops. This would result in all future ordinations in all four Churches being by laying-on of hands by bishops using a common ordinal and leading to interchangeability of ministries and full intercommunion.

The objections of the Catholic wing of the Church of England to the Anglican-Methodist reunion proposals ten years earlier were raised again now: Free Church ministers would not be re-ordained; women ministers in the other Churches would be allowed to celebrate holy Communion in the Church of England; unity with Rome would be hindered by any Covenant with nonconformist Churches; and the 'episcopal coinage' would be devalued. Though he was strongly in favour of the Covenant, these objections were put frankly to the diocesan synod in February 1982 by the archdeacon of Derby, Bob Dell, when asking it to agree to the Covenant in principle. In the event General Synod voted the proposal down. In the grass-roots deanery synods throughout the country the proposals also failed, with over one-third of the laity and nearly half the clergy opposed.

Desire for Christian unity is one thing, the will to achieve it another. It had long been true that denominational divisions are at least as much due to cultural, social and psychological factors as they are to issues of dogma and church order.[1] Perhaps the existence of the latter offer an acceptable excuse not to challenge these more deep-rooted, insidious and covert causes of division. Yet, in the end, only Christians care. The majority of people seem indifferent not merely to the question of whether the Churches unite or not but of whether they exist or not.

The 1990s

We are too near to the 1990s to be able to set these years in a broader perspective. Not only does the outcome of policies put in place in the 1990s lie in the future, but those involved in their formulation and implementation have too much invested in them to regard them with even-handed detachment. This is as true of the Church of England in Derbyshire as of any other area of social life. Further, as this is a social history and not a journal of record, a mere recital of events in the diocese in these years would be as out of place as it would be

---

[1] Roy Porter observes that 'by 1800 English piety was decisively shaped by social rank. Denomination itself had become a litmus of social position' [*English Society in the Eighteenth Century* (Penguin 1991), 184].

tedious.

For these reasons our detailed story ends here. Peter Spencer Dawes, who had been vicar of the parish of The Good Shepherd, Collier Row, Romford, and then archdeacon of West Ham, became bishop of Derby in 1988 on Cyril Bowles' retirement. His own retirement in 1995 prompted tributes to his 'wide accessibility, power as a preacher, theological scholarship, wide reading, sense of humour and serious pursuit of the truth.'[1] He and his successor, Jonathan Sansbury Bailey, who had been vicar of Wetherby, archdeacon of Southend, and suffragan bishop of Dunwich, and who was made bishop of Derby on Peter Dawes' retirement, were to lead the Church of England in Derbyshire through a period of even greater religious confusion and change.

But if detached analysis of these years is not possible, and a mere recital of their events too tedious, it is helpful to record contemporary impressions. A number of men and women, ordained and lay, from the north and south of the county and from rural and urban parishes, were asked to set down their perceptions of the diocese in the 1990s. What follows is based on their responses. Quotations are from respondents, unless indicated otherwise.

'Change like the Spring comes slowly and reluctantly'

This was said of the diocese in the north of the county, but it rings true of the Church of England generally in many places.

New forms of eucharistic worship were often accepted reluctantly, 'the impact of their newness softened by the comfortable presence of the familiar Book of Common Prayer at Matins and Evensong'. 'Them in Derby' burdened parishes, many deprived of an incumbent, with increasing financial demands. Small rural communities and parishes felt marginalised. This inevitably made some congregations resentful and inward looking. The continuing creation of new patterns of parochial organisation – a response to reduced numbers of clergy and financial constraints – meant that not a few of the clergy who remained were required to work together in unfamiliar team and group ministries. This has been 'a very difficult exercise' for many in both urban and rural parishes as one respondent observed.

Though new patterns of parochial ministry have been inevitable, they could

---

[1] *DDN*, July 1995.

result in very significant losses to the Church of England. There is now, one respondent commented, little place for the Anglican priest as 'poet or artist . . . or philosopher who could serve the diocese and the world at large' from a small rural parish. More importantly, for this respondent and for others, there is a danger that we will eventually lose some rural churches. They provide places of peace and serenity 'in the midst of endless bustle' and their loss 'will diminish us as a church and diocese, and then we will diminish others.' Above all, their loss will deprive us of ancient places where men and women have for centuries been engaged by (in a striking phrase) that 'awesome and probably wild God in our genes and our adaptive heritage who stalks us.'

These new patterns and new demands meant that a greater emphasis than hitherto was placed on the ministry of the whole church, with clergy and laity working together collaboratively. The 1998 *A Better Way* strategy for local ministry was based on the conviction that there must be a better way to promote the Church's ministry than by '*merely* spreading the clergy ever more thinly over the ground and lumping parishes together', as its strategy document put it. In putting in place a policy by which the ministry of the whole Church was offered by clergy and lay people together (in 'mutual equality . . . distinction of identity and diversity of function'), it offered a renewed vision to many parishes. The initiative was greeted warmly, because, as one respondent said, 'it had slowly dawned on priest and people that if the Church was to regain effectiveness it had to be by shared ministry – a priesthood of all believers based on Baptism.' This had long been believed, though the gap between conviction and action in the Church of England is closed at least as often by resource constraints as by the practical application of theological truths.

There was some opposition to this increased emphasis on the ministry of the whole congregation. It was said that it tended to undermine the central importance of the sacraments and therefore of the ministry of the ordained priest. Nevertheless, the *A Better Way* initiative 'as an attempt to rise above pragmatic responses to falling numbers of clergy and shortage of money' and as 'a blueprint for enabling struggling church communities to maintain their place of worship and improve their outreach to their community' was widely regarded as immensely significant, though a judgement as to its long-term effectiveness lies well in the future.

Money inevitably featured regularly on diocesan synod agendas throughout the

1990s. Bishop Peter Dawes' *Bishop's Initiative in Giving*, launched in 1990, combined with his resolute dealing with the management problems which had led to the financial crisis that he inherited, 'was possibly the most important thing he achieved ... . The outcome has been a lean, efficient central organisation, delivering excellent service from rationalised accommodation.' The limitation on the numbers of clergy employed in the diocese were to be much more the result of the application of national quotas than of what the diocese could afford. 'There has been an air of being in control and able to make ends meet in a way not shared by much of the Church' one respondent observed. This had, at least potentially, freed the Church of England in Derbyshire to address its primary work of worship and mission. If for no other reason than this, the diocese looks back to Bishop Peter Dawes' ministry as bishop of Derby with deep and lasting gratitude. Much remained for his successor to do, and the raising of clergy morale, and the giving of 'a much greater sense of direction to the diocese' was the fruit of the first years of Bishop Jonathan Bailey's ministry.

Worship is the Church's first work. Some clergy and laity had become increasingly frustrated by what one priest describes as 'the non-user-friendliness, and inappropriate wording of the little red book [the ASB Rite A booklet]', the most commonly used of the holy Communion services in the ASB, and some parishes produced their own service books which, while retaining the ASB rite, were more attractive to use. Of at least equal importance in some parishes in promoting greater congregational involvement in worship in the 1990s was the admitting of children to Communion before Confirmation, where permission had been granted by the bishop.

The ordination of women to the priesthood in 1994, though opposed by some and deeply regretted by others, was welcomed by many and came to be increasingly accepted in the parishes as the years passed. It came to be realised that 'the need of congregations for a particular person to whom they could relate [was] much more important than matters of gender or, indeed, of ministerial status – incumbent, priest-in-charge, NSM, Reader.' This is a very significant observation. The role of this 'particular person' (the traditional role of the 'parson') in no way undervalued the responsibility of the whole congregation to share in the Church's ministry, for the ministry of the 'particular person' came to be seen as one of service *to* the congregation and to the wider community. It was *representative of* the ministry of the whole Church, rather than one in which that ministry was exclusively lodged. This shift of emphasis – the returning (albeit very gradually) of the Church's ministry to the whole people of God – had been taking place since the late Middle Ages, but the 1980s and 1990s were to see it given greater impetus. This was due to many factors, not least financial constraints and the relative shortage of stipendiary clergy.

There was much else on the agenda of the diocese in the 1990s. Examples include the number of initiatives for and with young people; the development of a diocesan child protection policy; the *Decade of Evangelism* (in the event more an aspiration than an achievement); and the maturing of the charismatic renewal movement from 'the "happy-clappy" stereo-type', as one respondent put it. Ecumenical ventures such as the Padley Centre, the Derby Soup Run, Salcare in Heanor, and the response of the Churches to the victims of economic change in the mining and agricultural industries featured significantly in these years and showed the Churches' continuing involvement with social issues. So too did the rapid and effective diocesan response to the Church of England's report *Faith in the City* which attracted 'a much higher proportion of funding into the diocese [for local projects] than might have been expected for a diocese of our size and level of urban deprivation.'[1]

Yet there were those who believed strongly that while the diocese may have become leaner and fitter in the 1990s and had ended the decade in very good heart, its response to rapid social change was becoming more muted and less effective. It seemed to one inner-city priest that in the 1990s 'individualism whether in the name of our country, or small groups wielding power, became the important factor in public life', and increasingly a factor in Church life too.

'Certainty converts those who want it'

A priest with long and faithful service in urban ministry in the diocese wrote this:

---

[1] The later report, *Faith in the Countryside*, did not have the same impact; the extent of rural deprivation was not widely appreciated, and there was no national Church funding to support local projects addressing rural problems.

In the Diocese of Derby as elsewhere, the Church showed itself struggling to cope with the nature of social change and the incredible pace of that change. The Church of England's distinctive claim to be a broad church continued to be both a bane and a blessing. At one level it was a miracle that the whole held together at all. At another level, it frustrated progress, development and an effective response to the 'new' world that was rapidly establishing itself.

In the 1990s, the diocese of Derby had shown great commitment to the cause of social justice, yet for this priest, as for others, it had no clearer answer to the intractable problems around sexual orientation, the ordination of women, and crime and punishment than the Church nation-wide (perhaps not surprisingly). For him too, there was another issue to be faced:

> One root problem remained the nature and authority of the Christian Holy Book, which continued to be idolised as the time-locked voice of a deity that few recognised or wanted. This had a feel good factor for those within the Church who could still subscribe to this anachronism, but prejudiced much of the population against the Church.

He continued: 'As the decade closed the Diocese was left with the paradox that certainty converted those who wanted it and put bums on pews but alienated those who knew they no longer wanted certainty, yet had questions to be answered. How the Diocese reconciles these two poles will be the challenge of the new era.'

It is with the challenges and opportunities of that new era that we conclude.

Postscript

Beyond Christendom:
faith in the future

'Christendom' is a term now very rarely used. It used to be employed, as the *Oxford English Dictionary* has it in one of its definitions, as 'the Christian domain; the countries professing Christianity taken collectively.' No country now professes to be Christian. Every formerly Christian nation has now a very varied religious colouring. In 1995 in Great Britain there were more Muslims (586000) than Methodists (421000), and more Sikhs (350000) than Baptists (230000). Although many people still make some acknowledgement of the nation's Christian past, and the Churches, particularly the Church of England, are still cut into the fabric of national life to an extent which belies their decreasing numbers, we cannot say that we are a Christian nation and a part of Christendom. 'The present Christendom is merely titular and verbal' observed the 17th century German Lutheran Jacob Boehme[1], and so it is for us. In the mid-1990s no more than 15% of the adult population claimed membership of the traditional British Churches, lower than in any other European country. 'What these figures demonstrate most forcibly is that majority Britain, White Britain, was overwhelmingly a secular society.'[2] We are very far from that sense of an all-pervading Christendom felt by Richard Chenevix Trench, archbishop of Dublin from 1863 to 1884, for whom, a mere century and a half ago, it was 'commensurate and almost synonymous with the civilised world.'[3] In England

---

[1] John Ellistone, *The Epistles of Jacob Behmen* [Boehme], (English trans, 1866 edition), xxxiv, 16.
[2] Arthur Marwick, *British Society since 1945* (Penguin 1996), 460-1. The figure of 15% is taken from *Social Trends 1995*, 222. This is replicated for church attendance in the 1998 British Social Attitudes survey. These are questionnaire surveys. Peter Brierley's 1998 church census produced a figure for church attendance of 7.5% of the total population (*Religious Trends 2000/2001*, 12.3).
[3] *Notes on the Miracles of Our Lord* (1846), Preliminary Essay, vi.

we are far further than a mere stage or two beyond a Christendom so defined.

That is demonstrated by each of the numerical indicators we have considered.[1] However, contemporary sociologists of religion have been quick to point out that the decline in numbers attending the main Christian Churches must be set alongside other more positive indicators: the rapid growth of new Christian groups; the persistence (because of the importance) of civic religion (that is the role of the Churches at times of significance for society as a whole); and the considerable number of those who profess a private faith or affirm the place of the spiritual in their lives.[2] Taken together with the growth of new religious movements outside Christianity the evidence suggests that the notion that we are now a secularised nation, if by that is meant a nation without religion, is far from accurate.

'Secularisation' is a slippery word. It is best understood less as a term with a precise definition and more (like 'Reformation') as a marker indicating a series of complex and not necessarily interacting social, political and ethical, as well as religious, shifts of emphasis and interpretation. But imprecise though the concept of secularisation is it has been much used when discussing the state of Christianity in Britain. Here are two of very many definitions, one from a social historian and one from two sociologists of religion, all with knowledge of, and a degree of sympathy for, the Churches.

The social historian Edward Royle defines secularisation as 'the shift across a range of human institutions, activities and beliefs from views rooted in the transcendental and supernatural to ones rooted in the present and natural world.'[3] It signifies the attempt of people to live without religion. For the sociologists Robert Towler and Anthony Coxon, working with a narrower definition in their study of Anglican clergy, it is 'a process whereby the Church and its clergy lose control of some aspect or aspects of the non-religious affairs

---

[1] For a careful consideration of the significance of these indicators, see Peter Brierley, *The Tide is Running Out* (Christian Research 2000).

[2] See David Hay, *The Spirituality of the Unchurched*, a paper prepared for the British and Irish Association for Mission Studies, and published on the Internet [*BIAMS Home Page/HMC Home Page*, 1 September 2000]. Dr Hay notes a 60% rise in the number of those reporting a religious or spiritual experience over the period 1987–2000. However, he suspects that there has been 'no great change over the past few years in the frequency with which people encounter the spiritual dimension of their lives. What is probably changing is people's sense of the degree of social permission for such experience.' This is significant in itself.

[3] Edward Royle, op. cit., 343.

of a society.'[1] The *process* described in the second definition led to the cultural *shift* set out in the first. For all three, secularisation has been a very long-term process. It is no comparatively recent and negative consequence (as is commonly supposed) of 'materialism' or 'liberalism' or 'industrialisation' or 'urbanisation' or 'modernism'.

Nor is secularisation necessarily related to a decline in church attendance. Although the USA is a highly industrialised nation the incidence of church-going is high. Secularisation, in the sense of the exclusion of all religious privilege, is written into its constitution, yet religious observance is popular and seen almost as a defining element of the American way of life. In England the mid-19th century saw rapid industrialisation and economic growth, and, for the middle-classes at least, a fast-rising standard of living, yet it was also a time when church-going was at a much higher level than in the equally materialist mid-20th century. The social and cultural shift from a reliance less on the transcendent than on the immanent, less on heaven than on earth and less on God than on man has, therefore, not everywhere, always and inevitably been accompanied by a personal loss of faith in 'heaven' or 'the spiritual' or even in 'God'. Far from it.

This general shift of emphasis has been taking place for several hundred years and we have traced much of its progress in the story of the Church of England in Derbyshire. Its origins can be dated to the discoveries of Copernicus and Galileo. They first challenged the notion, held almost to be an article of faith by the Church, that the earth, and therefore man, was the very hub of the universe, thereby beginning the process empirical science was to follow in its undermining of traditional theological assumptions, a process so bitterly resisted by the guardians of theological orthodoxy.

The scientific revolution was to run parallel to, and interact with, the theological and political revolution we call the Reformation, but its consequences were to be more far-reaching. That said, the cultural changes brought about by the Reformation were themselves profound. For centuries the Church had dominated almost all walks of life: government, education, the law, medicine and diplomacy. The Reformation destroyed clerical control of the nation's great institutions, yet it left the largely Anglican land-owning gentry, and therefore the clergy dependent upon their patronage, very much in control of a predominately rural England, a control they maintained for at least

---

[1] Robert Towler and A.P.M. Coxon, *The Fate of the Anglican Clergy*, (Macmillan 1979), 191.

300 years. At the level of the parishes it has been said that 'there was an unprecedented merging of the church and the state, the spiritual and the temporal, the ecclesiastical and the landed interest . . . . According to William Cobbett, the clergy had "laid down the Bible, and taken up the statute book."'[1] As it has been said succinctly: 'gentility privileged Anglicanism'[2]. The Reformation, very long in its maturing, effectively secularised the Church.

It was not until the late 19th century that this secularising process began slowly to become one of the de-Christianisation, or at least of the unChurching, of the nation. As A.N. Wilson puts it, in the late 19th century

> for the first time in Europe a generation was coming to birth who had no God, or at least no God of any substance, and who found it difficult to justify religion except in the most basic of Utilitarian terms.[3]

We should not exaggerate the then pace or depth of this process. By 1930, as the diocese of Derby was beginning its life, it was still true that as a systematic view or interpretation of life, Christianity had few rivals. Yet a radical change in the religious subconscious of the nation had taken place. In the 19th century religious affiliations had a socially cohesive effect. Men and women associated with those churches and chapels that matched their political and economic circumstances, and would change religious allegiance to match their rising social aspirations. By the 1930s these communal and class ties had become weakened as English society became socially and culturally much more eclectic and plural: as Hugh McLeod puts it, 'the secularising effect of a pluralist society lay primarily in the fact that the religious community was ceasing to be a necessary source of identity and support.'[4] Throughout the life of the diocese of Derby its parishes have served a religiously plural, eclectic society which has owed allegiance to no one religious, or secular, ideology.

Secularisation is therefore primarily a wider social, rather than a narrowly religious, phenomenon[5]. The Churches are inevitably caught up in it, as much in the 20th century as in the past. The fact that secularisation co-existed, at least for a time, with a high level of church-going suggests that *the Churches themselves were a major secularising factor* in the later years of the 19th

---

[1] David Cannadine, *Aspects of Aristocracy*, (Penguin 1995), 24.
[2] Douglas Hay and Nicholas Rogers, *Eighteenth Century English Society*, (Opus 1997), 24.
[3] A.N. Wilson, *God's Funeral* (Abacus 2000), 56.
[4] Hugh McLeod, *Religion and the People of Western Europe 1989–1970* (OUP 1981), 141.
[5] For classic studies see Owen Chadwick, *The Secularization of the European Mind in the Nineteenth Century* (CUP 1975), and David Martin, *A General Theory of Secularization* (Blackwell, Oxford 1978).

century and the first decades of the 20th. This is the point that Jose Harris makes and that we considered earlier. The very zealousness of the Churches was a potent factor in their marginalisation. What Harris calls 'the expanding area of secularized neutrality' in Edwardian England was a stage in the much more long-standing and progressive shift from heavenly to earthly frames of reference, and one which the Churches themselves prompted. But this progressive shift was initially less a process of de-Christianisation (though that was taking place) than of what we have called the unChurching of the nation. Specifically Christian *and Church* affirmations and expressions of the transcendent in common life began first to be marginalised and then to be ignored, and the numerical strength of the Churches began to decline. From being an Estate of the Realm, part of the body politic, the Church of England became, seemingly, one voluntary organisation among others (and a numerically less significant one as the years passed) while still retaining its public service function at those times when, individually or collectively, people needed to engage with religion.

The 1960s may have been a watershed, but long before then the Christian Churches had become used to living with both frames of reference. As to the earthly frame, while Eric Hobsbawm is correct when, writing of the mid-20th century, he notes that 'the clergy now accepted the hegemony of the laboratory' he is wrong to dismiss them as mere hangers-on in the scientific revolution 'drawing what theological comfort [they] could from scientific cosmology, whose "Big Bang" theories, could, with the eye of faith, be presented as proof that a God had created the world.'[1] This ignores the very significant contribution to the conversation between theology and science by Edward Barnes in a previous generation, and Thomas Torrance and John Polkinghorne and John Hapgood and many others in this. More widely, it ignores the extent to which scientific methods of investigation had, for a century and more, influenced the literary criticism of the Bible and the study of Christian origins, and had thus been absorbed into the Church's ways of thinking. It also greatly underrates the ability of clergy and lay people generally to handle the methods and findings of science in a theologically sophisticated way. It is a symptom of the effect of the secular world-view that an historian of Eric Hobsbawm's sophistication can write of the clergy in this

---

[1] Eric Hobsbawm, *Age of Extremes: The Short Twentieth Century 1914–1991*, (Abacus 1995), 554–5.

way. The best of the Church's theologians had, for at least one hundred years, been developing a theology based upon the truths found both in the data provided by empirical science *and* in the poetry and story of Scripture[1] without reducing the one to the other. This is one of many examples of the modernising of the Church, and of the extent to which the secularising process for which it had been partly responsible, had, paradoxically, equipped it for a new age.

However, on one reading of the evidence this modernising had failed. Large numbers of people had become indifferent to the claims of a Church that had quite radically reformed its ways of thought, its structures, its worship and its understanding of ministry. Yet their indifference to the Churches by no means meant that they were indifferent to the questions the Churches had always attempted to address. The end of the 1960s saw a deepening sense of dis-ease and disillusion with the confident claims of secular reason. It did not deliver all that it seemed to promise in the Sixties, and the last decades of the 20th century have seen questions rather than answers dominating the public agenda, and the questions are the profound and age-old questions with which religion has always been concerned. Grace Davie makes just this point.[2] Given this, she continues,

> Religious life – like so many other features of post-industrial or post-modern society – is not so much disappearing as mutating, for the sacred undoubtedly persists and will continue to do so, but in forms that may be very different from those which have gone before.[3]

Post-modernism, of which this disillusion and questioning and mutating are symptoms, is but a development of modernism, but it is a development with which the Churches generally are as yet unfamiliar. All open, and therefore questioning, systems of thought have within them the seeds of their own mutation and re-formation. This must be true of theology and thus of the Churches. Holding fast to the timeless and transcultural Gospel, the Churches must continually reformulate and re-present its truths and, as they do so, to be

---

[1] they had long recognised that reason and revelation were not always and inevitably in conflict but that each enriched the other.

[2] Grace Davie, op. cit., 196.

[3] ibid., 198.

in the vanguard of social and cultural change if they are not to be reduced merely to drawing what comfort they can from such scant regard of a world that is passing them by accords them, becoming ever more entrenched and irrelevant, and thus effectively denying the very truths of the Incarnation by which they claim to live.

No one can tell what the next generations will see. Will they see the death of the Church, with Christianity vanishing quite slowly like the Cheshire Cat, with its grin – its residual influence – remaining for some time after the rest of it has gone? Or will they see the death of the Church in its old cultural forms and its evolution – indeed its resurrection – in a changed community of faith? Our history strongly suggests the second. The Church has adapted to fundamental societal change for two millennia. It has for centuries lived with that progressive shift to a materialist frame of reference we loosely call secularisation, and, prey to that process as it may have been, and contributing to it as it may have done, it has, at its best, responded to it and adapted positively to it. To a much greater extent than is often realised, it has humanised it (or rather has revealed the sacred within it) and in the proclamation and service of the Gospel has offered to it a prophetic witness and an ethical critique.

If that is not wishful thinking and is to be the long-term pattern, what does the future hold for the Churches in the short-term? Michael Moynagh and Richard Worsley in *Tomorrow: Using the future to understand the present*, published in May 2000, offer two possible scenarios for the year 2020. The first is that the mainline Churches will continue to fail 'to engage radically with the changing nature of society', to squander resources, and to persist in appointing clergy to nearly empty churches. Such congregations as there are will become 'more inward-looking and defensive, [and] increasingly separate from the rest of society' as they become more vulnerable and marginalised. The other scenario is much more positive. New congregations will be formed where people actually congregate, and that will often not be in church. There will be congregations meeting on other days of the week than Sunday, in other places than church buildings and at times of the day other than those traditionally used for worship. In the Church of England many more men and women in secular employment will be ordained to the priesthood and will lead the local Christian communities from which they were drawn. There will be a Christian revival, and although we will never recreate Christendom God will be worshipped and the Gospel will continue to be preached.

These are very simplistic scenarios, based less on analysis of trends than on speculation. Who can tell if either of them will match the reality? All that we can be confident of is what the history of Christianity, not least in Derbyshire, tells us. It is that those who are drawn to the religious quest (and that is a very significant proviso) will embrace a Christian religion which grows from them and belongs to them. In the long run they will reject whatever seems alien in religion however superficially attractive it may seem, and however strongly urged on them by those invested with religious authority. People will continue to believe in the Gospel so long as what they believe engages with their lives at the deepest level. The Churches will continue to decline numerically if they are *perceived* (whatever may be the reality) not to offer what people need from them. That is the brutal sociological reality however Christians might wish it otherwise or believe that it should be otherwise. The Church of England, as an arm of the state, once *enforced* religious observance and people were compelled to attend. It then *offered* its fellowship as a still respected, and constitutionally established, institution within the state and people chose not to attend. Can it change again and become what it has never been since the Middle Ages – a Church of and for *all* the people, offering, in the intimacy of a true communion which speaks to the deepest instincts of men and women, 'the blysse wyth-owten ende'?

We have yet to find out. Some may consider that the Church's past has destroyed the possibility of such a future. Yet, as S.C. Carpenter reminded us, Christianity has always been 'too spiritual for [the English] perfectly to comprehend, too exacting for them completely to obey, yet so humane that the English, who are intensely human, have never been able wholly to deny or wholly to resist its claim to sovereign rule.' The story of Christianity in Derbyshire shows how perceptive an historical judgement that was.

Glossary

Advowson   See Patronage

Anchorite   A hermit [from Gr. *ana* + *khōreō*, retire].

Anglo-catholic   'The modern name of the more advanced section of the High Church movement in the Church of England.' (*ODCC*) The term was first employed in 1838. See **High churchman, Oxford Movement**

Alternative Service Book, The   of the Church of England was authorised for use in 1980 in conjunction with *The Book of Common Prayer* of 1662. It was superseded by *Common Worship* in 2000. See **Common Worship**

Appropriation   'The practice common in the Middle Ages of permanently annexing to a monastery the tithes and other endowments which were intended for parochial use.' (*ODCC*) See **Tithe, Impropriation**

Archdeacon   An ordained man or woman with a defined area of jurisdiction in a diocese by delegation of its bishop. This area is known as an archdeaconry. Originally, an archdeacon was the senior deacon appointed to assist a bishop. He was the *oculus episcopi*, the 'bishop's eye'. Modern archdeacons have wide powers and responsibilities which may vary in detail from diocese to diocese, but in the main relate to faculty legislation, parsonages, benefice vacancies, the formal induction of incumbents (that is, placing them in possession of the 'temporalities' of the benefice), annual visitations (which include the admission of churchwardens), parish inspections, and clergy care and discipline. See **Visitation**.

Arminianism   Jacobus Arminius (1560–1609), Dutch Reformer. On the basis of Paul's *Epistle to the Romans*, he opposed Calvin's doctrines of predestination, arguing that Christ's death was for all and not only for the elect, and insisting that the sovereignty of God was compatible with human freewill. See **Calvinism**.

Articles of visitation   see **Visitation**

Baptism and Confirmation   By the sacrament of Baptism an individual is made one with Christ and a member of the Church. In Anglican theology Confirmation is not a sacrament in the strict sense. It is 'the occasion when the response of conscious faith required of candidates for Baptism, and, in the case of infants, vicariously made by the godparents, is openly affirmed, and candidates receive in their turn the bishop's blessing with the outward sign of the laying on of hands and prayer . . . that they may daily increase in the Holy Spirit.' G.W.H. Lampe, *The Seal of the Spirit* (1967), vii–viii.

Benefice [from Lat. *beneficium*, favour]. In the context of parish ministry, the office of incumbent of a parish conferring various 'rights and appurtenances'.

Broad Churchmen A term which came to be applied around 1848 to Anglicans who took the formularies of the Church of England in a broad and liberal sense, and held that it should be tolerant and comprehensive 'so as to admit of more or less variety of opinion in matters of dogma and ritual' *OED*. Unlike the 'High Church' and the 'Low Church', the 'Broad Church' had no coherence as a party.

Calvinism The theological system of John Calvin, Protestant reformer 1509–1564, in particular his related notions (a) of absolute predestination according to which God gratuitously determined that some, the elect, should be saved by Christ's atoning death, and others (through no fault of their own) should be damned for all eternity; and (b) of the indefectibility, or perfect and unfailing quality, of divine grace. Both doctrines derived logically from Calvin's extreme view of the utter omnipotence of God.

Canon [from Gr. *kanōn*, rule] There are several related meanings, those relevant here are: (a) as in Canon Law which is the body of rules or decrees of the Church. In the Church of England it comprised the 'Constitutions and Canons Ecclesiastical' agreed by the Convocations and ratified under the Great Seal by James I in 1603, and subsequently extensively revised. These are binding only on the clergy and authorised lay workers including Readers. Under the Synodical Government Measure 1969 the power to make canons was transferred from the Convocations to the General Synod; (b) a canon is a senior member of a cathedral or collegiate church (as, for example, Derby All Saints and Southwell Minster), anciently possessing a prebend [from Latin *praebenda* pension], a revenue derived from estates. In cathedrals canons are either residentiary (usually stipendiary) or honorary; (c) a priest living under a monastic rule, as, for example, an Augustinian canon.

Catechism [from Gr. *katēcheō*, to make hear, hence, to instruct]. A manual of Christian doctrine. In the Church of England, in the 1662 *BCP* it is described as 'An instruction to be learned of every person before he be brought to be confirmed by the bishop'. It consists of an exposition of the Apostles' Creed, the Ten Commandments and the Lord's Prayer (with explanations) followed by sections on the sacraments of Baptism and 'the Supper of the Lord'. Rubrics (or directions) to the clergy require the incumbent to instruct children in the Catechism 'upon Sundays and Holydays, after the second lesson at Evening Prayer' and that 'all Fathers, Mothers, Masters, and Dames, shall cause their Children, Servants and Prentices, (which have not learned their Catechism,) to come to the Church at the time appointed . . .' This form of religious education and preparation for Confirmation has long since been discontinued.

Cathedra   The bishop's chair [Gr. *kathedra]) in his principal church (hence 'cathedral').*

Chalice   The cup in which the wine is administered in the celebration of holy Communion.

Chancel   [Lat. *cancelli*, lattice]. Originally the part of a church nearest to, and including, the altar. It now designates the area reserved for the clergy and the choir east of the nave. In older churches the chancel is sometimes separated from the nave by a screen. The repair of the chancel was usually the responsibility of the rector of the parish, ordained or lay.

Chancellor   (from Lat. *cancellarius* porter, secretary [*cancelli*, lattice]). In its use in this book the term applies to (a) the diocesan bishop's senior legal representative and the principal legal officer of the diocese. The chancellor (often a judge and always a barrister) hears applications for, and grants, faculties, fixes tables of fees, and issues marriage licences through surrogates. He or she usually also presides in the Consistory Court. The Consistory Court is the court of first instance with regard to faculties and in discipline proceedings (other than on matters of doctrine and ritual) against the clergy. When acting thus, the chancellor acts as the bishop's Official Principal and Vicar-General, that is, he or she represents the diocesan bishop in the exercise of his coercive jurisdiction. There is thus no appeal to the bishop against his chancellor's judgment. (See **Registrar**). (b) a canon of a cathedral with (formerly) special responsibility for its school and library, but now usually with a wider educational accountability.

Chapel-of-ease   An Anglican church subordinate to its parish church provided for the ease or convenience of remote parishioners.

Chapter   [from Lat. *capitulum, caput*, head]. For a relevant definition see **Dean/ Provost and Chapter**

Charge   A formal address delivered by a bishop or archdeacon at a visitation of the clergy and churchwardens under his jurisdiction, and by a bishop to those to be ordained deacon or priest before their ordination.

Charismatic movement   A movement within some Churches to restore the *charismata* or spiritual gifts, especially those of 'speaking with tongues' and 'prophecy', to a central place in the life and worship of the Church. It is characterised by spontaneity and enthusiasm.

Church Commissioners The body established in 1948 from the amalgamation of Queen Anne's Bounty and the Ecclesiastical Commissioners. The latter had managed the revenues of the Church of England since 1835.

Church Congresses A series of unofficial gatherings of Anglican churchmen meeting for three days and held annually in different centres from 1861 to 1913, and, on less frequent occasions subsequently. The establishment of Church Assembly in 1919 made them less necessary and they were eventually discontinued. Official reports of the Proceedings were published.

Church rates A rate on all assessed property within a parish in England and Ireland, levied by resolution of the annual vestry, for the maintenance of the parish church and its services. This was enforceable in law. The assumption upon which church rates was based was that as the rites of the Church of England were available to every parishioner, the maintenance of the church should be a charge on all. Church rates were strongly resented by nonconformists on the ground that it was unjust for them to be required to maintain the parish church as well as their own places of worship. Eventually the Compulsory Church Rate Abolition Act was passed in 1868. Thereafter voluntary rates could be set, but these were subsequently superseded by voluntary contributions.

Churching of Women The *BCP* form of *Thanksgiving of Women after Childbirth*, commonly called the Churching of Women.

Churchwarden In the Church of England an honorary office of a parish or district church, held by a lay person chosen at the annual vestry (though, customarily, one churchwarden was appointed by the incumbent). Traditionally, the churchwardens were 'guardians of the parochial morals and trustees of the Church's goods.' (Macmorran). There are normally two churchwardens. They have a wide range of legal powers and duties. They are officers of the bishop by whom (or on his behalf by the archdeacon) they are formally admitted to office.

Common Worship: Services and Prayers for the Church of England. *The Book of Common Prayer* is the permanently authorised provision for public worship in the Church of England. The services and other material in *Common Worship* are authorised for use pursuant to Canon B 2 of the Canons of the Church of England until further resolution of the General Synod.

Convocations In the Church of England, the synods or assemblies of clergy in the provinces of Canterbury and York, constituted by statute, to consider ecclesiastical matters. The Convocations consist of two Houses, an Upper House of bishops and a Lower House of the clergy. They were originally convoked by Edward I. The Convocation of York was suppressed from 1698 to 1861, and of Canterbury effectively so from 1717 to 1852. The power of the Convocations to pass canons was passed to the General Synod under the Synodical Government Measure 1969.

Curate   Correctly, an ordained man or women with cure of souls, that is, the incumbent. The prayer for 'the whole state of Christ's Church' in the 1662 *BCP* thus prays for 'all Bishops and Curates . . .' Hence 'assistant curate', though this is usually but incorrectly shortened to 'the curate'.

Cure   [from Lat. *curare*, to take care of, hence, care, or charge] In the Church of England a cure is the spiritual charge of a parish. All those entrusted with the 'cure of souls', that is, the spiritual well-being of parishioners, hold a cure. This includes the bishop of the diocese. Traditionally, at the institution of an incumbent, the bishop formally shares the cure of souls, which is 'both mine and thine', with the new incumbent.

Daily Offices   [Med. Lat. *officium*, performance of a task, hence divine service] In the Church of England, the services of Morning and Evening Prayer, enjoined by the 1662 *BCP* 'Daily to be said and used throughout the year'. It is further required that these services 'shall be used in the accustomed Place of the Church, Chapel, or Chancel; except it shall be otherwise determined by the Ordinary of the Place.'

Dean/Provost and Chapter   The dean is the senior priest of a cathedral with responsibility for its worship, and, with the cathedral chapter, for the supervision and maintenance of the cathedral and its property. The chapter formerly comprised the canons, but its composition, in Derby and elsewhere, is now changed by constitution under the Cathedrals Measure 1999. The dean ranks next to the bishop of the diocese in seniority. Some great churches other than cathedrals, notably Westminster Abbey and Windsor, also have deans. The title 'Dean' is used of other ecclesiastical offices (e.g. Dean of the Arches, the presiding judge of the Court of Arches) and also of secular offices. In England the title 'Provost' was used of the heads of the cathedrals of newer dioceses (of which Derby was one) where the cathedral is also a parish church and where the provost was the incumbent. When the Cathedrals Measure came into force the title was abolished, and heads of all cathedral chapters are now known as deans.

Deanery   An *area* (in the towns) or a *rural* deanery is an association of parishes brought together primarily for administrative purposes. It has a synod which consists of a house of clergy and a house of laity and which exercises powers at the deanery level similar to those exercised at a diocesan level by the diocesan synod. The area or rural dean, who is also chair of the deanery synod, is normally (though not necessarily) the incumbent of a parish in the deanery. He or she is the bishop's officer and is appointed by him. The clergy meeting other than as the house of clergy comprise the deanery chapter with the area or rural dean as chair. Unrelated to this definition, a deanery is the residence of a dean.

Deism   Belief in the existence of God based on reason alone, thus rejecting notions of divine revelation, and the Christian doctrines of the supernatural. It is effectively the equivalent of 'natural theology'. A.J. Beresford Hope, a strong supporter of the establishment of the new diocese of Southwell, wrote of 'that decorous and philanthropic deism which is a growing peril of the age' [*English Cathedrals of the Nineteenth Century* (1861), 260].

Diocese   [from Gr. *oikēsis*, administration, from *oikeō*, to inhabit. Thus Lat. *di* + *oikēsis*]. The geographical area under the pastoral care of a bishop. See **See**.

Donative   A benefice or living once in the gift of an ecclesiastical body possessing ordinary jurisdiction, which, when the jurisdiction was dissolved passed to the grantees of the land. The owner of the living became the ordinary and could institute the incumbent without reference to the diocesan bishop. Donatives were finally abolished by the Benefices Act 1898. A bishop now has sole ordinary jurisdiction in his diocese. See **Ordinary**

Ecumenical movement   [Gr. *oikoumenē*, the whole inhabited world]. The movement in the Churches towards the recovery of Christian unity 'transcending differences of creed, ritual and polity' [*ODCC*]. The modern movement dates from the Edinburgh Missionary Conference held in 1910, and finds expression in the World Council of Churches, and, in this country, in Churches Together in England. See **Local Ecumenical Partnership**

Electoral Roll   In the Church of England, the Roll of those persons who have applied to be members of their church under the Church Representation Rules. Such persons have the responsibility for electing representatives on to the parochial church council and deanery synod.

Evangelical   'From the 18th century onwards applied to that school of Protestants which maintains that the essence of the Gospel consists in the doctrine of salvation by faith in the atoning death of Christ, and denies that either good works or the sacraments have any saving efficacy'[*OED*]. Most Anglican Evangelicals were Calvinist, following George Whitefield, though some worked closely with John Wesley, an Arminian in theology. (NOTE: with upper case 'E' usually signifying the movement within the Church of England)

Examining chaplain   According to the *BCP* ordinal archdeacons are formally responsible for enquiring about, and examining, candidates as to their fitness for ordination. However, canon 35 of 1604 required that either the bishop or priests appointed by him should undertake this task. The long-established process of national selection, professional training and assessment of candidates for ordination has largely replaced the function of examining chaplains.

Excommunication A formal ecclesiastical censure, imposed by one empowered to do so. In the mediaeval Church it took two forms: a lesser penalty of exclusion from the sacraments, and the much greater penalty of expulsion not only from the Church but from society.

Faculty Formal permission granted by the diocesan chancellor (in certain cases delegated to the archdeacon) to make additions or alterations to churches and churchyards, including permanent but moveable objects.

First Fruits and Tenths See **Queen Anne's Bounty**

Glebe [from Middle English, following Latin, *gl(a)eba*, soil, clod]. The historic lands belonging to the Church of England and assigned for the support of the parish priest. More recently these lands have been transferred to diocesan boards of finance who take responsibility for their administration.

Group Ministry A collaborative ministry covering two or more benefices, with different incumbents, in a partnership of equals. Group and team ministries can be established by pastoral schemes set up under the Pastoral Measure 1983. See **Team Ministry**

Gild or **Guild** [from OE *geld*, payment] A mediaeval urban (usually) confraternity with a common purpose which could be religious, charitable, commercial, or the practice and maintenance of a craft. Secondary common purposes could include mutual support in sickness or need, provision of funerals and masses for members, support of widows and orphans, and the commemoration of a patron saint and the maintenance of his or her chapel or altar.

High Churchman A term first used in the 17th and early 18th centuries denoting a member of the Church of England who gives a high place to the authority and claims of the bishops and the priesthood, and affirms the centrality of the sacraments as saving means of grace. From this is derived 'High Church' and 'High Church party'. It came to be applied, after 1833, to the adherents of the Oxford Movement.

Host [from Lat. *hostia*, victim] The consecrated bread in the eucharist, regarded as the sacrifice of the body of Christ.

Impropriation 'The assignment or annexation of an ecclesiastical benefice to a lay proprietor or corporation.' (*ODCC*) See also **Appropriation, Rector, Perpetual Curate, Vicar**

Incumbent [Lat. *incumbere*, from *cumbere/cubare*, to lie (down), in the sense of to be in possession] In the Church of England the holder of a parochial charge (benefice) as rector, vicar, perpetual curate etc.

Interim Rite (so called) The change in the structure of the 1662 holy Communion service in which the Prayer of Oblation and the Lord's Prayer are placed before, and not after, the receiving of communion.

Lambeth Conference The assembly of the bishops of the Anglican Communion world-wide under the presidency of the archbishop of Canterbury. It was first held in 1867, and meets once in every ten years.

Living See **Benefice**

Local Ecumenical Partnership An LEP exists 'where there is a formal written agreement affecting the ministry, congregational life, buildings, and/or mission projects of more than one denomination; and a recognition of that agreement by the sponsoring body, and by the appropriate denominational authorities.' (LEPs Consultation Report, Swanwick, March 1994). See **Ecumenical Movement**.

Low Churchman A term deriving from the early 18th century to designate a member of the Church of England who gives a low place to the authority of bishops and the priesthood, to the role of the sacraments as means of grace, and, generally, to matters of ecclesiastical organisation. Hence 'Low Church' and 'Low Church party'.

Matin(s) Before the Reformation an office of one of the canonical hours of prayer. It was supposed to be said in the middle of the night, but was often recited with another office, lauds, at daybreak, or on the previous evening. From 1548 it became a title for the order for public Morning Prayer in the Church of England.

Mass [derived from Latin *missa*, from *mittere*, to dismiss, perhaps from the concluding words of the Latin rite: *Ite, missa est*] A title of the eucharist, the sacrament of the altar, used in the Roman Catholic Church and by anglo-catholics in the Church of England for whom the title is commonly associated with a doctrine of eucharistic sacrifice. The word was retained by Thomas Cranmer in his 1549 *BCP* in the title 'The Supper of the Lord and the Holy Communion, commonly called the Mass', but was dropped in later editions. See **Host**

Methodism Originally a system of religious observance and discipline encouraged in 1729 in Oxford by John Wesley and those who followed him, including his brother Charles and George Whitefield. In 1784 John Wesley established the 'Yearly

Conference of the People called Methodists' from which the Methodist Churches subsequently derived. The term 'Methodist' has never been adequately explained. Its first recorded use was in 1733. It may have referred to the group's 'methodical' observance of the ordinances of the Church of England.

Metropolitan   The title of a bishop exercising jurisdiction in a province, that is, a group of dioceses. In England these bishops are the archbishops of Canterbury and York. The terms 'province' and 'metropolis' derive from the organisation of the early Church which generally followed that of the Roman empire.

Monastic orders   The principal orders of monks and nuns with communities, appropriated tithes and endowments, land-holdings, or grazing rights in Derbyshire before the Reformation were the Augustinians, an 11th cent. order observing a rule derived from the writings of St Augustine, bishop of Hippo in north Africa (died 430); the Benedictines, an order established *c*. 525 by St Benedict; the Cistercians, an order founded in 1098 as a stricter offshoot of the Benedictines; the Cluniacs, a 10th cent. order with a strict Benedictine rule and with their mother house at Cluny in central France; the Dominicans, founded in 1215 and following the rule of St Dominic; and the Premonstratensians, an order of canons founded at Premontre in France in 1119. See **Religious**

Nave   The main part of church to the west of the chancel. The term is thought to derive from the Latin *navis*, ship, an early symbol for the Church, but it may have evolved from the Greek *naos*, temple.

Ordinary   'In canon law, an ecclesiastic in the exercise of the jurisdiction permanently and irremovably annexed to his [or her] office.' (*ODCC*).

Oxford Movement   The movement for the revival of 17th century High Church doctrines and practices in the Church of England, which began in Oxford about 1833. Its leading figures were John Keble, Richard Hurrell Froude, Edward Bouverie Pusey and John Henry Newman.

Paten   The plate or flat dish, usually of silver, on which the bread is laid in the celebration of holy Communion.

Patronage   The right to present or appoint a person to a benefice is called an *advowson* [from Lat. *advocatio*] and the owner of this right is called the patron whether an individual or a corporation recognised by law.

Peculiar   A parish or church formerly exempted from the jurisdiction of the bishop of the diocese and his archdeacon and in which some other ecclesiastical body (for example, a dean and chapter of a cathedral) exercised jurisdiction. Most peculiars were abolished in the 19th century, though some, notably chapels in royal residences and including Westminster Abbey, remain. See **Donative**.

Perpetual Curate   When the monasteries were dissolved and appropriations were transferred to lay people and there was no regularly endowed vicar, the lay impropriator had to nominate a person to the bishop for him to licence to serve the cure. These curates became perpetual, and are now for most purposes regarded as the incumbents of parishes. The clergy in charge of churches and chapels augmented by Queen Anne's Bounty became perpetual curates, that is, the fact of augmentation of a parish chapelry made that chapelry a separate parish. In the 19th and 20th centuries clergy in charge of churches of separate parishes, district chapelries, ecclesiastical districts were perpetual curates as were ministers of new districts set up under the Church Building and New Parishes Acts, and the New Parishes Measure 1943. Perpetual curates are commonly called 'vicars'.

Plurality   Holding more than one benefice at the same time by the same person.

Proctors in Convocation   The elected representatives of the clergy of the Church of England, who together (with ex *officio members*) comprise the Lower Houses of the Convocations of Canterbury and York. See **Convocation**

Province   See **Metropolitan**

Queen Anne's Bounty   A fund created by Queen Anne in 1704 to receive the taxes of First Fruits or Annates (the very considerable sum paid on entry to any benefice, originally the first year's revenues) and tenths (a recurring annual charge of a much smaller sum) originally paid to the pope but taken into the royal revenues by Henry VIII. This fund was used to augment the income of poor benefices both by lot and to meet benefactions.

Quota/Parish share   The amount assessed to be paid by parishes to the diocesan Board of Finance.

Readers/Lay-Readers   In the Church of England a man or woman trained, and licensed by the diocesan bishop, to preach and to conduct religious services other than the sacraments and holy matrimony but including funerals (with the goodwill of the relatives and at the invitation of the parish priest). Readers are not ordained. They undertake pastoral and educational responsibilities in parishes under the direction of the incumbent. Under Canon B12 a lay person may be authorised by the bishop to distribute the sacrament of holy Communion to the people. In practice this is frequently a Reader, but is not necessarily so. The office dates from 1559. The Archbishop of Canterbury, Matthew Parker, realising that many former chantry chapels in outlying areas had been deprived of services, instituted an order of Readers in 1559. Readers were to read the service of the day together with a homily but not to preach. The order died out as the number of clergy increased. The present order of Readers is commonly dated from its establishment in Gloucester in 1866, though lay 'Scripture Readers' were at work in Derby in 1843.

Real Presence   A term used in the theology of the eucharist or holy Communion (especially in the Church of England) to signify, for those who hold to this view, that Christ is actually present in the consecrated bread and wine of the sacrament. It is to be contrasted, on the one hand, with the doctrine of transubstantiation, and, on the other, with merely commemorative or symbolic interpretations. It was recorded that Hugh Latimer (1485–1555) bishop of Worcester, Protestant reformer and martyr, held that 'this same presence may be called most fitly a real presence, that is, a presence not feigned, but a true and faithful presence' [John Foxe, *Book of Martyrs*, 1563]. See **Transubstantiation**

Rector   Historically, an incumbent entitled to all tithes and glebe income. A 'lay rector' was a lay person receiving the rectorial tithes of a benefice. He or she holds the freehold of the parish church but this gives no right of possession. A lay rector may still occasionally be responsible in law for the repair of the chancel of the parish church, though he or she can compound for this liability with the diocesan board of finance. The distinction between a rector and a vicar as the title of the incumbent is of no practical significance today except where it has a special meaning (as in 'team rector'). See **Appropriation, Impropriation, Tithe, Vicar**

Registrar/Bishop's legal secretary   A solicitor who is the diocesan legal officer of first resort and who acts in a legal capacity for the diocesan bishop in matters to do with his diocese, especially with regard to ordinations, institutions to benefices, faculties, consecrations of churches etc. The registrar implements the decisions of the chancellor, the principal legal officer of the diocese. See **Chancellor**

Religious   A technical term applied to any member of a religious order, that is, a community under vows of poverty, chastity and obedience.

Reservation   In the Church of England the practice of keeping bread (and occasionally wine) consecrated at holy Communion primarily for the administration of communion to those who are ill or house bound.

Rogation Days   [from Lat. *rogare*, to ask]. Days in the early summer on which prayers are offered, especially for the harvest. Three (minor) Rogation Days are prescribed in the 1662 *BCP* on the Monday, Tuesday and Wednesday before Ascension Day, being 'Days of Fasting, or Abstinence'.

Rural/Area deanery   See **Deanery**

Schools, Church Church schools are either Voluntary Aided or Voluntary Controlled schools. *Voluntary Aided schools* are owned by voluntary organisations (in this case the Church of England) rather than by the Local Education Authority (LEA). They are aided financially by the LEA and the Department for Education and Employment (DfEE) though the governors must raise 15% of the cost of external repairs, maintenance and capital schemes. The Church has a majority on the governing body of VA schools. The Church of England's *Voluntary Controlled schools* are owned by the Church but control has been ceded to the LEA, normally in those cases where the maintenance burden was too great to be met by the managers. The Church does not have a majority on the governing body.

See [from Lat. *sedes*, seat] Correctly, the official 'seat' of a bishop, otherwise known as his *cathedra* (Lat., throne). So, that which is committed to a bishop, his jurisdiction or diocese. 'To fill the vacant see' means be appointed a (usually) diocesan bishop, though suffragan bishops nominally possess a see. See **Diocese, Suffragan bishop**

Simony [the term derived by reference to Simon Magus, *Acts* 8:18]. The buying or selling of ecclesiastical preferment. This is no longer a practical issue.

Stipend The income of the clergy paid for the exercise of their ministry. Though technically it is not a salary (as, in law, beneficed clergy are self-employed) in almost every respect it is now treated as such.

Suffragan bishop Strictly, any bishop in relation to his archbishop (to whom he gives *suffraganeus* [Lat. from *suffragium*, assistance], but the term is usually employed of a stipendiary bishop appointed to assist a diocesan bishop. Although he is therefore an assistant bishop, that designation is normally given to other bishops in a diocese, either retired or holding some other appointment, who assist the diocesan bishop on occasion.

Surplice A surplice is a white liturgical vestment with wide sleeves. It can be worn by Anglican clergy when officiating at all services, and also by lay people (in choirs or when serving at holy Communion). The fees paid to clergy when officiating at the 'Occasional Offices', that is, at services as occasion may demand, such as weddings and funerals, at which a surplice is worn, are known as 'surplice fees'.

Team Ministry A collaborative ministry of clergy normally covering a single benefice with several churches, or two or more benefices held in plurality by the same incumbent. The incumbent of the benefice is styled 'team rector' and is the team leader, and other clergy (other than assistant curates) are designated 'team vicars'.

Terrier [from med. Lat. *terrarius* from *terra*, earth] An inventory of all lands, property and other possessions of parochial churches and chapels. Terriers are liable to regular inspection by archdeacons.

Thirty-Nine Articles of Religion   A series of theological statements accepted by the Church of England as normative, though they are not a creed nor are they expositions of a creed. They embody the Church's position in relation to the theological controversies of the 16th century. Earlier stages in their formulation led to this final form being approved by Convocation in 1571. 'The Articles were intended to mark the agreement of the Church of England with the Church Catholic, to define its attitude towards Rome and the reformed bodies, to assert the power and independence of the English State in its relation to the church as one of the forms of national life, and to preclude errors such as had arisen amongst those who had departed from Rome.' [*Dictionary of English Church History* 1948]. Before 1865 all beneficed Anglican clergy were required formally to subscribe to the doctrines of the Church of England as set forth in the *BCP* and the Thirty-Nine Articles as agreeable to the Word of God, but subsequently they have been required only to affirm that this is so.

Tithe   An early form of local income tax imposed to support the ordained ministry. It consisted of a 10% levy in kind or (eventually) by commutation on produce and on the profits of labour or on a mixture of both. 'Great tithes' were levied on crops, and 'small tithes' on cattle, chickens, eggs etc. Common land was not tithable. In 1918 tithe was converted to a tithe rent charge, fixed for seven years. From 1925 a proportion of rent charges was paid into a sinking fund and designed to redeem all tithe liabilities by 2010. The process was accelerated in 1936. By 1989 no benefice was dependent for income on payments arising directly or indirectly from historic tithes.

Title   A fixed sphere of work and an income as a condition of ordination, thus a first curacy following ordination.

Tory   see **Whig**

Transubstantiation   According to Roman Catholic doctrine, the conversion or transformation, in the eucharist, of the substance (that is, the deepest ontological reality) of the bread and wine into the body and blood of Christ, with only the appearances (and other 'accidents') of the bread and wine remaining. The proposition was defined as *de fide*, that is, as true doctrine (the denial of which would be heretical) at the Lateran Council in 1215, and reaffirmed by the Council of Trent in 1551. Some modern Roman Catholic theologians have sought to modify the expression of this doctrine by speaking of transubstantiation less in terms of ontology and more in those of symbol.

Translation   The transfer of a bishop from one see to another.

Vestry   A room or part of a church in which (where there is no separate sacristy) the vestments of the clergy, eucharistic vessels, and registers and other records are kept and where the clergy vest or robe. From this the annual vestry, held in Eastertide, takes its name. This is the assembly of parishioners to elect churchwardens and, formerly, to undertake other parish business. Originally this assembly met in the vestry. The annual vestry now only elects churchwardens, its other powers being transferred to the annual parochial church meeting.

Vicar   Historically, the incumbent of a benefice of which the tithes had been appropriated by a monastic house. Monks would be sent to act as the parish priest, but eventually a 'secular' priest (that is, one who had not taken monastic vows) was appointed as a substitute (*vicarius*). Today there is no practical distinction between inducted and instituted incumbents whether they are rectors, vicars or perpetual curates.

Vicar-general   see **Chancellor**

Visitation   The formal inspection, infrequently by a diocesan bishop or annually by archdeacons acting on behalf of the bishop, of the temporal and spiritual state of the Church in a diocese. The archbishops of Canterbury and York have the right to visit the dioceses in their provinces; for example, Archbishop Pecham visited Derbyshire during his visitation of the diocese of Coventry and Lichfield in 1280.

Whig   A member of the political alliance which, after the 1688 Revolution, sought to subordinate the power of the Crown to that of parliament and the upper classes. The Whigs passed the Reform Bill of 1832, and, later in the 19th century were succeeded by the Liberal party. Opposed to the Whigs were the Tories. They were opposed to the exclusion of James II, inclined to the Stuarts after the Revolution of 1689, but, after 1760, accepted George III and the established order of Church and state. They opposed the Reform Bill of 1832. They gave rise to the Conservative party. [*COD*]

Those interested in the careers of Anglican clergy in the modern period should consult Crockford's Clerical Directory, published annually from its first edition in 1858 (reliably indexed from 1860). It absorbed the rival Clergy List in 1917.

Index

Emboldened, italicized locators denote an illustration number; fn refers to footnotes.

BOOKS OF RELATED INTEREST ALSO PUBLISHED BY SCARTHIN BOOKS

DERBYSHIRE CHURCHES AND CHAPELS OPEN TO VISITORS
Compiled by Rodney Tomkins, illustrated by Elizabeth Stoppard, foreword by the Bishop of Derby
Illustrated paperback   128 pages   ISBN 1 900446 02 2

TRANSFORMATION OF A VALLEY: THE DERBYSHIRE DERWENT
By Brian Cooper, photographs by Neville Cooper
Illustrated hardback   328 pages   ISBN 0 907758 17 7

SQUIRE OF CALKE ABBEY: THE JOURNALS OF SIR GEORGE CREWE 1815-1834
Edited by Colin Kitching, foreword by Howard Colvin
Illustrated paperback   142 pages   ISBN 0 907758 84 3

THE HISTORY OF THE DERBYSHIRE GENERAL INFIRMARY 1810-1894
By V.M. Leveaux, foreword by Jeremy Taylor
Illustrated cloth-bound hardback   160 pages   ISBN 1 900446 00 6

THE DIARIES OF MARIA GYTE OF SHELDON, DERBYSHIRE 1913-1920
Edited by Gerald Phizackerley,
foreword by His Grace the Duke of Devonshire
Illustrated paperback   332 pages + 16 pages of plates
ISBN 0 907758 96 7

HISTORIC ORGANS IN DERBYSHIRE: A SURVEY FOR THE MILLENNIUM
By Rodney Tomkins, foreword by Nicholas Thistlethwaite
Illustrated cloth-bound hardback   304 pages   ISBN 0 907758 97 5

THE HOSPITALLER ORDER OF ST. JOHN OF JERUSALEM IN DERBYSHIRE HISTORY
By Gladwyn Turbutt
Illustrated cloth-bound hardback   64 pages   ISBN 1 900446 01 4